THE YALE EDITION

OF

HORACE WALPOLE'S

CORRESPONDENCE

EDITED BY W. S. LEWIS

VOLUME THIRTY-SIX

HORACE WALPOLE'S
CORRESPONDENCE
WITH
THE WALPOLE FAMILY

EDITED BY W. S. LEWIS
AND
JOSEPH W. REED JR
WITH THE ASSISTANCE OF
EDWINE M. MARTZ

NEW HAVEN
YALE UNIVERSITY PRESS
LONDON · OXFORD UNIVERSITY PRESS

1973

TABLE OF CONTENTS

LIST OF ILLUSTRATIONS

Grateful acknowledgment is made to the late Marquess and the Dowager Marchioness of Cholmondeley for permission to reproduce the portraits of Lady Mary Churchill, Sir Robert and Lady Walpole and Lady Malpas.

INTRODUCTION

A characteristic of Horace Walpole that has received less than its due from his biographers and that is apparent in this volume and the following three to his Conway cousins, is devotion to his family, Uncle Horace and brother Robert excepted.

In his first letter to his Dear Mama, which was written at the age of seven or eight, he hopes that she and everyone else at home including his 'cruataurs' are 'wall,' a concern he never lost for those he loved. In his second letter to her, which was written shortly afterwards, he asks for copies of 'yearl of assex' and 'Jan Shore,' early evidence of his interest in history and the theatre. The third letter to 'My Dearest Dear Mama' reports from Eton when he was just sixteen that the 'last dose has succeeded as well as the first and worked the same; it is impossible it could do ill as your dear hands mixed it.' The fourth and last letter to her, written only two days later, hopes that he had finished his physic, but since Dear Mama desires him to continue it he will. It is understandable that when Lady Walpole died four years later his grief was so deep and prolonged that his friends feared for his health. In the twenty months following her death we have only one letter from him;[1] in it he said he had got out of a house he could not bear. Sixteen years after his mother's death he was permitted by the Dean and Chapter of Westminster Abbey to put up a cenotaph for her in the Henry VII Chapel, and that was a comfort and satisfaction to him.

As his parents were estranged and he was wholly under the domination of his mother, Horace saw little of his father until his return from the Grand Tour in 1741. Lady Walpole had died four years earlier and Sir Robert's second wife, Maria Skerrett, his former mistress and the mother of Horace's sister who became Lady Mary Churchill, had also died. Sir Robert's political enemies were closing in on him, yet he had no more loyal supporter in the House than his youngest son to whom he had given a family borough while the young man was abroad. Father and son discovered each other; Horace

1. To Charles Lyttelton 18 Sept. 1737.

poured out his long suppressed affection for Sir Robert whose
enemies became his enemies and remained so ever afterwards:
Horace Walpole was a passionate partisan all his life. Love of pictures also brought father and son together. Horace wrote a catalogue,
the first of its kind in England, of Sir Robert's great collection, *Ædes
Walpolianæ: or, A Description of the Collection of Pictures at
Houghton-Hall in Norfolk, the Seat of the Right Honourable Sir
Robert Walpole, Earl of Orford.* It was dedicated to Lord Orford,
and appended to it was 'A Sermon on Painting, Preached before the
Earl of Orford at Houghton, 1742.' Sir Robert must have been delighted with its concluding panegyric that likens him to 'Moses himself! The Lawgiver, the Defender, the Preserver of Israel!' Father and
son were together constantly during Sir Robert's final illness, Horace collaborating with Dr Ranby in his *Narrative of the Last Illness
of . . . the Earl of Orford,* 1745, and recording his father's last
words.[2]

There are nine letters between Horace and his Uncle Horace
(three now first printed) that are remarkable for the younger man's
rudeness. As our footnote 1 to his letter of 7 May 1745 points out,
he wrote 'a full and true account of the bloody civil wars of the
house of Walpole' in which his uncle appears in a very bad light indeed.[3] That 'Old Horace' was something more than the unsavoury
buffoon that his nephew makes him out to have been is shown by
his successful embassies to The Hague and Paris. Although it appears that the younger Horace had right on his side in the civil wars
of the Walpoles, one must admire his uncle's temperance in answering his nephew's waspish attacks.

The only signs of friendliness between Horace and his eldest
brother, Robert, are Robert's gifts: a picture of Oliver Cromwell, and
a book of drawings, then attributed to Callot, that Robert gave Horace and that Horace prized so highly he kept it locked up in the
Glass Closet in the Strawberry Hill library. Robert, Horace wrote
to Mann, had 'been as much my enemy as it was in his power to be'
by withholding Horace's legacy from their father.[4] Since Robert died
in 1751 his relations with Horace did not improve with age, as Horace's did with his elder brother Edward.

2. Which we give in MANN x. 12.
3. The account is given in GRAY ii. 195 ff.
4. Ca August 1748 (MANN iii. 496).

Edward is one of the four people who figure most prominently in this volume. The other three are his daughter Maria Countess Waldegrave, later Duchess of Gloucester, Robert's son George, Earl of Orford, and Thomas Walpole, Horace's favourite Wolterton cousin.

We meet Edward in a violent letter he wrote Horace complaining of his much younger brother's 'contemptuous and arrogant' treatment of him.[5] We also have Horace's devastating rejoinder, over which he must have worked many angry hours and which he prudently withheld, contenting himself with a firm but dignified reply that must have made Edward dislike him more than ever, yet Edward acknowledged from the first Horace's unflagging kindness to his four illegitimate children by Dorothy Clement, whom Horace identified in his *Last Journals* as 'of Durham, a milliner's apprentice.'[6] When the children were ill he took them to Strawberry Hill out of their father's casually run houses and continued to be concerned for their welfare as long as he lived. We see him in the letters they wrote their Aunt Jane Clement and her niece Anne after Dorothy Clement died. In them Uncle Horace is the wise, affectionate counsellor and delightful companion. These letters, which have only recently come to light, show how beloved Uncle Horace was.

When Edward died Horace wrote Mann, 'My brother died yesterday evening with the same constant tranquillity which he had preserved through his whole illness. His almost unvaried health from soon after thirty to seventy-seven, his ample fortune, and unambitious temper, make his life and death rather to be envied than lamented. His boundless benevolence and charity had left him but very moderate wealth, which he has given chiefly to his eldest daughter, Mrs Keppel.'[7] To this valedictory Walpole added a footnote that summarizes Edward's life and character: 'Sir Edward Walpole second son of Sir Robert Walpole Earl of Orford had one son and three daughters: Edward, a colonel in the army, died young. Laura was married to Frederic Keppel Bishop of Exeter; Maria, married first to James, 2d Earl of Waldegrave, and secondly to his Royal Highness William Henry Duke of Gloucester; and Charlotte, married to Lionel Talmache Earl of Dysart. Sir Edward Walpole

5. *Post* 15 May 1745 OS.
6. *Last Journals* i. 93, n. 1.
7. To Mann 13 Jan. 1784, MANN ix. 466.

had parts, wit, humour, was an excellent mimic, and was very eloquent; but being very shy, lived a retired life, and for several of his
latter years scarce stirred out of his own houses. He was a very great
musician, composed admirably, particularly in a melancholy or
church style, and invented an instrument which he called a pentachord. He drew and painted, though seldom, but with much character, and wrote some copies of verses, a very few of which were
printed; and he drew up the pathetic, and just epitaph for his son-in-
law the Earl of Waldegrave in Navestock church in Essex.'[8] The letters in Appendix 4 to Jane Clement, Dorothy's sister who was living
in one of Sir Edward's houses carrying out some of the duties of a
housekeeper, show him as an exceedingly difficult man, but he ended
up by taking care of her for life.

Maria, his second and most beautiful daughter, was her Uncle
Horace's favourite. In addition to being beauty itself, he wrote
Mann, 'She has a great deal of wit and vivacity, with perfect modesty.' Her first husband was Lord Waldegrave, a most satisfactory
match, for which Uncle Horace took credit. 'I jumbled them together,' he wrote Mann, 'and he has already proposed. For character
and credit, he is the first match in England—for beauty, I think she
is. She has not a fault in her face or person, and the detail is charming. A warm complexion tending to brown, fine eyes, brown hair,
fine teeth, and infinite wit, and vivacity. Two things are odd in this
match; he seems to have been doomed to a Maria Walpole—if his
father had lived, he had married my sister: and this is the second of
my brother's daughters that has married into the house of Stuart—
Mr Keppel comes from Charles; Lord Waldgrave from James II. My
brother has luckily been tractable, and left the whole management
to me.'[9]

When Waldegrave died four years later Maria had produced the
three beautiful Ladies Waldegrave of Reynolds's picture that their
Uncle Horace had him paint for Strawberry Hill at one hundred guineas a Lady.[10] They were Lady Elizabeth Laura who married her cousin
the fourth Earl Waldegrave, Lady Charlotte Maria who married
Lord Euston later fourth Duke of Grafton, and Lady Anna Horatia
who married Lord Hugh Seymour. Their mother wrote Uncle

8. Ibid., n. 1.
9. 11 April 1759, MANN v. 285.
10. Reynolds's receipted bill for it is at Farmington.

Horace, 'My daughters boast much of your goodness to them,'[11] and again, 'Your manner of speaking of my dear girls makes me quite happy, so happy that it generally makes my eyes run over.'[12] In 1766, three years after her first husband's death, she married secretly the Duke of Gloucester, who was seven years her junior and who had fallen in love with her when he was only twenty. Walpole disapproved of the marriage from the first because he foresaw the unhappiness it would bring her, but when it was announced in 1772 he stood loyally by her while she suffered the consequences of the King's displeasure. He continued to give her admirable advice and the support she badly needed and did not get from her father. Her later life was a sad conclusion to its bright beginning. No longer beautiful and far from slender, her imperious temper lost her the affection of her royal husband who treated her badly, but she cultivated her Uncle Horace so assiduously that he left her £10,000. To her daughter Elizabeth Laura Waldegrave (1760–1816) he left £5000, Strawberry Hill, and his house in Berkeley Square. Uncle Horace gave Elizabeth Laura every comfort he could when her eldest son and husband died, but her memory is tarnished by her cutting out, from excessive propriety, paragraphs and pages of his memoirs and commonplace books in her possession.

The third major figure in this volume is Walpole's nephew George third Earl of Orford (1730–91).[13] Uncle Horace described him to Mann, at the age of twenty-five: 'To speak freely to you, my dear Sir, he is the most particular young man I ever saw. No man ever felt such a disposition to love another as mine to him; I flattered myself that he would restore some lustre to our house, at least not let it totally sink; but I am forced to give up him and all my Walpole-views. I will describe him to you if I can, but don't let it pass your lips. His figure is charming; he has more of the easy genuine air of a man of quality than ever you saw: though he has a little hesitation in his speech, his address and manner are the most engaging imaginable: he has a good breeding and attention when he is with you that is even flattering; you think he not only means to please, but designs

11. 10 Aug. 1777.

12. 14 Sept. 1777. HW describes an outing on the river with his great-nieces in his letter to Conway of 21 Aug. 1778.

13. For the fullest and best later account of him, see R. W. Ketton-Cremer, *A Norfolk Gallery*, 1948 pp. 162–87; for a discussion of his paternity, see *Lord Hervey's Memoirs*, ed. R. Sedgwick, rev. edn, New York, 1963, pp. 194–5.

to do everything that shall please you; he promises, offers everything one can wish—but this is all; the instant he leaves you, you, all the world, are nothing to him—he would not give himself the least trouble in the world to give anybody the greatest satisfaction—yet this is mere indolence of mind, not of body; his whole pleasure is outrageous exercise. Everything he promises to please you, is to cheat the present moment, and hush any complaint—I mean of words; letters he never answers, not of business, not of his own business: engagements of no sort he ever keeps. He is the most selfish man in the world without being the least interested: he loves nobody but himself, yet neglects every view of fortune and ambition. . . . You will ask me what passions he has; none but of parade—he drinks without inclination—has women,—not without inclination, but without having them, for he brags as much as an old man; games without attention; is immeasurably obstinate, yet like obstinate people, governed as a child. In short, 'tis impossible not to love him when one sees him; impossible to esteem him when one thinks on him!'[14]

From 1773 to his death in 1791 Orford was intermittently insane. His mother who, according to Walpole, 'was turned to stone sooner than Niobe,'[15] was living in Italy with a lover and couldn't be bothered with her son, nor could Uncle Edward. The responsible members of the family, including the Wolterton Walpoles, besought Horace to take charge of his nephew, and he did so after securing a signed request from all concerned that he act for the family, although, as he confessed, 'I don't understand, you know, a syllable of money and accounts.' Orford was living at Houghton with his faithful mistress, Patty Turk, eating and drinking excessively, celebrated as a sportsman and the last falconer in England, endangering his already overburdened estate with extravagance and neglect. Walpole found Houghton 'a rookery of harpies,' infested with 'rascally attorneys,' but, he wrote Mann, 'the vanity of restoring my family engrosses me.'[16] To his satisfaction and surprise he proved very good at it. 'When my mind reposes a little,' he continued to Mann, 'I smile at myself. I intended to trifle out the remnant of my days—and lo! they are invaded by lawyers, stewards, physicians, and jockeys! Yes,

14. 15 June 1755, MANN iv. 481–2.
15. To Lady Ossory 4 June 1773, OSSORY i. 118.
16. 13 July 1773, MANN vii. 497.

this whole week past I have been negotiating a sale of race-horses at Newmarket, and to the honour of my transactions the sale has turned out greatly.' When Orford recovered he promptly lost much of what had been 'gleaned from the ruin'; when he relapsed, as he did twice, Uncle Horace returned but refused to take care of anything except his nephew's personal safety. He continued to act when needed until Orford mercifully died and Walpole succeeded him as, so he said, 'the poorest earl in England.' He never took his seat in the House of Lords and had little satisfaction in his new honours during the five remaining years of his life.

The fourth chief figure in this family volume is Thomas Walpole (1727–1803), 'Old Horace's' second son. He and his son Thomas (1755–1840), a diplomat, became Walpole's devoted friends to whom he showed no hint or trace of his animosity towards their father and grandfather. The elder Thomas was a banker who lived much in Paris and who helped to secure for Horace the manuscripts left him by Madame du Deffand when they were held back by the 'chicaneries' of her executor, the Prince de Beauvau. Some of his son's spirited drawings and caricatures that Walpole owned are now at Farmington. Oddly enough, there is no mention in their correspondence of Thomas's *Letter . . . to the Governor and Committee of the Treasury of the Bank of England,* on the successful termination of a lawsuit in Grenada, which Walpole brought out at the Strawberry Hill Press in 120 copies,[17] a publication that is a far cry from the rest of its output and that is further proof of the affection and regard its director had for his cousin. How warmly the younger Thomas cherished Cousin Horace's memory is shown by a collection of six portraits that he formed in his old age. He called them all 'Horace Walpole,' but, alas, not one of them is. The last to be rejected is the Rosalba that has been reproduced over and over, most recently by us in our volume 17 shortly before we discovered that the sitter was, in fact, the second Viscount Boyne.

The one letter we have to Charles Churchill, Walpole's brother-in-law, shows how close Walpole was to him and his wife, Lady Mary, to whom for fifty years and more he wrote hundreds of letters, now all lost.[18] We have glimpses of her at Houghton as a young

17. Hazen, *SH Bibl.* 121–3; see *post* p. 204.
18. For an explanation of their disappearance, see W. S. Lewis, *Collector's Progress,* 1951, pp. 185–6.

girl playing the harpsichord, singing, and laughing with Horace at their rustic Norfolk neighbours. On her elevation to the rank of an earl's daughter she had to endure public and private slights, but this hatefulness assured her a special place in her brother's affection. Later we hear of visits to Strawberry Hill with one or more of her seven children. Two of them, George and Horace, came to Strawberry as their uncle's aides-de-camp when he, aged seventy-eight, received the Queen and eight princesses there, but Lady Mary and her family remain tantalizingly shadowy figures.

W.S.L.

MANUSCRIPTS AND BIBLIOGRAPHY

Most of the letters in this volume were at Strawberry Hill when Walpole died. Mrs Damer, who lived there until 1811, bequeathed them to her neighbour Sir Wathen Waller, 1st Bt, in 1828. They remained in the Waller family until they were sold at Sotheby's 5 Dec. 1921 (first Waller Sale). Many were bought in and resold at Christie's 15 Dec. 1948 (second Waller Sale).

Elizabeth Laura Countess Waldegrave took possession of Strawberry Hill when Mrs Damer moved out of it in 1811. On Lady Waldegrave's death in 1816 Strawberry and its contents were inherited by her son John James, 6th Earl Waldegrave. Some letters were apparently included in the bundle of 'private and family papers' in Walpole's Box A, which Walpole bequeathed to Lord Waldegrave (see Appendix 3). Some letters and the manuscript of Walpole's *Last Journals*, which includes transcripts of letters, remain in the possession of the Waldegrave family; other letters were sold, probably by Lord Euston as executor for the 6th Earl Waldegrave, to Richard Bentley (1794–1871), the publisher, to whose grandson the manuscripts descended. They were acquired from his estate in 1937 by W. S. Lewis.

The manuscripts of the four early letters from Walpole to his mother, Lady Walpole, and the three letters between Walpole and his father, Sir Robert, were bequeathed by Mrs Damer to Sir Wathen Waller, 1st Bt; they were included in the two Waller sales, and were bought by Maggs for W. S. Lewis.

There are twenty-nine surviving letters between Walpole and his brother, Sir Edward; twenty from and nine to Sir Edward, five of them previously unpublished. Five of these letters may have been included in Walpole's Box A, inherited by the 6th Earl Waldegrave; two of these remained at Strawberry Hill and then at Chewton until 1948, when W. S. Lewis acquired them from Lord Waldegrave; the other three were sold to Richard Bentley, and were acquired by W. S. Lewis in 1937. Fifteen letters have a Damer-Waller provenance before they were bought by W. S. Lewis. Six letters were owned in 1902 by Messrs J. P. Pearson, were sold in various sales (see *post* HW to Sir Edward 28 April 1769), and were acquired in 1941 by W. S. Lewis. Three letters are printed from Walpole's transcript in his MS of *Last Journals*, 'Journal Geo. 3d 1772,' now in the possession of Lord Waldegrave. One scrap of a letter was acquired by W. S. Lewis from W. A. Myers.

The letters between Walpole and various members of the Waldegrave family were probably among the papers inherited by the 6th Earl Waldegrave. These include the following:

30 letters, 14 to and 16 from the Duchess of Gloucester; 14 printed here for the first time.

One letter to and two from the Duke of Gloucester, the latter two previously unpublished.

12 letters from Lady Elizabeth Laura Waldegrave, and 4 from her husband, the 4th Earl Waldegrave, all printed here for the first time.

Two letters from the Hon. William Waldegrave, brother of the 4th Earl, and one letter to him, all previously unpublished.

One letter apparently to the 5th Earl Waldegrave.

One letter from Lady Charlotte Maria Waldegrave, previously unpublished.

From the letters bequeathed by Mrs Damer to Sir Wathen Waller, 1st Bt, there is one letter from Lady Dysart and one letter from the Hon. Frederick Keppel.

There are nine surviving letters between Walpole and his uncle, Horatio Walpole, Senior, 1st Lord Walpole of Wolterton; four from and five to 'Old Horace'; three are here printed for the first time. The four letters of 1751 survive in copies by 'Old Horace' now in the possession of David C. L. Holland; a draft of one of these in Walpole's hand is in the possession of W. S. Lewis. The four letters of 1756 have a Waldegrave-Bentley provenance before they were acquired by W. S. Lewis in 1937. One letter was acquired by W. S. Lewis from G. H. Last, of Bromley, Kent, in 1937.

One letter from Horatio Walpole, Junior ('Pigwiggin') which was bequeathed by Mrs Damer to Sir Wathen Waller, 1st Bt, was sold Sotheby's to Dobell in 1921, and has since then disappeared. A letter from 'Old Horace's' son, Robert Walpole, was sold Sotheby's 26 May 1964 to Maggs for W. S. Lewis. One letter to Rachel, Lady

Walpole of Wolterton, is printed for the first time from a photostat of the manuscript in the possession of the Earl of Leicester at Holkham.

There are 29 letters between Walpole and his cousin Thomas Walpole; 27 to and 2 from Thomas; 5 are printed for the first time. There are 8 letters from Walpole to Thomas Walpole the Younger, one printed for the first time. These letters were bequeathed by Thomas Walpole the Younger to his son, Sir Spencer Walpole; he passed them on to his daughter and she to her son, F. C. Holland. Most of these are now in the possession of his nephew, David C. L. Holland, except for one which is owned by H. Jock Lang, and one other which was among the letters sold by Lord Euston to Richard Bentley.

Between Walpole and his nephew, George, 3d Earl of Orford, there are six surviving letters, three to and three from Lord Orford; two printed here for the first time. Four letters were sold by Lord Euston to Richard Bentley, and were acquired by W. S. Lewis in 1937. One letter has a Damer-Waller history until its sale to Maggs for W. S. Lewis. One letter is printed from Walpole's transcript in his MS 'Memoirs of the Reign of King George the Third' (foul copy), Volume I.

The few surviving letters between Walpole and the Cholmondeleys were among the letters which Mrs Damer bequeathed to Sir Wathen Waller, 1st Bt: one from George, 3d Earl Cholmondeley, one from the Hon. Robert Cholmondeley, three to and from Mrs Robert Cholmondeley, of which two are published for the first time.

Of the letters between Walpole and the Churchills, only five survive: one to Charles Churchill, which was privately printed by Robert Walpole in 1833, passed into the possession of Miss Lucy Larner, and has since disappeared; one from Charles Churchill, one from his daughter Lady Cadogan, and one to his daughter-in-law Mrs Horace Churchill, were in the Damer-Waller group; one other letter from Lady Cadogan is now in the possession of Lord Kenyon, Gredington Whitchurch, Salop.

Four letters to the Clements, one to Jane and three to Anne, all previously unpublished, were preserved by the Clement family and were acquired from a descendant of theirs in 1959 by W. S. Lewis.

We wish to correct an error concerning four manuscript letters, two to and two from Dr Charles Burney now in the Berg Collection of the New York Public Library. The letters are listed in Miss Joyce Hemlow's *Catalogue of the Burney Family Correspondence 1749–1878* (New York and Montreal, 1971, pp. 29–30) as to and from Horace Walpole, whereas correctly they are to and from his nephew George, 3d Earl of Orford. The dates are: 17 April 1791 to Orford, 30 April 1791 from Orford, [April, 1791] to Orford, and 8 Nov. 1791 from Orford.

In the transcription of the text we have followed the editorial method described in the earlier volumes of this edition. Spelling and capitalization have been normalized, except for proper names and certain characteristic words such as 'cotemporaries.' Walpole's punctuation has been followed exactly, but that of his correspondents has been normalized to some extent. In biographical notes we assume the use of the *Dictionary of National Biography,* the *Complete Peerage,* and the *Complete Baronetage;* and for Members of Parliament, Romney Sedgwick, *The History of Parliament. The House of Commons 1715–1754,* 1970, and Sir Lewis Namier and John Brooke, *The History of Parliament. The House of Commons 1754–1790,* 1964. In citing eighteenth-century newspapers, such as the *Daily Advertiser,* we omit the year if it is the same as that of the letter we are annotating. All English books are assumed to be published in London, and all French books in Paris, unless otherwise stated.

W.S.L.
E.M.M.

ACKNOWLEDGMENTS

Our first acknowledgment is due Lord Waldegrave, who has kindly let us publish for the first time the letters from his ancestress, Maria Walpole Countess Waldegrave, afterwards Duchess of Gloucester, to Horace Walpole. And as usual, we have drawn on Lady Waldegrave's unrivalled knowledge of the Walpoliana at Chewton House. From the outset of this undertaking forty years ago Lord and Lady Waldegrave have been its constant friends, eagerly abetting it in every way they can and so making an invaluable contribution to Walpolian studies. We are greatly indebted to the Dowager Marchioness of Cholmondeley for photographs of the family portraits at Houghton and her unflagging interest in the Yale Walpole.

Professor F. A. Pottle of our advisory committee and Mrs Marion S. Pottle have made valuable suggestions. Dr Warren Hunting Smith has read the typescript and proof at every stage and has enriched the footnotes and appendices with his contributions. We also wish to thank Mr Lars Troide and Mr John Riely for editorial assistance.

The Walpole staff has done much of the work of seeing this correspondence through the press; Mrs Louis L. Martz has been in charge of the work on this volume. We are grateful to Mr David Mandel and Miss Barbara Stoops for verifying the footnotes and references, and to Mrs Victoria Wolf and Mr Edward Michewicz for assistance with the typing.

Since some of the annotation of the correspondence was done at Wesleyan University, we wish to thank the following research assistants there, some of whom received financial support from the Work-Study Program of the Federal Government: Mr Stephen J. Voorhies, Mr John Thurner, Mrs Ellen D'Oench. Miss Antoinette Knight and Miss Helen Zawisa assisted with the typing. Specific inquiries were answered by Miss Sylvia Joan Jurale of the Olin Library, Wesleyan, and by Mr John W. Spaeth, Jr.

W.S.L.
J.W.R.

CUE-TITLES AND ABBREVIATIONS

Ædes Walpolianæ,
Works ii . . . Horace Walpole, *Ædes Walpolianæ: or, A Description of the Collection of Pictures at Houghton Hall in Norfolk, the Seat of . . . Sir Robert Walpole;* in vol. ii of *The Works of Horatio Walpole, Earl of Orford,* 5 vols, 1798.

Army Lists . . . [Great Britain War Office], *A List of the General and Field Officers as they rank in the Army,* London, 1740–1841.

BERRY . . . *The Yale Edition of Horace Walpole's Correspondence: The Correspondence with Mary and Agnes Berry,* New Haven, 1944, 2 vols.

Biddulph . . . Violet Biddulph, *The Three Ladies Waldegrave,* London, 1938.

Chatham Corr. . . William Pitt, Earl of Chatham, *Correspondence,* ed. W. S. Taylor and J. H. Pringle, 1838–40, 4 vols.

CHATTERTON . . *The Yale Edition of Horace Walpole's Correspondence: The Correspondence with Thomas Chatterton . . . ,* New Haven, 1951.

Cobbett, *Parl. Hist.* . *The Parliamentary History of England,* ed. William Cobbett and John Wright, 1806–20, 36 vols.

Coke, 'MS Journals' . Photostats of unpublished journals (1775–91) of Lady Mary Coke in the possession of Lord Hume.

COLE . . . . *The Yale Edition of Horace Walpole's Correspondence: The Correspondence with the Rev. William Cole,* New Haven, 1937, 2 vols.

Collins *Peerage,* 1812 . Arthur Collins, *The Peerage of England,* ed. Sir Samuel Egerton Brydges, 1812, 9 vols.

Cunningham . . *The Letters of Horace Walpole, Earl of Orford*, ed. Peter Cunningham, 1857–9, 9 vols.

Daily Adv. . . . *The Daily Advertiser.* Film in the Yale University Library from the file of the Library of Congress.

DALRYMPLE . . . *The Yale Edition of Horace Walpole's Correspondence: The Correspondence with Sir David Dalrymple. . . ,* New Haven, 1951.

Des. of SH, 1784 . . Horace Walpole, *A Description of the Villa,* Strawberry Hill, 1784, 2d edition.

'Des. of SH,' *Works* ii . Horace Walpole, 'A Description of the Villa of Mr Horace Walpole at Strawberry Hill near Twickenham,' in vol. ii of *The Works of Horatio Walpole, Earl of Orford,* 1798, 5 vols.

DNB . . . . *Dictionary of National Biography,* ed. Leslie Stephen and Sidney Lee, reissue, 1908–9, 22 vols.

DU DEFFAND . . . *The Yale Edition of Horace Walpole's Correspondence: The Correspondence with Mme du Deffand,* New Haven, 1939, 6 vols.

GEC . . . . George Edward Cokayne, *The Complete Peerage,* revised by Vicary Gibbs *et al.,* 1910–59, 13 vols; *The Complete Baronetage,* Exeter, 1900–9, 6 vols.

Geo. III's *Corr.,* ed. Fortescue . . . *The Correspondence of King George the Third from 1760 to December 1783 . . . ,* ed. Sir John Fortescue, London, 1927–8, 6 vols.

GM . . . . *The Gentleman's Magazine.*

GRAY . . . . *The Yale Edition of Horace Walpole's Correspondence: The Correspondence with Thomas Gray, Richard West and Thomas Ashton,* New Haven, 1948, 2 vols.

Grenville Papers . . *The Grenville Papers, being the Correspondence of Richard Grenville, Earl Temple, K. G., and the Right Hon. George Grenville . . . ,* ed. William James Smith, London, 1852–3, 4 vols.

Hazen, *Bibl. of HW* . Allen T. Hazen, *A Bibliography of Horace Walpole,* New Haven, 1948.

Hazen, *Cat. of HW's Lib.* . . . Allen T. Hazen, *A Catalogue of Horace Walpole's Library*, New Haven, 1969, 3 vols.

Hazen, *SH Bibl.* . . Allen T. Hazen, *A Bibliography of the Strawberry Hill Press*, New Haven, 1942.

Hist. MSS Comm. . . Historical Manuscripts Commission.

HW . . . . Horace Walpole.

Isenburg, *Stammtafeln* . Wilhelm Karl, Prinz von Isenburg, *Stammtafeln zur Geschichte der europaeischen Staaten*, Berlin, 1936, 2 vols.

'Journal Geo. 3d 1772' . *Journal of the Reign of King George the Third, from the beginning of the year 1772; by Horace Walpole; being a supplement to his Memoires*, HW's transcript in his MS of *Last Journals*, in the possession of Lord Waldegrave.

Journals of the House of Commons . . [Great Britain, Parliament, House of Commons] *Journals of the House of Commons . . . Reprinted by Order of the House of Commons*, 1803, 51 vols.

Ketton-Cremer . . Robert Wyndham Ketton-Cremer, *Horace Walpole*, London, 1940.

Last Journals . . Horace Walpole, *The Last Journals of Horace Walpole during the Reign of George III from 1771–1783*, ed. A. Francis Steuart, 1910, 2 vols.

MANN . . . . *The Yale Edition of Horace Walpole's Correspondence: The Correspondence with Sir Horace Mann*, New Haven, 1954–71, 11 vols.

MASON . . . *The Yale Edition of Horace Walpole's Correspondence: The Correspondence with William Mason*, New Haven, 1955, 2 vols.

Mem. Geo. II . . Horace Walpole, *Memoirs of the Reign of King George the Second*, 2d edn, ed. Henry R. V. Fox, Lord Holland, 1847, 3 vols.

Mem. Geo. III . . Horace Walpole, *Memoirs of the Reign of King George the Third*, ed. G. F. Russell Barker, 1894, 4 vols.

MONTAGU . . . *The Yale Edition of Horace Walpole's Correspondence: The Correspondence with George Montagu*, New Haven, 1941, 2 vols.

MORE . . . . *The Yale Edition of Horace Walpole's Correspondence: The Correspondence with Hannah More . . .* , New Haven, 1961.

Namier and Brooke . Sir Lewis Namier and John Brooke, *The House of Commons 1754–1790*, London, 1964.

NBG . . . . *Nouvelle biographie générale*, ed. Jean-Chrétien-Ferdinand Hoefer, 1852–66, 46 vols.

OED . . . . *A New English Dictionary on Historical Principles*, ed. Sir James A. H. Murray *et al.*, Oxford, 1888–1928, 10 vols.

Old Westminsters . *The Record of Old Westminsters*, ed. G. F. Russell Barker and Alan H. Stenning, 1928, 2 vols. *A Supplementary Volume*, ed. J. B. Whitmore and G. R. Y. Radcliffe, [1938?].

OSSORY . . . *The Yale Edition of Horace Walpole's Correspondence: The Correspondence with the Countess of Upper Ossory*, New Haven, 1965, 3 vols.

Sedgwick . . . Romney Sedgwick, *The House of Commons 1715–1754*, London, 1970.

SELWYN . . . *The Yale Edition of Horace Walpole's Correspondence: The Correspondence with George Selwyn . . .* , New Haven, 1961, 2 vols.

Sir Spencer Walpole . *Some Unpublished Letters of Horace Walpole*, ed. Sir Spencer Walpole, London, 1902.

SH . . . . Strawberry Hill.

Toynbee . . . *The Letters of Horace Walpole, Fourth Earl of Orford*, ed. Mrs Paget Toynbee, Oxford, 16 vols, 1903–5; *Supplement*, ed. Paget Toynbee, 3 vols, 1918–25.

Works . . . *The Works of Horatio Walpole, Earl of Orford*, 1798, 5 vols.

WSL . . . . W. S. Lewis.

LIST OF LETTERS

The dates of the letters to Walpole are in italics. Missing letters are marked by an asterisk after the date. Letters printed here for the first time are marked by a dagger (†); those printed in full for the first time are marked by a double dagger (‡). Page references to earlier editions are given in the preliminary notes to the letters.

LETTERS BETWEEN WALPOLE AND HORATIO WALPOLE, SR, LORD WALPOLE OF WOLTERTON

LETTERS BETWEEN WALPOLE AND LADY MARY CHURCHILL

LETTERS BETWEEN WALPOLE AND THE DUCHESS OF
GLOUCESTER

LETTER TO WALPOLE FROM LADY DYSART

LETTERS BETWEEN WALPOLE AND LADY ORFORD

LETTERS BETWEEN WALPOLE AND GEORGE, 4TH EARL OF CHOLMONDELEY

LETTERS BETWEEN WALPOLE AND ANNE CLEMENT

LETTERS BETWEEN WALPOLE AND HORATIO, 2ND LORD WALPOLE OF WOLTERTON

LETTER TO WALPOLE FROM ANNA MARIA KEPPEL

LETTERS BETWEEN WALPOLE AND THOMAS WALPOLE THE YOUNGER

To Lady Walpole, 1725 *bis*

Printed from the MS now WSL; first printed, Toynbee *Supp.* i. 2, where it is illustrated. Damer-Waller; sold Sotheby's 5 Dec. 1921, lot 48, bought in; resold Christie's 15 Dec. 1947, lot 29, to Maggs for WSL.
Endorsed (by HW); My 2d letter to my mother.

DEAR Mamy I hope you and Papy are Wall my duty to prince William[1] a my coussens wats nothiing but I want yearl of assax and Jan Shore[2] and I am very Wall. now pray my Servica to Dolle and mrs gravenner[3] and mr nelson[4] and mrs Sellwin and mrs neve[5] is very wall and I sent the Dice for you becaus I thaght you had non and my cousens are all very wall. mr wesson[6] gives his Service to you and if you lik my chiken I will send you som more of them and pray Desire of mr Jankins[7] to send me som more paper

HORACE WALPOLE

1. William Augustus (1721–65), cr. (1726) D. of Cumberland, 2d son of George II.

2. HW's copies of John Banks, *The Unhappy Favourite: or the Earl of Essex,* and Nicholas Rowe, *The Tragedy of Jane Shore,* and three other plays, the five bound in one volume, were sold SH iii. 142 (Hazen, *Cat. of HW's Lib.,* No. 1907).

3. Presumably Anne Grosvenor (1679–1750), a friend of Lady Walpole. Later, through Sir Robert's influence, she was appointed under housekeeper (1738) and housekeeper (1739) of Somerset House (GRAY i. 220, n. 17). See also Conway to HW 14 May 1740 OS. None of HW's letters to her has been recovered.

4. Not identified.

5. Isabella Le Neve (ca 1686–1759), long a member of Sir Robert Walpole's household, acting as governess and companion for Lady Mary Walpole; later a member of HW's household (MONTAGU i. 62, n. 27; MANN ii. 36, n. 37).

6. Edward Weston (1703–70), son of the Rev. Stephen W. Weston, Bp of Exeter; educated at Eton (1717–20) and King's College, Cambridge (B.A. 1723, M.A. 1727); fellow of King's 1723–31; tutor at Bexley, Kent, to the four Townshend cousins and to HW in the summer of 1725 and again at Twickenham in 1726 (Lady Townshend to Edward Weston 1 Jan., 17 July 1725 NS, and Sir Robert Walpole to Weston 19 Sept. 1726 OS, MSS now WSL; extracts printed in Hist. MSS Comm., 10th Report, App. pt i, 1885, pp. 239–40; R. A. Austen-Leigh, *Eton College Register, 1698–1752,* Eton, 1927, p. 365; 'Short Notes,' GRAY i. 3).

7. —— Jenkins (d. 1736), Sir Robert Walpole's steward.

To Lady Walpole, Friday 28 September 1733 OS

Printed from the MS now WSL; first printed, Toynbee *Supp.* i. 3. Damer-Waller; sold Sotheby's 5 Dec. 1921, lot 49, bought in; resold Christie's 15 Dec. 1947, lot 30, to Maggs for WSL.

Address: To the Honourable the Lady Walpole at Chelsea Middlesex.

Postmark: 29 SE WINDSOR.

Eton,[1] Sept. 28, 1733.

My dearest dear Mama,

I CAN gladly let you know now that this last dose has succeeded as well as the first and worked the same; it is impossible it could do ill as your dear hands mixed it, which made me take it with the greatest pleasure. I received my dear Mama's present with all the joy that I could anything from you: I have also received the box with the breeches. As to my cousin Harry,[2] Mr Bland[3] has given you so exact an account, that I think it needless for me to mention him. My sentiments always sympathize so exactly with my dear Mama's, that I don't doubt but you can read in your own heart how much I long to be with you.

I am my dear Mama

your most affectionate son

HOR. WALPOLE

1. HW entered Eton 26 April 1727 and left 23 Sept. 1734 ('Short Notes,' GRAY i. 4–5; R. A. Austen-Leigh, *Eton College Register, 1698–1752*, Eton, 1927, p. 356).

2. Hon. Henry Seymour Conway (1719–95), HW's lifelong correspondent and most intimate friend, 2d son of Francis Seymour Conway (1679–1732), cr. (1703) Bn Conway, by his 3d wife Charlotte Shorter (d. 1734), HW's aunt; he was at Eton in 1732 (ibid. 80).

3. Rev. Henry Bland (ca 1703–68), D.D., 1747; prebendary of Durham, 1737; HW's tutor at Eton and apparently Conway's tutor as well; he was the son of Dr Henry Bland, Provost of Eton (ibid. 32).

To Lady Walpole, Sunday 30 September 1733 OS

Printed from the MS now WSL; first printed, Toynbee *Supp.* i. 3–4. Damer-Waller; sold Sotheby's 5 Dec. 1921, lot 50, bought in; resold Christie's 15 Dec. 1947, lot 31, to Maggs for WSL.

Address: To the Honourable the Lady Walpole at Chelsea Middlesex.

Postmark: 1 OC WINDSOR.

Eton, Sept. 30th 1733.

My dearest dear Mama,

I HOPE you are well, I am very well. My love to Dolly and Grave.[1] I was in hopes I had finished my physic, but since my dear Mama desires it, to be sure I will take it again, and I will send the box back tomorrow. I could almost wish the Prince of Orange[2] hanged for keeping me so long from seeing my dear Mama. I gave Mr Bland your letter, and he gave me the enclosed for you.[3]

I am my dear Mama

your most affectionate son,

Hor. Walpole

I have no heats at all now.

1. Mrs Grosvenor (see *ante* HW to Lady Walpole 1725 *bis*).

2. William Charles Henry (1711–51), Prince of Orange 1732–51; Stadtholder, as William IV, 1747 (MANN iii. 346, n. 7; 394, n. 1); m. (14 March 1734) Princess Anne (1709–59), eldest dau. of George II. 'His Highness the Prince of Orange being certainly expected here in a very short time, the nobility and other persons of distinction are preparing very splendid suits of clothes for the occasion' (*Daily Adv.* 21, 26 Sept.). But it was announced, *sub* 30 Sept., that 'The Prince of Orange's departure from Holland was put off for a month' (GM 1733, iii. 494). The *Daily Adv.* 3 Oct. reported, 'We are assured that his Highness the Prince of Orange is expected at Hampton Court about Saturday sennight, and that great preparations are making there for celebrating his marriage with the Princess Royal on the 22d instant, her Royal Highness's birthday'; he arrived 7 Nov. 'off Woolwich . . . being attended from thence by the Hon. Horatio Walpole Esq.' (GM 1733, iii. 605). See also J. H. Plumb, *Sir Robert Walpole: The King's Minister*, 1960, pp. 288–90.

3. Both letters are missing.

CATHERINE, LADY WALPOLE, BY MICHAEL DAHL

To Sir Robert Walpole, Tuesday 27 July 1736 OS

Printed from the MS now WSL; first printed, Toynbee *Supp.* i. 4–5. Damer-Waller; sold Sotheby's 5 Dec. 1921, lot 51, bought in; resold Christie's 15 Dec. 1947, lot 32, to Maggs for WSL.

King's College, July 27, 1736.

Honoured Sir,

THE pleasure I received at Houghton[1] is completed by hearing you returned safe to Chelsea; though I could always wish you there, where you are, and have so much reason to be, happy. As fine as it is, I should not have felt half the satisfaction, if it had not been your doing: I wish all your other actions could afford you as much ease to enjoy their success, as those at Houghton do: But as I know how little leisure you have, I will not detain you by endeavouring to express in a long letter, what the longest could never do, my duty and admiration. I beg these short lines and all my actions may convince you how much

I am, Sir,

Your most dutiful son,

Hor. Walpole

To Sir Robert Walpole, 1741

Missing; mentioned by Mann to HW 24 Sept. 1741 NS: 'We could not make out what 220 [HW] had wrote to 705 [Sir Robert Walpole]'[1] (Mann i. 146).

---

1. Houghton Hall, Sir Robert's Norfolk seat, described by HW in *Ædes Walpolianæ*, 1747. Toynbee inferred from HW's letter to Charles Lyttelton of the same date that this marked HW's first visit to Houghton, but Gray in his letter of 3 July [1735] wishes HW 'a good journey' there (Gray i. 84).

1. For the cipher used by HW and Mann in their correspondence, see Mann i. p. liii.

To SIR ROBERT WALPOLE, March 1741

Missing; mentioned by HW to Conway 25 March 1741 NS: 'I wrote last post to Sir Robert, to wish him joy; I hope he received my letter.'

From ROBERT[1] or EDWARD[2] WALPOLE, February 1741

Missing; mentioned by HW to Joseph Spence 21 Feb. 1741 NS: 'I had a letter from one of my brothers last post to tell me from Sir Robert that he would have me leave Italy as soon as possible, lest I should be shut up unawares by the arrival of the Spanish troops;[3] and that I might pass some time in France if I had a mind.'

From SIR ROBERT WALPOLE, Saturday 16 July 1743 OS

Printed from the MS now WSL; first printed, Toynbee *Supp.* iii. 110–11. Damer-Waller; sold Sotheby's 5 Dec. 1921, lot 169 to Wells, who gave it to Thomas Conolly of Chicago; sold by him (together with other letters) to WSL, 1937.
Endorsed (by Sir Robert): H. Walpole.

Houghton, July 16th 1743.

Dear Horace,

IT IS a subject not to be enlarged upon by letter, but I am desired to have it recommended to such young gentlemen in the army as are of our acquaintance, to make an acquaintance with young Mr Townshend,[1] who now serves as a volunteer with Lord Dunmore.[2]

---

1. Robert Walpole (1701–51), eldest son of Sir Robert Walpole; cr. (1723) Bn Walpole; 2d E. of Orford, 1745.

2. Hon. Edward Walpole (1706–84), 2d son of Sir Robert Walpole; K.B., 1753; M.P. Lostwithiel 1730–4, Great Yarmouth 1734–68; Clerk of the Pells, 1739.

3. At this time HW was staying with Horace Mann at Florence; he continued in Italy until some time after 19 July. Philip V, heir of the Spanish Hapsburgs, in the dispute over the Austrian succession, was particularly interested in the Italian provinces, but the invasion here threatened did not take place until the following autumn.

———

1. Hon. George Townshend (1724–1807), 4th Vct Townshend, 1764; cr. (1787) M. Townshend; M.P. Norfolk 1747–64; served on the staff of Lord Dunmore 1743–5; Brig.-Gen. in the expedition against Quebec, 1759, when he took command of the army after the death of Gen. Wolfe and received the surrender; Gen., 1782; Field Marshal, 1796.

2. John Murray (1685–1752), 2d E. of Dunmore, 1710; Ensign at the battle of

CATHERINE, LADY WALPOLE, AND HORACE,
BY CHARLES JERVAS

He was in the last action,[3] and by all accounts behaved well, but it is apprehended, he is fallen into some company who far from encouraging him in the way he is in, dissuade him all they can from going on.

I cannot but imagine, it would be of service to him, if Harry Conway,[4] and Mr Churchill[5] would unaffectedly make an acquaintance with him, where he could learn no notions, but what would be of service to him. I know we are treading upon thorns when we are meddling with the concern of that family. My Lady[6] must know nothing of the matter, nor the young man suspect anything but accidental matters.

Desire Mr Pellham[7] to put the enclosed letter to Lord Loudoun[8] into the next packet for the army. You may let him know, that it is wholly upon the subject of Mr Townshend, at the request of my Lord,[9] but 'ware—my Lady.

I mend apace in all respects,[10] but cannot yet sleep anights.

Yours most affectionately,

Orford

Blenheim, 1704; Brig.-Gen. at the capture of Vigo, 1719; Lt-Gen., 1739; made a Knight Banneret by the King for the victory at Dettingen; Gen., 1745. See Newcastle's letter to Dunmore recommending George Townshend, in C. V. F. Townshend, *The Military Life of Field-Marshal George First Marquess Townshend*, 1901, p. 6.

3. At Dettingen, 16 June; after the battle George Townshend wrote, 'I could give such an account of the declining condition of our army and interests of Germany as would make the most indifferent person weep. . . . the more I consider the situation of our armies and the temper of those who direct them, the conduct of the French from our first sight of them, the accounts I learn from the inhabitants of this country and the opinion of people in general, all seem to agree in the verdict Inglorious' (ibid. 36).

4. Who was also with the British army in camp at Hanau after the battle of Dettingen; see Conway to HW 8 July 1743 NS.

5. Charles Churchill (?1720 – 1812); M.P. Stockbridge 1741–7, Milborne Port 1747–54, Great Marlow 1754–61; Lt 6th Dragoon Guards, 1736; Lt 2d Foot Guards, 1739. He married HW's half-sister, Lady Mary, in 1746.

6. Etheldreda or Audrey Harrison (d. 1788) m. (1723) Charles Townshend, 3d Vct Townshend, 1738; she was notorious for the freedom of her speech. George was removed from her allegedly Jacobite influence by his relations, the Pelhams, and placed in the family of the Duke of Cumberland (DNB). See also Sir Lewis Namier and John Brooke, *Charles Townshend*, 1964, pp. 5–6.

7. Hon. Henry Pelham (1695–1754), secretary at war 1724–30; paymaster general 1730–43; first lord of the Treasury and chancellor of the Exchequer 1743–54.

8. John Campbell (1705–82), 4th E. of Loudoun 1731; aide-de-camp to the King 1743–5; Gen., 1770.

9. Charles Townshend (1700–64), 3d Vct Townshend, 1738; M.P. Great Yarmouth 1722–3; lord lieutenant of Norfolk 1730–8.

10. From a fall down the stairs at Houghton, when he 'cut his forehead two inches long to the pericranium, and

To SIR ROBERT WALPOLE, 1744

Missing; answered *post* 14 July 1744.

From SIR ROBERT WALPOLE, Saturday 14 July 1744 OS

Printed from the MS now wsl; first printed, Toynbee *Supp.* iii. 116. For the history of the MS see *ante* 16 July 1743 OS.

Memoranda (in HW's hand; those marked with an asterisk were crossed out as he used them):

* Lady Rich[1] broke her heart so often

* Winningt.[2] wife din'd to save dinner—& have turn'd their stomachs.

One lamp light when but one in town.[3]

organ made by apoth. of glister pipes.[4]

* Churchill's child *opera comique*[5]

Mr Champigni[6] Prs of Wales. *never aging counting till the tenth.[7]

* Mrs Hamilton[8] to tack   Charles Stanhope[9]   Molly Henley[10]

Houghton, July 14th 1744.

Dear Horace,

I THANK you for your correspondence,[11] and the accounts you have given me of the busy world, I must be in your debt from

another gash upon his temple, but most luckily did himself no other hurt' (HW to Mann 19 July 1743 OS, MANN ii. 277). Sir Robert wrote Pelham 13 July: 'Horace will give you an account of my accident. . . . It has been said, this comes of dining with Tories' (William Coxe, *Memoirs of the Administration of . . . Henry Pelham*, 1829, i. 83).

---

1. Elizabeth Griffith (ca 1692–1773), m. (1714) Sir Robert Rich, 4th Bt (SELWYN 295, n. 33). HW wrote Mann 22 July 1744 OS: 'She has so often broken her heart about singers, that the *rent* must be very large by this time' (MANN ii. 481–2).

2. Thomas Winnington (1696–1746), M.P. Droitwich 1726–41, Worcester 1741–6; a Tory who later supported Sir Robert Walpole (OSSORY i. 252). The incident to which the memorandum refers has not been traced, although Winnington is mentioned in HW to Mann 22 July 1744 OS and in HW to Sir Charles Hanbury Williams 7 July 1744 OS (MANN ii. 481; SELWYN 56).

3. Unexplained.

4. Unexplained.

5. The younger Charles Churchill's daughter (d. before 28 July) by Giulia Frasi, opera singer; HW wrote this bon mot to Mann 22 July 1744 OS (MANN ii. 481; Sir George Grove, *Dictionary of Music*, 5th edn, ed. Blom, 1954, iii. 488).

6. Possibly Jean Champigny (1717–?87), Chevalier, French historian (NBG).

7. HW had seen the Princess of Wales at Ranelagh 7 July 1744 (SELWYN 57), but the specific reference is not traced.

8. Possibly Bridget Coward (d. 1775), m. (1719) Hon. George Hamilton (d. 1775), 6th son of James, 6th E. of Abercorn; or the wife of the Hon. Charles Hamilton (1704–86). 9th son of Lord Abercorn (*Scots Peerage*, ed. Paul, Edinburgh, 1904–14, i. 60–1). For HW's allusion to the numerous Hamiltons who received positions in the Prince of Wales's household through Lady Archibald Hamilton's influence, see MANN i. 279 and n. 60.

9. (1673–1760), M.P. (Sedgwick ii. 433–4).

10. Unexplained.

11. Missing.

hence where nothing occurs worthy of a fine gentleman. The amusements arising from the inanimate world afford no relish to men of taste. The wild beasts of the woods, the flocks and herds, wear neither breeches nor petticoats, and are wholly inconversable, and though they are not impertinent, and have *no pretty quarrels*, yet where's the wit in bleating and lowing, or even the dumb show of love, where there is no coquetting, jilting and deceiving! At my age, and to my age alone they are entertaining, who can admire the words of nature in plain simplicity. But still I have some comfort from these rural insipid pastimes. They really contribute to the amendment of my health. I am much better since I came hither[12] and truly I think by being here, all the disagreeable symptoms I had, are gone, and this I verily believe will make you partake in my pleasures. I know what would add to them, when you can persuade yourself to sacrifice the joys of the *beau-monde* to your amusements of a dull rural life.[13]

But we all love to please ourselves, and may it always be in your power to make yourself as happy as I wish you, for I am most truly

Yours most affectionately,

ORFORD

---

12. He had been at Houghton since 24 June (SELWYN 49; MANN ii. 467).

13. HW left London 20 Aug. OS and arrived at Houghton 22 Aug.; he stayed until early October (DALRYMPLE 23; Con-way to HW 1 July, 2 Sept. 1744 NS). HW had persuaded Sir Charles Hanbury Williams to accompany him, but Williams became ill and did not go (MANN ii. 498; SELWYN 63–5, 67–71).

To Horatio Walpole, Sr,[1] Tuesday 7 May 1745 OS

Printed for the first time from the MS now wsl; acquired, 1937, from G. H. Last, Bromley, Kent.

Endorsed (by 'Old Horace'): Nephew Horace May sept 1745 Rd 9.

Arlington Street, May 7th 1745.

Dear Sir,

I CAN'T lose the first moment to repeat to you how very much you have obliged me.[2] I hope I shall never feel it less warmly than I do now, and that I shall always be as eager to show you my gratitude, as I now am to have the opportunity.

I hope you have received the letter from my brother:[3] he promised me to write you one; pray let me know if he has; I know he does not love the trouble; but if he has not, I will not rest till he has. In the meantime, I beg you will keep this letter, by which I assure you my brother gave me the most absolute promise of choosing your son[4] the next Parliament for Castlerising.[5] Mr Churchill[6] is not dead, but past recovery.

You will have had, Sir, many accounts of our great misfortune:[7] as nobody from their experience and zeal will take it more to heart than you, I wish I could send you any more favourable particulars.

1. Horatio Walpole (1678–1757), cr. (1756) Bn Walpole of Wolterton; 'Old Horace'; HW's uncle; M.P. 1710–56. He was later the subject of several controversies with HW, so violent that HW wrote detailed accounts of them and jokingly contemplated the publication of two volumes of 'Horatiana . . . or a full and true account of the bloody civil wars of the house of Walpole, being a narrative of the unhappy differences between Horatio and Horace Walpoles' (Montagu i. 186). One of these, 'A Narrative of the Proceedings on the intended Marriage between Lord Orford and Miss Nicholl' is an appendix to Gray ii. 193ff. 'He ['Old Horace'] knew something of everything but how to hold his tongue, or how to apply his knowledge. . . . His mind was a strange mixture of sense alloyed by absurdity, wit by mimicry, knowledge by buffoonery, bravery by meanness, honesty by selfishness, impertinence by nothing' (*Mem. Geo. II,* i. 140–1).

2. Unexplained.

3. Robert Walpole, who had succeeded as 2d E. of Orford on the death of his father 18 March 1745 OS. His letter is missing.

4. Horatio Walpole (1723–1809), 2d Bn Walpole of Wolterton, 1757; cr. (1806) E. of Orford; 'Pigwiggin.'

5. The Walpole family had controlled it for year; see *post* 15 May 1745 OS; L. B. Namier, *Structure of Politics at the Accession of George III,* 2d edn, 1957, p. 145; J. H. Plumb, *Sir Robert Walpole: The Making of a Statesman,* Boston, 1956, pp. 57–61, 99–104.

6. Lt-Gen. Charles Churchill (ca 1679–1745), M.P. for Castle Rising 1715–45; he died 14 May 1745 (Sedgwick i. 551–2; GM 1745, xv. 276). Richard Rigby (1722–88) was returned in his place (*post* 15 May 1745 OS, n. 2).

7. The British defeat at the battle of Fontenoy (then called Tournay) 11 May 1745 NS (30 April OS).

SIR ROBERT WALPOLE, BY CHARLES JERVAS

The Dutch mail of yesterday indeed softens our loss a good deal, and reduces it to four thousand men.[8] We have no accounts of what the French have suffered; but it can't be considerable, for though our troops fought so desperately, it was against cannon, rather than men. We had but two small batteries, and those at too great a distance to have effect; while the French had their whole train of artillery. Sure Koninsegg[9] is most blameable! We had but forty-four to fourscore thousand: fought between two incessant batteries, the most considerable of which, we had no notice of. 'Tis not known whether the Duc d'Harcourt[10] or the Count de Saxe[11] commanded them: they talk of the King's or the Dauphin's[12] coming up with the Household Troops. Our Guards have suffered exceedingly: the young men have highly distinguished themselves, and very fatally![13] There never were so many officers lost. There are certainly killed, Sir James Campbell,[14] Gen. Ponsonby,[15] Col. Carpenter,[16] Kellet,[17] Gee,[18] Hallct,[19] Bob Douglas,[20] Lord Morton's[21] brother, young Ross[22] of the House of Commons, Col. and Major Montagu's brothers,[23] and Lord

8. Reported in *Daily Adv.* 11 May.

9. Lothar Joseph Dominik (1673–1751), Graf von Königscgg und Rothenfels; imperial field marshal and councillor; in command of the Austrian Netherlands since 12 Feb. 1745 (MANN iii. 20, n. 27; Constant von Wurzbach, *Biographisches Lexikon des Kaiserthums Oesterreich*, Vienna, 1856–90, xii. 229–31). The *London Gazette Extraordinary* 11 May reported, 'His Royal Highness the Marshal Konigsegg, and the Prince of Waldeck, resolved . . . to attempt it, though the enemy was advantageously posted, as well as superior in number' (GM 1745, xv. 246).

10. François, Duc d'Harcourt (1689–1750), Maréchal de France, 1746.

11. Hermann-Maurice, Comte de Saxe (1696–1750), Maréchal de France, 1744; he was in command (MANN iii. 39, n. 4).

12. Louis XV and Louis (1729–65), respectively.

13. The account of the battle and list of dead and wounded is in the *London Gazette Extraordinary* 11 May OS (GM 1745, xv. 246–9).

14. Hon. Sir James Campbell (ca 1667–1745), K.B., 1743; Lt-Gen., 1742 (MANN iii. 42, n. 3).

15. Hon. Henry Ponsonby (d. 1745), Col.

of the 37th Foot, 1735; Maj.-Gen., 1743 (ibid. 43, n. 4).

16. Robert Carpenter (d. 1745), Capt., 1734; Col. (army rank) (ibid. 43, n. 5).

17. William Kellet (d. 1745), Lt, 1726; Capt. of the 2d Regiment of Foot Guards (ibid. 43, n. 11).

18. William Gee (d. 1745), Lt-Col. of the 20th Foot (ibid. 43, n. 9).

19. Not identified.

20. Hon. Robert Douglas (ca 1703–45), Col. of the 3d Regiment of Foot Guards; M.P. (ibid. 43, n. 6; Sedgwick i. 618).

21. James Douglas (ca 1702–68), styled Lord Aberdour 1730–8; 14th E. of Morton, 1738.

22. Hon. Charles Ross of Balnagowan (1721–45), Lt and Capt. of 3d Foot Guards, 1741; M.P. Ross-shire 1741–5; in Dec. 1741 it was charged that Ross was under age when elected, but he was not unseated (ibid. i. 244, n. 10; Sedgwick ii. 393).

23. Edward Montagu (d. 1745), Lt-Col. of the 31st Foot; Christopher Montagu, army chaplain, also died about this time; Charles Montagu (d. 1777), Maj. in the 11th (Sowle's) Regiment, was wounded (MONTAGU i. 11 and n. 2; MANN iii. 43, n. 8; Conway to HW 14 May 1745 NS; GM 1745, xv. 248; *Daily Adv.* 17 May).

Charles Hay,[24] who had both his legs shot off. Lord Cathcart[25] is wounded in the face, Lord Ankram[26] in the back of his head, Lord George Sackville[27] in the breast, Lord Petersham[28] in the foot, Jack Mostyn[29] and Vanbrugh;[30] all slightly; so is Lord Albemarle[31] who was beat down by the wind of a ball. 'Tis said young Honeywood[32] who suffered so much at Dettingen, has lost a leg. I am so lucky to have lost no friend. Harry Conway,[33] and Lord Malpas[34] who arrived the night before, are both safe. I forgot among the killed, poor Berkeley,[35] Lady Betty Germain's[36] favourite nephew. Lord Dunmore,[37] Elliot,[38] Gen. J. Campbell,[39] Fitzroy[40] and several others were not got up, which makes the greatest noise. Hildsley[41] who led up

24. Lord Charles Hay (d. 1760); he was severely wounded and reported killed, but recovered to receive the formal compliments of officers and men (F. H. Skrine, *Fontenoy*, 1906, p. 171, n.).

25. Charles Cathcart (1721–76), 9th Bn, 1740. 'The black patch over the "Fontenoy" scar on his cheek (of which he was very proud) appears in all his portraits' (GEC iii. 106, n. *b*).

26. William Henry Ker (d. 1775), styled E. of Ancram 1722–67; 4th M. of Lothian, 1767; aide-de-camp to the D. of Cumberland 1745–6; Gen., 1770; M.P. 1747–63.

27. George Sackville (1716–85), later (1769) Germain, cr. (1782) Vct Sackville; M.P., P.C.; commander-in-chief of the British forces in Germany under Prince Ferdinand of Brunswick until he was dismissed from the service after the battle of Minden.

28. William Stanhope (1719–79), styled Vct Petersham 1742–56; 2d E. of Harrington, 1756; Gen., 1770; M.P. 1741–56 (MANN iii. 43, n. 4).

29. John Mostyn (1709–79), Gen., 1772; M.P. 1741–68.

30. Charles Vanbrugh (d. 1745, of wounds received at Fontenoy), son of Sir John Vanbrugh (ibid. iii. 43, n. 12).

31. William Anne van Keppel (1702–54), 2d E. of Albemarle, 1718; aide-de-camp to the King 1724–34; Lt-Gen., 1745; served at Dettingen (1743) and Culloden (1746); commander-in-chief of the forces in Scotland, 1746; K.B., 1725; K.G., 1749; Governor of Virginia 1737–54; ambassador to France 1749–54.

32. Philip Honywood (ca 1710–85), of Marks Hall, Essex; Lt-Col. of 3d Dragoons, 1743; Gen., 1777; M.P. 1754–84. He sus-

tained nine wounds at Dettingen, the most dangerous very near the brain (ibid. ii. 261, n. 25; Namier and Brooke ii. 635–6).

33. Henry Seymour Conway was a Lt-Col. on the D. of Cumberland's staff and one of his six aides-de-camp (MANN iii. 43, n. 13).

34. George Cholmondeley (1724–64), styled Vct Malpas, HW's nephew; M.P. 1754–64; served as a volunteer at Fontenoy; Col. 65th Foot 1760–4 (Namier and Brooke ii. 213–14).

35. Henry Berkeley (d. 1745), son of the Hon. Henry Berkeley (MANN i. 459, n. 18).

36. Lady Elizabeth Berkeley (1680–1769), m. (1706) Sir John Germain, Bt (d. 1718).

37. See *ante* 16 July 1743 OS, n. 2. That Dunmore and other officers did not arrive in time for the battle is mentioned in Philip Yorke to H. Walpole, Sr, 4 May 1745 OS; see HW to Conway 27 May 1745 OS, n. 8.

38. Probably George Augustus Eliott (1717–90), cr. (1787) Bn Heathfield of Gibraltar; wounded at Dettingen and Fontenoy with the 2d Horse Grenadier Guards; aide-de-camp to George II 1756–9; Gen., 1778; commander-in-chief in Ireland 1774–5; Gov. of Gibraltar during a siege of four years 1779–83; K.B., 1783.

39. John Campbell (ca 1693–1770), 4th D. of Argyll, 1761; Gen., 1765; M.P. 1713–61; K.T., 1765.

40. Charles Fitzroy (?1713–82), later (1749) Fitzroy Scudamore; M.P. 1733–82; Capt. 5th Foot, 1735; Capt. and Lt-Col. 1st Foot Guards, 1740; Second Maj., 1747 (Namier and Brooke ii. 436–7).

41. Francis Hildsley or Hildesley (fl.

Harry Conway's company, who was about the Duke, as his aide-de-camp, was killed. The Blues and Highlanders particularly distinguished themselves, well; the Dutch cavalry, ill, for they ran away.[42] Boetzlaer's[43] brother is killed. The Dutch are very zealous and warm to repair this loss: Tournay must be gone, but they depend much on the citadel's holding out, which is reckoned the strongest in Europe.[44] The King was gone on Friday;[45] and was out of sight of Sheerness when the messenger came up, that was sent after him; he has since been blown back into Harwich, but whether he will come back or not!—

This, Sir, is all I can venture to tell you on good grounds; for I won't send you the thousand idle reports: I wish I had any room to give you a better prospect!

I beg my best compliments to my aunt[46] and all your family, and pray, Sir, believe it is from my heart and not to finish my letter of course that I assure [you] I am

Yours most devotedly

HOR. WALPOLE

PS. The Prince[47] said to Hop,[48] 'Ce n'est qu'une écratigneure [égratinurc]'—He replied, 'Monseigneur, c'est un coup mortel, s'il n'est remedié d'abord.'

1705–58) was wounded at Fontenoy but survived to be promoted for gallantry (*Notes and Queries* 12th ser. iii. 12; *Army Lists*, 1740, p. 12; Charles Dalton, *George the First's Army 1714–1727*, 1910–12, ii. 265–7). For Conway's account of the battle see his letter to HW 14 May 1745 NS.

42. 'The Dutch had orders only to defend themselves in case they should be attacked, which they were not. . . . Their worthy ambassador [at Paris] . . . owned their troops did nothing, but ascribed it to a pique of their old generals for having the Prince of Waldeck put over their heads' (Morton to Newcastle, Parks, 16 May NS, BM Add. MSS 32804, f. 332; MANN iii. 43, n. 14a).

43. Jacob Filips Boetzelaer (1711–81), Baron, Dutch envoy extraordinary to England 1744–5, minister plenipotentiary 1745–7 (*Repertorium der diplomatischen Vertreter aller Länder*, Vol. II, ed. Friedrich Hausmann, Zurich, 1950, p. 245). His

brother, Karel Boetzelaer (d. 1745), Baron, was Lt-Col. and Capt. in the Dutch Guards (*Daily Adv.* 7 May; *London Gazette* 7–11 May, No. 8430, *sub* Hague, 18 May NS).

44. See Conway to HW 26 May 1745 NS and n. 7.

45. 3 May, when the King took a barge from Whitehall; he sailed 10 May for Holland, landed there 12 May and proceeded to Hanover (MANN iii. 39, n. 6, 44; GM 1745, XV. 274).

46. Mary Magdelaine Lombard (ca 1695–1783), m. (1720) Horatio Walpole, 'Old Horace.'

47. Frederick Louis (1707–51), P. of Wales 1727–51; see the ballad written in French by the Prince two days after the news of Fontenoy reached London (MANN iii. 45–6).

48. Hendrik Hop (1686–1761), Bn; Lt-Gen.; Dutch envoy extraordinary to England 1723–61 (ibid. iii. 212, n. 6).

From SIR EDWARD WALPOLE, Wednesday 15 May 1745 OS

Printed from the MS now WSL; first printed (misdated 17 May 1745), Cunningham i. 355–6. The MS was sold, probably by Lord Euston as executor to the 6th Earl Waldegrave, to Richard Bentley (1794–1871), the publisher, to whose grandson it descended; acquired from the latter's estate in 1937 by WSL through the good offices of John E. Hodgson.

Pell Mell,[1] May 15, 1745.

Sir,

CASTLE Rising is a family borough.[2] Lord Orford's son[3] ought to be brought in there preferably to anybody. Next to him, I, and then you, my uncle[4] and his children[5] have the next claim; then the Townshends[6] and the Hammonds.[7] Who all together make so large a number that I did not imagine there was a possibility of a recommendation of mine taking place. Otherwise, as I have frequently wished it, I should have spoke to my Lord long ago, but I always thought he was bound to offer it to some one of them, whether they applied or not. And in case they should all of them decline it, I did imagine my Lord must have, out of his own particular friends, more than one, whom he would wish to distinguish by so great a favour. For which reason, besides the consideration of our near relations, I

1. Sir Robert had given Edward a freehold in Pall Mall (HW, 'Account of my Conduct,' *Works* ii. 365; MANN iii. 32, n. 3).

2. It had been one since the early eighteenth century; see H. L. Bradfer-Lawrence, 'Castle Rising and the Walpoles,' *Supplement to Blomefield's Norfolk*, ed. Ingleby, 1929, pp. 29–46; L. B. Namier, *Structure of Politics at the Accession of George III*, 2d edn, 1957, pp. 145–6; J. H. Plumb, *Sir Robert Walpole: The Making of a Statesman*, Boston, 1956, pp. 57–8, 99–101. Gen. Charles Churchill, an old friend of Sir Robert Walpole, had represented the borough for thirty years (1715–45). His death on 14 May created a vacancy and caused the quarrel between HW and Edward over the patronage for this borough. Richard Rigby (1722–88), HW's friend, and later the Duke of Bedford's political manager, was returned 24 Oct. and served until 1747 (Sedgwick ii. 383–4), when he was replaced by Lord Luxborough (MANN iii. 419; Sedgwick ii. 192). HW visited Rigby for three weeks in June 1745 (MONTAGU i. 14).

3. George Walpole (1730–91), son of Robert Walpole; styled Vct Walpole; 3d E. of Orford, 1751.

4. *Ante* February 1741, n. 2.

5. His sons were Horatio Walpole ('Pigwiggin'); Thomas (1727–1803); Richard (1728–98); and Robert (1736–1810). See *ante* 7 May 1745 OS.

6. The sons of HW's aunt, Dorothy Walpole, Lady Townshend; see *ante* HW to Lady Walpole, 1725, n. 3.

7. The sons of HW's aunt, Susan Walpole (1687–1763), m. (1707) Anthony Hamond (d. 1743): Richard (d. 1776); Robert (d. 1750); and Horace (1718–86) (Sir Bernard Burke, *Landed Gentry*, 1851, i. 533; see also Sir William Hoste, *Memoirs*, 1833, i. 5, n.).

should have thought it presumption in me to apply, though there is no one thing I should covet more than thus to support a friend, and by it, to give myself an additional credit and weight in Parliament. How you came never to think of me who stand so directly before you, or if you did think of me, how you happened to imagine that I was not to be consulted in an affair of this consequence, where birth and seniority[8] give me so just and natural a pretension, I cannot conceive. It is so contemptuous and arrogant a treatment, that it is not easily to be forgot. For to be sensible yourself how very desirable a thing it is, either in a private view in regard to a friend, or in the eye of the world, in respect to one's self, and to think that I either did not desire it or did not know its advantages, is to despise me beyond measure.

But your conduct to me has always been of the same kind and has made it the most painful thing in the world to me to have any commerce with you. You have, I must confess, showed a great disposition to me and to my children[9] at all times, which is agreeable to the good nature, that I shall ever do you the justice to think and say you possess in a great degree. But it has been mixed with what I dare say you can't help and never meant offence by, but still what I am not obliged to bear, such a confidence and presumption of some kind of superiority, that, my sentiments not tallying with yours upon that head, it has been very unpleasant. You have assumed to yourself a preeminence, from an imaginary disparity between us in point of abilities and character that, although you are a very great man, I cannot submit to. And you have crowned the whole with this most evident proof that I have not mistaken you. Therefore since the conditions of your friendship and kindness are such that I must be subject to direct injuries, such as this cruel wrong done me now, or those kinds of hurts that a man feels most when they have the face of kindness, I must be excused if I beg it of you as a favour, never to be kind to me again.

I am your humble servant

Ed. Walpole

8. Edward was HW's senior by 11 years.
9. His four children by Dorothy Clement (ca 1715–ca 1739), a milliner, were: Laura (ca 1734–1813), m. (1758) Hon. Frederick Keppel, Bp of Exeter; Maria (1736–1807), m. 1 (1759) James Waldegrave, 2d E. Waldegrave; m. 2 (1766) William Henry, D. of Gloucester; Edward (1737–71); Charlotte (1738–89), m. (1760) Lionel Tollemache, styled Lord Huntingtower, 5th E. of Dysart.

To Sir Edward Walpole, ca Thursday 16 May 1745 OS

Printed from the MS now WSL; first printed, Cunningham i. 356–60; reprinted, Toynbee ii. 91–6. For the history of the MS see *ante* 15 May 1745 OS. Dated with reference to *ante* 15 May 1745 OS, to which this letter is a reply. *Endorsed* (by HW): This answer not sent.

BROTHER, I am sorry you won't let me say, Dear Brother, but till you have still[1] farther proved how impossible it is for you to have any affection for me, I will never begin my letters as you do.

Sir,

Before I enter upon your letter,[2] I must be so impertinent even as to give my elder brother advice, and that is the next letter you write, to consider whether the person it is addressed to, has any dependence upon you, or which I am sure your heart will tell you I have not, any obligation to you. If they have neither, they may happen to laugh at your style.

Castle Rising is a family borough. This is your first proposition, but not very definite. It is a borough in *our* family, but I never heard, that it was Parliamentarily entailed upon every branch of our family. If it was, how came Mr Churchill to be always chose there? However, before I ever undertake anything again, I will certainly examine our genealogical table, and be sure, that[3] Lord W.,[4] yourself and all our eleven first cousins,[5] have no mind to the same thing.

Lord Orford's son ought to be brought in there preferably to anybody. Lord Orford's son is but fifteen, and consequently incapable of being brought in anywhere these six years.

Next to him I and then you. N.B. We are both in already,[6] though to be sure you are right in the order of succession, which you seem to be perfectly master of.

Otherwise as I have long wished it, I should have spoke to my Lord long ago. I[7] spoke to my Lord lately, and have got it.[8]

1. 'Have' crossed out after 'still.'
2. *Ante* 15 May 1745 OS.
3. 'Not one of' crossed out and 'Lord W., yourself and all' written above.
4. Walpole, their nephew.
5. 'After you' crossed out after 'cousins.' HW refers to their eleven surviving male cousins in the paternal line.
6. Edward was at this time sitting for Great Yarmouth and HW for Callington.
7. 'Did' crossed out after 'I' and 'speak' altered to 'spoke'; 'long ago' crossed out and 'lately' written above.
8. Apparently HW's cousin 'Pigwiggin' was considered first; then HW proposed Rigby, although Oxford University expressed opposition to his candidacy (Sedgwick ii. 383).

I always thought he was bound to offer it to some one of them. He does not seem to have been of your opinion.

To give myself an additional credit and weight in Parliament. You might have left out *additional.*

How[9] you came never to think of me. For your sake I won't answer this.

Or how you happened to imagine I was not to be consulted. I will ask you another question, how you happen to imagine it was necessary for me to consult you? Have you ever given me any encouragement to consult you in anything? How must I consult you? By letter? You never would see me either at your own house or here![10]

Whose birth and seniority give me so just and natural a pretension —To my father's estate before me, to nothing else that I know of.

It is so contemptuous and arrogant a treatment. Those words I return you, being full as proper and decent from me to you, as from you to me, whose birth, though thank God not my seniority, is as considerable as yours.

As to the desirableness of this affair, your whole paragraph may be very political, but is not argumentative.

But your conduct to me has always been of the same kind. As you are so kind afterwards as to explain what my conduct has always been to you, I shall certainly not endeavour to refute this passage but submit myself to your own acknowledgments.

The most painful thing in the world to have any commerce with you; I believe it, for I have always seen it, and in vain endeavoured to make it more tolerable to you.

You have I must confess showed a great disposition to me and to my children at all times. Thank you.

Good nature, which I think and say you possess in a great degree. Dear brother, I wish I could think the same of you.

It has been mixed with what I dare say you can't help, and never meant offence by. I may if I please believe the same of your letter.

A confidence and presumption of some kind of superiority. This I must answer a little fuller, as being the only thing in your letter, which you have not confuted yourself. I won't appeal to everybody

---

9. 'Your' crossed out after 'How.'
10. The authority you affect over me is ridiculous, and for consulting you, good God! Do you think you ever judge so dispassionately, as that any man living would consult you? (HW).

that has ever seen me with you, but to yourself. Lay your hand on your heart, and say, if I have not all my lifetime to this very instant, treated you with a respect, a deference, an awe, a submission,[11] beyond what, I say to my shame, I ever showed my father; and you ought to be ashamed too, who made it necessary for his peace and for my own, that I should treat you so. I never disputed your opinion, I never gave my own, till you had yours: this was confidence and presumption!

You have assumed to yourself a preeminence, from an imaginary disparity between us in point of abilities and character. Who told you so? Not your eyes, but your jealousy. I'll tell you, brother, the only superiority I ever pretended over you, was in my temper.

Although you are a very great man. I leave that expression to support[12] itself upon its own force, meaning and elegance.

Since the conditions of your friendship and kindness are such that I must be subject to direct injuries. What those *direct injuries* are may be collected from what you have said above of my constant behaviour to you and your children at all times, or still more clearly, from the next paragraph, wherein you call 'em, *Those kinds of hurts that a man feels most when they have the face of kindness.* This by all truth is the only hurt I am ever conscious of having done you.

Before I take notice of the conclusion of your letter, I must mention a few other things. In your letter to our brother,[13] who has still less deserved your monstrous behaviour to him, having always had that affection for you, which I was always desirous of having, you tell him he gives away his interest; and in the same letter are for recommending a friend of yours. Whatever your injustice may make you think of me and my friends; neither my brother Orford, nor[14] I hope any man else thinks his interest in worse hands, when given at my suit, than at yours. You tell him too, your honour is concerned in this—'Tis a strange point of honour you have always laid down to yourself of opposing everything I wish. 'Tis your own fault that I rake up your wrongs with me. Because I was always silent, did you imagine I was always ignorant? In my mother's lifetime, you accused me of fomenting her anger against you. The instant she died, did I

11. 'Which' crossed out after 'submission.'
12. 'That' crossed out after 'support'; '&' crossed out after 'force.'

13. Robert, E. of Orford; the letter is missing.
14. '&' crossed out and 'nor' written above; 'no' crossed out after 'hope' and 'any' written above.

not bring you all my letters to her[15] which she had kept, in never a one of which, was your name mentioned, but to persuade her to continue[16] that love to you, which your behaviour has always laboured to extinguish in the hearts of all your relations. As to my father, I well know how ill you always used him on my account. Your writing against Dr Middleton[17] who came to make me a visit at Houghton of two days, is one instance among many. Your converting[18] all the jealousy you used to have of Lady Mary,[19] into a friendship with her, to prevent her loving me, is another. I only touch on these. Know, brother, that you never came where my father was, that I did not beg and beseech him, never to take notice of me before[20] you. This I have living witnesses to prove. For your transports of jealousy, about my speaking in Parliament,[21] I will say nothing, but this: was it reasonable I should be silent there, because you had no ambition of making a figure? oh! brother, so far from having that self-conceit you attribute to me, all my family and acquaintance know, that no man has a greater opinion of your parts; no man has commended you more. I have always said, all the world would love you, if you let them: and for your love to your father, I have always declared, that of all his children I was convinced you loved him the best.[22] What have you said of *me* behind my back?

---

15. Of which only four have been recovered.

16. 'Have' crossed out and 'continue' written above; 'for' crossed out after 'love' and 'to' written above.

17. Conyers Middleton (1683–1750), D.D., author, controversialist, HW's correspondent. He had taken some pains to become acquainted with HW at Cambridge, apparently in hopes of preferment through Sir Robert's offices, but HW genuinely liked him (Ketton-Cremer 43–4). 'My brother hated Middleton. . . . once when Lord Montford brought Middleton for one night only to Houghton, my brother wrote my father a most outrageous letter, telling him that he knew I had fetched Middleton to Houghton to write my father's life' (HW to Mann 22 Dec. 1750 OS, Mann iv. 215). The visit to which HW refers probably took place in 1741 (Cole's account of Middleton, Dalrymple 306).

18. 'Making over' crossed out and 'converting' written above.

19. Lady Maria (Mary) Walpole (ca 1725–1801), m. (1746) Charles Churchill; HW's half-sister.

20. 'You' written over 'him' and then crossed out after 'before.'

21. HW spoke for the first time in the House of Commons 23 March 1742, 'against the motion for a secret committee on my father. This speech was published in the magazines, but was entirely false, and had not one paragraph of my real speech in it' ('Short Notes,' Gray i. 12). The committee was to inquire into 'the conduct of Robert Earl of Orford during the last ten years,' and the motion passed the House by a vote of 252 to 245. The evidence it collected was inconclusive (ibid., n. 77). For the true text of the speech, see HW to Mann 24 March 1742 OS, Mann i. 376–7.

22. HW wrote Mason 2 May 1773 of Sir Edward, 'who I have often said, adored his father, and of all his children loved him the best' (Mason i. 70).

I have done, brother, though by this example, believe I have not said the hardest things that I could to you.

You conclude with disclaiming all friendship with, and relation to me. After the vain pains I have taken to deserve that friendship, and the regard I have in vain had to that relation I don't know whether[23] I ought not readily to embrace this entire rupture. However as I think you are good-natured when you are cool, and must have repented this unmerited ill treatment, I can forgive you,[24] and for this last time offer you my friendship: at the same time assuring[25] you, that I despise your anger, and if you[26] persist in disclaiming my brotherhood, the only cover that you have for your abuse, I must tell you, that you *shall* treat me like a gentleman.

Yours or not

as you please

Hor. Walpole

PS. If you have anything farther to say to me, it must be in person, for I will not read any more such letters—nor will I be affronted.[27]

PS. If I have entered upon more points than your letter led me to, it was from my heart's being full of resentment for a long[28] series of your injustice to me, and from being glad to take the opportunity of making you sensible of it, by this expostulation, which I have never been able to do by the most submissive behaviour, and by every instance I had in my power of showing you, how much I wished you would be my friend. But that is past; if you have any-

---

23. 'This entire rupt' crossed out after 'whether.'

24. Three years later, when Edward planned to use HW's house for his daughter Laura (who was ill) without asking the owner's permission, HW wrote Montagu, 'I can conceive forgiveness; I can conceive using people ill—but how does one feel to use anybody very ill without any provocation, and then ask favours of them?' (14 July 1748, Montagu i. 61). Six years later HW proved his forgiveness when Edward had been made victim by a gang that charged him with sodomitical assault; HW came up to London and helped to convict the conspirators (W. S. Lewis, *Horace Walpole,*

[New York], 1960, p. 23). Later he collected Edward's drawings and directed that they be preserved in his family, and paid tribute to his 'unaffected heroism' at his death (HW to Lady Ossory 19 Jan. 1784, Ossory ii. 432). After a long tribute to his brother in *Last Journals* (i. 102) HW concludes, 'This tribute to his virtues I pay with pleasure, and it may be credited, for to me he was never affectionate, though, but for one short period, we always lived on fair terms.'

25. 'Telling' crossed out and 'assuring' written above.

26. 'Not' crossed out after 'you.'

27. This postscript has been crossed out.

28. 'Of' crossed out after 'long.'

ROBERT, LORD WALPOLE, BY JOHN WOOTTON

thing farther to say to me, it must be in person, for I will not read any more such letters—nor will I be affronted.

To Sir Edward Walpole, Friday 17 May 1745 OS

Printed from the MS now WSL; first printed, Cunningham i. 360; reprinted, Toynbee ii. 96. For the history of the MS see *ante* 15 May 1745 OS.
Endorsed (by HW): This answer sent.

May 17, 1745.

Dear Brother,

YOU have used me very ill without any provocation or any pretence. I have always made it my study to deserve your friendship, as you yourself own, and by a submission which I did not owe you. For consulting you in what you had nothing to do, I certainly did not, nor ever will, while you profess so much aversion for me. I am still ready to live with you upon any terms of friendship and equality, but I don't mind your anger, which can only hurt yourself, when you come to reflect with what strange passion you have treated me, who have always loved you, have always tried to please you, have always spoke of you with regard,[1] and who will yet be, if you will let me,

Your affectionate brother

and humble servant

HOR. WALPOLE

To Robert, 2d Earl of Orford, Saturday 7 September 1745 OS

Missing; mentioned by HW to C. H. Williams 7 Sept. 1745: 'I am ashamed of sending you such a scrap of a letter, but I have found so many that I must answer, besides a long one I am obliged to write to my brother about his wife, that I hope you will forgive me' (SELWYN 95). 'My Lady O. is arrived; I hear she says, only to endeavour to get a certain allowance' (HW to Mann 6 Sept. 1745 OS, MANN iii. 104).

1. On 25 May HW wrote Montagu of Sir Edward, 'There is nothing in the world the Baron of Englefield has such an aversion for, as for his brother' (MONTAGU i. 14).

From GEORGE, LORD WALPOLE, ?September 1748

Missing; mentioned by Lord Chedworth to HW 23 September 1748: 'But Lord Walpole told me before I had your letter that he had wrote to you concerning this affair [he thought 'that his father is so angry with him, that . . . he is unwilling to return'] and said he had not heard from you lately and that he did intend to send his servant to you if he did not hear from you soon.'

From SIR EDWARD WALPOLE, Monday 29 May 1749 OS

Missing, except for a scrap, now WSL; bought June 1962 from W. A. Myers.

May 29, 1749.

. . . house at Tickenham does not co
the plan of your improvements . . .[1]

I am yours etc.

ED. WALPOLE

From HORATIO WALPOLE, SR, Thursday 20 June 1751 OS

Printed with the appendix 'The Nicoll Affair' in GRAY ii. 214–15.

To HORATIO WALPOLE, SR, Friday 21 June 1751 OS

Printed with the appendix 'The Nicoll Affair' in GRAY ii. 215.

From HORATIO WALPOLE, SR, Friday 21 June 1751 OS

Printed with the appendix 'The Nicoll Affair' in GRAY ii. 216.

To HORATIO WALPOLE, SR, Saturday 22 June 1751 OS

Printed with the appendix 'The Nicoll Affair' GRAY ii. 205–6.

1. HW began making his improvementsof SH in 1748.

From CHARLES CHURCHILL, ca Friday 19 June 1752 OS

Missing; HW mentions to Conway 23 June 1752 OS 'what Mr Churchill writes me, the distress and poverty of France.'

To LADY MARY CHURCHILL, Thursday 27 August 1752 OS

Missing; listed in HW's memoranda on HW to Conway 23 Aug. 1752 OS.

To SIR EDWARD WALPOLE, ca Thursday 6 December 1753

Missing; mentioned by HW to Mann 6 Dec. 1753: 'I have but just time to send my brother an account of his succession[1] . . . you shall let me go make my brother happy' (MANN iv. 403).

To the HON. THOMAS WALPOLE, Thursday 5 September 1754

Missing; listed in the catalogue of Charles F. Heartman, Metuchen, N.J. (10 April 1926) as item 605: 'A.L.S., 1 page, quarto. Strawberry Hill. Sept. 5th, 1754.'

To LORD ORFORD, ca Tuesday 25 March 1755

Missing; mentioned in HW's 'Short Notes,' GRAY i. 26: 'In March 1755 I was very ill used by my nephew Lord Orford upon a contested election in the House of Commons, on which I wrote him a long letter with an account of my own conduct in politics.'

---

1. 'In December died Erasmus Shorter Esq. the last and youngest of my mother's brothers. He dying without a will, his fortune of £30,000 came in equal shares between my brother Sir Edward, me, and my cousins, Francis Earl of Hertford, Colonel Henry Seymour Conway and Miss Anne Seymour Conway' ('Short Notes,' GRAY i. 25). See also MONTAGU i. 156–7 and MANN iv. 403, n. 8.

From Lord Orford, Saturday 10 April 1756

Printed for the first time from the MS now WSL. For the history of the MS see *ante* 15 May 1745 OS.
Dated by HW to Lord Orford 10 April 1756, a reply to this letter.
Endorsed (by HW): Ld Orford to Hor. Walpole Junior.

Saturday, three o'clock.

Dear Sir,

IT was with great concern that I found the other day, and still find, that we differ in opinion, concerning the mutual entail[1] that Mr Walpole[2] and myself have thought proper to make of our estates, on the heirs male of the family; because, whenever I have the misfortune to think differently from you, I always suspect my own judgment; I am, notwithstanding after the most cool deliberation on this affair, still of opinion, that it is a very prudent and justifiable agreement, and what, I am firmly persuaded, my grandfather[3] (if alive) would have come into. I own myself so very ignorant of the doctrine of chattels, as not to be able to determine what difference my father's[4] death and the marriage of my cousin's[5] has made in the goodness of the bargain: nor indeed has it any weight with me, because if the measure is a right one, the advantage the younger branch of our family may possibly reap from it, ought not to hinder the getting it into execution. With regard to Mr Walpole, the many obligations I have to him, and the good will I bear his children, have I own inclined me to wish, if I have no issue myself, that the estate might one day be joined with the name, nor do I think, if you consider the advantages that[6] what I will call the female part of the family, and especially that favourite daughter of Sir Robert's[7] received by his will,[8] you will not[9] be of opinion, that they have any

1. 'In April 1756 my uncle Horace Walpole having drawn in my nephew Lord Orford to alter the settlement of his estate, I entered into a new dispute with my uncle on behalf of my nephews Lord Malpas and Mr Cholmondeley and my sister Lady Mary Churchill, who were all injured by that disposition; and I wrote an account of that whole affair' ('Short Notes,' GRAY i. 26–7). HW's account, 'Case of the Entail of the Estate of Sir Robert Walpole Earl of Orford,' now WSL, is printed for the first time as Appendix 1 to this volume.
2. 'Old Horace.'
3. Sir Robert Walpole.
4. Robert, 2d E. of Orford, had died 31 March 1751.
5. Presumably Horatio Walpole, Jr, 'Pigwiggin.'
6. 'This' crossed out after 'that' in MS.
7. Lady Mary Churchill.
8. Sir Robert's will provided that the £12,000 advanced into the Exchequer by

injustice done them by this preference—I am now to thank you for the great frankness you have expressed in this affair, which I shall always esteem as a very great obligation; and as a proof of your friendship for me: I must likewise desire you will reck⁹ᵃ this matter secret, not that I apprehend that it will not bear the strictest examination from every unprejudiced person, but because, I have no inclination to appear in print, and that I think it rather impertinent to trouble the public with family concerns. I am dear Sir,

Yours most sincerely,

ORFORD

I have sent you a copy of the settlement.[10]

To LORD ORFORD, Saturday 10 April 1756

Printed for the first time from the MS now WSL. For the history of the MS see *ante* 15 May 1745 OS.
Endorsed (by HW): To Lord Orford.

Arlington Street, April 10, 1756.

My dear Lord

AS when you parted from me last, you did me the honour to thank me for what I had said to you, I take the liberty to send you the enclosed paper,[1] and beg you will read it coolly at your leisure. The facts contained in it are undeniable; and as I was so happy as to convince you that you had been overseen[2] in the fallacious bargain that had been offered to you, and showed you how much you would be tied up by it in the disposition of your estate whenever my uncle should die, so I will still hope that your justice and good nature will

his wife Maria Walpole before her marriage, to which he was entitled, be held for their daughter until her marriage, together with lands in the counties of Somerset and Salop and all of his jewels except those otherwise disposed of (will of Sir Robert Walpole).

9. 'Think' crossed out after 'not.'
9a. 'To reckon, consider, think' (OED).
10. Missing; probably the 'will of 1756'

(see Appendix 1, n. 1); HW refers to this document in his letter to 'Old Horace' *post* 13 April 1756.

1. Evidently a summary of arguments about the entail, but probably not HW's 'Case of the Entail,' printed as Appendix 1.

2. Originally 'overreached'; 'reached' crossed out, 'seen' written above.

carry equal conviction on the other topics:—but I shall say no more on that head—I only beg you for your own sake to be expeditious in dissolving a compact so unequal and so prejudicial to yourself.

I will not keep you, but[2a] to say one word in my own justification; I owed it to you, to my nephews,[3] to my sister,[4] and to their children[5] to set this affair in its true light; and I can[5a] honestly say, that so far from speaking or acting for any interest of my own, I evidently act against my interest. I have known above these two years that you had cut off the entail[6] of your estate: you will bear me witness, my Lord, that I never once gave you the most indirect hint that I wished you to resettle it, though I myself was cut off; and had you died without a will, the estate would have fallen into my brother's[7] power, whose laudable affection for very deserving though natural children,[8] might have induced him to leave the estate from me, if he died first. By your new settlement, I am secured—and yet, my Lord, so little do I expect, so little do I wish to outlive you and my brother, so averse am I from being benefited by an act[9] that is so deeply to wound the rest of my nearest relations, that I most fervently wish to see this security revoked—I desire to see myself exposed to every art that my uncle can use to hurt me; and when he will thus injure innocent children, and so many people who have never offended him, what must I not expect he will attempt against me who have detected so many of his mysterious dealings! I do not doubt but he will leave no means untried[10] to prejudice me even with you, my Lord, for saving you from his arts—and though I know

2a. 'Two' inserted after 'but' and then crossed out.

3. Sons of George, 3d E. of Cholmondeley: Vct Malpas (*ante* 7 May 1745, n. 34) and the Hon. Robert Cholmondeley (1727–1804), divine, m. (1746) Mary Woffington (ca 1729–1811).

4. Lady Mary Churchill.

5. The children of Vct Malpas were George James Cholmondeley, later 4th E. of Cholmondeley, and Hester Cholmondeley (1755–1828), who m. (1773) William Clapcott Lisle. Robert Cholmondeley's children were George James (1752–1830), Horace (b. 1753), Robert Francis (1756–77), Henrietta Maria (1754–1806), Hester Frances (1763–1844). Lady Mary Churchill's children were Charles (ca 1747–85), Robert (b. 1748), George (d. 1808), Henry,

Horatio (1759–1817), Mary (b. 1750), Sophia (before 1759–97) (Collins, *Peerage*, 1812, iv. 34–5; Mann viii. 524, n. 5; Hertford to HW 17 July 1764, n. 5; Selwyn 357; du Deffand iv. 440).

5a. 'Not' crossed out after 'can.'

6. His father, Robert, 2d E., and grandfather, Sir Robert, 1st E., had left large debts: 'He . . . has very prudently cut off the entail in order to raise a necessary sum of money' ('Case of the Entail,' Appendix 1).

7. Sir Edward Walpole.

8. See *ante* 15 May 1745 OS, n. 9.

9. The will of 1756 (see Appendix 1, n. 1).

10. 'Unused' crossed out and 'untried' written above.

MARY WALPOLE, LADY MALPAS, BY THOMAS HUDSON

nothing that would hurt me more than the loss of your affection, justice and honour compel me to act the part I do. I will say no more, my Lord, but that I do not desire you to make any secret of what[11] I have said to you—both my purpose, and the means I have employed to obtain it are honest, and I scorn disguise and mystery.

I am my dear Lord

Yours most sincerely

Hor. Walpole

PS. After this experience I hope you will not let my uncle persuade you to have any more private transactions with him—I desire not to be trusted myself, but, my dear Lord, consult the Duke of Grafton,[12] Mr George Townshend, or some other man of as great honour, and of whose friendship you are equally persuaded: their regard for you will make them see[13] what your careless and open honest heart prevents your attending to.

To Horatio Walpole, Sr, Tuesday 13 April 1756

Printed from the MS now wsl; first printed, Cunningham ix. 485–6; reprinted, Toynbee iii. 410–11. For the history of the MS see *ante* 15 May 1745 OS. *Endorsed* (in an unidentified hand): H.W. to H.W. Senior.

Arlington Street, April 13, 1756.

Sir

MY Lord Orford having sent me a copy of a paper which it seems you call *a mutual entail*,[1] but which in reality is an act to set aside your brother's grandchildren and daughter,[2] and finding my name inserted in it[3] (a strong presumption of how little you think there is of substantial on your part of the transaction) I must

11. 'Any thing' crossed out and 'what' written above.
12. Charles Fitzroy (1683–1757), 2d D. of Grafton; styled E. of Euston until 1690; Viceroy of Ireland 1720–4; P.C., 1715; K.G., 1721; F.R.S.
13. HW inserted 'them' after 'see' instead of after 'make.'

1. See *ante* 10 April 1756, n. 1.
2. Vct Malpas, Robert Cholmondeley (sons of Mary Walpole, Lady Malpas), and Lady Mary Churchill, 'my nephews and sister,' as HW says below; see Mann ix. 132 and n. 8.
3. See 'Case of the Entail,' Appendix 1.

desire my name may be omitted; and this, without supposing or pretending to suppose that I sacrifice the least prospect of interest; but I cannot suffer my name to stand with my consent as accessory to a deed so prejudicial to my nephews and to my sister, and so entirely annulling the will of my father, that great man, to whom you and I, Sir, owe all we have, and without whom I fear we had all remained in obscurity!

If this is denied me, I shall immediately execute the strongest act the law can invent or allow (and I don't know what the law cannot invent, and I do know that what it can invent, it will allow) to debar myself from ever receiving any benefit from your fortune, if the most improbable of all events[4] should happen, its coming to our line; and as a record of my disapprobation of this compact.

However, Sir, as no interest of my own is concerned, as I plead for those who are nearest and most dear to me, and as I think it so serious a thing lightly and without any reason to set aside the will of the dead,[5] and of what dead! I will, notwithstanding all our differences, still act the part of a relation, and even of a friend towards you, and as such, I most solemnly entreat and recommend to you to be content with all the obligations[6] you received from my father, and not exclude his grandchildren and his daughter from his estate. At least, I will not be a party to setting aside the disposition which he made of a fortune (acquired by himself) in favour of his own posterity.

I am Sir

Your humble servant

Hor. Walpole

---

4. 'Circumstances' crossed out and 'events' written above.

5. 'Wish' or 'with' inserted above 'dead.'

6. Sir Robert secured for his brother Horace the place of secretary to Gen. James Stanhope, minister to Spain, in 1706, which appointment began Horace's diplomatic career (J. H. Plumb, *Sir Robert Walpole: The Making of a Stateman*, Boston, 1956, pp. 122–3).

From HORATIO WALPOLE, SR, Tuesday 13 April 1756

Printed for the first time from the MS now WSL. For the history of the MS see *ante* 15 May 1745 OS.
Endorsed (by HW): H.W. Senior to H.W. Junior.

Cockpitt, April 13, 1756.

Sir

AS what has passed between Lord Orford and me relating to the mutual entail of our estates, has been done with the entire free will and in concert with his Lordship, I shall as soon as I have communicated your letter to me of this day[1] on the subject, to him, and taken proper advice upon it, return you an answer;[2] in the meantime I can assure you that I shall always endeavour, and I am not conscious of having ever done otherwise, to act the part of a relation and even of a friend towards you. I am

Sir
Your most humble servant

H. WALPOLE

From HORATIO WALPOLE, SR, Wednesday 14 April 1756

Printed for the first time from the MS now WSL. For the history of the MS see *ante* 15 May 1745 OS.
Endorsed (by HW): H.W. Senior to H.W. Junior.

Cockpitt, April 14, 1756.

Sir

I HAVE communicated to Lord Orford your letter to me of yesterday,[1] and am with his approbation to acquaint you, that you seem not to understand rightly, what has passed between his Lord-

1. See *ante* HW to 'Old Horace' 13 April 1756.
2. See *post* 'Old Horace' to HW 14 April 1756.

1. *Ante* HW to 'Old Horace' 13 April 1756.

ship and me, relating to the mutual entail of our estates, and therefore it may not be improper to give you a plain and true state of this affair.

My late, dear, good and great brother after having entailed his estate upon Sir Ed[ward] Walpole and you, and your heirs male respectively, gave the reversion of it, to Lord Malpas, and his brother and their heirs male, and in default of such issue to Lady Mary Churchill etc., and it is well known that this disposition of your father's arose merely upon my declining to accept of an offer he made me of a mutual entail of our estates upon our two families, which I own I could not agree to at that time, because the settlement must then have been made upon such very unequal terms, as might hazard the doing a most irreparable injury to my own family; for it would, had I come into it, have been in the power of the present Lord Orford, when he came of age,[2] to have defeated any settlement of my brother's estate, that could have been made with respect to me and my family; whereas the entail which would have been made by me of my estate upon my brother's family, would always have stood good, and no son of mine could have altered, or cut it off; although the very foundation and consideration of these reciprocal entails would have been destroyed; but Lord Orford and I in our proceeding have strictly pursued the great object and original intention of your father in the disposition of our respective estates, and have acted agreeably to what my brother had much at heart, and had himself more than once proposed to me, and consequently no person has the least pretence, either in right or reason to censure or complain of our having acted contrary to what he designed.

As to that part of your letter, which gives me notice of your executing the strongest act the law can invent to debar yourself from receiving any benefit from my fortune,[3] if it should ever come to your line, I can only say, that as this is as much in your power to do, as it was in Lord Orford's and mine to do, as we have done, it must be left to your discretion to execute this purpose, when, and in what manner you please.

I shall never forget the infinite, and inexpressible obligations I have to my late dearest brother, your father, and as I am sure I never have been, nor ever shall be, wanting to show my grateful sense of

2. Lord Orford came of age in 1751.   3. Which HW threatened in *ante* HW to 'Old Horace' 13 April 1756.

HORATIO WALPOLE, SR, LORD WALPOLE OF WOLTERTON,
BY J. B. VAN LOO

them, I shall be ready to perform all possible acts of kindness and friendship towards you and the rest of our relations.

I am Sir

Your humble servant

H. WALPOLE

To HORATIO WALPOLE, SR, Wednesday 14 April 1756

A draft, printed from the MS now WSL; first printed, Cunningham ix. 487; reprinted, Toynbee iii. 411–12. For the history of the MS see *ante* 15 May 1745 OS.

Endorsed (by HW): H.W. Junior to H.W. Senior.

Arlington Street, April 14, 1756.

Sir

I SHOULD not think a letter with so little solidity in it as yours[1] required any reply,[2] if I could not answer it by a plain matter of fact, which you seem totally to have forgot, but of which many living witnesses can put you in mind. The reason you constantly gave my father for not accepting the mutual entail, was,[3] sometimes, that you yourself would not pass over your own daughters, sometimes that your wife[4] would not let her estate go from her own daughters.[5] As to that plausible[6] reason, as you think, that this Lord Orford might have cut off the entail,[7] it is easy to observe how you confound[8] terms; you say, your sons could not have cut off your entail; but would[9] not your grandson as well as your brother's grandson have such a power?[10] You are forced to destroy the parallel, before[11] you can produce a semblance.

1. *Ante* 14 April 1756.
2. 'Answer' crossed out and 'reply' written above.
3. 'Th' crossed out after 'was.'
4. Mary Magdelaine Lombard (see *ante* 7 May 1745, n. 46).
5. Mary, Henrietta Louisa, and Anne (Collins, *Peerage*, 1812, v. 672).
6. 'You' crossed out after 'plausible.'

7. See *ante* 'Old Horace' to HW 14 April 1756.
8. 'Change' crossed out and 'confound' written above.
9. 'Could' crossed out and 'would' written above.
10. 'I am Sir your humble servant Horace Walpole' crossed out after 'power.'
11. 'The parallel' crossed out after 'before.'

As to[12] Lord Orford's approving what you say to me, it surprises me a little, for in the last conversation I had with him, he owned he was sensible that the compact he had inconsiderately made with you was very prejudicial to himself for this reason, that considering the great[13] difference of your ages, if you should die in a year,[14] he would in honour remain tied up not to alter his will, and consequently had given away from himself the propriety of his estate; he thanked me for what I said to him, and his last words to me were, 'Sir, I will see you again in two days, and by that time[15] I will have dissolved the bargain.'[16]

With regard[17] to your taking upon you to decide what was my father's[18] great object, I am not casuist enough to interpret between the act and the will of the dead: were I to advise in this case, you had better rest the whole upon[19] the power the law gives you; that perhaps will not be disputed. Of the equity and gratitude the world[20] will judge, as they will of your professions, which must[21] be tried by your actions.

I am, etc.

To Lady Mary Churchill, ca Friday 22 October 1756

Missing; mentioned by Conway to HW 28 Oct. 1756: 'Lady A. is much obliged to you for writing to Lady Mary as I find she has her box [at the Opera] at heart.' Lady Ailesbury had asked HW 21 Oct. 1756 to write to Lady Mary.

12. 'What' crossed out after 'to.'

13. 'Your great' crossed out and 'the great' written above.

14. 'Old Horace' died within the year, 5 Feb. 1757.

15. 'Then' crossed out and 'by that time' written above.

16. 'I am Sir your humble servant Hor. Walpole' crossed out.

17. 'To Lord Orford and' crossed out and 'to' written above; 'you' altered to 'your.'

18. 'Intent' crossed out after 'father's.'

19. 'Your legal power, than' crossed out after 'upon.'

20. 'Must and' crossed out after 'world.'

21. 'They will cons' crossed out and 'must' written above.

From Lord Orford, Monday 7 February 1757

Printed from the MS now WSL; first printed, Toynbee *Supp.* ii. 98–9. Damer-Waller; sold Sotheby's 5 Dec. 1921, lot 168, bought in; resold Christie's 15 Dec. 1947, lot 53, to Maggs for WSL.

Dated by reference to the death of 'Old Horace' (5 Feb. 1757) and HW's letter to Mann 13 Feb. 1757, in which HW says, 'to my mortification [I] am forced to stand for Lynn' (MANN v. 57).

Lynn, Monday.

Dear Sir

HAVING considered with my friends here on a proper person to represent the town,[1] on the vacancy occasioned by Lord Walpole's decease[2] they were all unanimously of opinion that you were the only person who from your[3] near affinity to my grandfather[4] whose name is still in the greatest veneration and your own known personal abilities and qualifications, could[5] stand in the gap on this occasion and prevent opposition and expense and perhaps disgrace to the family—upon these grounds I have taken the liberty to nominate you a candidate and having canvassed[6] the town in your name have the pleasure to inform you that I have not met with a single negative so that your election[7] will be entirely secure. I have wrote to the Duke of Devonshire[8] to desire he would vacate your seat[9] and Sir John Turner[10] will settle the time of issuing out the writ for your re-election. As I know you do not love trouble if it will not be convenient to you to leave London at this season, a letter of excuse[11] for your not[12] appearing the day [of] the election to the Mayor[13] which I will deliver to him, will be all that will be necessary. And I beg you

1. King's Lynn.
2. On 5 Feb.; his eldest son, 'Pigwiggin,' who had sat for King's Lynn since 29 June 1747, was accordingly removed to the House of Lords.
3. 'His' crossed out and 'your' written above in MS.
4. Sir Robert Walpole had represented King's Lynn 1702–12, 1713–42.
5. 'Who' crossed out before 'could.'
6. Originally 'upon canvassing'; 'upon' crossed out, 'having' written above, 'canvassing' altered to 'canvassed.'
7. HW was returned in a by-election

24 Feb.; he sat for King's Lynn until his retirement from Parliament in 1768.
8. William Cavendish (1720–64), 4th D. of Devonshire; prime minister from Nov. 1756 to June 1757.
9. HW represented Castle Rising 1754–7.
10. (1712–80), 3d Bt; M.P. King's Lynn 1739–74.
11. Missing.
12. 'Next' crossed out and 'not' written above.
13. Benjamin Nuthall (Hamon Le-Strange, *Norfolk Official Lists*, Norwich, 1890, p. 196).

will likewise be pleased to acquaint my friend Mr Charles Boone[14] that with his good leave I shall name him to succeed you at Castle Rising.[15]

I hope that these reasons will convince you of the necessity there was for me to declare you a candidate so precipitately, and that as it will be attended with no trouble or expense to you that you will concur with my wishes, and those who in this place are the hearty friends to our family. If at the next general election you should choose to return to Castle Rising[16] you will have my consent, as at that time I may be able to fix upon some one who may be agreeable to the town—

I am dear Sir

Yours most entirely

ORFORD

Pray direct to me at Houghton.

To LORD ORFORD, February 1757

Missing; implied in postscript of *ante* 7 Feb. 1757.

From SIR EDWARD WALPOLE, Thursday 6 July 1758

Printed from the MS now WSL; first printed, Toynbee *Supp.* ii. 108–9; reprinted, Biddulph 25. Damer-Waller; sold Sotheby's 5 Dec. 1921, lot 191, bought in; resold Christie's 15 Dec. 1947, lot 57, to Maggs for WSL.

Pall Mall, July 6, 1758.

Dear Brother,

YOUR great kindness to my daughters[1] entitles you to every mark of respect from them, in which light I take the liberty to

---

14. (?1729–1819), elected 25 Feb., sat for Castle Rising 1757–68, 1784–96.
15. See *ante* 15 May 1745 OS, n. 2.
16. HW did not choose to return to Castle Rising but stood again for King's

Lynn in the general election of 1761 and was re-elected (MONTAGU i. 316, 337, 350; Namier and Brooke i. 341).

---

1. See *ante* 15 May 1745 OS.

acquaint you with proposals of marriage to my daughter Laura[2] from Mr Fred. Keppel[3] of Windsor, which as soon as he is so fortunate as to increase his income by farther preferment he will immediately carry into execution.[4]

I am your affectionate and obedient servant

ED. WALPOLE

PS. I give £*8000* down, and probably two more some other time,[5] which, observe, differs widely from some time or other.

2. The eldest of his daughters.

3. Hon. and Rev. Frederick Keppel (1729–77), canon of Windsor, 1754–62; Bp of Exeter, 1762. Sir Edward wrote him (letter now WSL) 4 July 1758: 'The friendship you and I have lived in for some time past cannot but make your proposal very acceptable to me.'

4. The marriage took place 10 Sept. 'As to the time of putting your design in execution I must leave that entirely to yourselves and your own convenience. It would undoubtedly be best to wait for farther preferment, for fear you should find £600 a year too little to live so genteelly upon as you would wish to do and as you have been used to and are able to do now upon £400 a year while you are single' (ibid.). HW wrote Mann 9 Sept. 1758, 'We are very happy with the match' (MANN v. 239; see also HW to Selwyn 19 Aug. 1758, SELWYN 150, n. 1).

5. 'I can at present give my daughters £8,000 apiece and I will do the utmost in my power to make it up [to] ten apiece before I die. That however must be looked upon as a very precarious expecta-tion. I did always propose to give them £5,000 down upon marriage, but it will be absolutely necessary in respect to the smallness of your income, to give the whole £8,000 down with Laura, which I will very readily do. And I wish it was more. Your proposal of settling her fortune upon her and her children is very generous and I don't doubt it will give you a secret satisfaction that you did it, if you should have children' (Sir Edward Walpole to Frederick Keppel 4 July 1758). At her husband's death, left with four small children and insufficient income, Laura Keppel received from Sir Edward an estate at Windsor of £800 a year, a house in town and a coach. 'He has indeed been a most bountiful father always, and has not made his children wait for his death' (HW to Mann 4 Jan. 1778, MANN viii. 349). Lady Elizabeth Laura Waldegrave in a letter written within a few days of Bp Keppel's death, remarks that Sir Edward 'would do everything . . . that a father could do' for Laura that 'she should have everything comfortable about her' loc. cit., n. 9).

From the HON. FREDERICK KEPPEL, Sunday 17 June 1759

Printed from Toynbee *Supp.* iii. 161. Damer-Waller; sold Sotheby's 5 Dec. 1921, lot 154, to Maggs, with lot 155. It has since disappeared.

Sunday, Windsor, June 17th '59.

Sir,

I TAKE the liberty of informing you, that this day your niece Mrs Keppel was brought to bed of a daughter.[1] I hope you will excuse this freedom, which I should not have taken, had I thought Mrs Keppel indifferent to you.

I am

Sir

Your most obedient humble servant

FRED. KEPPEL

To LORD ORFORD, Monday 22 November 1762

Printed from HW's transcript in his MS 'Memoirs of the Reign of King George the Third' (foul copy), Vol. I, p. 79; a draft by HW is inserted as p. 79a; the MS is in the possession of Lord Waldegrave; first printed, Cunningham iv. 47; reprinted, Toynbee v. 277.

Arlington Street, Nov. 22, 1762.

My dear Lord,

I MUST preface what I am going to say, with desiring you to believe that I by no means take the liberty of giving you any advice; and should the proposal I have to make to you be disagreeable, I beg you to excuse it, as I thought it my duty to lay before you anything that is for your advantage, and as you would have had reason to blame me if I declined[1] communicating to you a lucrative offer.

1. Anna Maria Keppel (1759–1836), m. (1790) the Hon. William Stapleton, army officer, son of Sir Thomas Stapleton, 5th Bt and brother of Thomas, 12th Bn Le Despenser (OSSORY i. 382 and n. 2).

1. 'Delivered' crossed out and 'declined' written above in the draft.

I last night received a letter from Mr Fox,[2] in which he tells me that hearing the Parks, vacant by Lord Ashburnham's[3] resignation[4] are worth £2200 a year,[5] he will, if you desire to succeed him, do his best to procure that employment for you, if he can soon learn that it is your wish.

If you will be so good as to send me your answer, I will acquaint him with it; or if you think it more polite to thank Mr Fox himself for his obliging offer,[6] I shall be very well content to be, as I am in everything else, a cipher, except when I can show myself

My dear Lord

Your very affectionate humble servant

Hor. Walpole

From Charles Churchill, Monday 19 March 1764

Missing; mentioned *post* HW to Churchill 27 March 1764.

2. Henry Fox (1705–74), cr. (1763) Bn Holland. Fox wrote HW 21 Nov. 1762 that if Orford accepted the Parks, 'I doubt not of his and his friend [Charles] Boone's hearty assistance, and I believe I shall see you, too, much oftener in the House of Commons. This is offering you a bribe, but 'tis such a one as one honest good-natured man may without offence offer to another' (Selwyn 167–8). HW replied 21 Nov. that he hoped Lord Orford would accept the offer, but added, 'I cannot even flatter myself with having the least weight with my Lord Orford'; he did not want to be 'involved in this affair any otherwise than as a messenger' (ibid. 168–9).

3. John Ashburnham (1724–1812), 2d E. of Ashburnham. He resigned as Ranger of St James's and Hyde Parks and lord of the Bedchamber, 19 Nov. 1762, in the general secession of Newcastle's friends from office following the King's 'affronts' to the Duke of Devonshire (ibid. 167, n. 2).

4. 'Dismission' crossed out and 'resignation' written above in the draft.

5. 'This post was not worth £2,200 a year by itself, but with the Bedchamber, as Lord Ashburnham had held it. Lord Orford was already lord of the Bedchamber, so, though I did not know it at that time, the offer was grossly fallacious. Fox however might be ignorant too of this circumstance' (HW's note to Fox's letter, cited ibid. 167, n. 1); the salary for lord of the Bedchamber was £1,000 a year (ibid.).

6. Lord Orford accepted the offer. 'Without preface or apology, without recollecting his long enmity to Fox . . . and without a hint of reconciliation, to Fox he went, accepted the place, and never gave that ministry one vote afterwards; continuing in the country, as he would have done if they had given him nothing' (*Mem. Geo. III* i. 172). The announcement of his appointment appeared in the *London Gazette*, No. 10283, 29 Jan. – 1 Feb. 1763.

To LADY MARY CHURCHILL, ca Sunday 25 March 1764

Missing; mentioned *post* HW to Charles Churchill 27 March 1764.

To CHARLES CHURCHILL, Tuesday 27 March 1764

Printed from the text privately printed in July 1833 by Robert Walpole, son of Robert Walpole, 4th son of 'Old Horace.' In his prefatory note to it Robert Walpole states that the letter is 'now printed for the first time with the consent of the possessor of the original,' not saying who the owner was, 'in a form suited to the size of the pages of the volumes published by Lord Dover' of Walpole's letters to Mann, 1833. The original MS was in the possession of Miss Lucy Larner of Aylsham, Norfolk, in July 1901 (correspondence with Mrs Paget Toynbee now WSL), but it has since disappeared. Reprinted Toynbee vi. 39–41.

Arlington Street, March 27, 1764.

Dear Sir,

I HAD just sent away a half-scolding letter to my sister,[1] for not telling me of Robert's[2] arrival, and to acquaint you both with the loss of poor Lord Malpas,[3] when I received your very entertaining letter of the 19th.[4] I had not then got the draught of the Conqueror's kitchen, and the tiles you were so good as to send me;[5] and grew horribly afraid lest old Dr Ducarel,[6] who is an ostrich of an

1. Lady Mary Churchill; the letter is missing. Lord Hertford wrote HW 17 July 1764 that he had seen Mr Churchill at Paris: 'I was much disappointed in not being able to see Lady Mary, but Lady Hertford promised to entertain her today at dinner before she returned to Compiègne. Mr Churchill seems very uncertain where he shall dispose of himself and his children. His first intention upon leaving Caen seems to have been for Nancy or some town in Lorraine, but I think at present he is rather inclined to go to some old château in the neighbourhood of Paris which the proprietor does not inhabit.'

2. 'Robert and Horace both mentioned in this letter, were sons of Mr Churchill' (Robert Walpole's note). The Churchills' second son, Robert (b. 1748, d. unmarried) (MANN iii. 465, n. 18).

3. Who died 15 March 1764, on his

return from Ireland; HW wrote Mann 18 March, 1764 'He arrived in town last Monday, grew immediately worse, it turned to an inflammation in his bowels, and carried him off in five days' (MANN vi. 210; see *ante* 7 May 1745 OS, n. 34).

4. Missing.

5. In the China Room at SH was 'A tile from the kitchen of the Conqueror at Caen in Normandy' ('Des. of SH,' *Works* ii. 414). In William Bawtree's extra-illustrated copy of *Des. of SH*, 1784 (now WSL; Hazen, *SH Bibl.* 128), opp. p. 13 is a water-colour drawing of one of the tiles.

6. Andrew Coltee Ducarel (1713–85), antiquary and HW's occasional correspondent. HW acknowledged the gift of his *Anglo-Norman Antiquities Considered, in a Tour through Part of Normandy*, 25 April 1767 (Hazen, *Cat. of HW's Lib.*, No. 3274).

antiquary, and can digest superannuated brickbats, should have gobbled them up. At my return from Strawberry Hill yesterday, I found the whole cargo safe, and am really much obliged to you. I weep over the ruined kitchen, but enjoy the tiles. They are exactly like a few which I obtained from the cathedral of Gloucester, when it was new paved;[7] they are inlaid in the floor of my china-room.[8] I would have got enough to pave it entirely; but the canons who were flinging them away, had so much devotion left, that they enjoined me not to pave a pagoda with them, nor put them to any profane use. As scruples increase in a ratio to their decrease, I did not know but a china-room might casuistically be interpreted a pagoda, and sued for no more. My cloister is finished and consecrated;[9] but as I intend to convert the old blue and white hall next to the china-room, into a gothic columbarium,[10] I should seriously be glad to finish the floor with Norman tiles. However, as I shall certainly make you a visit in about two months, I will wait till then, and bring the dimensions with me.

Depend upon it, I will pay some of your debts to Monsieur de Lislebonne;[11] that is, I will make as great entertainments for him as anyone can, who almost always dines alone in his dressing-room; I will show him everything all the morning, as much as anyone can, who lies abed till noon and never gets dressed till two o'clock; and I will endeavour to amuse him with variety of diversions every evening as much as anyone can, who does nothing but play at loo till midnight, or sit behind Lady Mary Coke[12] in a corner of a box at the opera. Seriously though, I will try to show him that I think distinctions paid to you and my sister favours to me, and will make a point of adding the few civilities which his name, rank, and alliance with the Guerchys can leave necessary. Monsieur de Guerchy[13] is adored

7. See HW to Bentley Sept. 1753.

8. 'In the floor some very ancient tiles with arms, from the cathedral at Gloucester' ('Des. of SH,' *Works* ii. 405).

9. The 'Great Cloister,' 13 ft by 56 ft, open to the lawn.

10. 'It was not executed' (HW's note to his letter to Mann 20 Nov. 1757, MANN v. 157). Bentley's drawings for it are now WSL and are also annotated by HW, 'not executed.'

11. François-Henri d'Harcourt (1726–1804), Comte de Lillebonne; Duc d'Harcourt, 1783. The Churchills visited him at Chitry in 1771 (DU DEFFAND iii. 83). There

is no other record of his visiting SH in 1764; for his visit to SH in 1766 see ibid. i. 42.

12. Lady Mary Campbell (1727–1811), 5th and youngest daughter of John Campbell, 2d D. of Argyll; m. (1747) Edward Coke, styled Vct Coke. HW shared box No. 3 on the ground tier with Lady Mary, Lady Ailesbury, Lady Strafford, Lord Hertford and Gen. Conway (MORE 8, n. 1; 14, n. 1).

13. Claude-Louis-François de Regnier (1715–67), Comte de Guerchy, French ambassador to England 1763–7 (MANN vi. 175, n. 7). His wife was Lillebonne's cousin.

here, and will find so, particularly at this juncture, when he has been most cruelly and publicly insulted by a mad, but villainous fellow, one Deon,[14] left here by the Duc de Nivernois,[15] who in effect is still worse treated. This creature, who has been made minister plenipotentiary, which turned his brain, as you have already heard, had stolen Nivernois's private letters, and has published them, and a thousand scandals on Monsieur de Guerchy, in a very thick quarto.[16] The affair is much too long for a letter, makes great noise, and gives as great offence. The council have met today to consider how to avenge Guerchy and punish Deon.[17] I hope a legal remedy is in their power.

I will say little on the subject of Robert;[18] you know my opinion of his capacity, and I dare say think as I do. He is worth taking pains with; I heartily wish those pains may have success! The cure performed by James's powder[19] charms me more than surprises me. I have long thought it could cure everything but physicians.

Politics are all becalmed. Lord Bute's[20] reappearance on the

14. Charles-Geneviève-Louis-Auguste-André-Timothée de Beaumont (1728–1810), Chevalier d'Éon, a former secretary to the Duc de Nivernais and minister plenipotentiary in his place (see HW to Mann 9 April 1764, ibid. vi. 216–17). He later created a sensation when he appeared to have changed into a woman.

15. Louis-Jules-Barbon Mancini-Mazarini (1716–98), Duc de Nivernais, diplomatist and writer. HW had met him in England when Nivernais was negotiating for the treaty of peace in 1763. They remained lifelong friends and occasional correspondents. In 1785 HW printed at Strawberry Hill Nivernais's translation of the 'Essay on Modern Gardening' (DU DEFFAND i. 174, n. 16).

16. Lettres, mémoires et négociations particulières du Chevalier d'Éon . . . avec M.M. les Ducs de Praslin, de Nivernois, de Sainte-Foy, et Regnier de Guerchy, ambassadeur extraordinaire, etc., published 23 March, 'imprimé chez l'auteur aux depens du corps diplomatique,' in royal quarto, price one guinea, one printing for 'S. Vanderbergh, bookseller in Exeter-Change in the Strand' (Daily Adv. 27 March) and the other 'for J. Dixwell, in St Martin's Lane, near Charing Cross' (ibid.). HW's annotated and extra-illustrated copy of the latter, stamped with his arms, is now WSL

(Hazen, Cat. of HW's Lib., No. 2374; MANN vi. 216, n. 4).

17. 'Yesterday [9 July] at noon came on before Lord Mansfield, at the King's Bench Bar, Westminster, the trial of M. d'Éon, for a libel on . . . the French ambassador; a special jury was empanelled on the occasion; but no evidence appearing on M. d'Éon's behalf, he was found guilty; and sentence is to be pronounced tomorrow, being the last day of the term' (London Chronicle 7–10 July, xvi. 30). After d'Éon was cited to receive sentence, he absconded (MANN vi. 248, n. 9).

18. Robert Churchill (n. 2 above).

19. Robert James (1705–76), friend of Dr Johnson, invented the famous fever powder, composed of antimony and phosphate of lime. HW was a 'fanatic believer in its efficacy.' For a discussion of its effect upon Goldsmith, see Frederick A. Pottle, 'James's Powders,' Notes and Queries 4 July 1925, cxlix. 11–12; see also Sir D'Arcy Power, 'Medicine,' Johnson's England, ed. Turberville, Oxford, 1933, ii. 276.

20. John Stuart (1713–92), 3d E. of Bute, 1723; prime minister. 'The great Northern Star has again appeared at Court, at the private levee at the Queen's House, and this day at the House of Lords, to attend Mr Norborne Berkeley's peerage' (Newcastle to Legge 23 March,

LADY MARY CHURCHILL, BY ARTHUR POND

scene, though his name is in no playbill, may chance to revive the hurly-burly.

My Lord Townshend[21] has not named Charles[22] in his will,[23] who is as much disappointed, as he has often disappointed others. We had last night a magnificent ball at my Lady Cardigan's.[24]

> Those fiddles play'd that never play'd before,
> And we have danc'd, where we shall dance no more.[25]

We, that is, the *totum pro parte;* you do not suspect me, I hope, of any youthfullities; *d'autant moins* of dancing; I that have rumours of gout[26] flying about me, and would fain coax them into my foot. I have almost tried to make them drunk, and inveigle them thither in their cups; but as they are not at all familiar *chez moi,* they formalize at wine, as much as a middle-aged woman, who is just beginning to drink in private.

Adieu, my dear Sir, my best love to all of you; as Horace[27] is evidently descended from the Conqueror, I will desire him to pluck up the pavement by the roots, when I want to transport it hither.

Yours affectionately,

HORACE WALPOLE

BM Add. MSS 32957, f. 232, cited MANN vi. 219, n. 21; see also HW to Hertford 27 March 1764).

21. Who died 12 March 1764 'on the road coming from Bath' (*St James's Chronicle* 13–15 March; HW to Hertford 18 March 1764).

22. Hon. Charles Townshend (1725–67), 2d son of Lord Townshend; chancellor of the Exchequer, postmaster general, one of the commissioners of the Admiralty. 'He had almost every great talent, and every little ability. His vanity exceeded even his abilities' (*Mem. Geo. III* iii. 72). See HW to Hertford 15 Feb. 1764; Sir Lewis Namier and John Brooke, *Charles Townshend,* 1964, pp. 102–3.

23. 'Lord Townshend . . . has left everything to his eldest son [George, 4th Vct]. The lady he kept was not mentioned in his will' (Lady Mary Cornwallis to Capt. William Cornwallis 26 March 1764, Hist. MSS Comm., *Various Collections,* Vol. VI, 1909, p. 306). 'But there is said, or supposed to be, £50,000 in the funds

in his mistress's name, who was his housemaid' (HW to Hertford 18 March 1764).

24. Lady Mary Montagu (ca 1711–75), younger daughter and co-heir of John, 2d D. of Montagu, m. (1730) George Brudenell, 4th E. of Cardigan, 1732, cr. (1766) D. of Montagu. Her villa was on the Thames at the foot of Richmond Hill (MORE 2, n. 5). HW described her ball to Hertford 27 March 1764: 'Three sumptuous suppers in three rooms. . . . I was curious to see how many quarrels my Lady must have gulped before she could fill her house . . . for there were very few of her own acquaintance, chiefly recruits of her son and daughter.'

25. Not traced.

26. It did not develop; his next major attack was in June of 1765.

27. Horatio (Horace) Churchill (1759–1817), fifth son of Charles and Lady Mary Churchill (MANN v. 279, n. 10). He apparently helped to get the tiles for HW at Caen (n. 5 above).

From LORD CHOLMONDELEY,[1] Thursday 19 April 1764

Printed for the first time from a photostat made when the MS was owned by Sir Wathen Waller, Bt. Damer-Waller; sold Sotheby's 6 Dec. 1921, lot 201, bought in; resold, Christie's, 15 Dec. 1947, lot 59, to Messrs Batsford and sold by them to an unidentified client.

Thursday night, April the 19th 1764.

Dear Brother,

YOU will I am confident from your humanity and the regard and attention you have shown to Lady Malpas,[2] excuse these few lines. I have heard that Lord Besborough[3] last year let the little house in the neighbourhood of the great one he has built.[4] This is the thing in the world would be the most convenient to my daughter. I am willing in all shapes to alleviate her misfortunes and restore peace of mind if possible; if this can be rented all purposes are answered without any awkward compliments or forced civilities from anyone.

Your intimacy and friendship[5] may perhaps open the way to such a *tentative* for I am not intimate enough with my Lord to try the experiment.

Good nature wants no incentatives [*sic*], therefore shall conclude this letter without further apology, being with true affection and esteem

Dear Brother

Your most obedient humble servant

CHOLMONDELEY

1. George Cholmondeley (1703–70), styled Vct Malpas, 1725; 3d E. of Cholmondeley, 1733; M.P. East Looe 1724–7, Windsor 1727–33; Col. in the army, advancing to Lt-Gen., 1759; lord privy seal 1743–4. He m. (1723) HW's sister Mary (1705–32). HW had called him 'A vain empty man, shoved up too high by his father-in-law, Sir Robert Walpole, and fallen into contempt and obscurity by his own extravagance and insufficiency' (*Mem. Geo. II*, i. 173).
2. Hester Edwardes (ca 1727–94), m. (1747) George Cholmondeley (1724–64)

styled Vct Malpas (MANN iii. 340, n. 3; vi. 210); for her husband's death see *ante* 27 March 1764, n. 3.
3. William Ponsonby (1704–93), 2d E. of Bessborough, 1758; M.P., P.C.
4. Roehampton or Parksted (now Manresa House), at Roehampton, Surrey. The 'villa' was designed by Sir William Chambers (John Harris, *Sir William Chambers*, 1970, p. 245).
5. HW speaks of Bessborough's affability (MONTAGU ii. 313), but was not 'intimate' with him.

From Lady Mary Churchill, late July 1764

Missing; mentioned by HW to Hertford 3 Aug. 1764: 'I received a letter from Lady Mary today, telling me she was that instant setting out from Paris, but does not say whither.' Hertford answered 21 Aug. 1764, 'Mr Churchill and Lady Mary are gone into Champagne, but I do not find they are yet settled at any place.'

To Lady Mary Churchill, early November 1764

Missing; mentioned by Hertford to HW 10 Nov. 1764: 'I sent the letter you enclosed to me for Lady Mary Churchill the first moment I could. Mr Foley, who is Mr Churchill's banker, was fortunately here [Fontainebleau] and undertook to forward it. They are I believe at Nancy, at least in some part of Lorrain.'

From Charles Churchill, ?July 1765

Missing; mentioned by HW to Mann 12 Aug. 1765: 'I have had a letter from Mr Churchill who has been at Nancy' (Mann vi. 324).

To Sir Edward Walpole, Friday 13 September 1765

Missing; listed in 'Paris Journals,' du Deffand v. 376; it was sent to England 13 Sept.

To the Hon. Robert Cholmondeley,[1] Monday 30 September 1765

Missing; listed in 'Paris Journals,' du Deffand v. 376.

1. *Ante* 10 April 1756, n. 3.

To Lady Mary Churchill, Saturday 5 October 1765

Missing; listed in 'Paris Journals,' du Deffand v. 376.

To Lady Mary Churchill, Wednesday 13 November, 1765

Missing; listed in 'Paris Journals,' du Deffand v. 377.

To the Hon. Robert Cholmondeley, Monday 30 December 1765

Missing; listed in 'Paris Journals,' du Deffand v. 378.

To Lady Mary Churchill, Saturday 8 February 1766

Missing; listed in 'Paris Journals,' du Deffand v. 379.

To ?Sir Edward Walpole, ca Friday 14 March 1766

Missing. HW's list of 'letters written from France,' du Deffand v. 380, records a 'red box E. W.,' sent to England 14 March by Mr Sackville; and his list of 'things sent to England,' ibid. 404, includes a 'red snuff-box with urn E. W. by Mr Sackville,' sent to England 13 March.

To Lady Mary Churchill, Thursday 3 April 1766

Missing; listed in 'Paris Journals,' du Deffand v. 381.

From the Hon. Thomas Walpole, early July 1766

Missing. In his letter to Thomas Walpole of 18 July 1766, HW returned Pitt's letter to Thomas Walpole which the latter probably sent HW earlier in July.

To the Hon. Thomas Walpole, Friday 18 July 1766

Printed from a photostat of the MS owned in 1937 by Francis Caldwell Holland, Hillside House, West Horsley, Surrey; first printed in *Some Unpublished Letters of Horace Walpole*, ed. Sir Spencer Walpole, 1902, pp. 9–10; reprinted, Toynbee vii. 24. The MSS of the letters to and from Thomas Walpole the Elder and the Younger were inherited by Sir Spencer Walpole from his father, Thomas Walpole the Younger. Sir Spencer left the MSS to his son-in-law, F. C. Holland, and he to his nephew, David C. L. Holland, in whose possession they now are.
Enclosure: William Pitt to Thomas Walpole, ca July 1766, missing.

Arlington Street, July 18, 1766.

Dear Sir,

I AM extremely obliged to you for the testimony you have borne in my favour, and much flattered by the sight of Mr Pitt's letter,[1] which is too valuable not to restore to you. You shall not be ashamed of having been my surety, for what little assistance I can give Mr Pitt, especially by my connections, he may depend upon; and he may as much depend upon it, that I have nothing to ask, nor shall ever trouble him with a solicitation. To see an upright, reputable and lasting administration, is all my wish. I was born in politics, but do not design to die in them. The return of L[ord] T[emple][2] will greatly facilitate everything, and I hope even Mr Pitt's recovery,[3]

---

1. Missing.
2. Pitt offered Temple the office of first lord of the Treasury, but Temple insisted that his brother George Grenville be brought into the ministry as well. Pitt refused and also denied Temple's other demands (*Mem. Geo. III*, ii. 243–5; MANN vi. 435–6).
3. HW apparently thought this a political illness, but there is evidence that it was real. 'It was given out that he had a fever, and he retired to Hampstead. . . .

On the 16th [Lord Temple] . . . was with Mr Pitt till seven in the evening, dined, and took the air with him, when such high words passed, that the coachman overheard their warmth, and Mr Pitt was so much agitated that his fever increased, and he would see nobody, not even the Duke of Grafton, whom he had sent for to town' (*Mem. Geo. III*, ii. 243). 'In a word, three hot nights in town rendered a retreat hither [North End House, Hampstead] necessary; where I

which is so essential to his country. I again thank you, dear Sir, and am

your faithful

humble servant

Hor. Walpole

To the Hon. Thomas Walpole, Wednesday 4 November 1767

Printed from a photostat of the Holland MS; first printed, Sir Spencer Walpole 10–12; reprinted, Toynbee vii. 145–7. For the history of the MS see *ante* 18 July 1766.

Arlington Street, Nov. 4th 1767.

Dear Sir,

I AM exceedingly obliged to you for the sight of such curious papers.[1] I heard the transaction last night from Mr C[onway][2] to whom Lord C[amden][3] had told it with great concern, for you, and from the part he had been forced to take in it.[4] What can I say of a man, who was born to astonish the world from the greatest things to the least? Which sort of madness is it? real? or affected?[5] No matter. I heartily pity you, yet do not see how so good-natured a man could act otherwise, for you are not a Grenville.

brought yesterday a feverish heat and much bile, and have almost lost it already' (Pitt to his wife, 15 July 1766, *Chatham Corr.* ii. 444).

1. Thomas Walpole had shown HW letters he had received from Lady Chatham (Pitt had been created E. of Chatham in 1766) 'begging in the most pathetic terms that he would sell them Hayes [Place] again.' T. Walpole had purchased the property at Hayes from Pitt in Nov. 1765. In 1767 Pitt decided that the air at Hayes would aid his health and desired to buy it back. T. Walpole had invested a great deal in improvements and at first refused, but relented, fearing that 'Lord Chatham's ill health would be imputed to him' (*Mem. Geo. III*, iii. 30–3).
2. Henry Seymour Conway; see Hertford to HW 17 Sept. 1767.
3. Sir Charles Pratt (1714–94), cr. (1765)

Bn Camden of Camden Place and (1786) Vct Bayham of Bayham Abbey and E. Camden; lord chancellor, July 1766 – Jan. 1770; lord president of the Council, March 1782 – March 1783, Dec. 1784 – April 1794.
4. Thomas Walpole had consulted Lord Camden, Pitt's lifelong friend, in his distress over reselling Hayes. Evidently Lord Camden was instrumental in his decision to sell. T. Walpole wrote Pitt 30 Oct. 1767 that he had seen Camden and had decided to restore Hayes to Pitt. Lord Camden wrote Lady Chatham 30 Oct. 1767 that his part was 'extremely painful, having been witness to the distress of both parties. If this sacrifice shall prove instrumental in the recovery of Lord Chatham's health, Mr Walpole will be well paid; and I am afraid that nothing short of that will make him completely happy' (*Chatham Corr.* iii. 289–90).
5. When HW heard of the transaction

Well! Sir, but we shall want this strange man, and may his singularity be as useful as it has been! You judge very right about Portugal[6]—Oh! no, it is not over—there are more storms too, I think, than one gathering abroad.[7]

Mr Conway has at last obtained the King's and the Duke of Grafton's[8] consent to his not taking *any part* of the profits of secretary of state.[9] He is in debt, and may ruin himself, and yet I own I could not bring myself to dissuade him from this step.

Lord Orford I hear has compromised Ashburton.[10] Palk[11] is to come in for this session, and Sullivan[12] and Charles Boone[13] next Parliament.[14] The latter is well off. I do not know what he means to do with Castlerising[15]—By what I hear of his circumstances, the best thing he can do, will be to sell it—but he seldom does the best thing, even for himself, which is the only excuse I know for the rest of his behaviour. The lawyers think he gets ten thousand pounds for

between his cousin and Chatham he was 'at that time persuaded . . . of Lord Chatham's madness,' and he quotes Lord Camden as saying the same thing (*Mem. Geo. III* iii. 30). Chatham was probably suffering from manic-depressive psychosis, and was incapacitated until 1769 (Namier and Brooke, iii. 298).

6. Portugal had 'seized the Rio Grande' in Brazil in a quarrel with Spain over some American possessions. 'This was thought a desperate act of D'Oyeras [Œiras] to involve us in their protection; or, if we abandoned them, as an excuse for leaning towards the family compact' (*Mem. Geo. III* iii. 78).

7. HW expresses his fears in ibid. iii. 77.

8. Augustus Henry Fitzroy (1735–1811), 3d D. of Grafton, 1757; M.P.; P.C., 1765. At this time he was first lord of the Treasury and had been acting virtually as prime minister during Chatham's illness.

9. Conway had been made Lt-Gen. of the Ordnance on Lord Townshend's elevation to the viceroyalty of Ireland. 'Conway was indeed most averse to accept the Ordnance and retain the Seals [of secretary of state], and wished heartily to give up the latter; and when compelled to keep both, would not accept the very lucrative emoluments of Secretary' (ibid. iii. 71). 'Mr Conway has acted nobly, and refused the emoluments of secretary of state, which amount to above five thousand pounds a year, contenting himself

with the profits of Lieutenant-General of the Ordnance, which do not exceed eleven hundred, and waiting for a regiment' (HW to Mann 29 Oct. 1767, MANN vi. 559–60).

10. Thomas Walpole was to replace HW in his seat for King's Lynn upon his retirement, giving up his seat for Ashburton which he had held since 1761. Ashburton was in Lord Orford's patronage; he agreed 'that Palk was to sit only until the general election, when the candidates were to be Orford's nominee and Palk's friend, Laurence Sulivan' (Namier and Brooke iii. 245).

11. Robert Palk (1717–98), cr. (1782) Bt; M.P. Ashburton 1767–8, 1774–87, Wareham 1768–74 (ibid. iii. 245).

12. Laurence Sulivan (ca 1713–86), M.P. Taunton, 1762–8; Ashburton 1768–74; director of the East India Co. intermittently (ibid. iii. 508–9; *Mem. Geo. III* iii. 309).

13. See *ante* 7 Feb. 1757, n. 10.

14. Parliament was prorogued to 24 Nov., and preparations were being made for the general election of 1768, the Septennial Act requiring the dissolution of the Parliament of 1761 before 19 May 1768 (Ossory i. 29, n. 3).

15. Jenison Shafto (ca 1728–71), gambler and owner of race-horses, was returned on Orford's interest in March 1768, and Thomas Whately (ca 1728–72) was returned on Lord Suffolk's interest (Namier and Brooke iii. 426–7, 627).

himself by Harris's[16] death, and he demands it in ready money directly—but I do not believe he gets it, except for his life.

I heartily wish Lord Walpole may open his eyes on the behaviour of his false friends. I do not think the parts of the Opposition at all united.[17] I will take great care of the papers for you and am, dear Sir,

your most obliged

humble servant,

Hor. Walpole

From the Hon. Robert Walpole,[1] Wednesday 15 February 1769

Printed for the first time from the MS now wsl. Sold Sotheby's 26 May 1964 (Property of a Gentleman), lot 552, to Maggs for wsl.

Paris, Feb. 15, 1769.

Dear Sir,

I LAST night delivered your letter[2] to Madame du Deffand and have the pleasure of sending you one from her.[3] This gives me

16. John Harris (ca 1690 – 5 Oct. 1767), M.P. Helston 1727–41; Ashburton 1741–67; Lord Orford's step-grandfather; he was the second husband of Orford's maternal grandmother Margaret Rolle (Namier and Brooke ii. 590).

17. The Opposition to the ministry of Grafton and Conway consisted of two factions, the Duke of Bedford's and Lord Rockingham's. George Grenville was allied to Bedford's. On the first two days that Parliament met (24 and 25 Nov.) the Opposition's division became apparent: Grenville made two speeches which greatly offended the Rockingham faction. Partly as a result of this the Bedford faction broke with Grenville and, declaring themselves tired of opposition, sought to join the Administration. 'The Rockinghams, who have no reason to be angry with anybody but themselves, which nobody likes to be, do not know with whom to be most angry: George Grenville is distracted that the ministers will not make America rebel, that he may be minister and cut America's throat, or have

his own throat cut; and everybody else, I suppose, will get places as soon as they can' (HW to Mann 2 Dec. 1767, Mann vi. 565–7; Mem. Geo. III iii. 81–100).

1. Robert Walpole (1736–1810), HW's first cousin, 4th son of 'Old Horace,' m. 1 (1780) Diana Grosett (d. 1784); m. 2 (1785) Sophia Stert (ca 1769–1829); secretary of the English embassy (1768–9) and minister plenipotentiary (1769–71) at Paris; envoy extraordinary and plenipotentiary at Lisbon 1771–1800 (Ossory ii. 400; gm 1829, xcix pt i. 573). While in Paris he became well acquainted with Mme du Deffand who wrote HW 4 July 1769, 'Il a une politesse rustique que ne me déplaît pas; je le crois un bon garçon, je suis parfaitement bien avec lui' (du Deffand ii. 257).

2. HW to Mme du Deffand 9 Feb. 1769, missing, listed in 'Paris Journals' 'by Mr [Robert] W[alpole's] gent.' (ibid. ii. 198, v. 388).

3. Probably Mme du Deffand to HW 13 Feb. 1769 (ibid. ii. 198).

an opportunity of thanking you for your kind remembrance of me and of assuring you how happy I shall always be in testifying my sense of it to[4] you or by the means of those who you shall recommend, or with whom you are connected.

Your correspondence from hence is too interesting and too well informed, for me to pretend to contribute in any manner to your entertainment. Those who wish well to both countries may flatter themselves that the weakness (moral and political) of the two nations may contribute to the continuance of peace. I am, dear Sir

Your most affectionate relation

and obedient Servant,

Rob. Walpole

From Mrs Robert Cholmondeley,[1] Wednesday 15 March 1769

Printed from the MS now wsl; first printed, Toynbee *Supp.* iii. 213–14. Damer-Waller; sold Sotheby's 5 Dec. 1921, lot 106, to Wells, who gave it to Thomas Conolly of Chicago; sold by him (together with other letters) to wsl, 1937.

Wednesday the 15.

I HOPE, Sir, that with this note you will get a book[2] that Madame du Deffand did me the honour to entrust me with to get conveyed to you. I waited on her this evening with my Lord Cholmondeley and Lord Malpas.[3] She received them as she does everybody that has the honour to be related to you or even known to you, with politeness and kindness. But I doubt *mon cher père* was too agreeable to be much relished by a person of her sense.[4] She suffers

---

4. 'Towards' altered to 'to.'

1. Mary Woffington (ca 1724–1811), dau. of John Woffington, Dublin bricklayer, and sister of Peg Woffington, the actress; m. (1746) the Hon. Rev. Robert Cholmondeley, HW's nephew (J. Dunbar, *Peg Woffington and her World*, Boston, 1968, pp. 10, 110–11, 134–5, 177–8). HW introduced her to Mme du Deffand; see DU DEFFAND i. 299, ii. 206, and *passim*.

2. Jean-François, Marquis de Saint-Lambert, *Les Saisons*, Amsterdam [Paris],

1769, including *Fables orientales*, of which Mme du Deffand wrote 16 March 1769, 'C'est Mme Cholmondeley qui s'est chargée de vous le faire tenir par le courrier de l'ambassadeur' (ibid. ii. 212, 214, nn. 2, 3).

3. Her father-in-law and his grandson, George James Cholmondeley (1749–1827), styled Vct Malpas 1764–70; 4th E. of Cholmondeley, 1770; cr. (1815) M. of Cholmondeley.

4. 'Mme Cholmondeley m'amena hier son beau-père avec son petit-fils. Ah! Mon-

me because you protect me and as I have no pretensions I trust I am
not impertinent. She is wonderfully good to me, and though I am
sensible it is for your sake she is so kind to me yet I could wish she
knew how grateful I am for her more than civilities.[5]

If you won't allow me to thank you, you must to bless you, for I
do assure you my spirits were so depressed till you revived them by
procuring me the honour of Madame [du] Deffant's acquaintance
that I don't know what might have been the consequence. But now
I am as happy as I can be out of England; ten thousand thanks to
you for my present tranquil state. I hope I shall deserve the continuance of your favours. I am sure it shall be my study to deserve
'em.

I am with unfeigned gratitude

Your most obliged and most humble servant

M. CHOLMONDELEY

To Mrs Robert Cholmondeley, ca late March 1769

Missing; mentioned by Mme du Deffand to HW 7 April 1769; 'Wiart le
traduira fort bien, il a traduit votre dernière lettre à Mme Cholmondeley'
(DU DEFFAND ii. 222).

sieur, quel Milord! J'avais vu un facétieux
il y a quelques jours qui contrefait les
Anglais en caricature extrêmement outrée,
elle me paraîtrait moins aujourd'hui, vous
avez là un étrange beau-frère. Il est cependant très poli; j'ai bien peur qu'il n'en
dise pas autant de moi; quand il partit,
j'appelai Mme Cholmondeley pour la prier
de me faire l'honneur de souper chez moi
dimanche, et d'amener monsieur son
neveu et de faire en sorte que je peux me
dispenser d'avoir monsieur son beau-pere.
Cela n'est-il pas extrêmement incivil et
même impertinent?' (Mme du Deffand to
HW 16 March 1769, ibid. ii. 211–12).

5. See ibid. ii. 210.

To Sir Edward Walpole, Friday 28 April 1769

Printed from the MS now WSL; first printed, Toynbee *Supp.* i. 178–81. With this letter were HW's letters to Sir Edward Walpole of 21 April 1777, 22 April 1777, A.M. and P.M., 25 April 1777, 11 Feb. 1778. Owned in 1902 by Messrs J. P. Pearson, London; sold by them, Sotheby's 19 July 1911, lot 157, bought in and re-offered by Pearson, catalogue 16, lot 464; sold Anderson Galleries, 2 Feb. 1927 (A. Conger Goodyear of Buffalo sale), lot 349, where this letter was reproduced in facsimile; offered by Walter M. Hill, Chicago, 1933. Sold American Art Association, 12 March 1936 (Marsden J. Perry of Providence sale), lot 535; offered by Walter M. Hill, Dec. 1936, lot 166; sold Morley's Auction Rooms, Philadelphia, 14 April 1941, lot 214, to Rosenbach for WSL. The six letters with HW's 'Elegy to the Memory of Mary, Lady Hervey,' a copy in Kirgate's hand of Lord North's letter to HW of 9 Feb. 1778 and a copy in Kirgate's hand of HW's reply 11 Feb. 1778, were bound together before 1918 by Pearson. A copy of HW's letter to Lord Orford 5 Oct. 1778, also bound with these at one time, has since been detached.

Endorsed (by Sir Edward): My brother's letter when he sent Lady Hervey's Epitaph April 28, 1769. Epitaph on Lady Hervey by Mr H. Walpole.

Dear Brother,

I WILL certainly send you the epitaph on Lady Hervey[1] as soon as I have time to copy it out, which shall be some time today:[2] I cannot refuse it to you, though I have to everybody else, because Lord Bristol[3] would not like it should appear before it is inscribed on the intended monument. I am sure I may depend that you will not let it go out of your hands.

1. Mary Lepell (1700–68), friend and correspondent of HW; widow of John, Lord Hervey of Ickworth. She d. 2 Sept. 1768. HW wrote the epitaph 18 Nov. 1768 'at the desire of her son George William Hervey, Earl of Bristol. I wrote the elegy for the monument . . . to be erected in the church at Ickworth in Suffolk' ('Short Notes,' GRAY i. 43). It was inscribed on a flat stone in the pavement of the chancel of Ickworth church with only minor variations from the original, and is signed, as Lord Bristol requested, 'Hon. Horace Walpole Esq. fecit.' A manuscript copy in HW's hand is now WSL (epitaph printed in HW's *Fugitive Verses,* ed. W. S. Lewis, 1931, pp. 149–50 and Toynbee *Supp.* i. 180–1).

2. HW's copy accompanied this letter.

3. George William Hervey (1721–75), styled Lord Hervey of Ickworth; succeeded his father as 2d Bn Hervey of Ickworth, 1743, and his grandfather as 2d E. of Bristol, 1751; Lady Hervey's son. His letter of thanks to HW (18 Dec. 1768, Toynbee *Supp.* i. 179, n. 3) seems to suggest that HW revised an earlier version of the epitaph ('Short Notes,' GRAY i. 43, n. 296; 183, n. 17).

I never heard Mrs Macaulay[4] was supposed to write Junius,[5] nor know anything of her owning those papers. I have heard they were written by a merchant, which is not very probable. In general I think opinions are divided between Lord George Sackville,[6] *Will. Burke*,[7] not *Edmund,* and Mclean.[8] For myself, I think both the style and matter make it most probable that the first is the author— some circumstances however are against that opinion. The attack on Weston[9] looks like the second, as one should suppose the author well acquainted with the Secretary's office; some persons too think the style resembles that of the occasional writer three years ago, who was certainly Will. Burke: but to me Junius is a more concise and better writer. I am not acquainted with either Mclean's style or parts. In short, you see I have told you what I *don't* know.

Yours ever

H. W.

4. Catherine Sawbridge (1731–91), m. 1 (1760) George Macaulay; m. 2 (1778) William Graham; the historian and republican, of whom Dr Johnson declared, 'To endeavour to make *her* ridiculous, is like blacking the chimney' (*Boswell's Life of Johnson,* ed. G. B. Hill and F. L. Powell, Oxford, 1934–50, ii. 336; MANN vii. 145 and n. 29).

5. The *Letters* of Junius were first published in the *Public Advertiser* at intervals between 21 Jan. 1769 and 21 Jan. 1772; for the early editions see T. H. Bowyer, *A Bibliographical Examination of the Earliest Editions of the Letters of Junius,* Charlottesville, Va., 1957, *passim.* HW's copy of the 1770 edition, now WSL, is Hazen, *Cat. of HW's Lib.,* No. 2215. HW's 'Hints for discovering Junius' (BM Add. MS 32559, f. 107; facsimile in *Athenæum,* 1891, lxiv pt 1. 122) suggests Charles Wolfran Cornwall, M. P.; others suspected of writing the letters were Edmund Burke, John Wilkes, Lord Temple, and HW himself; Sir Philip Francis has

been considered a strong candidate (MANN vii. 165, 188, 247–8; Namier and Brooke ii. 467–8; *Letters of Junius,* ed. C. W. Everett, 1927, pp. 382–7), but T. H. Bowyer (op. cit. p. xix) concludes that 'the identity of Junius remains unsettled.'

6. *Ante* 7 May 1745 OS, n. 27.

7. William Burke (ca 1729–98), Edmund Burke's cousin; undersecretary of state 1765–7; M.P. Great Bedwyn 1766–74 (*Old Westminsters* i. 143–4; Namier and Brooke ii. 153–8).

8. Lauchlin Macleane (?1727–78), M.D., 1755; army surgeon; served with Wolfe at the taking of Quebec; under-secretary of state 1766–8; M.P. Arundel 1768–71 (ibid. iii. 93–4).

9. Edward Weston was under-secretary of state 1730–46, 1761–4; chief secretary for Ireland 1746–51; he was attacked by Junius in the tenth letter, 21 April 1769, as the supposed author of *A Vindication of the Duke of Grafton* (Everett, op. cit. 52; see also *Grenville Papers* iv. 468 and n. 1).

From Sir Edward Walpole, Monday 22 May 1769

Printed for the first time from the MS now wsl. The MS remained at Strawberry Hill, and then at Chewton until 1948 when Lord Waldegrave sold it to wsl.

Address: To the Honourable Mr Horace Walpole.

Pall Mall, Monday, May 22, 1769.

MR Littlehales,[1] whom I told you I would apply to for the valuation of the perpetual advowson,[2] tells me that it is worth at least £*1400* and that he can get it any day he pleases. Therefore he will be the proper person to sell it for our friend.[3]

Your tragedy[4] is in a very high style, very uncommon and very affecting. Your fondness for Shakespear has given you a great deal the air of his plays, which I need not tell you.

As to the Hymns,[5] they must be Chorus. I know your intention in them, and if I can not do them I can so direct as that they shall be done, probably to your mind.

I am affectionately yours

E. W.

---

1. Probably Baker John Littlehales (d. 1782) of Lincoln's Inn (GM 1782, lii. 551).

2. 'The "patronage" of an ecclesiastical office or religious house; the right of presentation to a benefice or living' (OED).

3. Presumably Catherine Daye (ca 1724–75), HW's half-sister, natural daughter of Sir Robert Walpole by Carey Daye. Sir Robert had bequeathed the 'perpetual advowson, free disposition, and right of patronage and presentation of, in, and to the Church of Pelden [Peldon] in . . . Essex' to Catherine Daye; HW in making arrangements for her two insane sisters (Elizabeth Hunter Daye and Rachel Davison Daye) mentions the advowson in turn in his will, in which he provides for the possibility that Catherine Daye had attached the advowson or annuities appending to it in her last will (SELWYN 350, 359). This advowson was apparently not connected with the living provided by Sir Robert for Catherine Daye's prospective husband, Edmund Keene, rector of Stanhope, co. Durham (see *post* 5 May 1770; COLE ii. 371–4; MANN iv. 346).

4. *The Mysterious Mother*, completed 15 March 1768 and printed at SH June–Aug. 1768 ('Short Notes,' GRAY i. 43; Hazen, *Bibl. of SH* 79).

5. There are two hymns: the first is sung by 'a procession of children' issuing from a castle in Act II, scene ii; the second is an anthem, sung by 'a procession of friars' in Act IV, scene ii. Sir Edward was 'a fine musician, and even invented a most touching instrument, which, from the number of its strings, he called a pentachord. . . . In pathetic melancholy he chiefly shone' (*Last Journals* i. 102). A MS folio of Italian operatic arias owned by him was later given to Charles Wesley; it is now BM Add. MS 24307 (*British Museum Catalogue of Manuscript Music*, ed. Augustus Hughes-Hughes, 1906, ii. 334–5).

From Mrs Robert Cholmondeley, ?October 1769

Missing; implied in Mme du Deffand to HW 6 Oct. 1769: 'La nièce vous rendra compte de la visite que la grand'maman fit à Panthémont' (DU DEFFAND ii. 273).

To Mrs Robert Cholmondeley, Sunday 15 October 1769

Printed for the first time from a photostat of the manuscript kindly supplied by its owner, Sir John Riddell, Bt, of Morpeth.

Address: À Madame Madame Cholmondeley à la communauté de St-Joseph rue St-Dominique faubourg St-Germain à Paris.

Postmark: EK.

Strawberry Hill, Sunday, Oct. 15, 1769.

Dear Madam,

I HAVE sent Madame du Deffand such journals of all that did not happen to me, that I have nothing more to say about nothing.[1] My journey however did not seem complete, till I got hither today: I am now quite arrived. Mrs Clive[2] and Mrs Mestivyer[3] have been here this evening, and made great inquiries after you, and send as many compliments. As cards are still green,[4] the former bears retirement with great heroism: but I doubt she will be as tired as any philosopher, when all her acquaintance are gone to town. She is charmed with a rural life while she is in the middle of an assembly.

Fontainebleau I fear has thinned St-Joseph[5] terribly. You will be a great resource to my dear old friend; and as you have taste to

1. HW had left Paris the evening of 5 Oct., and had sent letters (all missing) to Mme du Deffand that evening, 7, 8, 9, 10, and 13 Oct. (DU DEFFAND ii. 272, 276, 279). He arrived at Arlington Street 13 Oct.

2. Catherine ('Kitty') Raftor (1711–85), actress, HW's tenant at Little SH. See MONTAGU i. 269–70 for HW's account of an evening there in 1760 when Mrs Cholmondeley was present.

3. Mrs Clive's sister, who also lived at Little SH (see OSSORY ii. 57).

4. I.e., Mrs Clive is enjoying being called on by her new neighbours.

5. Mme du Deffand, 'my dear old friend' of the next sentence, lived at the Convent of St Joseph. She refers to this paragraph in her letter to HW 23 Oct. 1769 (DU DEFFAND ii. 292).

judge of her merit, and sensibility to feel her situation, will be a more real comfort to her than those who go to her from fashion, from air, or from idleness. I wish nothing more seriously than her happiness, and will contribute my share to it, as often as it is possible, both by writing and making her visits. I am glad *son capitaine* the Abbé[6] remains at Paris: his wit and cheerfulness are never exhausted. Pray make my particular compliments to him, to Mlle Sanadon,[7] to my good friend the Comte de Grave,[8] to Madame de la Valière,[9] to Monsieur de Pondeveylle,[10] and to Mesdames de Jonsac[11] and Broglie;[12] in general to *tout ce qui s'appelle la rue St-Honoré.* A kiss apiece at Panthémont[13]—don't mistake and give one of them to the Abbess.[14]

I know nothing, but that there is a civil war in Spitalfields,[15] is going to be a rebellion in the City,[16] and a revolution all over England.[17] Paoli[18] and Mrs Macaulay have quarrelled without meet-

---

6. Jean-Jacques Barthélemy (1716–95), abbé; antiquarian; numismatist; writer. 'Son capitaine' doubtless refers to his being secretary of the Swiss Guards, an appointment made in 1768 (ibid. ii. 9 and n. 1). He had intended to go to Fontainebleau, but changed his mind (ibid. ii. 289).

7. Mme du Deffand's companion; see ibid. i. 366.

8. Charles-François (1726–88), Comte de Grave.

9. Anne-Julie-Françoise de Crussol (1713–93), m. (1732) Louis-César de la Baume le Blanc, Duc de la Vallière.

10. Antoine Ferriol (1697–1774), Comte de Pont-de-Veyle. Mme du Deffand's friendship and liaison with him lasted for fifty years (ibid. iv. 91).

11. Élisabeth-Pauline-Gabrielle Colbert (d. 1786), m. (1736) François-Pierre-Charles Bouchard d'Esparbez de Lussan, Marquis de Jonzac (ibid. i. 3).

12. Louise-Augustine de Montmorency (b. 1735), m. (1759) Charles-François, Comte de Broglie (ibid. ii. 240).

13. The Abbaye de Panthémont, situated on the Rue de Grenelle, in which Mrs Cholmondeley's daughters, Henrietta Maria and Hester Frances, were pupils (ibid. ii. 230, 233, 400, 404).

14. Marie-Catherine de Béthizy de Mézières (d. 1794), whose mother was English, sister of General Oglethorpe (ibid. ii. 230, n. 3).

15. The weavers of Spitalfields had been petitioning for a reprieve for three weavers who stood under sentence of death; protests arose in 'riots . . . so hopefully nursed up against the execution of the weavers,' who were executed 20 Dec., 'for cutting and destroying work in the looms' (HW to Mann 31 Dec. 1769, MANN vii. 163 and n. 1; see also *Mem. Geo. III* iii. 262–3).

16. 'A dissolution would be big with every evil imaginable. Yet I fear the tempest is mounted too high to evaporate without some serious mischief. The City of London is full of faction. In short, the evils of vast wealth, luxury, license and ambition, are ripened to a head' (HW to Mann 6 Nov. 1769, MANN vii. 151).

17. HW wrote Mann 13 Oct. 1769 that England 'approaches by fast strides to some great crisis, and to me never wore so serious an air, except in the rebellion' (ibid. vii. 145).

18. Pasquale Paoli (1725–1807), Corsican patriot. He was in England seeking support for his cause, recognition of the independence of Corsica upon the expiration of its treaty with the Republic of Genoa. At that time the French troops were to evacuate the island and leave the Corsicans at liberty to take possession of ports gar-

ing;[19] and Lord Chatham and the Grenvilles[20] are reconciled though they have met. The Russian fleet is somewhere[21] and the Duke of Cumberland[22] everywhere. I don't know whether any of this news is new to you: but as news at Paris are like other things not the worse for being hashed over again, you must not wonder if I am not yet as fresh as the *Public Advertiser,* but repeat what I heard such an age ago as yesterday. While I am in this remembering way, thank you a thousand times for the charming purse you sent me.

When the General[23] returns, which I reckon will be about the end of the campaign at Fontainebleau, I shall be glad to hear how it terminates. You know how much I interest myself for our grand'-maman.[24]

Mr Cholmondeley,[25] I imagine, is not in town. Pray forgive me if I have not inquired after your papa.[26] Good night, *ma belle nièce;* I shall write to your aunt[27] on Friday, though the Lord knows what I shall find to say from hence, where I am quite alone.

Yours ever,

H. W.

risoned by them. Instead the French made a new treaty with the Genoese in May which frustrated these hopes. Paoli had arrived 19 Sept. (ibid. vii. 27, 139).

19. Catherine Macaulay (*ante* 28 April 1769, n. 4) had volunteered a constitution for Corsica in the form of an open letter to Paoli. HW noted in his MS *Journal of the Most Remarkable Events of . . . 1769,* p. 23: 'Mrs Macaulay offers to visit him; he replies he had no women to receive her. She resents it and they do not meet'; she was also reported to have offered her house to Paoli (*Boswell in Search of a Wife,* ed. F. Brady and F. A. Pottle, New York, 1956, p. 160, n. 9; MANN vii. 145, n. 29).

20. They were under attack by Wilkes; see HW to Mann 31 Dec. 1769, ibid. vii. 163.

21. HW reported 8 Oct. that the fleet was 'on the coast of Yorkshire' (ibid. vii. 146); Thomas Whately reported it 7 Oct. as 'by this time at Spithead' (*Grenville Papers* iv. 468); in December it reached the Aegean and threatened the Dardanelles (MANN vii. 146, n. 34).

22. Henry Frederick (1745–90), cr.

(1766) D. of Cumberland, younger brother of George III. Probably a reference to rumours of his scandalous amour with Henrietta Vernon, Lady Grosvenor, revealed in December (see HW to Mann 31 Dec. 1769, ibid. vii. 165 and nn. 14, 15).

23. John Irwin (1728–88), Maj.-Gen.; K.B., 1775 (DU DEFFAND ii. 93).

24. Louise-Honorine Crozat du Châtel (1735–1801), m. (1750) Étienne-François de Choiseul-Stainville, Duc de Choiseul. 'J'ai annoncé à la grand'maman votre arrivée pour le mois d'août, et celle du Général. "Je serai fort aise," m'a-t-elle écrit, "de revoir le General, mais mille et mille fois plus de revoir mon Horace"' (Mme du Deffand to HW 18 July 1769, DU DEFFAND ii. 264).

25. Her husband.

26. Her father-in-law, Lord Cholmondeley, since her own father was dead (see *ante* 15 March 1769; J. Dunbar, *Peg Woffington and her World,* Boston, 1968, p. 10).

27. Mme du Deffand, whom Mrs Cholmondeley calls 'la chère tante' *post* 13 Jan. 1770. HW's letter of Friday 20 Oct. is missing (DU DEFFAND ii. 288).

To Mrs Robert Cholmondeley, early January 1770

Missing; mentioned *post* 13 Jan. 1770, and also in Mme du Deffand to HW 12 Jan. 1770: 'Elle est fort glorieuse de la lettre qu'elle a reçue de vous, elle m'en a dit des choses qui me plaisent infiniment, mais elle ne m'a point offert de me la lire, et je ne l'en ai pas priée' (du Deffand ii. 337).

From Mrs Robert Cholmondeley, Saturday 13 January 1770

Printed from the MS now wsl; first printed, Toynbee *Supp.* iii. 217–18. Damer-Waller; sold Sotheby's 5 Dec. 1921, lot 106, to Wells who gave it to Thomas Conolly of Chicago; bought from him by wsl in 1937.

Jan. the 13.

Dear Sir,

THE moment I received your commands[1] I sent to Mr I-forgot-his-name,[2] but I have his address *en cas* he should require a re-membrancer. I sent to him for I was confined with a swelled face at the time and could not go out.[3] He promised to get 'em all if possible, but he feared there were some uncomatable, that is, he fancied there was neither print nor picture existing of some of the list, but if there was he certainly would get 'em. He is to bring them to me as he collects them and I shall send 'em to you as they come in unless you order me to the contrary.

You may depend upon my perfect obedience in everything as a proof of my duty. I supped [with Mme du Deffand] the night before last for the first time since I received your orders and went away before some of the company.[4] I have begged of her in your name, be-

1. A list of prints referred to below, presumably in HW's missing letter to Mrs Cholmondeley, ca early Jan. 1770.

2. Not identified.

3. Mme du Deffand wrote HW 12 Jan. 1770, 'Je m'étais prescrit tout ce que vous me conseillez pour votre nièce; ne craignez pas qu'elle me fasse veiller, il y a plus de quinze jours qu'elle n'est restée le soir chez moi, et en dernier lieu j'ai été quatre jours sans la voir, elle se disait fort malade' (du Deffand ii. 337).

4. According to Mme du Deffand's account 12 Jan. 1770, 'Avant-hier elle vint fort languissante, mais elle arriva hier avant cinq heures en chantant, en riant, enfin d'une gaîté extrême; elle est un peu folle, je ne m'y attacherai jamais, mais cependant elle est quelquefois fort aimable, et le fond de son caractère n'est pas

cause I know she will do for you what she would not do for any other person living, to leave off tea, but without effect for she assured me as I suppose she has you, Sir, that it not only agrees with her but does her infinite good. I really think *la chère tante's* health as good as ever I have known it. Her faintings were more owing to the sudden effects of cassia[5] than to weakness, though I think if she[6] could prevail upon herself to dine rather than sup it would be much better for her. Nobody can work that miracle but you, nor even you unless you were on the spot to force her. Come then, dear Sir, for her sake, I'm sure the certainty of seeing you every year would add many to her life.[7] I'm sure it would. Come then, Sir, and make her happy and everybody that knows you.

I would fain say something, but I cannot, yet I am very grateful, indeed I am, I wish you would allow me to say, affectionate. I am

with great respect

your most obliged

and most humble servant,

M. CHOLMONDELEY

I don't know whether the Duke of Bedford's illness[8] is good or bad, but I suppose I shall by the next post.

mauvais, elle n'est ni fausse ni imprudente, elle a un bon cœur, beaucoup d'esprit; elle n'est point intéressée, tout au contraire, elle a de la générosité et de la fierté' (ibid.).

5. 'An inferior kind of cinnamon, esp. the bark obtained from *Cinnamomum Cassia;* thicker, coarser, less delicate in flavour, and cheaper than the true cinnamon' (OED).

6. 'Should' in MS.

7. HW was to visit Paris again in 1771 and 1775. His earlier visits had been in 1739, 1741, 1765–6, 1767 and 1769.

8. He suffered a paralytic stroke in the spring of 1770 and remained partially paralysed until his death 14 Jan. 1771 (DU DEFFAND ii. 336; *Mem. Geo. III* iv. 172; MANN vii. 262).

From SIR EDWARD WALPOLE, Saturday 5 May 1770

Printed from the MS now WSL; for the history of the MS see *ante* 22 May 1769.
Address: To the Honourable Horace Walpole in Arlington Street.

Sat., May 5, 1770.

MR Coppinger[1] has answered our proposal[2] as follows:
'I cannot possibly have any objection, on behalf of my friend,[3] to go on with Mrs Daye's purchase, upon you and your brother entering into a bond to indemnify the purchaser, in case of any deficiency of assets, therefore beg she will send an order to Mr Coleman to deliver me the deeds in order to prepare the necessary conveyance. The security must be extended to the interest as well as principal, for you will recollect, the purchase is of a contingency, and there is no income to set off against the interest of the money paid down for the purchase.'

This last observation, which is the real state of the case, has staggered me; and will do as much by you, for besides that it may[3a] subject us eventually to the payment of a great deal of interest money, there will be such an interchanging of securities that we shall not know where we are. The difference out of the *1000* guineas, when the £*400* debt is discharged by Mrs Daye, should be made a deposit with a security from Mrs Daye to us, the interest of which will not be equal to the interest upon a *1000* guineas which we are to be bound for, and the account not to be made up or settled till the Chancery suit shall end—with which (if it should ever end) the confusion of this account will not end, but grow worse to those that will be farther removed from information than we are now, who are not very much masters of the affair at present nor likely to improve in it.

1. Presumably Fysh Coppinger, lawyer, admitted Lincoln's Inn 1751 (Hertford to HW 21 June 1773, n. 1).

2. Apparently a joint proposal made by HW and Sir Edward to set aside a sum of money for security to cover a purchase by Catherine Daye (see *ante* 22 May 1769, n. 3). They were to provide a thousand guineas, with interest to be paid by Catherine Daye to them, but because the property being purchased was a 'contingency,' with no income accruing from

it, they were also to provide security for the interest on the principal. Apparently one of the 'deeds' which she was to deliver to Coppinger was also tied up in Chancery, and Sir Edward was fearful that their security would be tied up for years in the confusion.

3. The people involved in this negotiation have not been identified.

3a. 'Will' crossed out and 'may' written above.

So that I believe we must lay aside our proposal of being bound for the purchase money. As for me, if Luxborough[4] were now sold for the money I hope to get for it, I would much rather pay my half of the £400 than think of any other method, and if it sells for my sum or the thereabouts I will be ready to pay it; but till then I can't. When you have turned all I have said in your thoughts, you will probably have another conversation with me upon it, and I beg you will let me know beforehand what day and time you will come, that I may have nobody with me. All tomorrow forenoon will be employed about my Luxborough matters with a friend[5] who is helping me through the mire.

Yours very affectionately etc.

ED. WALPOLE

From the HON. ROBERT CHOLMONDELEY, Monday 11 June 1770

Printed from the MS now WSL; first printed, Toynbee *Supp.* ii. 140, iii. 220. Damer-Waller; sold Sotheby's 5 Dec. 1921, lot 106, to Wells; given by him to Thomas Conolly of Chicago, from whom WSL acquired it in 1937.

Memoranda:

$$\begin{array}{r} 300 \\ 150 \\ 23 \\ 127 \\ \hline 600 \end{array}$$ H.W.

Monday, June 11th 1770.

Dear Sir,

I AM obliged to address you on a melancholy occasion which is the death of my father, who died last night[1] of a carbuncle in his back. He has been so bad ever since it came that I had it not in my power to wait on you, having never left him. You are a joint trustee

---

4. In Essex, Sir Edward Walpole's seat (*Last Journals* i. 96, n. 1), which he was trying to sell. The Ds of Gloucester wrote Jane Clement ca 30 Oct. 1772: 'I have just had a letter from my father to tell me he *believes* he has sold Lux[borough]: but not one word of the price—or my money: had

he met with some fresh misfortune I should have had a sheet of paper full of it—this letter is short' (MS now WSL).

5. Not identified.

---

1. He died at his house in Piccadilly 10 June (erroneously reported as 11 June

named in the will with General Cholmondeley.[2] Had you been in town[3] we should have begged the favour of you to have been present at the opening of it. Lord Cholmondeley[4] desires to join with me in love to you.

I am, dear Sir,

ever yours most affectionately,

ROB. CHOLMONDELEY

To MRS ROBERT CHOLMONDELEY, late August 1770

Missing; mentioned by Mme du Deffand to HW 12 Sept. 1770: 'Enfin la lettre à votre nièce m'apprend que vous souffrez, et il faut que je passe quatre ou cinq jours sans avoir de vos nouvelles' (DU DEFFAND ii. 460–1).

From MRS ROBERT CHOLMONDELEY, early October 1770

Missing; mentioned by Mme du Deffand to HW 9 Oct. 1770: 'Je fais serment que j'ai gardé le plus profond silence sur l'inquiétude que m'a donnée votre maladie; que je n'ai point prié votre nièce d'écrire, que c'est par vous que j'apprends qu'elle a écrit, que je ne suis nullement en confidence avec elle, et que je pousserai la discrétion jusqu'à ne lui point parler du chagrin qu'elle m'attire' (DU DEFFAND ii. 473).

From MRS ROBERT CHOLMONDELEY, late October 1770

Missing; mentioned by Mme du Deffand to HW 5 Nov. 1770: 'Votre nièce a la fantaisie d'écrire sans insinuation ni instigation de ma part et tout est perdu. Vous ne me croyez pas quand je vous dis que c'est à mon insu; cela est si vrai pourtant qu'elle ne sait pas un mot de tout ceci' (DU DEFFAND ii. 476).

in *Daily Adv.*). 'He . . . had a constitution to have carried him to an hundred, if he had not destroyed it by an intemperance, especially in drinking, that would have killed anybody else in half the time' (HW to Mann 15 June 1770, MANN vii. 217).

2. Gen. James Cholmondeley (1708–75), the younger brother of the deceased. The late Earl left a small estate (£2,500 a year) but an elaborate will (ibid.; DU DEFFAND ii. 423 and n. 4).

3. HW was at Strawberry Hill (MONTAGU ii. 306).

4. George James Cholmondeley (1749–1827), 4th E. of Cholmondeley, grandson of the deceased (*ante* 15 March 1769, n. 3).

To SIR EDWARD WALPOLE, Wednesday 7 August 1771

Missing; listed in 'Paris Journals,' DU DEFFAND v. 393.

To SIR EDWARD WALPOLE, Thursday 22 August 1771

Missing; listed in 'Paris Journals,' DU DEFFAND v. 393.

From SIR EDWARD WALPOLE, Tuesday 19 May 1772

Printed from HW's transcript in his MS of *Last Journals,* 'Journal Geo. 3d 1772,' f. 41, in the possession of Lord Waldegrave; first printed, *Last Journals* i. 93.

Pall Mall, Tuesday evening, May 19, 1772.

Dear Brother,

I OWE it to you in friendship; and your kindness to my children[1] to give you a kind of paternal right to be informed of every event of a consequence to them. I have this moment received an express from Lady Waldegrave[1a] with the Duke of Gloucester's[2] permission to acquaint me with their marriage, which was in 1766.[3] The clergyman who I always thought married them,[4] called here this morning;

---

1. Sir Edward Walpole, second son of Sir Robert Walpole, prime minister, and Earl of Orford, was never married, but by Dorothy Clement of Durham, a milliner's apprentice, had four natural children; Edward, who was in the army and died in 1771; Laura, married to Dr Frederic Keppel, Bishop of Exeter and Dean of Windsor, fourth son of William Anne Earl of Albemarle; Maria, first married to James second Earl of Waldegrave Knight of the Garter and governor of King George III and secondly to his Royal Highness William Henry Duke of Gloucester third son of Frederick Prince of Wales; and Charlotte, of whom her mother died in child-

bed, and who was wife of Lionel Talmach Lord Huntingtower; eldest son of Lionel Earl of Dysart, whom he succeeded in the title in 1771 (HW's note in the transcript, f. 40v.).

1a. Her letter is printed *post* Sir Edward Walpole to HW 20 May 1772, Enclosure.

2. William Henry (1743–1805), brother of George III, cr. (1764) D. of Gloucester; Maj.-Gen. in the Army, 1767; Lt-Gen., 1770; Gen., 1772; Field Marshal, 1793.

3. See *post* Sir Edward Walpole to HW 20 May 1772, n. 6.

4. Mr Baddeley. This was a mistake; they were married by a Dr Morton, as

SIR EDWARD WALPOLE, BY JOSEPH HIGHMORE

but would not come up as I had a good deal of company, but pressed to see Mrs Clement,[5] who was gone to Ham to Lord Dysart.[6] He said he would come again tomorrow. I had not then received the express, but figured to myself that his visit was on account of the marriage, for I have no sort of acquaintance with him. I fancy he will be here tomorrow; and I suppose we are to settle what is proper to be done for the security and proof, for they will not yet awhile make it public, or she take the title; which probably will be best till they have taken time to see what the King will do in it.[7]

I think it incumbent upon me to communicate it to you[8] as early as I know it myself

and am very affectionately yours

ED. WALPOLE

PS. This is confusedly wrote as I have people with me and have but just got her letter.

---

will appear afterwards (HW's note in the transcript, f. 40v.). The Duchess of Gloucester wrote Jane Clement 24 Aug. 1772, refusing to name the clergyman to her father: 'I do not think there is much chance of seeing my father, and indeed I dread it, for I know the first question he will ask is who married me, which I will *not* tell him' (MS now WSL). See *post* ca 25 May 1772, n. 1.

5. Aunt of Lady Waldegrave (HW's note in the transcript, f. 40v.). Jane Clement (ca 1722–98), sister of Maria Walpole's mother, Dorothy Clement.

6. Lionel Tollemache (1734–99), styled Lord Huntingtower; 5th E. of Dysart, 1770. His wife was HW's (and Jane Clement's) niece.

7. See *post* Sir Edward Walpole to HW 20 May 1772, n. 8.

8. HW wrote in *Last Journals*: 'I was a good deal embarrassed at the receipt of this letter. I had opposed the match till I had found it was to no purpose; and had continued steadfastly to avoid having any hand in it. I was determined still not to avail myself of an alliance that I had condemned, nor to pay court to my niece when she had carried her point, since I had declined doing so while her situation was uncertain. On the other hand, as I concluded the Duke of Gloucester would be forbidden the Court, like the Duke of Cumberland, I had no sort of inclination to engage in a quarrel with the King and Queen in support of a cause that I had disapproved, especially as my taking part for my niece would seem to contradict all my declarations. I did not desire to be abandoned by all the world . . . and reduced to live almost in solitude with the Duke and Duchess of Gloucester, who would not love me for what was passed' (i. 93–4).

To Sir Edward Walpole, Wednesday 20 May 1772

Printed from HW's transcript in his MS of *Last Journals*, 'Journal Geo. 3d 1772,' ff. 41–2, in the possession of Lord Waldegrave; first printed, *Last Journals* i. 94–5; reprinted, Toynbee viii. 166–8.

Arlington Street, May 20th 1772.

Dear Brother,

I AM much obliged to you for the mark you have given me of your friendship in acquainting me with Lady Waldegrave's marriage: and I give you many thanks for the justice you do me in believing that I interest myself extremely in the welfare of all your children.

Though entirely out of the secret of the match, I never doubted it from the long conviction I have had of Lady Waldegrave's strict virtue and many excellent qualities: since it is accomplished, I hope in God it will prove as great felicity to her, as it is an honour to her and her family. When I have said this with the utmost truth, it would be below me to affect much zeal and joy for the attainment of an object, which at the beginning I said all I could to dissuade her from pursuing, on the sincere belief that it was not likely to tend to her happiness.[1] When I found I had no chance of prevailing, I desisted; and having no right to question her, I forbore all mention of the subject. For her sake I did not approve the connection; for my own I could take no part in it, without being sure of the marriage. As both friendship for her and regard for my own honour dictated this conduct, I can neither repent it, nor deny it. Your daughter, I think, has too nice a sense of honour herself to blame me; and the Duke of Gloucester, I hope, will not be sorry that his wife's relations (for it is justice to you to say that you have always been more anxious about her character than her fortune) were infinitely more afraid of any disgrace that might happen to her, than they were ambitious of

---

1. 'I determined . . . to act as neutral a part as I could, and at once decline all share in the honours or disgrace of my niece. This was a conduct, I own, more prudent than affectionate or heroic; but I was cured of sacrificing myself for others: I had done with the world, and wished to pass in tranquillity the remainder of a turbulent life, in which I had given proof enough of spirit and disinterestedness. For these reasons I the next morning sent my brother this letter' (*Last Journals* i. 94).

an honour so much above their pretensions. It is not to make my court that I say this. I have no vanity to gratify, I have no wishes that were not satisfied before. I receive the honour done to the family with great respect for the Royal Person who confers it, but with no pride for myself, having never aspired above the privacy of my situation. To you and to your daughter I sincerely hope the event will prove a source of great happiness, and shall always be with proper deference for her, and with cordial good wishes for her and you

dear Brother, yours most affectionately

Horace Walpole

From Sir Edward Walpole, Wednesday 20 May 1772

Printed from HW's transcript in his MS of *Last Journals*, 'Journal Geo. 3d 1772,' f. 42, in the possession of Lord Waldegrave; first printed, *Last Journals* i. 95–6.

Enclosure: The Duchess of Gloucester to Sir Edward Walpole, 19 May 1772.

Wednesday, May 20, 1772.

IF I had seen you today, I should have shown you a letter[1] which I cannot resist sending you a copy of, to be preserved among your valuable collection of papers: in which, or any other top company, I think it highly deserves a place, for it strikes me as one of the sweetest samples of sense, language, and goodness of heart that I ever saw.

At the same time it will be a necessary information to you of what they wish to be our conduct on the occasion.

The substance of it, though not put together so well as it is in that letter, was what I wrote to her about a year and half ago, intended for his perusal. And it was my way of thinking from the beginning: for, as you very kindly observe in yours of today,[2] my solicitude was for her good, not her great name. And indeed if she were Queen of

---

1. See enclosure below.

2. *Ante* HW to Sir Edward Walpole 20 May 1772.

England, I do not believe, as near as St James's is, that ever I should go thither.3

Yours, etc.

E. W.

PS. Be assured she has the highest respect for you imaginable.

[Enclosure4]

St Leonard's,5 May 19, 1772.

My dear and ever honoured Sir,

YOU cannot easily imagine how much every past affliction has been increased to me, by my not being at liberty to make you *quite* easy. The duty to a husband being superior to that we owe a father, I hope will plead my pardon, and that instead of blaming my past reserve you will think it commendable.

When the Duke of Gloucester married me (which was in September 1766)6 I promised him, upon no consideration in the world to own it *even to you* without his permission: which permission I never had till yesterday, when he arrived here in much better health and looks than ever I saw him;7 yet, as you may suppose, much hurt at all that has passed in his absence:8 so much so, that I have had

3. Sir Edward lived so very retired a life, that he had not at this time stirred once out of his house since the 13th of the preceding December, when he had arrived from his seat, Luxborough, in Essex (HW's note in the transcript, f. 41v.). The Duchess wrote Jane Clement ca 3 July 1772, 'I was at Ham last week. . . . I saw my uncle [HW], who told me how very much he had been surprised at a visit my father made him. Lord Hertford was there who said he never saw my father look better, that he had not seen him of ten years, and thinks he looks younger than ever' (MS now WSL).

4. Printed from HW's transcript in his MS of *Last Journals*, 'Journal Geo. 3d 1772,' ff. 42–3, in the possession of Lord Waldegrave; first printed, *Last Journals* i. 96–7.

5. 'At St Leonard's Hill, in Windsor Forest, near his own lodge at Cranbourn, he [the Duke] built her a palace' (*Mem. Geo. III* iii. 269). The Duchess moved

there in March 1768 (DU DEFFAND ii. 9 and n. 3).

6. They were married privately 6 Sept. 1766 by her chaplain at her house in Pall Mall with no witnesses. This secrecy later caused doubts that the marriage had taken place (see *post* ca 28 May 1773).

7. He arrived at St James's 18 May 1772, 'in perfect health' (*London Chronicle* 20 May, xxxi. 482). He had gone to the Continent in late summer, had fallen seriously ill in Leghorn of diarrhœa and a suspected ulcer of the large intestine, and rumours reached England that he was dead (MANN vii. 333–7, 341–7; DU DEFFAND iii. 133).

8. The King by trying to hinder the declaration of the D. of Gloucester's marriage or to prevent it, by the Marriage Bill, was the cause that the Duke now owned it (HW's note in the transcript, f. 41v.). The prime cause of these official precautions had been the marriage of the Duke of Cumberland in Oct. 1771. On 20

great difficulty to prevail upon him, to let things as much as possible, remain as they are. To secure *my* character, without injuring his, is the utmost of my wishes: and I dare say that you and all my relations will agree with me, that I shall be much happier to be called Lady Waldegrave and respected as Duchess of Gloucester, than to feel myself the cause of his leading such a life as his brother[9] does, in order for me to be called Your Royal Highness. I am prepared for the sort of abuse the newspapers[10] will be full of—very few people will believe that a woman will refuse to be called Princess if it is in her power.

To have the power is my pride; and not using it, in some measure pays the debt I owe the Duke for the honour he has done me.

Feb. 1772 the King requested that Parliament institute a new provision to 'guard the descendants of his late Majesty' (*Last Journals* i. 23). The resultant Royal Marriage Act (12 Geo. III, c. 11, debated from 21 Feb., passed 24 March) required the King's consent for marriages contracted by descendants of George II under 25, and the consent of Parliament for those over 25, and made all persons who assisted or were present at such a marriage guilty of felony (*Statutes at Large*, ed. Owen Ruffhead, 1763–1800, xi. 335; MANN vii. 390, n. 1). HW wrote in *Last Journals* (i. 28, 115), 'The precipitation which strode over all these most important considerations spoke not only pride, passion, and the obstinacy of impatient prerogative, but looked as if some secret reason, which even a short time might defeat, lurked beneath. And this reason was supposed to be the possibility of the Duke of Gloucester's return, whose health was much mended. This advantage taken of a favourite and dying brother's absence did not indicate much affection or justice. People went further, and suspected that the Duke was only contracted to Lady Waldegrave; in which, though his marriage, if accomplished, could not be annulled, yet, the act once passed, could never be completed without the King's consent; and how relenting his Majesty was on that article the bill itself explained.' 'The King had not notified the Marriage Bill to the Duke of Gloucester till in the very letter in which he told him of his mother's death—thus heaping indignity on cruelty.'

9. The Duke of Cumberland (HW's note in the transcript, f. 42v.); see *post* 16 Sept. 1772.

10. The *Gazette de France* (23 Aug. 1771) had referred to the marriage, an indiscretion which became the pretext for the dismissal of two directors of the *Gazette* (DU DEFFAND iii. 92–3), and the *London Chronicle* 12–14 Dec. 1771 had reported it in passing: 'The marriages of two noble personages will be referred to the consideration of Parliament next session' (xxx. 574), but the Duchess probably had more in mind the *North Briton's* censure of the union in 1769. The *Morning Chronicle* of 28 May carried a purported account of this present letter: 'It was confidently reported on Monday last that the Dow—r Lady W——ve has declared her marriage to his R. H. the Duke of G——r, in a letter to her father, with the *consent* of her *royal husband.* This report (which has been current in the *bon ton,* and since it was first whispered, remains *uncontradicted*) adds that they were married in the year 1766, and that her Ladyship declares, in the epistle to Sir E——d W——e, that there is no issue by the marriage. When we recollect the attention that has always been paid by *Majesty* to this amiable Lady, and the grant of *five thousand pounds* per annum on the Irish list, given last July, we have little reason to doubt that the Court has been ignorant of the alliance, though it has been long a doubtful question to the public' (MANN vii. 415, n. 6).

All I wish of my relations is, that they will show the world that they are satisfied with my conduct,[11] yet *seem* to disguise their reasons.

If ever I am unfortunate enough to be called Duchess of Gloucester, there's an end of *almost* all the comforts I now enjoy; which if things can go on as they are now, *are many*.

From the DUCHESS OF GLOUCESTER, Saturday 23 May 1772

Printed from HW's transcript in his MS of *Last Journals,* 'Journal Geo. 3d 1772,' f. 44, in the possession of Lord Waldegrave; first printed, *Last Journals* i. 99.

Dated by HW: 'On the 23d I received this note from her.'

My dear Sir,

MY father writes me word that he showed you my letter,[1] and that you approve of my conduct,[2] which is an addition to my present happiness.

From SIR EDWARD WALPOLE, Saturday 23 May 1772

Missing; mentioned in *Last Journals* i. 99: 'The same day [23 May 1772] my brother wrote to me, with an account of the great respect and court which Lady Waldegrave told him had been paid to the Duke by all sorts of people, and that he intended to have a levee, to which he had expressly desired Sir Edward would not go, as it would distress him, the Duke (from the difficulty of receiving or not receiving him as a father).'

11. For HW's opinion, see *post* 24 May 1772.

1. *Ante* 19 May 1772, enclosed in Sir Edward's letter to HW of 20 May 1772.
2. See HW's reply *post* 24 May 1772.

To the Duchess of Gloucester, Sunday 24 May 1772

Printed from HW's transcript in his MS of *Last Journals*, 'Journal Geo. 3d 1772,' ff. 45–6, in the possession of Lord Waldegrave; first printed, *Last Journals* i. 100–1; reprinted, Toynbee viii. 168–9.

Arlington Street, May 24, 1772.

My dear Madam,

IT is very true what your father has told you, that I never was so struck with admiration of anything as I was with your letter to him.[1] It shows the goodness of your heart, of your understanding, and of your conduct; and a greatness of mind that makes you worthy of your fortune. You will not think this flattery, for *you know* I am incapable of flattering you—and it cannot be designed as a compliment to your rank, when I approve, as I do exceedingly, your waiving it.[2] The Duke of Gloucester has thence a satisfaction that few princes taste, the conviction that you married him from inclination, not from ambition.[3] I do not ask your pardon for having opposed that inclination,[4] because I did it from fearing it would not tend to

---

1. *Ante* Ds of Gloucester to Sir Edward Walpole 19 May 1772, enclosure in Sir Edward's letter to HW of 20 May 1772. 'It struck me with astonishment, admiration and tenderness. . . . What proper spirit! . . . what sense in her conduct! . . . This letter proved two things. I have always thought that feeling bestows the most sublime eloquence, and that women write better letters than men. I, a writer in some esteem, and all my life a letter-writer, never penned anything like this letter of my niece. It is great, it is pathetic, it is severe, and it is more than all these—it is the language of Virtue in the mouth of Love' (*Last Journals* i. 97).

2. The letter to her father had been signed Maria Gloucester but she did not adopt this style in letters to HW until 16 Sept. 1772 (see HW to Mann 20 Sept. 1772, MANN vii. 433). The Duchess wrote Jane Clement 24 Aug. 1772: 'That I do *not* call myself Duchess of Gloucester, it is *ridiculous* that I do not. My God what are people made of—I have two letters from him [HW], extolling me to the third heaven for not assuming the title! He wonders likewise that we do not join

forces with the Cumberlands! I own I wish to know for what?' (MS now WSL).

3. HW wrote in *Last Journals* (i. 97–8): 'She wrote a letter to her sister Dysart that did not breathe total self-denial. That she recounted with pleasure the magnificent presents the Duke had bought her was natural. . . . She desired her sister to make confidences of her marriage to persons likely not to keep the secret. . . . Her letter concluded with desiring Lady Dysart to omit the word *Dowager* in the subscription of her letters. . . . These symptoms convinced me that the natural ambition of her temper would not be long smothered.'

4. HW's earlier opposition was based on the 'improbabilities of marriage, the little likelihood of the King's consent, and the chance of being sent to Hanover separated from her children. . . . She yielded to copy a letter I wrote for her to the Duke of Gloucester, in which she renounced his acquaintance in the no new terms of not being of rank to be his wife, and too considerable to be his mistress. . . . The Prince renewed his visits with more assiduity. . . . I had done my duty. . . . I

your happiness. Nor can I repent my conduct and silence since:[5] you cannot disesteem me for it; and his Royal Highness cannot be sorry to have found that his wife's relations had too much honour to be proud even of his favour to you, till they were satisfied of your marriage. The Duke, I hear, is to have a levee[6] on Thursday: as I would not dare to take any liberty, and certainly would as little omit any mark of veneration and gratitude to his R.H. after the honour he has done to the family, I went to your father to consult him on what would be most proper for me to do. Having never had the honour of being presented to his R. H. or of kissing his hand, it would be presumption in me to approach him without that testimony of duty: but at the same time, as the motives of my past absence are well known, my going through that ceremony just now would be a positive declaration of my being assured of your marriage. Sir Edward is clear that such a step at this time would be the most improper imaginable,[7] and very repugnant to that amiable and wise moderation you have adopted; and he bid me tell you how very wrong he thinks it

studiously avoided him. . . . I preferred my honour to her favour, and left her to her own conduct. Indeed my own father's obligations to the royal family forbade me to endeavour to place a natural daughter of our house so near the throne' (*Mem. Geo. III* iii. 268–9).

5.The relationship had been the subject of considerable gossip since 1764, and although HW knew of the marriage much earlier, he had not acknowledged it until this letter. His private acknowledgment and public ignorance is perhaps best characterized in his letter to Mann of 31 Dec. 1769: 'The Dukes of Gloucester and Cumberland are as little spared, the former for having taken a wife for himself, so says the *North Briton*, observe *I* do not say so, and the latter for having taken another man's' (MANN vii. 165).

6. 'On the 28th the Duke of Gloucester had his levee, which was exceedingly crowded. . . . Perhaps he had a mind to feel the pulse of the public' (*Last Journals* i. 106; see also *post* ca 25 May 1772).

7. HW was in a quandary: 'Lady Waldegrave's noble conduct had captivated me, and I was determined to take her part in the most disinterested manner. Still, as she did not declare her marriage openly . . . and as I had . . . always declared that I never would go to him [the Duke] till I was certain my niece was his wife, not his mistress, my appearance would be the most clear avowal of the marriage. The case seemed to me too delicate to risk the decision myself' (*Last Journals* i. 99). At this point in the MS of *Last Journals* a large section is cut out (half of f. 44 and most of f. 45); the passage concludes, 'in [my letter] . . . I meant to show all manner of respect to the Duke, and even to my niece, now become my superior, and withal a proper and spirited sense of what I owed to myself.' The Duchess wrote Jane Clement 24 Aug. 1772 that HW was '*shocked* that *the Duke* has not been to my father— perhaps you think that, that is all for my father's sake—I do not. He knows the Duke cannot go to him till he has been with my father, therefore stands up for my father's honour—but I can tell him, the Duke will never go to him for advice; he will do what he likes himself, he will be drove by *nobody*' (MS now WSL). And she wrote her aunt 3 Oct. 1772, 'If I thought my father would come and see us . . . I would write to him and ask him . . . but, if you think he would not come I will not ask him, for I do not like to lay the Duke open to any more refusals' (MS now WSL).

would be for me to go to the Duke's levee. Let me beg you therefore, dear Madam, to acquaint his R. H. with the reasons why I am not one of the first to express my zeal and gratitude, together with my joy for his recovery and return. I have the utmost respect and attachment to his person; the more sincere, as I have no views, no ambition, no pride to gratify. My wishes are completely satisfied in your having acted as became the names you bore. The accession of dignity without your excellent qualities would never have made me, so much as I am, either in affection or respect

> Your most obedient
>
> humble servant,
>
> Horace Walpole

From the Duchess of Gloucester, ca Monday 25 May 1772

Missing; mentioned in *Last Journals* i. 101: 'To this letter [*ante* 24 May 1772] I received a very civil letter from my niece, approving my non-appearance at the Duke's levee, and telling me she had communicated to him what I had said. At the same time she expressed great uneasiness[1] at having heard that her father had shown her letter; which he had done with so little caution that the very words of it almost were quoted about the town. He had, in particular, shown it to one Touchet,[2] a broken merchant of a very bad character, but much in his esteem, and much more connected with Lord Holland, to whom he immediately reported the contents, as well as to many others. The Duke was exceedingly hurt at this indiscretion, and Lady Waldegrave complained to her father of that imprudence. Sir Edward owned the charges, but, having seen me so pleased with his daughter's letter, concluded I had been as little guarded as himself, and imputed the publicity of it to me as well as to himself.' See also *post* HW to Ds of Gloucester after 25 May 1772, missing.

1. The Duchess expressed more than uneasiness in her letter to Jane Clement of 24 Aug. 1772: 'Had he acted differently about the letter I wrote him I should have told him [who performed the marriage ceremony]; it is very lucky indeed that I did not put it in that fatal letter; that letter has been, I may almost say, my ruin, for I am certain but for that, the Duke would have been at the head of the Army—now he never will—but my father has ever been my greatest enemy.

Was he as indifferent to the world as I am he would not be so fond of worldly honours. . . for my being a Princess is no more than that to him' (MS now wsl). Her trust in her father was not soon restored. When she was pregnant she wrote again to her aunt 19 Nov. 1772 not to mention her 'present condition. . . . As soon as my father knows it he will talk of it to everybody' (MS now wsl).

2. The Duchess wrote Jane Clement 21 Sept. 1772: 'I am a little uncomfortable

To the DUCHESS OF GLOUCESTER, after Monday
25 May 1772

Missing; mentioned in *Last Journals* i. 101–2: 'I, who . . . had been over-circumspect from the very beginning of the amour, was astonished when my brother told me what he had written to his daughter; but on my giving him various proofs how little foundation there was for his involving me in the charge, he handsomely promised to clear me to Lady Waldegrave, and I myself sent her a minute account of the caution I had observed.'

From the DUCHESS OF GLOUCESTER, Wednesday
16 September 1772

Printed from HW's transcript in his MS of *Last Journals*, 'Journal of Geo. 3d 1772,' ff. 52–3, in the possession of Lord Waldegrave; first printed, *Last Journals* i. 129–30.

Pavilions,[1] Sept. 16, 1772.

My dear Sir,

I AM just now too much flurried to do more than write you the matter of fact. The Duke has sent Mr Legrand[2] to the King[3] to

about Mr Touchet, I wish you would speak to him. This is the story: about two years ago I borrowed £800 of Mr Fordyce, upon bond—in less than a year afterwards I gave Mr Touchet £400 to pay half, but took no receipt—more fool I. Well, some time afterwards I asked Mr Touchet if he had paid Mr F. the £400? He said he had put it in the shop, which was as well. Now, as things have turned out you see it was not as well, for there goes the £400, and I still owe Mr F. £800, and as I suppose that bond is part of his effects I shall have the whole to pay, for I have no voucher for the 400. Now between you and I and the post I think this transaction looks a little odd in our friend Mr T. If the £400 *only* remains due, I should wish my father to pay it, and then I have no more to do with it' (MS now WSL). 'I fear Touchet is what he has long been thought. As to my money, the bill in Chancery will still be the excuse for the non-payment of that. I was forced to send poor Tomkyns 100 by Ned

Roberts, with a promise of the other 200 at Christmas' (Ds of Gloucester to Mrs Clement 27 Oct. 1772, MS now WSL).

———

1. At Hampton Court, where the Duke of Gloucester sometimes resided (HW's note in the transcript, f. 51v.). Pavilions or Pavillions, the lodge belonging to the Duke of Gloucester as Ranger of Hampton Court Park, one of four small rectangular buildings designed by Wren at the four corners of the Bowling Green (OSSORY ii. 22, n. 2; Biddulph 54).

2. He had been Governor to the Duke of Gloucester (HW's note in the transcript, f. 51v.). Later (1777) HW described him as 'now his treasurer, a plain, honest, dull man, incapable of deviating from a Royal command' (*Last Journals* ii. 57), and the Duchess saw him as 'honest but . . . insufferably stupid and tiresome' (to Jane Clement 4 Jan. 1777, MS now WSL).

3. The Duke 'had not been able to

own his marriage, and the King is now gone to town to inform his ministers that the Duke of Gloucester is under the same proscription as the Duke of Cumberland.[4] You will perhaps wonder why we have changed our plan: but the Duke found it too inconvenient[5] to go on as we were.

The King must be displeased, but his behaviour has been such upon the occasion, that we have all the reason in the world to be grateful to him.[6] I must do Mr Legrand the justice to say that his be-

find a moment for declaring his marriage to the King, who would not be alone with him for a minute' (*Last Journals* i. 114), and the King persisted in his determination not to be told. He 'told Mr Legrand that he had not thought they were married; and on Legrand's urging the publicity of her letter to her father, the King said he had heard it, but did not believe what the servants said. He added, that, as nobody knew of this notification but he and Legrand, it might still remain undeclared, and Legrand saying that was impossible, the King begged the Duke would take time. Legrand went away, and, returning the next morning, told the King the Duke had taken a day to consider, but could not alter his resolution. The King *cried*, and protested he had not slept all night, and had not told the Queen. . . . Legrand begged him not to push the Duke too far; he did not know what might be the consequence' (ibid. i. 131–2). The Duke's letter of 13 Sept. 1772 announcing his marriage to the King is quoted by John Brooke, *King George III*, New York, 1972, p. 277.

4. Henry Frederick (*ante* 15 Oct. 1769, n. 22), youngest surviving brother of George III, m. (2 Oct. 1771), without the King's knowledge or consent, the Hon. Anne Luttrell (1743–1808), widow of Christopher Horton of Catton Hall. This marriage and the rumour of the Duke of Gloucester's marriage started the agitation that resulted in the Royal Marriage Bill, March 1772. Since his runaway marriage and their return from France in December 1771, the Duke and Duchess of Cumberland had been privately forbidden the Court, and it was 'a general secret . . . that the same persons must not go

to St James's and to the new married couple' (HW to Mann, 15 Dec. 1771, MANN vii. 358). The prohibition 'overawed people for the first month; in the second they stole a visit to Gloucester or Cumberland House, went to Court early in the third, and, being spoken to as usual, troubled their heads no more about the matter. It soon grew [to be] a dead letter' (Lady Louisa Stuart's 'Memoir,' in Lady Mary Coke, *Letters and Journals*, ed. J. A. Home, Edinburgh, 1889–96, i. pp. xcvi–xcvii). The *London Chronicle* 3–5 Sept. 1771 (xxx. 226) carried a report that the Duke of Gloucester had spoken to the Duke of Cumberland prior to his departure for Europe in Aug. 1771, requesting that he be more civil to the Duchess, that 'his behaviour to the Lady . . . was mean and inhuman, and showed a want of every social feeling'; he asked him to reform 'the impropriety and wickedness of his conduct.'

5. It was on the Duchess finding herself breeding (HW's note in the transcript, f. 52v.). The Duchess wrote Jane Clement 19 Nov. 1772, 'Some people think it will be a happy event for me, as now Parliament must think of me, for let me be what I will, my children must be Princes. . . . I am well convinced that whatever is, is right' (MS now WSL).

6. His behaviour at the birth of their child, in the inquiry into the marriage, and during the Duke's illness in 1777, gave her little to be grateful for. But the Duchess never actually deceived herself about the King's attitude; for instance, she wrote Jane Clement 24 Aug. 1772, 'His [Majesty] never does a seemingly good-natured thing without a bad motive' (MS now WSL).

haviour upon the occasion was manly and friendly. This letter is scarcely to be read, but as it is only for your perusal, it shall go. I am,

Dear Sir,

affectionately yours,

MARIA GLOUCESTER

To the DUCHESS OF GLOUCESTER, Thursday 17 September 1772

Printed from HW's transcript in his MS of *Last Journals*, 'Journal of Geo. 3d 1772,' f. 53, in the possession of Lord Waldegrave; first printed, *Last Journals* i. 130–1; reprinted, Toynbee viii. 201.

Dated by the introductory phrase in *Last Journals* (i. 130): 'The very next morning [i.e. after the receipt of the Duchess's letter of 16 Sept. 1772] as early as I could, I sent a servant to the Duchess with this letter.'

HAVING long known, Madam, that your understanding is as good as your heart is excellent, I must believe that you have not changed a plan of conduct[1] which I thought so right, without having still stronger reasons for what you have done. I am very happy to hear, that, though forced to act impartially, his Majesty has softened his justice with kindness. It must be my prayer as well as expectation, that your virtues will reconcile the King to you, and ease his Royal Highness's mind of the only pang which I flatter myself you will ever occasion to him.

My wish is to pay my duty to you,[2] Madam, immediately, and to the Duke, if I might be allowed that honour; but as I think that would be too great a liberty to take without his Royal Highness's permission, I must hope that the kind familiarity which you still show me, Madam, and which I burn to return, but restrain from a proper respect, will prescribe the conduct to me which his Royal

1. 'To let things as much as possible, remain as they are' (*ante* Ds of Gloucester to Sir Edward Walpole, 19 May 1772).

2. HW, in introducing this letter in *Last Journals* (loc. cit.), wrote, 'I was now to determine what part to take, and, as the Duke was now disgraced and my niece oppressed, I . . . resolved to offer to incur the King's prohibition and pay my court to them.' See *post* 17 Sept. 1772, n. 2.

From LADY DYSART,[1] Tuesday 20 October 1772

Printed from a photostat of the MS in the Bodleian Library; first printed, Toynbee *Supp.* iii. 229–30. Damer-Waller; sold Sotheby's 5 Dec. 1921 (1st Waller Sale), lot 118 with lot 117 to Maggs.
Address: To the Honourable Mr H. Walpole Strawberry Hill near Twickenham.
Postmark: 23 OC [?]IPSWICH.

Helmingham, October 20th 1772.

My dear Sir,

YOU was so ill when I saw you last, I cannot help troubling you with a few lines to inquire how you do, flattering myself I shall have the satisfaction of hearing you're quite recovered or at least much better.[2] As I know writing is very disagreeable if not well, I beg you won't trouble yourself, but let your housekeeper[3] inform me, as I hope you're convinced, it is not out of form I inquire, but a real anxiety about your health.

The Duke and Duchess of Gloucester came to Ham that Sunday evening.[4] I told your message. She said she wanted you to ask Mr Conway for a place in the Ordnance, and she would pay the salary till he could come into pay;[5] but as you, Sir, and I know, she has so

1. Charlotte Walpole, HW's niece (*ante* 15 May 1715 OS, n. 9). See HW's comment on her marriage in his letter to Mann 5 Oct. 1760, MANN v. 439–40.

2. He was ill with the gout. 'I . . . am now confined to my bed with the gout in every limb, and in almost every joint. I have not been out of my bedchamber these five weeks today [that is, since 19–20 Sept.]' (HW to Cole 7 Nov. 1772, COLE i. 285). He reported himself 'quite free from pain' by 8 Jan. 1773 (ibid. i. 292).

3. Margaret Young (fl. 1760–86), HW's housekeeper at SH (OSSORY i. 75 and n. 11).

4. Possibly 4 or 11 Oct.; see Hertford to HW 10 Oct. 1772.

5. HW wrote in *Last Journals*, 'The Duchess of Gloucester had a relation by her mother's side [Jack Vilett; see next note], who, though of a good gentleman's family, was an upper officer to and a favourite of the Duchess of Northumberland. Sir Edward Walpole had neglected

to serve this gentleman; and as he and I shared an office in the Customs, the Duchess of Gloucester asked me to bestow one on her relation, or to desire Lord Hertford to provide for him, or General Conway to appoint him a supernumerary officer in the Ordnance, she offering to pension him till he should come into a salary. I desired I might serve him myself, if I should find an opportunity, but I did not care to apply to Lord Hertford, from whom I had obtained several little favours, nor did I think it reasonable the Duchess should so soon expect another from him. To General Conway there were still stronger reasons against my addressing myself. He had greatly distinguished himself by a large, extensive, and economic reform of the abuses—gross abuses —in the office of Ordnance; he was the last man in the world to overcharge an office; and he was actually at this moment going to quit his post in disgust—was this the hour in which he would trans-

much to do with her money and is so generous, I should be very sorry to have [it] that way; she don't consider how pensions run up. I'd have no doubt if it is in your power you will do it most readily. Mr Vilett[6] knows nothing at present, that my sister has applied for him. I am, my dear Sir

Your obliged and affectionate niece,

C. DYSART

PS. My Lord desires his best compliments.

From the DUCHESS OF GLOUCESTER, October 1772 *bis*

Missing; mentioned *post* ca 23 Oct. 1772.

To the DUCHESS OF GLOUCESTER, ca Friday 23 October 1772

A draft, printed for the first time from the MS now WSL. For the history of the MS see *ante* 15 May 1745 OS.

Dated by the reference in *Last Journals* i. 151.

Madam,

I HAD flattered myself that having entirely cleared Mr C. and Lady A.[1] from an aspersion which I was sure could not be true, for undoubtedly nobody ever heard either of them say that they

gress his principles?' (i. 140). The last comment relates to the Conway-Hertford episode of this month (see *ante* HW to Ds of Gloucester, October 1772, notes).

6. Jack Vilett (d. 1779) (GM 1779, xlix. 215). The Duchess's efforts in his behalf are detailed in letters to Jane Clement: 'I presume my father will not give Jack Villet a Clerkship. Send me word whether he will or not, for if he has refused I will ask my uncle for one; and you may tell my father so. If there is no vacancy just now in either of the offices [of Customs], I would willingly pay the £50 a year till there was one, if my father would appoint

him' (21 Sept. 1772); 'I have spoke to my uncle about Vilett; he wishes he could talk to you upon the subject, but I fear that is not very easy to do—unless you could go to London for a day or two and then come to Strawberry, as Mr Walpole is very ill with the gout you will be sure to find him' (ca 28 Sept. 1772); 'My uncle can do nothing for Vilett, he told me his situation. I know he would if he could' (19 Nov. 1772).

———

1. Henry Seymour Conway and his wife Caroline Campbell, Lady Ailesbury.

should go to Gl[oucester] H[ouse] only in their way to C[larence] H[ouse],[2] and for their thought of going thither, after paying their duty to your R.R. H.H., I must confess I do not see the[3] crime of their doing what almost everybody else has done, even before appearing at Gl[oucester] H[ouse]. I did flatter myself that they would not still lie under your R. H.'s displeasure for that intention; but as your R. H. has upon second thoughts expressed your disapproval of them, and has declared that you will receive them only as I wrote I thought it my duty not to introduce two persons so disagreeable into your R. H.'s presence; and as Mr C. stands at this moment in the highest point of respect and esteem with all the world, and as Lady A. is the Duke of Arg[yll]'s[4] daughter, I owed it to my friendship and regard to them not to expose them to a slight[5] which I do not see how they deserve. I have therefore told Mr C. how unhappy I was to have proposed what has proved so very unwelcome to your R. H., and as he is the last man in England to intrude himself anywhere in an unbecoming manner, he will pay all the respect that remains in his power to pay to your R. H. by[6] abstaining from the honour of kissing your hand, till he and Lady A. shall be less under your displeasure.[7]

2. That is, before they went to the Duke and Duchess of Cumberland (see *ante* 16 Sept. 1772, n. 4).

3. 'Their' crossed out before 'the.'

4. John Campbell (ca 1693–1770), 4th D. of Argyll, 1761.

5. 'Slights' crossed out before 'a.'

6. 'And will abstain from the' crossed out before 'by.'

7. See Appendix 5. Hertford was bearing the brunt of her displeasure, rather than Conway: 'I would throw the warrant at Lord Hertford's head for he is acting a base vile part. I suppose my uncle and I shall quarrel for I shall tell him so' (Ds of Gloucester to Jane Clement 23 Oct. 1772, MS now WSL).

From the DUCHESS OF GLOUCESTER, Sunday 25 October 1772

Printed from HW's transcript in his MS of *Last Journals*, 'Journal of Geo. 3d 1772,' f. 66, in the possession of Lord Waldegrave; first printed, *Last Journals* i. 151–2.

Dated by its position in *Last Journals;* HW's reply is 27 Oct. 1772.

St Leonards, Sunday evening.

My dear Sir,

FOR I will call you so, though you have Madam'd me[1] up to the highest heavens—your letter[2] grieves me, because I think you have taken mine wrong. I was hurt with Lord Hertford's conduct,[3] and when a thing strikes me, I am too honest to conceal it. I never could look favourable upon Lord Hertford, whilst I believed those reports; and I cannot look grave upon any one without giving a reason. My author I will not tell, but my author is a good one.[4] The message from you to the King[5] could not cause the foreign ministers to be forbid visiting the Duke, after having had no message for six weeks.[6] This I only mention to show you that I cannot accuse you, however willing you may be to take it. I am at dinner, therefore am not very explicit, but I choose to send an immediate answer, because I see you are much hurt, and I should be very sorry to be the cause of an unnecessary moment's pain to one I have such a real regard for. I had rather find Lord Hertford innocent; but although I may have wrote when I was too warm,[7] your usual candour, however partial to him, will make you grant that I have reason to be hurt, though he may only have been officious. As to General Conway, perhaps what I said of him had better have been omitted; but you know I am blessed with Walpole-hastiness; and it did appear extraordinary, that he (just at the time I heard of his brother's conduct)

1. See *ante* 17 Sept., ca 23 Oct. 1772.

2. *Ante* ca 23 Oct. 1772.

3. It is clear from HW's reply and from *Last Journals* (i. 151) that her suspicions were groundless that Lord Hertford had brought about the King's prohibition of visits to the Duke of Gloucester.

4. HW marked his transcript at this point, with an asterisk, but his note was lost with the destruction of ff. 64, 65 (see

ante HW's notes on letters to Ds of Gloucester Oct. 1772).

5. Presumably HW's announcement, forwarded to the King through Lord Hertford, of his determination to attach himself to the Duke of Gloucester's court (see *post* 27 Oct. 1772; *Last Journals* i. 136).

6. See the preceding letter.

7. This probably also accounts for HW's destruction of the 'long minute account,' described in *Last Journals* i. 151.

accepted of so trifling a compensation[8] for what to the world appeared great injuries, and of which he complained as such.

However I am sorry I have given you any pain, but hope you will not be a real sufferer by it, and if you will think no more about it no more will I. I am not vindictive; I have vented myself to you, and had rather think for the best than the worst, and if you please, here it shall drop. But whether you will or not, I will still subscribe myself

Most affectionately yours

MARIA GLOUCESTER etc.

To the DUCHESS OF GLOUCESTER, Tuesday 27 October 1772

Printed from HW's transcript in his MS of *Last Journals*, 'Journal of Geo. 3d 1772,' f. 67, in the possession of Lord Waldegrave; first printed, *Last Journals* i. 152; reprinted, Toynbee viii. 209–10.

The transcript has had about five lines cut from HW's introduction to the letter, beginning 'To this I sent the following answer' (top of f. 67r.).

Strawberry Hill, Oct. 27, 1772.

I THANK you extremely, my dear Madam, for your answer[1] to my letter, and for the permission of concealing what is passed from the two persons in question,[2] who, I am sure, would suffer as much as I have done; but I had rather bear anything from my friends and for my friends, than give them the pain and the world the pleasure of knowing it.

I wish I had strength to add a few more explanations, Madam, that would be for your satisfaction, or was able to send you a letter, which as far as my confused head can recollect, would be a better justification of the *elder*,[3] than all I have said; but I am not capable

---

8. Conway kissed hands 23 Oct. for the post of governor of Jersey; he was succeeded by Sir Jeffrey Amherst as lieutenant-general of the Ordnance (*Daily Adv.* 16, 24 Oct.; see also Hertford to HW 22 Oct. 1772).

---

1. *Ante* 25 Oct. 1772. The Duchess wrote Jane Clement 27 Oct. 1772, 'My uncle and

I have had some intercourse about Lord Hertford—he defends him—but my opinion remains the same'; and again ca 30 Oct. 1772, 'My uncle and I have tiffed and made up again—I hope he is right—but I own I have my doubts about the Earl of Hertford' (MS now WSL).

2. Conway and Hertford.

3. When HW had recovered sufficiently

yet of searching for it, nor can employ anybody to look for it. I must therefore wait till I am better.

Indeed I am so low and faint today, that I must stop; and will take advantage, my dear Madam, of your late reproof[4] for my too abundant ceremony, though nothing can ever make me forget the respect I owe to the Duke of Gloucester's wife—no, not even the kindness of my niece.

I am, etc.

From the Duchess of Gloucester, early November 1772

Missing; removed from HW's MS of his *Last Journals*, 'Journal Geo. 3d 1772,' but his notes to this letter on ff. 66v. and 67v. survive, and are now printed for the first time:
1. Lord Hertford.
2. Not long after this letter, there appeared in the *London Evening Post* of Dec. 15th the following extraordinary paragraph and verses, confirming the Dss of Gloucester's suspicions of the Lutterel family: Temple Lutterel,[1] brother of the Dss of C[umberland] was a poet and probably author of the following verses:

To the Author of the London Evening Post;
Milbank Dec. 10th (where Lady Delaval, wife of Sir John[2] lived).

Sir, A *partie quarrée,* consisting of two Royal Princes and their amiable consorts, having agreed to pass an evening in writing some little productions of wit, you here receive the genuine performance of her Royal Highness the Dss of Cumberland, a strong proof that her pregnant wit is not inferior to her high station.

I am your humble servant
Elizabeth Delaval[3]

Upon the Royal Marriage Act.
Great Apsley[x] disdaining to pull off his hat,
Or submit[#] to the least alteration,

from the gout he found Hertford's letter and sent it to the Duchess as an enclosure with his letter *post* 15 Nov. 1772.
4. See *ante* 25 Oct. 1772.

1. Hon. Temple Simon Luttrell (?1738–1803), M.P. Milborne Port 1775–80 (Mann viii. 383, n. 7).

2. John Hussey Delaval (1728–1808), Bt, 1761; cr. (1783) Bn Delaval; m. (1750) Susanna Robinson Potter (d. 1783).
3. (d. 1785), dau. of Sir John, m. (1781) George Thicknesse (later Thicknesse Touchet), 19th Bn Audley, 1777.

Makes the Marriage Act pass for his Lordship's own brat,
  O'er the credulous part of the Nation.
Thus the Hedge-sparrow sits on the vile cuckoo's nest,
  And inverts Nature's laws topsy-turvy;
But the scabby production now hatched will attest
  The thick blood of Chief Justice Macscurvy.xx

x He did not take off his hat when receiving the bill from the Commons.4
He said he would not suffer an iota of the Marriage Act to be altered.
xx Lord Mansfield.

These verses were afterwards formally disavowed.

x This certainly alluded to the command of the Army, which the King certainly never intended the Duke should enjoy.5 The Duke sometimes thought of resigning his regiment, which I endeavoured by every way I could convey advice to him, without being named, to prevent. It would have rejoiced the King as it would destroy the possibility of that command; nor would it be easy for the Duke to come into the army again, for as his was the *first* Regiment of Guards, which would immediately be given away, what pension or emolument would satisfy a military Lord in lieu of *that* Regiment? and the Duke could not accept an inferior one.

xx The D[uche]ss of Gl[oucester] had told me at the Pavilions it was what the D. of C[umberland] wished.

To the Duchess of Gloucester, Sunday 15 November 1772

Printed from HW's transcript in his MS of *Last Journals,* 'Journal Geo. 3d 1772,' ff. 68–9, in the possession of Lord Waldegrave; first printed, *Last Journals* i. 154–5; reprinted, Toynbee viii. 214–16. The textual introduction to this letter, its notes and the caption 'November' were presumably cut out when the bottom half of f. 67 and top half of f. 68 were removed, perhaps by Elizabeth Laura, Lady Waldegrave.

Enclosure: Hertford to HW ?late September 1772, missing.

Strawberry Hill, Nov. 15, 1772.

THAT you have many enemies,1 my dear Madam, I do not doubt: your merit and fortune will raise you numbers of such in those, who have not the former, and are given up to the pursuit of the latter. Lies will be the consequence, as your very merit will pre-

4. Henry Bathurst (1714–94), cr. (1771) Lord Apsley, was lord chancellor 1771–8.
5. See *ante* ca 25 May 1772, n. 1.

1. Apparently a reference to the Duchess's missing letter complaining of the Luttrell family; see preceding letter, HW's notes.

vent them from hurting you, were they to speak nothing but truth. All I take the liberty to beseech of you is, not to let your own honest warmth and sincerity add to the number. At least wait till you can make your resentment felt as well as known—or what is more like you, till it will be noble to forgive. You are now in a position, in which your every word will be weighed, and, if possible, misinterpreted. In this country nobody escapes; and you are capable of being hurt, till the King and Duke are reconciled. I know how ready you are to bear anything for the Duke's sake: therefore for his sake bear ill nature: and when your own virtue is so great as to be willing to waive the honours due to his wife, rather than obstruct his R. H.'s return to Court, carry the sacrifice so much farther, as not to let the malicious know you know them, since by that frankness you will whet their claws in this only moment in which they can hurt his R. H. by keeping him from the King.

You will say it is very fine in me to preach, who am warm and imprudent like you and your father—but that is the very reason, my dear Madam, why I do preach. I have felt the inconvenience of incautious anger, and wish my experience may all turn to your service.

That lies swarm in plenty I know by ancient and recent personal experience too. I was told two days ago that a lady said, I had been the cause of the last full publication of your marriage, and that the King believed so. I did not vouchsafe to make an answer. You know, Madam, better than anybody does or can, how true that assertion is. If the King has been told such a gross untruth, I shall certainly be one of the least proper persons in the world to convey to his Majesty what you wish he should be told of your self-denial: yet it does you so much honour, it is such just gratitude to his R. H. and I am so indifferent about myself, that I shall certainly take care your declaration shall be made known to his Majesty—nor have I any doubt but Lord Hertford will be happy to be the messenger.

He knows too well the King's affection for the Duke not to be sure he shall execute a welcome office by doing anything that may tend to a reconciliation between the royal brothers; and his letter,[2] which I have already mentioned to you, Madam, and which I here enclose, will convince you Lord Hertford could not think for one moment that he should make his court to his Majesty by inflaming the difference between him and the Duke of Gloucester. The letter

2. Missing.

I give you my honour and oath in the most solemn manner is the genuine identic [*sic*] letter that I received at the time; nor has Lord Hertford the most distant idea or suspicion of what he was accused, or of my sending you his letter. I do both, in justice to him and myself, to prove to you, my dear Madam, that I would not put your interests into his hands, if I were not thoroughly convinced of his zeal to obey you. He is now in Suffolk, or shooting in Norfolk with my *excellent* nephew.[3] As soon as I am able to see him in town or here, which I have not yet done, I will not lose a moment. I will only beg you to return me his letter, because, though so strong a vindication of him, I am not sure he would like my showing it—but the goodness of my intention must justify me.

PS. 21st. I wrote the above some days ago, but was in too much pain then and for almost all the week since to finish it: and as Lord H[ertford] was not in town,[4] nor I able to go thither, there was no hurry. In my tedious and sleepless nights I have thought this matter over and over; and should the method you prescribe, not succeed, I think there might be still more direct and more efficacious ways taken[5]—but I know it does not become me to give advice; and therefore I can only show my zeal by implicit obedience, which you may always depend upon, my dear Madam, in

Your R. H.'s most faithful humble servant

H. W.

---

3. Lord Orford, who '. . . disobliged his whole family by very unworthy behaviour' (HW's note in the transcript, f. 68v.); see Hertford to HW 10 Oct. 1772.
4. See Lady Hertford to HW 16 Nov. 1772.
5. 'I meant by the last paragraph that the Duchess should either write to the King herself, or . . . that the Duke should go to the King by surprise, fling himself at his feet, and ask his pardon. . . . I knew the King's pusillanimity, which could not say *no* to a man's face' (*Last Journals* i. 156). The approaching confinement of the Duchess forced the delay of this plan (see *post* 22 Nov. 1772).

From the DUCHESS OF GLOUCESTER, Sunday
22 November 1772

Printed from HW's transcript in his MS of *Last Journals*, 'Journal Geo. 3d 1772,' ff. 69–70, in the possession of Lord Waldegrave; first printed, *Last Journals* i. 156.

Gloucester Lodge, Sunday Nov. 22d 1772.

My dear Sir,

I HAVE kept your servant so long that I will not write a long letter. I am very sorry that you are still so ill.[1] As to what I wrote to you last, it may rest for a time, as the King will soon be informed of my sentiments in another manner.[2] My not being upon any intimate footing with the Duchess of Cumberland[3] I still beg you will take all opportunities to say. I am, and shall always be civil to her; it is not possible I ever can be more—but I am running into a letter when I only meant a cover. I am, my dear Sir,

Your most obliged and

affectionate,

MARIA GLOUCESTER, etc.

PS. Observe we have changed the name of this place.[4]

1. See *ante* 20, 27 Oct. and 15 Nov. 1772, *post* 16 Dec. 1772.

2. 'The event . . . became public in the beginning of December. In one word, the Duke of Gloucester sent notice to the King that the Duchess was breeding; and she herself wrote to her father to inform me of it. Here, I believe, was the true reason of the Duke's formal declaration of his marriage. . . . I am inclined to think [it] will rather delay than advance the reconciliation' (*Last Journals* i. 156–7). See also HW to Mann 22 Dec. 1772, MANN vii. 452.

3. 'She certainly had had no reason to be pleased with the little cordiality shown to her by the Duchess of Gloucester' (*Last Journals* i. 244), who wrote Jane Clement 21 Sept. 1772: 'The Duke and Duchess of Cumberland drank tea here yesterday. . . . They are two very happy people, for he . . . does not repent what he has done; and *she* is fully convinced that no one ever became royalty better—and is as much at her ease with the Duke of Gloucester, as if she was a Princess born. The Duke ordered me to keep her at a distance, so I was very reserved which kept her in very good order; but she is very underbred and you see at once that she has never kept good company. She will be disappointed, for she told a friend of mine, before I saw her, that she and I should have a box at the opera together and a great many jolly parties. . . . She looks like an actress—and is very flaunting in her dress—is a bad likeness of Rob Seymour' (MS now WSL). See also MANN vii. 345.

4. (To Gloucester Lodge) (HW). It was the lodge at St Leonard's Hill (Biddulph 106).

From Sir Edward Walpole, Tuesday 15 December 1772

Missing; mentioned *post* 16 Dec. 1772.

From Sir Edward Walpole, Wednesday 16 December 1772

Missing; mentioned *post* 16 Dec. 1772.

To the Duchess of Gloucester, Wednesday 16 December 1772

Printed for the first time from the MS now WSL; acquired, Sept. 1959 (in a collection), from Miss Eleanor Forster of Tynemouth, Northumberland, a descendant of the Clement family.

Arlington Street, Dec. 16, 1772.

My dear Madam,

I MOST sincerely wish your R.H. joy of the news[1] with which my brother has acquainted me,[2] and for the communication of which I give you my most sincere thanks. May I beg, if I may take that liberty, to offer my most respectful congratulation to his Royal Highness on the same occasion?

My brother informed me last night that there was a clerkship vacant in our office,[3] which would not interfere with Collier,[4] and to which I might nominate. I immediately desired to offer it to Mr Vilett.[5] This moment I have received a letter[6] from Sir Edward, who says, that he is of opinion that the place, which indeed brings in but £45 a year, but the first and best thing I had to offer, would by no means do for Mr Vilett, and that Mrs Clement[7] is clearly of the same

1. That she was expecting a child.
2. The letter from Sir Edward is missing; but see *ante* 22 Nov. 1772, n. 2.
3. In the Customs.
4. Not identified.
5. See *ante* Lady Dysart to HW 20 Oct. 1772, nn. 5, 6.
6. The two letters of 15 and 16 Dec. from Sir Edward are missing.
7. The Duchess wrote Jane Clement 18

Dec. 1772: 'I do not care where Vilett gets a place if he has one to take him out of service, and therefore I wish he had the place in the Customs which Mr Walpole offered. I have wrote to Mr Walpole, to say that if he is to be in the Pells Office, if he could be named as supernumerary, I will very willingly pay him the £50 a year till he gets upon pay' (MS now WSL).

sentiment; but that to oblige you, Madam, he will give him the first clerkship of £50 a year that shall fall in the Pells, if he himself is alive at the time; and that according to appearances, there must one fall before it is long. It is, he says, and I am persuaded so, a much genteeler and easier thing, and that Mr Villet should have had one long ago, had he suspected such a thing would be acceptable. I am very happy this turns out so well, and though one can not wish any-one dead, I shall be glad, if the event happens, to have contributed in the least degree, Madam, to what you wish.

I am

with all the respect your R.H. forbids me to detail

Your most faithful humble servant

Hor. Walpole

PS. Allow me to present mine and Mr Pennicot's[8] gratitude, which is great indeed.

I came to town two nights ago, but am still moved from the bed to my couch by two servants.

From the Duchess of Gloucester, ca Thursday 17 December 1772

Missing; mentioned in the Duchess's letter to Jane Clement 18 Dec. 1772 (see *ante* 16 Dec. 1772, n. 7).

From Lord Orford, Thursday 11 March 1773

Missing; mentioned by HW to Mann 12 March 1773; 'The physicians have fancied my poor nephew cured; but yesterday he wrote a letter that proved the very reverse' (Mann vii. 467). Lord Orford had fallen into 'a kind of de-lirium' on or around 28 Jan., brought on (according to HW) by self-treatment for 'a cutaneous or some scorbutic eruption' (HW to Mann 17 Feb. 1773, ibid. vii. 460 and nn. 4–5). Orford remained indisposed till the end of the year. See Appendix 6.

8. The Rev. William Pennicott (1726– 1811) of Exeter College, Oxford (B.A., 1746), rector of Long Ditton, Surrey 1758– 1811 (Cole ii. 200 and n. 5).

To Lady Orford,[1] ca Friday 2 April 1773

Missing; mentioned by HW to Mann 2 April 1773: 'I am very glad of Lady Orford's message, as it gives me an occasion of writing to her, and laying the whole scene before her, as I have done in the enclosed, which I beg you will take care she should receive safe. My brother and I are very earnest to have her come over, as we really do not know how to act. If you see her, I will rely on your adding your persuasion to ours. I doubt very much of her son's recovery, though as the physicians say they expect it, at least intervals of sense, I have given her those hopes, not being willing to say the contrary against their opinions' (MANN vii. 470–1).

From Lady Orford, May 1773

Two letters, missing; mentioned by HW to Mann 15 June 1773: 'My Lady Orford has employed great art and pains, after a study of six weeks, to write a letter without any meaning, which with very ordinary talents might have been written in half an hour. In order to guard every outwork of interest and cunning, she has left the *heart* of the place naked. . . . A week after her long-meditated letter, came another, desiring I would admit Sir John Pringle to her son. . . . All you may hint . . . is, that her Ladyship's letter was so indefinite, and betrayed so little confidence in Sir Edward and me, that you conclude from the dryness and dissatisfaction of my answer, that I understood it as a rebuke to my officiousness, and that I had only said, that Sir Edward and I, finding our zeal received so coldly, should not trouble her Ladyship any farther' (MANN vii. 487–8).

1. Margaret Rolle (1709–81), dau. of Samuel Rolle of Heanton Satchville, Devon, m. (1724) Robert Walpole, 2d E. of Orford, 1745; Bns Clinton (*s.j.*), 1760. After the birth of their son (1730) she 'made it a point . . . not to let her husband lie with her; and at last stipulated for only twice a week' (HW to Mann 17 June 1746 OS, MANN iii. 203). In 1734 she eloped with the Rev. Samuel Sturgis, Fellow of Kings College, Cambridge, with whom she lived in Florence. In 1745 she was legally separated from Lord Orford. After his death in 1751 she married Sewallis Shirley, with whom she had been said to 'cohabit most lovingly' for some years (HW to Mann 1 April 1751 OS, ibid. iv. 239, n. 12). She lived in England with Shirley until their separation in 1754; and in 1755 returned to Italy, where she died.

To the DUCHESS OF GLOUCESTER, ca Friday 28 May 1773

Missing; mentioned in *Last Journals* i. 226: 'At night [28 May] the Duchess lent me the Archbishop's [Frederick Cornwallis (1713–82), Abp of Canterbury, 1768] letter, which I returned the next morning, but wrote to beg she would never let it go out of her hands again, as it was of the highest importance to her and the child.' Early in May the Duke of Gloucester asked the King to send officers of the Council to attend the Duchess's lying-in. The King's reply, that 'at a proper time after the delivery of the Duchess, your marriage, as well as the birth of the child, shall be properly inquired into' (ibid. i. 206), was 'a thunderstroke to the Duchess, at the eve of childbirth' (ibid. i. 207). The Duke requested an inquiry into the marriage '*as soon as may be,*' and the King appointed the Archbishop, Chancellor Bathurst and Dr Terrick, Bp of London, to 'report their opinions to him, which he would have entered into the Council books.' The committee met with the Duke and Duchess on 23 May and the Duke 'told them he had been married on such a day to the Dowager Lady Waldegrave, at her own house in Pall Mall, by her own chaplain Dr Morton, who was now dead; "and, my Lords, we had no witnesses." ' Depositions were taken and 'the Duchess's obvious pregnancy was presented' (ibid. i. 208, 218). See also the Duke's letter of 25 May 1773 to Sir Edward (Appendix 2). On 26 May 'the three Lords made their report, expressed their satisfaction and the King ordered all the depositions . . . entered in the Council books.' The letter HW refers to, addressed by the Archbishop to the Duke (dated 27 May 1773) reported that 'His Majesty was pleased to say, that, as your Royal Highness was satisfied with the proofs of the validity of your marriage, and did not desire to have it further authenticated, his Majesty . . . does not think it necessary to take any farther steps in it' (the full text is in *Last Journals*, i. 226), thus, according to HW, removing 'all ground of cavil' and assuring 'the indissolubility of his marriage and the rights of his child.' But he adds, 'The King through the whole showed so much pride, ill-nature, duplicity, and pusillanimity, that one may almost conclude the whole had been concerted and conducted by himself, the Queen, her women, and a man as silly as her women—Lord Rochford. . . . Satisfactory as the Archbishop's letter was at last, I soon learnt that the avowal had been wrung most reluctantly from a mind that had harboured disingenuity to the last moment . . . and which, as deceit pursued to its inmost retreat never pardons, his Majesty resolved not to forgive' (ibid. i. 226–7; see also Biddulph 86–99). On 29 May, three days after her parents' marriage had been declared valid, Princess Sophia Matilda of Gloucester (d. 1844) was born.

To the Hon. Thomas Walpole, Thursday 1 July 1773

Printed for the first time from a photostat of the Holland MS; for the history of the MS see *ante* 18 July 1766.

Arlington Street, July 1st 1773.

Dear Sir,

I SHALL take it as a particular favour if you will do me the honour of meeting your brother Lord Walpole[1] here tomorrow at twelve o'clock. I have been advised that it is not prudent in me to undertake the care of Lord Orford's affairs[2] without the specific request of his nearest relations; and that it will be necessary for me to have it for my justification to Chancery. My strength, which was always very inconsiderable, is so much weakened by my late long illness,[3] that I doubt whether I shall be able to go through the fatigue and multiplicity of details with which I find every part embarrassed. I am however willing to risk myself in order to do some good, if I can; and as I find nobody else will submit to the burthen, I think it my duty to do it, if I can on proper authority. All I ask for the security of myself and my character is that each of my near relations will in writing give me these few words, *It is at my request and with my approbation that Mr H.W. takes into his hands the conduct and management of Lord Orford's affairs during his insane state of mind.* My brother[4] has given me this satisfaction. I have demanded the same of Mr Sharpe[5] in Lady Orford's name; I have insisted that she shall send me one[6] to the same effect, without which I can not nor will venture to proceed. I have acquainted Lord Walpole with the intent of my invitation, and I thought it right, Sir, to advertise you beforehand, that I might not seem to do anything by surprise. Sir Edward has been so good as to go farther, and say that he shall look on whatever I do as his own act—but I did not desire so much, nor do. I mean to be accountable to the family for my conduct; and shall be ready to satisfy them on every step I take, and to

1. Horace Walpole, 2d Bn Walpole of Wolterton.
2. See *ante* 11 March 1773, heading.
3. HW is referring to the severe attack of the gout he suffered the preceding autumn and winter.
4. Sir Edward's letter is missing.

5. Joshua Sharpe (d. 1788), lawyer of Lincoln's Inn, who served as Lady Orford's legal adviser (MANN iv. 547, n. 5; vii. 464).
6. Mentioned by HW to Mann 9 Sept. 1773 (ibid. vii. 514).

produce the vouchers for all. I will neither receive or pay any money myself, but see all paid into a banker's hands, and direct the banker to pay the necessary bills.

If it is not convenient to you, Sir, to call here tomorrow, I will beg you to send me a line to the purport I have mentioned. It is all I ask of my family to support me in so painful an office.

I am, dear Sir,

Your obedient humble servant

Hor. Walpole

From Lady Orford, August 1773

Missing; mentioned by HW to Mann 9 Sept. 1773, Mann vii. 514 (see *post* 9 Sept. 1773, heading).

To the Hon. Thomas Walpole, Saturday 4 September 1773

Printed for the first time from a photostat of the Holland MS; for the history of the MS see *ante* 18 July 1766.

Address: To the Honourable Thomas Walpole in Lincoln's Inn Fields London.

Postmark: ISLEWORTH 6 SE FREE.

Endorsed: Private Walpole papers 1773 & after.

Enclosure (in Kirgate's hand).

The cover for this letter was used by Thomas Walpole for the draft of his reply to HW *post* ca 11 Sept. 1773.

Strawberry Hill, Sept. 4, 1773.

Dear Sir,

THE honour you and my relations have done me, of trusting to me the conduct of my nephew's affairs, makes it my duty to acquaint them and you with every step of any consequence I take; as I shall continue to do while I have any share in the management. I am just come from Houghton,[1] whither I went to inform myself

1. He returned 29 Aug. (HW to Conway 30 Aug. 1773).

as well as I could of the state of my Lord's affairs, and to see what could be done to put them into any order. I flatter myself that the reform I have made will show I have not been an unprofitable steward. I wish I could add, that I had found any prospect of doing essential good; but everything is so much worse than my expectation or even fears suggested, that I know not from what quarter any salvation can come. The most that can be done, will be to stop the torrent, which in another year would have swept away even the ruins. The house itself is in the worst repair, the wings exposed to the weather in every room, the water-house falling, the church unroofed, the walls and pales half down—but these are light in comparison—My Lord has contracted debts of every kind, and when the bills are all come in, I think they will exceed forty-four thousand pounds, independently of the debts of his father and grandfather, which leaves him infinitely poorer than a beggar. He has sold the perpetuity of the livings of Harpley and Bircham, and was on the point of selling that of Massingham.[2] He has been plundered in the grossest manner by every species of dependant; and some of his *friends* I doubt have not spared him even since his misfortune began—How ineffectual, Sir, can be my efforts to correct such devastation—yet I have attempted to do something. I have got rid of his dogs[3] and most of his horses;[4] the rest will be sold in the beginning of October. He kept in his own hands a farm of near four hundred a year. This I hope to be able to let soon—the more necessary, as he has a steward,[5] who though he cannot read or write, casts accounts so

2. All three of these Norfolk parishes were in Orford's patronage (Blomefield's *Norfolk*, v. 161, 229; ix. 11).

3. 'He is recorded as having at one time fifty brace of greyhounds, and it was his fixed rule never to part with a single whelp, till he had a fair trial of his speed; consequently he had . . . a collection of very superior dogs. . . . He introduced every experimental cross, from the English lurcher to the Italian greyhound' (Thomas Goodlake, *The Courser's Manual*, Liverpool, 1828, p. xiv; see also R. W. Ketton-Cremer, *Norfolk Gallery*, 1948, p. 180). See Hertford to HW 21 June, and HW to Lord Townshend 24 Aug. 1773.

4. 'To be sold by auction by Mr Bever, at Newmarket, on Saturday next, the 10th instant, at ten o'clock. All the horses, etc.,

in training, subject to their engagements, with the hunters and hacks, the property of a nobleman.' 'To be viewed, and catalogues had as soon as possible. The remainder of the stud of brood mares, colts, and fillies, will be sold at Newmarket in next October meeting' (*Daily Adv.* 3, 5–8, and, slightly changed, 9 July; OSSORY i. 134, n. 5). One of his horses, Stoic, had fetched 500 guineas (HW to Lady Ossory 26 June 1773, ibid. i. 133 and n. 20), but the appraisals seem to have been sanguine (ibid.).

5. William Withers kept Orford's cash books 1774–80; another steward was William Moone (*post* 22 April 1777, n. 2; OSSORY i. 141–2); and Carlos Cony, Orford's solicitor, was sometimes called a steward (*post* 21 April 1777; 5 Oct. 1778, n. 1).

well, that for seven years my Lord has received nothing from his farm, and has sometimes bought corn and hay.

The expense of Houghton, even with the necessary servants that are left, and keeping it weather-proof, will I hope not exceed four hundred a year. Many of his farms are let without leases, are greatly underlet, and consequently may be essentially raised. I have already increased one, as you will see by the enclosed, above an hundred and forty pounds.[6] The retrenchments already made are very considerable, as appears by the same abstract. I do not reckon the reduction of the consequences of so many horses, grooms and thieves, though I do not doubt but those consequences amounted to above double what I have struck off. The minute particulars of all I have done are too voluminous for a letter; but I shall be ready and glad, Sir, to explain and satisfy you in any articles you wish to be informed of. I desire to have every particle of my conduct scrutinized, as long as I have anything to do with the management—not out of vanity, for alas! it is impossible to be more unequal than I am to the task. I never understood money, farms, bullocks, sheep, or any kind of country affairs—much less horses and Newmarket, and mortgages. All I can say is, that I spare no time, application and trouble, and seek to get the best information I can—yet with all my zeal, I must think myself unequal to the task, as I find I am in every respect; at the same time meeting with the greatest discouragements. Lady Orford uses me ill,[7] though I take off from her a burthen she ought to bear in my place. I have no legal power to do[8] many right and necessary things; I expose myself to many risks; I am forced to make a thousand enemies, and to do hard things against my nature. I am in dread of doing unjust things, either by my Lord on one side, or by his tenants on the other; and while I mean nothing but to do right,

6. Three days earlier HW had thought that his re-leasing had been even more successful, only to watch the agreements one by one fall through (HW to Lady Ossory 1 Sept. 1773, Ossory i. 141–2).

7. Mann was trying to get her to send HW the necessary permission to take over his nephew's affairs (Mann vii. 505–45). Later she summarized her feelings toward her mad son and HW's efforts in his behalf: 'I am much obliged to Mr Walpole. It is impossible not to admire both his style and his sentiments, which are just and delicate. His account of Lord Orford is the most affecting, as it leaves no room to flatter oneself with his ever recovering his senses, and shows what he must suffer by the great attention necessary to preserve his wretched life in spite of himself. Mr Walpole's goodness for him ought to be rewarded in a better world than this' (quoted by Mann to HW 18 Dec. 1773, ibid. vii. 534).

8. 'Make' crossed out and 'do' written above in the MS.

my ignorance may draw me into doing wrong. In short, dear Sir, I am very desponding. I grudge no pains, though I sacrifice my whole time and happiness. If I thought all my care and anxiety could be recompensed with retrieving the affairs of my family, I should have more courage; but Lord Orford seems to have involved himself so deeply, that I do not see whence restoration can come. All I pretend to, is to have put his affairs into some method; an abler person may perhaps do more, and may avail themselves of what has cost me so much care. I will trouble you no farther now. You understand these things better than I do, and therefore I imagine will only see them in a still worse light than they appear to

dear Sir

Your most obedient humble servant

Hor. Walpole

[Enclosure]

Abstract of what has been done by Mr Moone and Mr Walpole, in August 1773.

Retrenched by Mr Moone in expenses at Houghton and Earsewell [Eriswell, Suffolk].

By discharging servants at Houghton	194 = 1 = 0
More that go at Michaelmas	93 = 5 = 0
Ditto 5 horses and boys at Newmarket	269 = 12 = 0
Lodgings at Newmarket	26 = 5 = 0
By discharging servants at Earsewell	42 = 6 = 0
The fishery there given up	9 = 9 = 0
Another fishery in Norfolk ditto	4 = 4 = 0
The gardener at Houghton	50 = 0 = 0
Dogs and horses at Houghton	400 = 0 = 0
Beagles	100 = 0 = 0
	1189 = 2 = 0

The account of the horses and dogs cannot yet be made up, as the horses will not all be sold till October, nor are all the dogs yet gone, but the expense of both, amounting to a very great sum, will be all retrenched.

All my Lord's debts and bills have been called for, but are not come in yet, though many are.

Part of a farm, kept in my Lord's own hands, has been let at an advanced rent, the increase amounting to

per annum 75 = 10 = 0

Brown's farm let to Spurgeon, and increased—per annum 74 = 0 = 0

149 = 10 = 0

To Lady Orford, Thursday 9 September 1773

Missing; mentioned by HW to Mann 9 Sept. 1773: 'I have received a satisfactory, and even flattering, letter from Lady Orford this very day; and I enclose an answer to it, which I hope will be more welcome to her, than hers was to me, for it now pins me down to the oar, and the best part of the remainder of life must be given up to this painful duty. I shall do everything in my power to please her, and to do justice to her son and my family. I shall not often trouble her with letters, as she cares so little to be troubled, but you may assure her and she may depend upon it, that if she will at any time but give me a hint through you or Mr Sharpe, I will do whatever she commands. I have told her the truth, that nothing should have persuaded me to go on but the approbation of my Lord's own mother' (MANN vii. 514).

From the Hon. Thomas Walpole, ca Saturday 11 September 1773

Printed for the first time from a photostat of the Holland MS; for the history of the MS see *ante* 18 July 1766.

Only a draft of this letter survives; it was written on the cover of HW's letter *ante* 4 Sept. 1773.

Dated by Lord Walpole's reply to Thomas Walpole of 13 Sept. 1773. Thomas Walpole is replying to HW's letter of 4 Sept., but the beginning of the letter shows that the reply was delayed.

Dear Sir,

ON my arrival in town last night I received the letter[1] you was so kind to write to me concerning Lord Orford's affairs. I shall immediately transmit it to Lord Walpole who I am sure will be as ready as I am to acknowledge the obligation by which you bind the whole family in taking upon you the administration of a mass so

1. *Ante* 4 Sept. 1773.

complicated with error, neglect and imposition. What you have already done by the note you are pleased to communicate to me shows that however unpractised you may have been in affairs of this sort, nobody is more able in the execution,[2] which I will attribute to your zeal if you will not allow it to your talents, though[3] such as you possess will always avail[4] in whatever undertaking they are exercised, and you hold[5] a rank with respect to Lord Orford which gives you an authority no other of his relations could have. Notwithstanding the considerable retrenchments you have made and the increase of income you have made with the prospect of pushing this farther, I am not less affected[6] than you are at the heavy load of debt that is hanging over us, against which I see no prospect of relief[7] of but in the success of our prayers for your life, Lord Orford's life, and the death of Lady Orford, from whose ashes[8] may afford that assistance which her existence denies. I have a true sense of your condescension in entering into a detail of this vexatious business, in which I have so little right to interfere and no means of affording you any assistance. As one of a family to whom you so generously sacrifice a long-enjoyed and well-employed retirement, I shall ever acknowledge myself with the sincerest gratitude.

To Lady Orford, Thursday 4 November 1773

Missing; mentioned by HW to Mann 4 Nov. 1773: 'I not only write all my letters myself, but am forced to take copies of them too, for it is of too much consequence to me not to know what I say; and many I cannot trust to a copyist, as you will see by the enclosed, which I send you open, for I cannot write it over a third time. Put a seal that my Lady will now know; but make yourself master of the contents first, that you may be able to assist me if necessary, and say I sent you a summary account of the matter. . . . Mr Sharpe would have persuaded me against this step; everybody else approves it. In short, I could do nothing else' (Mann vii. 523).

2. 'Able in the execution' written above 'fit for the business' in the MS.

3. 'I have experience to know that' crossed out after 'though.'

4. 'To' crossed out after 'avail.'

5. 'Stand' crossed out and 'hold a rank' written above.

6. 'Alarmed' crossed out after 'less.'

7. 'Remedy' crossed out and 'relief' written above.

8. 'Alone' crossed out after 'ashes.'

To the Duchess of Gloucester, Thursday
27 January 1774

Printed from the MS now WSL; first printed, *Last Journals* i. 366–9; reprinted, Toynbee viii. 409–13. For the history of the MS see *ante* 15 May 1745 OS.

In *Last Journals* HW wrote, 'At night, having well considered the affair, I wrote her the following letter in hopes it would open the Duke's eyes on the imprudence of his plan, when he saw how very strong the arguments were against it' (i. 365–6).

Jan. 27, 1774.

Madam,

THE most proper mark of respect that I can show to the Duke or to your Royal Highness on a subject of such momentous importance,[1] is to use as few words as possible. I am not wise enough to advise, much less to decide upon it, nor do I know a man in England who I think could advise the Duke upon it with good effect. All I can do is to suggest what comes into my mind on the most intense thought and coolest reflection, submitting my sentiments with the utmost deference to his Royal Highness's judgment.

No man living has a higher opinion of the Duke of Richmond's[2] unequalled honour and integrity, than I have. I respect his spirit and abilities, and am as sure as I can be of anything that he is incapable of an unworthy action. Still I should not recommend him for the mover, if the question is resolved upon. The Duke of R[ichmond] is particularly unwelcome to his Majesty; and the measure will be thought the more hostile, if proposed by his Grace.[3]

1. 'They were exceedingly embarrassed in their affairs and greatly in debt. On the 27th of January the Duchess sent for me, and told me the Duke had ordered her to speak to me on their situation; that he intended to apply to Parliament; but she expressed herself so mysteriously that I did not clearly understand whether his Royal Highness proposed to ask for a settlement on her or for an additional income for himself—I thought the latter, and spoke only on that. . . . I was much struck with the extreme impropriety of so ill-advised a measure, that was totally hopeless of success, and that only could tend to widen the breach, and draw a

Parliamentary approbation of the King's rigour. I saw it would draw ruin on the Duchess herself' (*Last Journals* i. 364–5).

2. Charles Lennox (1735–1806), 3d D. of Richmond, 1750; General of the Army, 1782; Field Marshal, 1792; ambassador to Paris 1765–6; P.C., 1765; secretary of state for the Southern Department, 1766; m. (1757) Mary Bruce (1740–96), dau. of 3d E. of Ailesbury, and Henry Seymour Conway's stepdaughter. HW was devoted to both the Duke and Duchess.

3. 'That Duke' crossed out after 'by' in the MS. HW wrote in *Last Journals* (i. 365, 369), 'I loved the Duke of Richmond too well to embark him in a step

The question itself seems to me most unlikely of success. The ministers will plead that when the King however necessitous, does not ask for an increase of income, from the present distressed situation of the country, it cannot be reasonable to augment the revenue of his brothers. An increase of the King's own revenue might be supposed to include the charge of his own children; but an addition to that of his brothers, would not lessen the burthen of his own issue. And it would infallibly be urged that so numerous a progeny as his Majesty's, makes it imprudent to establish a precedent of such large revenues for each prince of the Royal Family.

In any case, so great is the power of the Crown, and so infamous the servility of Parliament, that there cannot be the shadow of hope that an increase could be obtained for the two royal Dukes, against the King's inclination.

But a question moved and lost, as undoubtedly this would be, could only make his Royal Highness's case worse, if possible, than it is at present. His Royal Highness's father, though heir-apparent to an old King, could not obtain an increase of income, when parties ran high, and were almost equally divided. His R.H. the Duke of Gloucester, can hold out neither hopes nor rewards, and, in a very low ebb of Opposition, would obtain scarce any support. When so few pay common respect by waiting on him, though not discountenanced for it, would they vote for him? no, not all that now pay their duty to him.

The question moved and lost, would change the state of the case to his R.H.'s disadvantage. His treatment may now be thought hard. When he should have had recourse to opposition, which a Parliamentary application would be called, the courtiers would term it an hostile measure, and thus claim a sanction for their servility, by affecting to support offended Majesty.

The King himself would then too plead that he only acted by the opinion of Parliament, who did not think it reasonable to increase the income of the two Princes. And the most moderate ministers, if any such there are, who may have wished a reconciliation between the King and his brothers, will then oppose it, as concluding that by

that would not only be a personal affront to the King, but would be universally condemned, and thence become universally ridiculed. . . . I showed the letter to the Duke of Richmond, who entirely agreed with my sentiments, and had no mind to be made the instrument.'

voting against them, they have made the two royal Dukes their personal enemies.

Thus every door to a reconciliation in the R[oyal] Family would be shut, and no advantage gained. On the contrary, his R.H. would only let the world know how few friends stand by him. When so few even of the Opposition wait on him, I doubt whether they would be heartier friends to his interest.

These seem to me insurmountable difficulties. It is still more arduous for me to chalk out an alternative.

I presumed to tell your R.H. Madam, when you first mentioned this great point to me, that I thought the first step in wisdom to be taken was to engage the favour of mankind to the Duke's cause by showing he had done everything rather than act in what might be called a hostile manner.[4] His R.H. will, I flatter myself, forgive me if I use even an improper term. Will it be too free-spoken, in so important a moment to say, that previous to an application to Parliament which should in prudence be the last resort, it would recommend even that application[5] if the Duke could show he had tried every method of softening his Majesty's displeasure? Nobody knows so well as his R.H. how to mix dignity with propriety. Could not his R.H. Madam, blend those two in a representation of his youthful error, of his concern for having afflicted an affectionate brother and King, of tenderness for a wife, and a sweet little innocent Princess,[6] calling on His Majesty's piety for forgiveness,[7] and by touching his heart[8] on his own conjugal and parental affections; and above all by stating his own anxious cares on the incertitude of the fate of persons so dear to him as your R.H. and the infant Princess his daughter? These, Madam, are noble motives, and would

---

4. 'Measure' crossed out and 'manner' written above.

5. 'By showing that' crossed out after 'application.'

6. 'By' crossed out after 'Princess.'

7. HW had suggested this to the Duchess in conversation before he composed this letter: 'Before the application . . . to the King . . . I thought the Duke ought, previous to all other conduct, to ask his Majesty's pardon. "The King . . . is not only, Madam, his Royal Highness's King, but elder brother, and I advise nothing but what I would practise. I would not submit to ask pardon of any other man living, but of my brother; and *you know*, Madam, that I have asked pardon of your father, when he has been the person in the wrong, only because he is my elder brother [*ante* 16, 17 May 1745 OS]. I would have the Duke ask the King's pardon, and then entreat the Bench of Bishops to be mediators, and urge to his Majesty's piety the duties of forgiveness and reconciliation"' (*Last Journals* i. 365; see Appendix 2). The King was not reconciled to his brothers until 1780 (Ossory ii. 198).

8. 'By' crossed out after 'heart.'

justify a tender and fraternal application to his Majesty's heart, and would distress it far differently from a question in Parliament. They would engage the compassion of the disinterested world, and in the last resort would corroborate in the strongest manner[9] all arguments in Parliament; where it would certainly be asked if his R. Highness had used any intercession with the King his brother.[10] When[11] the Duke had tried all other methods in vain, such application could not be condemned: and the preference of all softer methods, first would redound to his R.H.'s honour.

Having said thus much, Madam, I think my conscience and duty oblige me to add, that I think it indispensably incumbent on those who have the honour to be related to your R.H. to give you no advice but such as may tend to repair the breaches which the Duke's tenderness for you has occasioned in the R[oyal] F[amily]. The good of his R.H. calls on you and on us to consult his welfare in the first instance. You have always told me how desirous you are of sacrificing yourself for him. I know the uprightness of your heart, Madam, and I know you spoke truth. Advise him to whatever is most for his benefit and credit. Do your duty by him, and trust to a just God for your reward. In the presence of that God I have given you the best advice in my power. I am sure I have not displeased[12] you by my freedom: I hope I have not offended his R.H. but I declare on my conscience and honour, that I know not what better advice to give,[13] and I sign it with my name, as the firm opinion of, Madam

Your R.H.'s

most faithful

and devoted humble servant

Hor. Walpole

---

9. 'Representa' crossed out after 'manner.'

10. 'Where . . . brother' is an interlineation.

11. 'Had' crossed out before 'When.'

12. 'Offended' crossed out and 'displeased' written above.

13. 'To this letter I received no answer. The next time I saw the Duchess she told me she had given the Duke the letter, who

From Lord Orford, ca February 1774

Missing; mentioned by HW to Mme du Deffand 1 March 1774: 'Mon neveu m'écrit des lettres d'une sagesse extrême, mais on me dit qu'il songe à reprendre ses liaisons avec Newmarket, qui sera la pierre de touche' (DU DEFFAND iv. 24).

To Lady Orford, ca February 1774

Several letters, missing; mentioned by HW to Mann 2 Feb. 1774: 'I have done with her: I shall write her one more letter to tell her her son is quite recovered, and then forget her. . . . I sent my late letters to Lady O. in Sir W[illiam Hamilton]'s packet, but I think it safer to convey the enclosed by you' (MANN vii. 548, 551). ' "I received the letter you enclosed from Mr Walpole, and hope that he has long since received mine" ' (Lady Orford to Mann, quoted in Mann to HW 12 March 1774, ibid. vii. 558).

From Lady Orford, ca February 1774

Several letters, missing; mentioned by HW to Mann 23 Feb. 1774: 'I have had mighty civil dispatches from my sister-in-law. She desires the continuation of our correspondence, which I shall now and then obey. I may be obliged to renew it, and therefore it is best to keep it up' (MANN vii. 557). One of these letters arrived the night of 21 Feb. with a letter from Sir William Hamilton: ' "The last I got Sir William Hamilton to put into his packet for fear of accidents, as I should be extremely sorry he should think I neglected my acknowledgments for so much goodness. I think I wrote you that I had sent him a letter for Lord Orford for him to deliver or not as he thought proper" ' (Lady Orford to Mann, quoted by Mann to HW 12 March 1774, ibid. vii. 558–9; HW to Sir William Hamilton 22 Feb. 1774). 'I have received a gracious epistle from the Countess, enclosing one to her son, open, and full of commendations of my behaviour' (HW to Mann 28 March 1774, ibid. vii. 560).

said I had mistaken the affair, and he would explain it to me. This intimated that he meant to ask a provision for her and the child, rather than for himself— yet my arguments were equally good against both; and though the Duke never said a word to me on the business more, it was plain he thought so too, for he laid aside his design. I believe, however, that he did not like my freedom, though for some time he treated me with more regard' (*Last Journals* i. 369). In May of this year the Duke moved again for a provision for his family, but it was rejected by the King. In April 1778 a bill was passed to include the Duke and Duchess of Gloucester's two children in the Parliamentary provision for the King's children (ibid. i. 369–71, ii. 156–7; *post* HW to D. of Gloucester 17 Jan. 1775, Ds of Gloucester to HW 10 Aug. 1777).

From Sir Edward Walpole, Monday 25 April 1774

Printed from the MS now WSL; first printed, Toynbee *Supp.* iii. 231–2. Damer-Waller; for the history of the MS see *ante* 6 July 1758.
Address: To Mr Hor. Walpole in Arlington Street.

Pall Mall, Monday April 25, 1774.

Dear Horace,

I AM quite stunned with this unfortunate event of the sudden decline and danger of Monsieur Pontdeveylle;[1] for my young client[2] certainly thought his fortune made: which now will be very precarious. And as he is of a frame and make to be easily shaken, I fear the consequences of it to him—his mind is stouter than his body; and I do not always see what he feels. But I believe this unhappy disappointment strikes deep. —Your goodness to him I am sure he feels; and so do I. Which makes it a delicate point to urge it any farther—He is indeed an invaluable young man; has many great and good qualities; has an admirable understanding; tried integrity, and uncommon powers in his two professions.—His affairs are in such a situation, that he cannot go in less than three weeks: nor indeed is he established enough in his health to venture abroad immediately. But at all events will certainly set out in three weeks at most.[3]

He is much mended by Dr Jebb's[4] kind attention to him—vast quantities of bark have done more for him than anything he has yet tried; and perhaps it will restore him and save him—He will be with me all tomorrow evening. And it would be a vast consolation to him to see you, if you could call in.

Yours very gratefully and faithfully

Ed. Walpole

1. Antoine Ferriol, Comte de Pont-de-Veyle (see *ante* 15 Oct. 1769, n. 10); his ill health is mentioned by Mme du Deffand 17 April: 'Pont-de-Veyle est très malade, et si dangereusement, qu'il y a fort peu d'espérance' (DU DEFFAND iv. 40).

2. Mr Bishop, an actor and dancer, friend of Sir Edward, who wanted HW to solicit Mme du Deffand's influence with Pont-de-Veyle in Bishop's behalf; HW wrote a letter of recommendation and Mme du Deffand introduced him to Pont-de-Veyle (*post* 16 July 1774; DU DEFFAND iv. 28–31, 34–6, 50–1, 55).

3. He arrived in Paris 18 May (Mme du Deffand to HW 18 May 1774, ibid. iv. 55).

4. Richard Jebb (1729–87), cr. (1788) Bt; M.D. Marischal College Aberdeen, 1751; physician to George III, 1762, and to the Prince of Wales, 1787 (*Last Journals* i. 505; OSSORY i. 175, n. 3; *London Chronicle* 12–14 July 1787, lxii. 41).

From SIR EDWARD WALPOLE, Saturday 16 July 1774

Printed from the MS now WSL; first printed, Toynbee *Supp*. iii. 233–4. Damer-Waller; for the history of the MS see *ante* 6 July 1758.
Address: To the Honourable Horace Walpole at Strawberry Hill Twickenham Middlesex.
Postmark: 16 IY.
Endorsed (by HW): From Sir Edw. Walpole.

Pall Mall, July 16, '74.

Dear Horace,

I HAVE not yet thanked you by letter or in person, which I have very sincerely done in every other shape, for your great goodness to Mr Bishop;[1] amply manifested in the extraordinary condescension and benevolence of the Marquise du Deffand towards him.[2] I did not indeed take notice of it before, as he was appointed to the stage; and I imagined I should have some instance of his success to recount to you when I should acknowledge your kindness to me. I find since, that he exhibits himself this month and by a letter from another friend of mine now at Paris, I hear that he meets with uncommon encouragement and approbation among the people of the profession.

If in your correspondence with Madame du Deffand she should mention anything[3] about him worth my knowing I dare say you will favour me with a line. And when he returns to England I shall hope for your protection for him.

I am most affectionately yours

ED. WALPOLE

PS. I beg when you write that you will desire the Marquise to accept my best respects and to believe that I have the deepest sense

1. Sir Edward had perhaps asked his daughter for help in this matter at an earlier date. The Duchess of Gloucester wrote Jane Clement ca 28 Sept. 1772: 'I have had the so long expected request for Bishop, and have not given a favourable answer. . . . we have more pages and dependants than we know what to do with. . . . [The Duke] never will stir a finger to help me with my dependants' (MS now WSL); and again on 18 Dec., 'I have paid Ned Bishop £50' (ibid.).

2. See *ante* 25 April 1774, n. 2, and below, n. 5.

3. On 21 Feb. 1775 Mme du Deffand wrote HW: 'Je suis ravie du succès du petit danseur et fort aise que monsieur votre frère soit content de moi' (DU

of her great benevolence and condescension⁴—she was so exceedingly attentive to your request, that she ordered her carriage and took him to Monsieur Pontdeveylle's.⁵—I have no words to thank her in for so very gracious and so efficacious an act of patronage as that—it is a substantial proof of a most high respect and affection for you. Which, when I read your letter of introduction,⁶ so elegant it is, so full of kindness to me and humanity to the young fellow, I do not in the least wonder at, nor that she sets so great a value upon your friendship—which whatever you may think, I do no less than she.

From LORD CHOLMONDELEY,¹ ca October 1774

Missing; mentioned by HW to Conway 29 Oct. 1774: 'Lord Cholmondeley sends me word he goes to Paris on Monday: I shall send this and my other letter by him.'

To the DUKE OF GLOUCESTER, Tuesday 17 January 1775

Printed from the MS of HW's draft now WSL; first printed, Cunningham vi. 175–8; reprinted, Toynbee ix. 139–43. For the history of the MS see *ante* 15 May 1745 OS.

Endorsed (by HW): To the Duke of Gloster.

Jan. 17, 1775.

Sir,

YOUR R.H.'s commands are so much a law to me, that though deeply conscious of the inequality of my understanding to so arduous a question, and full of fears lest a word should drop from me that should lead your R.H. into any step prejudicial to yourself or

DEFFAND iv. 160). HW saw Bishop in Paris ('Paris Journals,' 23 Aug. 1775, ibid. v. 344).

4. 'Je suis honteuse de ses [Sir Edward's] remercîments pour ce qui ne m'a donné ni peine ni embarras' (Mme du Deffand to HW 24 July 1774, ibid. iv. 77).

5. 'Votre petit homme est arrivé. Je le menai hier chez Pont-de-Veyle, il est content da sa figure, c'est un maître de langue qui est son interprète. Pont-de-

Veyle lui a dit d'aller chez Rebel ou Berton, qui sont les directeurs de l'Opéra' (Mme du Deffand to HW 18 May 1774, ibid. iv. 55).

6. ?HW to Mme du Deffand 13 May 1774, missing (ibid.).

1. George James Cholmondeley (1749–1827), 4th E. of Cholmondeley, HW's grand-nephew.

to the Princesses[1] your daughters, I venture to lay my thoughts at your R.H.'s feet, only entreating,[2] if they appear to have any weight in them, that your R.H. would not adopt them till they have been approved by better judgments than mine.

Before I speak, Sir, on the question whether your R.H. should take any measure in Parliament, for procuring a provision for your family,[3] permit me, Sir, to state an apprehension that has struck me from the conversation I had the honour of having with you the last time I saw you. Your R.H. expressed doubts whether there might not be some idea of calling the legitimacy of your children in question.[4] Alas! Sir, if it is possible that any human mind should have such an idea, would not a motion in Parliament be the likeliest method of bringing that horrid intention into execution? The Parliament is so infamous, that it could, I firmly believe, be brought to lend its assistance to anything. As your R.H.'s hints of carrying[5] any part of your cause thither, has not alarmed, may one not suppose, that, not alarming, it pleases! What will either House not do! what has either refused to do! Consider, Sir, how many would be glad to colour over their mean desertion or neglect of you, by calling into question the validity of your marriage, and consequently of the birth of your children. Shame is apt to fly to crimes for a veil. I have no difficulty in speaking on this question: Your R.H. must authenticate the legitimacy of your children, before you think of a provision for them. I rest it there, Sir, not to trouble you with unnecessary words.

In regard to the question your R.H. was pleased to put to me, on some motion for a provision, I will consider it in two lights; in the

---

1. Their second daughter, Princess Carolina Augusta Maria, was born 24 June 1774 but died only two months after this letter (14 March 1775). See Geo. III's *Corr.*, ed. Fortescue, iii. 168, 187.

2. 'That' crossed out after 'entreating' in MS.

3. The King wrote Lord North 16 Jan. 1775, 'I cannot therefore bring myself on a repetition of this application to give him hopes of a future establishment for his children, which would only bring a fresh altercation about his wife whom I can never think of placing in a situation to answer her extreme pride and vanity. Should he be so ill-advised as to have

a provision for her and the children moved in Parliament the line of conduct to be held is plain . . . that it is natural the King should not apply to Parliament for provisions for the children of a younger branch of his family when he has not as yet done it for his own numerous offspring; . . . I am certain you know my way of thinking too well to doubt that should any accident happen to the Duke I shall certainly take care of his children' (Geo. III's *Corr.*, ed. Fortescue, iii. 165).

4. See *ante* ca 28 May 1773, heading.

5. 'Bringing' crossed out and 'carrying' written above.

first, whether it would be proper for any Lords to take it up—This, Sir, I am sorry to say, lies in a small compass, and extends to a very few Lords in the Opposition; your R.H. knows already my opinion, that a few opposing Lords would only do your cause signal mischief, and would give the pretended sanction, that I fear is wished for, to doing nothing for you—and therefore, if I am not wrong, not to be attempted. The Duke of R[ichmond] with whom I have talked,[6] fears nothing, Sir, but hurting your cause.[7] He is so personally obnoxious,[8] that he thinks a motion from your R.H. and himself, would only be considered, certainly represented, as factious—his Grace's tenderness and delicacy would not suffer him to add, that none of his friends would support him, though he knows they would not. What could be expected, Sir, from a measure so generally abandoned? When could it be revived with success, unless, not only times, but men should be totally altered?

I can then, Sir, have but one idea left, the same I suggested on Monday,[9] if your R.H. should still think the present season a proper one, though it is probable that nothing will be stirred this year in relation to an increase of the revenue of the Crown. I must throw myself on your R.H.'s great goodness and generosity, before I presume to utter what I have farther to say. You have indeed, Sir, commanded me, given me leave to speak what I think, and I dare not at such a crisis but speak what I think. Be not offended, Sir, my heart burns to serve you —but I will not waste your time on my idle apologies. My sincerity must be proved by my actions.

I have said, Sir, how infamous I think Parliaments. I have not so bad an opinion of all mankind in general. Humanity can operate, when interest is silent. It seems essential in my opinion to any future service that your R.H. may reap from a motion in Parliament that the cry of mankind should be raised loud in your favour. That can only be excited by stating your sufferings[10] and by being able to prove that you have done everything in your power to reconcile his Majesty, and to deprecate his anger. The plan[11] I should humbly

6. 'This morning' crossed out after 'talked.'

7. The Duke of Gloucester had hoped to engage the Duke of Richmond to be the mover in Parliament for the provision when he had been considering it early in 1774 (see *ante* 27 Jan. 1774).

8. I.e., in disfavour with the King (ibid.).

9. 'Last night' crossed out and 'on Monday' written above.

10. 'Oppressions' crossed out and 'sufferings' written above.

11. 'My p' crossed out before 'The plan.'

offer to your R.H. for your conduct will best explain my meaning, laying it before you, Sir, with the utmost deference and diffidence; far from presuming to dictate, but obeying from perfect submission.

I should begin, Sir, by writing an ostensible letter to the King asking pardon for a natural, youthful error,[12] regretting his displeasure, entreating a return of his fraternal affections, stating my own ill health,[13] and how much that must be augmented by his resentment, and at least imploring he would give that relief to a sick body[14] and wounded mind of promising he would make a proper provision for persons so dear to me as my wife and children. As[15] heightening the picture a little would not add to your R.H.'s disorder, I would beg the comfort of taking leave of him in so critical a situation of my health. If this should have no effect, Sir, I would just before leaving England, in my place in the House of Lords, acquaint their Lordships, that I was grieved that his Majesty was so much offended at a youthful error, which as it was neither repugnant to religion, or law at that time, I had flattered myself had not been irremissible. That I had done but what the heir of the Crown, James II when Duke of York had done and been forgiven,[16] and what had very frequently[17] been done by other Princes[18] of the royal blood, and by Kings of England themselves. That I had never refused any match that had been proposed, and had only chosen for myself, when no wife had been sought for[19] me. That I had preferred legal matrimony to the dissoluteness of youth; that I had selected a woman of blameless virtue, and that I had done what their Lordships could not disapprove, I had chosen a lady from their own

12. Neglecting to obtain the King's approval for his marriage (see *ante* 19 May 1772, enclosure in 20 May 1772, and n. 8).

13. About a week later the Duke of Gloucester was 'very ill . . . extremely ill. It was reported and believed that he was dead. . . . The physicians . . . gave no hopes yesterday' (HW to Mann 25 Jan. 1775, MANN viii. 74).

14. 'Distempered body' crossed out before 'sick.'

15. 'If' crossed out before 'As.'

16. James II when Duke of York married in 1660 Anne Hyde (1637–71), dau. of Edward Hyde, 1st E. of Clarendon. She was later to become the mother of Queen Mary and Queen Anne. Her father was 'frantic with rage' when he heard of the marriage and there was a controversy over the circumstances of the ceremony, in which it was confessed that 'they were not fully married till about a month or two before she was brought to bed; but that they were contracted long before, and time enough for the child to be legitimate' (Samuel Pepys, *Diary*, ed. Wheatley, i. 326, *sub* 23 Feb. 1661).

17. 'Constantly' crossed out and 'very frequently' written above.

18. 'Sons' crossed out and 'Princes' written above.

19. 'Proposed to' crossed out and 'sought for' written above.

class into which Princes of the Blood used to marry. I would then acquaint them with the steps I had in vain taken for reconciliation. I would entreat them to be mediators with the King for remission of my fault, in marrying without his approbation: I would acquaint them with the precarious state of my health, which obliged me to leave the kingdom and my family unprovided for; and I would beg them as Christian peers and his Majesty's Great Council, to endeavour to repair the breaches in the Royal Family; and if anything should happen to me, to intercede with his Majesty's piety and forgiveness, to make a suitable provision for two innocent young Princesses of his own blood who had never offended him; and I would add, that to avoid any suspicion of intending to disturb[20] his Majesty's mind, I declined[21] making any present Parliamentary application for my children, but would leave to the wisdom of their Lordships to take the most proper time of being intercessors[22] for me and my family with my royal brother. This address, Sir, to the Lords I would deliver[23] in writing, and would desire it might be entered on the Journals. I would then retire and leave them.

But now, Sir, after taking such a latitude of liberty, whom shall I entreat to be intercessor[24] for me with your R.H.?—Your own excellent heart, Sir. No, you cannot be offended at zeal, even if it has passed its due bounds. On my soul, Sir, I think that what I have said, is the best method I can devise for obtaining your R.H.'s object. No highflown loyalty, nor grovelling self-interest has dictated my words. If Parliament is against you, the majority of mankind must be gained over by acting as they would advise.[25] If I advise you, Sir, to stoop beyond what your royal heart would suggest, it is for the sake of your children, who will plead, when I fail. If you are in the right, in the world's eye, whatever it costs your feeling, it will be of use to them. The circumstances may change; your health I trust in God will be reestablished, and the more sacrifices you have made, the higher you will stand in the esteem of mankind. I still flatter myself you will enjoy all the happiness and dignity due to your virtues and

20. The 'ing' of 'disturbing' is crossed out and 'intending to' is interlineated before 'disturb.'

21. 'Avoided' crossed out before 'declined.'

22. 'Mediators and' crossed out before 'intercessors.'

23. 'Leave' crossed out and 'deliver' written above.

24. 'Mediator' crossed out before 'intercessor.'

25. 'Prescribe' crossed out and 'advise' written above.

birth. I am not likely to see that moment nor should profit by it if I did—but I have done my duty as your true servant, and if I was now at my last hour, I could not give you any other advice than what I now presume to lay at your feet, etc. etc.

PS. If your R.H. should deem this advice timid, I beg it may be tried by this test, whether your R.H. thinks[26] that any one of your enemies[27] would be glad I had[28] given this advice; undoubtedly,[29] Sir, the more you take care to be in the right yourself, the more you put those, who hurt you with the King in the wrong.

To Lady Orford, ca Wednesday 15 February 1775

Missing; enclosed by HW to Mann 15 Feb. 1775: 'I am now going to write a letter to his mother to ask a trifling favour, which I care not whether she grants or refuses—but it was at the request of another [Charles Boone had asked HW to request of Lady Orford a church living which was in her gift; HW had never met the clergyman who wanted it.] Here is the letter; I beg you to give or send it, accordingly as she is at Florence or Naples' (Mann viii. 82; see also ibid. viii. 105).

From Mary Churchill,[1] July 1775

Printed from a transcript (by R. W. Ketton-Cremer, 1966) of the MS in the possession of Lord Kenyon, Gredington, Whitchurch, Salop. The MS is small, folded several times, and was probably kept inside the snuff-box it mentions. Presumably the box, which has since disappeared, was one of 'two papier-maché snuff-boxes, one presented by Miss Churchill' (sold SH xvi. 114 to Lady Walsingham, mother-in-law of the 3d Bn Kenyon).

Dated conjecturally by Mme du Deffand's allusion to the Churchills' visit to Spa in her letter to HW of 9 July 1775: 'Vous allez perdre madame votre sœur et toute sa famille; vous ne me dites point où ils iront après Spa' (du Deffand iv. 206–7).

Address: To the Honourable Horatio Walpole.

I beg your pardon, Sir, if I take the liberty of sending you this beautiful snuff-box, but I thought there would be always something

---

26. Originally 'you think Sir'; 'r' added to 'you,' 'R.H.' interlineated, 's' added to 'think,' 'Sir' crossed out.

27. 'The Court' crossed out and 'your enemies' written above.

28. 'Wish me to have' crossed out and 'be glad I had' written above.

29. 'For' crossed out before 'undoubtedly.'

1. HW's niece, Mary Churchill (b. 1750), dau. of Charles Churchill and Lady Mary

wanting in your cabinet of curiosities² if you had not the views of Spa amongst other fine paintings; a gentleman³ who sets out to-morrow for England furnishes me an opportunity of having the pleasure of sending them to you.

We flatter ourselves you will be glad to hear the waters have done us great good, especially to my brother⁴ and me.

My Papa and Mama desire me to say everything that is kind from them to you. I hope you will forgive my troubling and believe me to be

Dear Sir

Your most obedient humble servant

M. CHURCHILL

To CATHERINE DAYE, Thursday 17 August 1775

Missing; listed in 'Paris Journals,' DU DEFFAND v. 395.

To the DUCHESS OF GLOUCESTER, Monday 21 August 1775

Missing; listed in 'Paris Journals,' DU DEFFAND v. 395.

From the DUCHESS OF GLOUCESTER, ?August 1775

Missing; mentioned by HW to Mann 8 Dec. 1775: 'I know nothing directly, having received but a single letter from her Royal Highness since they set out. I need not say to you, that I never had such an honour from the Duke'ᵢ (MANN viii. 147–8).

Dated by HW to Mann 10 Oct. 1775 (ibid. 134): 'I know nothing of their Royal Highnesses nor have heard of them since they were at Strasburgh'; Mrs Keppel received a letter dated Strasbourg 26 Aug. from the Duchess (Laura Keppel to Jane Clement 9 Sept. 1775, MS now WSL).

Walpole; m. (7 Aug. 1777) as his 2d wife, Charles Sloane Cadogan (1728–1807), 3d Bn Cadogan, 1776, cr. (1800) E. Cadogan. She was divorced (1796) in a cause of crim. con. with the Rev. Mr Cooper (1766–1834) (OSSORY i. 368, nn. 2, 3).

2. In the Glass Closet of the Great North bedchamber, 'a snuff-box with views of Spa; given by Miss Churchill' ('Des. of SH,' *Works* ii. 500).

3. Not identified.

4. Probably Horace Churchill (*ante* to Charles Churchill 27 March 1764, n. 27).

1. He had apparently never replied to HW's letter of 17 Jan. 1775.

To Lady Mary Churchill, 29 August 1775

Missing. Listed in 'Paris Journals,' du Deffand v. 396.

To the Duchess of Gloucester, Monday 4 September 1775

Missing; listed in 'Paris Journals,' du Deffand v. 396; sent to Venice 4 Sept., as HW wrote Mann 10 Oct. 1775, 'I wrote twice to Venice.'[1] (Mann viii. 134); mentioned by HW to Mann 7 Sept. 1775: 'I have written to her, without naming you, to dissuade their fixing at Rome'[2] (ibid. viii. 125).

To the Duchess of Gloucester, Monday 11 September 1775

Missing; listed in 'Paris Journals,' du Deffand v. 396, sent on 11 Sept.; see HW to Mann 10 Oct. 1775, Mann viii. 134, and *ante* 4 Sept. 1775, heading.

To the Duke of Gloucester, December 1775

Missing; answered *post* 17 Jan. 1776. The letter which the Duke is answering may have been written to the Duchess.

1. The Duke had written the King in January requesting permission to go abroad and again applying for financial provision for his family; the King granted only the permission to travel (Geo. III's *Corr.*, ed. Fortescue, iii. 164–5; *ante* 17 Jan. 1775). 'The Duke and Duchess had left England . . . for the Duke's health, from the distress of his finances, and worn out by the persecutions of the Court' (*Last Journals* i. 504–7, 525). The death of their second child, Princess Carolina Augusta Maria, in March of this year and the King's refusal to permit her burial in the Royal Vault at Westminster had added to their unhappiness (ibid. i. 360, 363, 445–8; Mann viii. 86). They set out for Italy from Dover 24 July (*Daily Adv.* 25 July) and arrived in Calais 25 July where they 'were received with proper respect . . . by order of the French Court. . . . The King of France invited them to Versailles, but they excused themselves, which was ill-judged, as it would have been of great use to the Duchess to be owned there' (*Last Journals* i. 470–1).

2. Before he left England the Duke had told Lord Rochford he was going 'To Rome, my Lord, the only place where the Pretender and I can live.' 'The Duke could not go to any other capital, as the King's ambassadors were not allowed to pay their duty to him' (*Last Journals* i. 525 and n. 2). In 1771 the Duke and his suite had lived in Sir Horace Mann's house and 'mortified my particular friend . . . by unmerited slights'; HW referred to 'the disagreeable position you are in from the absurdity of your inmates' (ibid. i. 94; HW to Mann 14 Jan. 1772, Mann vii. 363–4). HW wished to spare Mann another embarrassment either from a repetition of the earlier slights or from the official protocol Mann was under as the King's diplomatic representative; see HW to Mann 10 Oct. 1775, ibid. viii. 134.

From the DUCHESS OF GLOUCESTER, December 1775

Missing; mentioned by HW to Mann 28 Jan. 1776: 'I have had a letter from the Duchess, who tells me the Pope[1] has been a perfect knight-errant in courtesy and gallantry, and enjoined all manner of attentions to them from his college[2] and nobility'[3] (MANN viii. 174). Perhaps it was received by HW 24 Jan., since 'one of the Duke of Gloucester's suite, arrived at Cumberland House from Rome, with letters from his Royal Highness' the night of 23 Jan. (*Daily Adv.* 25 Jan.).

From the DUKE OF GLOUCESTER, Wednesday 17 January 1776

Printed for the first time from a photostat of the MS in the possession of Lord Waldegrave.

Teodoli Palace Rome[1] January 17, 1776.

Dear Sir,

I HAVE the pleasure to inform you that the Duchess my wife was safely delivered of a son[2] on Monday last the fifteenth of January in the *presence of my family*. They are both well. The Duke and Duchess of Saxe Gotha,[3] and the Margrave of Anspach,[4] are to be

1. Giovanni Angelo Braschi (1717–99), became Pope as Pius VI in Feb. 1775.
2. Of cardinals.
3. On the Duke's visit in 1771, Pius VI's predecessor, Clement XIV, had issued the Duke of Gloucester a most cordial invitation to come to Rome (Mann to HW 29 Oct. 1771, MANN vii. 343) and 'The Stuarts had once more the mortification of seeing a Prince of the rival Blood, and a Protestant, distinguished with peculiar honours by a Pope, who even conversed with him' (*Mem. Geo. III*, iv. 241).

___

1. A palace on the Corso just opposite the church of Santa Maria Maddalena al Corso, near the Palazzo Chigi on the Piazza Colonna (MANN viii. 181, n. 7).
2. William Frederick (1776–1834), Duke of Gloucester, 1805; styled Prince William

of Gloucester; Gen., 1808, Field Marshal, 1816. The Duchess wrote Jane Clement 16 Feb. 1776, 'Last Monday [12 Feb.] the month was up. My boy was christened; all the English 32 present; we are overrun with English . . . as to Sophia, she thrives nobly, such a face for breadth you never beheld! William, too, comes on very much, but he is small boned so that he does not yet cut a great figure; I think him like his father, excepting his mouth and that is like mine' (MS now WSL). See also GM 1776, xlvi. 138.

3. Ernst (1745–1804), D. of Saxe-Gotha, 1772; m. (1769) Charlotte (1751–1827) of Saxe-Meiningen. The Duke was a nephew of the Duke of Gloucester's mother (MANN viii. 181, n. 8).
4. Karl Alexander (1736–1806) of Brandenburg-Ansbach, Margrave of Ansbach 1757–91, Margrave of Bayreuth 1769–91.

the sponsors. It being the Duchess's wish the child will be called William Frederick.

I am now to thank you for your letter,[5] and so would that little dear angel Sophia, if she had not a little of the fallen angel and therefore is rather perverse.[6] I do not mean a pun, though her excessive impetuosity causes her to fall about ten times a day.

I remain, dear Sir,

Yours sincerely

WILLIAM HENRY

From the DUCHESS OF GLOUCESTER, ca March 1776

Missing; mentioned by HW to Mann 17 April 1776: 'The Duchess of Gloucester had told me with great concern the danger of Lady Lucy [Mann]' (MANN viii. 191).

From LADY CHARLOTTE MARIA WALDEGRAVE,[1] Saturday 25 May 1776

Printed from the MS now WSL; first printed, Toynbee *Supp.* iii. 243–4. Damer-Waller; sold Sotheby's 5 Dec. 1921, lot 189, to Wells who gave it to Thomas Conolly of Chicago, from whom WSL bought it, 1937.
Address: The Honourable Horace Walpole Strawberry Hill near Twickenham Middlesex.
Postmark: 25 MA.

Saturday night, May 25th 1776.

My dear Sir,

I AM sorry to say that Laura[2] is not at all better than she was yesterday; her fever is the same as it was yesterday morning, she

---

5. Missing.
6. 'Uncontrollable' crossed out before 'perverse.'

---

1. (1761–1808), second dau. of the Ds of Gloucester, by her first husband, the 2d E. Waldegrave; m. (1784) George Henry Fitzroy (1760–1844), styled E. of Euston, 4th D. of Grafton, 1811. They

had ten children (Collins, *Peerage*, 1812, i. 220).
2. Lady Elizabeth Laura Waldegrave (1760–1816), 1st dau. of the Ds of Gloucester, by her first husband, the 2d E. Waldegrave. She m. (1782) George Waldegrave (1751–89), styled Vct Chewton 1763–84, 4th E. Waldegrave, 1784, son of her uncle John, 3d E. Waldegrave.

was bled again this morning and she has been very much troubled all today with the strangurys.³ I wish I could have given a better account of her but I have told you everything exactly as Dr Jebb told me. I had flattered myself she would have been better today but as soon as she is a little better, she relapses again into her former state and I fear she will be a great while before she is quite recovered. I hope you will excuse this short note but I am impatient to read a letter I have just received from the Duchess.⁴

I am your most dutiful niece,

C. M. WALDEGRAVE

To the DUCHESS OF GLOUCESTER, September 1776

Missing; mentioned by Mann to HW 12 Oct. 1776 *bis:* 'I took the opportunity of conveying your letter to the Duchess by one of the Prince of Sweden's officers. . . . It was to be delivered as yesterday' (MANN viii. 247).

To SIR EDWARD WALPOLE, Monday 21 April 1777

Printed from the MS now WSL; first printed, Toynbee *Supp.* i. 260–3. For the history of the MS see *ante* 28 April 1769.

Endorsed (by Sir Edward): My Brother April, 21 —77 from Eriswell.

Barton Mills,¹ Monday night, April 21st 1777.

Dear Brother,

I GOT to Eriswell² between seven and eight; my Lord was in bed, and is very mad, though he has momentary intervals, and knows

3. The word denotes either a disease of the urinary organs characterized by slow and painful emission of urine, or a condition of strangling or choking (OED).

4. Of Gloucester, who wrote Jane Clement 20 July 1776, 'Will you write my sister word . . . how very sensible I am of the very great goodness she and her Lord have shown to Laura: indeed it is not possible to be more grateful than Laura is; she says that she is so happy at Exeter that she could *only* find it increased by seeing me—she is truly grate-

ful, when anyone is good to her, she is not likely to forget it. The other two are very happy with Lady Dy[sart]. This is a very delightful summer for them all' (MS now WSL). See also Appendix 5.

1. HW was staying at The Bull, an inn at Barton Mills, near Mildenhall, Suffolk (OSSORY i. 349, n. 2; MANN viii. 292, n. 1). See Appendix 6.

2. Three miles from Mildenhall. Lord Orford was living in the parsonage house there (ibid. viii. 292, nn. 1–2).

his servants, but it does not last, and then he takes them for other persons. The medicines have operated sufficiently, yet he is not better.

Mr Bewley[3] was gone on his own affairs, but returned on having had my letter sent to him, soon after I arrived. I found Mr Cony[4] and a neighbouring parson[5] (not Mr Ball[6] himself) who on my saying Dr Monroe[7] desired my Lord might be brought immediately to town, exclaimed, as did Cony, that it would kill my Lord to remove him from Eriswell, in which he delighted. I own I was very angry, and said, I did not understand such language. That I had taken the best physical advice, Dr Jebbe's and Dr Monroe's, and that having taken advice, I was come to execute it, not to ask other advice, and that though I would seek the best advice; when I had got it, I should be very peremptory in following it. That I had never heard of a madman being consulted on the place of his habitation; and that if he did not know his servants for two minutes, he probably did not know his house. I asked them if that wretched hovel[8] was a proper habitation for the Earl of Orford—or if it ever had been so? That I was determined to carry him to London, and would place him in the face of the whole town, where everybody might see or learn the care that was taken of him; and that in one word, I would not return to London without him. The parson had nothing to say and took his leave, to which I had no objection. Mrs Turke[9] representing too that

---

3. William Bewley (ca 1726–83), surgeon and apothecary of Great Massingham, Norfolk; friend of Joseph Priestley and Dr Charles Burney; 'the Philosopher of Massingham' (CHATTERTON 121, n. 1). HW's letter to him is missing.

4. Carlos Cony (fl. 1774–91), son of Edwin Cony (high sheriff of Norfolk, 1734); Lord Orford's solicitor in 1777 (MASON i. 323, n. 1). He was put in charge of the sale of the pictures at Houghton the following year (see *post* 1 Oct. 1778, n. 1; 5 Oct. 1778, n. 1). HW wrote Mann 28 April 1777, 'On my arrival, his mistress, his steward and a neighbouring parson . . . cried out, I should kill him if I conveyed him [to London] from that paradise' (MANN viii. 293–4). Withers was keeping Orford's accounts, and Moone was also a steward (*ante* 4 Sept. 1773, n. 5), but Moone evidently was elsewhere (*post* 22 April 1777).

5. Not identified.

6. Thomas Ball (ca 1734–89), D.D., 1777; rector of Eriswell; HW identified him as 'One Ball, minister of Eriswell, a jockey parson' (MANN viii. 293, n. 6).

7. Dr John Monro, physician at Bethlehem Hospital (OSSORY i. 350, n. 10).

8. 'The single chamber without a bed is a parlour seven feet high, directly under my Lord's bedchamber, without shutters, and so smoky, that there is no sitting in it unless the door is open' (HW to Mann 28 April 1777, MANN viii. 293).

9. Martha ('Patty') Turk (ca 1737–91), Lord Orford's mistress. HW describes her as 'forty, red-faced, and with black teeth, and with whom he has slept every night these twenty years' (ibid. viii. 295). 'The fond, faulty Patty loved him with a blindness of passion . . . was good, faithful, kind, friendly and praiseworthy' (Madame d'Arblay, *Memoirs of Doctor*

my Lord would not bear to quit Eriswell, I would not reprimand her then, but bade Cony tell her, that if she tried to hinder his going to town, she should not accompany him, and I made her promise she would not oppose it. I told her that Dr Jebbe had heard when my Lord was last in town, that he had betrayed symptoms of his disorder returning, which they will not allow—but Dr Jebbe is not to be doubted; and these people have shown that they concealed the illness to the last moment they could.

Indeed Eriswell is in every light one of the most improper places upon earth, for besides its being so out of the way of all help, it is built of lath and plaster, and if left a moment alone, he might escape with the greatest ease.[10] It has not a decent lodging room, and there are ponds close to it. I would not answer for his safety a quarter of an hour there.

He has got the waistcoat[11] on, Dr Monroe's man[12] is happily arrived, and since my letter arrived, three men have watched him constantly.

I asked Mr Bewley if he had acted from himself, whether he would not have sent us an account immediately; he said, certainly yes.

Cony was in great agitation, shed tears, and begged to know how he had offended me. I answered, that I had nothing to say; that I thought it very extraordinary he should send a message of such consequence by the coach, and that I should not enter then into any other particulars; it was not a proper time. He begged to know my commands. I said, I had none to give. That you and I had thought of nothing but my Lord's health and safety, and had no time for other considerations. He asked if he must go on with my Lord's affairs as usual. I said, he knew best what he had to do. That when my Lord's safety was ascertained; it would be proper to wait and see whether this disorder went off, or whether his Lordship remained in his present melancholy state. If in the latter, I supposed the family would take legal advice about his affairs, as they had medical about his person. That I could not guess what would or could be done;

Burney, 1832, i. 101–2; see also iii. 149; Lord Townshend to HW 30 Nov. 1791; DU DEFFAND iii. 436, iv. 9).

10. 'On the window being opened . . . he tried . . . to make to it, was outrageous at being opposed (for he always had at least two men in the room) and at last the guard was forced to take him in his arms and fling him on the bed. I have ordered bars for the window; and he has a handkerchief around his legs' (HW to Lord Ossory 22 April 1777, OSSORY i. 350).

11. A strait-jacket.

12. Not identified; sent from London by Monro (ibid. i. 350, n. 10).

and that all I knew was, who would not be the person that would undertake my Lord's affairs. He then begged leave to return home about his own business, which I very gladly advised him to do.

This is all I can tell you hitherto, and I hope you approve thus far. I dare to say every dirty artifice will be tried to prolong the stay at Eriswell, but I am not to be duped or terrified by such managements, and as the two first actors[13] have thought proper to decamp, it will not encourage the others.[14] I will not stir a step but with prudence and for Lord Orford's good and in the most open and avowed manner. We have no view, no end to answer, but doing a melancholy duty to which we are called by necessity. Low mercenary people will suspect us from consciousness, but I defy them and will not swerve from what is right. I will write again tomorrow night.

Yours ever

H. Walpole

To Sir Edward Walpole, Tuesday 22 April 1777

Printed from the MS now wsl; first printed, Toynbee *Supp.* i. 263–4. For the history of the MS see *ante* 28 April 1769.

Endorsed (by Sir Edward): By Express April 22, 1777—from Eriswell. From my brother.

Eriswell, Tuesday morning, April 22d 1777.

Dear Brother,

DR Beevor,[1] a physician of Norwich, is here, and thinks my Lord Orford has so considerable a degree of fever and flux upon him as not to be without danger. He consequently cannot be removed at present. Dr Beevor wishes Dr Jebbe would come down, though there is no immediate necessity—I wish it still more, and so will you, I

---

13. 'Authors' crossed out and 'actors' written above.

14. An echo of Voltaire's *Candide,* 'pour encourager les autres'; see Chute 555, n. 2.

1. John Beevor (1727–1815), son of Thomas Beevor, grocer and brewer of Norwich; M.D., 1764; brother of Thomas Beevor, 1st Bt (Ossory i. 349, n. 5).

know, that nothing possible may be neglected for my Lord's recovery. If Dr Jebbe will be so good as to be here on Thursday evening, Dr Beevor will meet him. The latter thinks that when the fever goes off, his Lordship will still for some time, though perhaps a short one, remain disordered. I have sent for Moone,[2] because I wish to have as many of his own servants here as we can. My Lord is not constantly furious; at present he is only quite silent, though he has shown his tongue, which he would not do before today; and he is very weak. I will not leave him, but stay till I can bring him safely to town.

Yours ever

H. WALPOLE

To Sir Edward Walpole, Tuesday 22 April 1777 *bis*

Printed from the MS now WSL; first printed, Toynbee *Supp.* i. 264–5. For the history of the MS see *ante* 28 April 1769.

Endorsed (by Sir Edward): My Brother Tues. Evening. April 22, 1777 from Eriswell.

Eriswell, Tuesday night 22d.

Dear Brother,

I HAVE an opportunity of sending a line, and take it, to thank you for sending Moone, and to tell you how much I applaud your idea of carrying[1] my Lord first to High Beach,[2] as going to his own house will better reconcile him to being removed. If you should happen not to have yet taken a house, it will be prudent to defer it till he is at Highbeech. He has been pretty quiet all day, except one effort to get to the window which was opened by the doctor's order as the room smoked, and indeed in this hovel there is not one that does not. My Lord has had some sleep too today, and is certainly not worse. My cousin Lord Walpole's[3] son[4] has been so kind as to come

2. William Moone (ca 1725–97), Lord Orford's steward; clerk of the Exchequer ca 1770–97; Lord Orford's deputy as Ranger of St James and Hyde Parks 1763–91 (ibid. i. 135, n. 8).

1. 'Him' crossed out after 'carrying' in the MS.

2. High Beech, in Essex, between Loughton and Waltham Abbey. Lord Orford was there when HW wrote to Mann 14 May 1777 (MANN viii. 300–1; see also OSSORY i. 350, n. 12).

3. Horatio Walpole, 2d Bn Walpole of Wolterton.

4. Hon. Horatio Walpole (1752–1822),

and dine here from Newmarket,⁵ which has been a great comfort to me. I have not time to say more now.

Yours ever

Hor. Walpole

To Sir Edward Walpole, Friday 25 April 1777

Printed from the MS now wsl; first printed, Toynbee *Supp*. i. 265–7. For the history of the MS see *ante* 28 April 1769.
Endorsed (by Sir Edward): My brother April 25 1777.

Barton Mills, Friday night, April 25, 1777.

MY Lord Orford has continued very quiet; though he has not got out of his chair all day, and his water came away in the night without his knowing it, which Dr Beevor told me was the worst symptom remaining. He eat the leg and wing of a chicken today, and helped Mrs Turk, who dined with him, and talks in a whisper to her. I came away at six o'clock, and since that, his footman has been here in the inn, and says he will dine below tomorrow, and talks of taking the air on Monday. I should think the physicians would not approve this, having ordered him to be kept perfectly quiet—but I have no power to hinder it, and Dr Beevor cannot come again till Tuesday, and is above forty miles off.¹ In truth I shall not believe my Lord is rational, till he is unreasonable—at least the extravagant things he did last time as soon as he was pronounced sane, were just what the people about him declared² were marks of his being as he had used to be. They and I differ a little in the denomination.

I have told Dr Beevor I will stay here till I have seen him the doctor on Tuesday. I think I shall be wished away sooner, and wish it myself much more, but it is proper the physical people should give me my dismission, especially as Dr Jebbe was so clear last night that my Lord is not at all in his senses; and should any accident happen,

2d E. of Orford (n.c.), 1809; 'I give you ten thousand thanks . . . for sending my cousin to me, who was great comfort, to me, as he is very sensible, good and perfectly right-headed' (HW to Lord Ossory 22 April 1777, ibid. i. 349).
    5. The Bull, where HW was staying,
was about eight miles north of Newmarket (Mason i. 306, n. 1).

1. At Norwich.
2. 'Declared' written over 'pretend' in MS.

they that were so sorry to see me arrive, would be the first to charge the neglect on me. I flatter myself I act exactly as you would have me, and I take such care to do everything of the little I do with so many witnesses, all belonging to my Lord, that I trust not a motion of mine can with a shadow of truth or justice reflect on you; though if there is any fault, I give it you under my hand, that the fault is my own not yours, who told me last Sunday, and frequently three years ago, that it would kill you, if the burthen of the estate should fall upon you.[3] Neither of us have ever acted as interested men; and characters, I hope, do not change totally at seventy and sixty. We can say with the strongest truth that no man under Lord Orford's misfortune was ever treated with the tenderness, attention, and even respect that he has been—yet I see that the experience of thirteen months has not removed the jealousies. I could not bear the suspicion, if I did not see at the same time that those jealousies are founded on the dirtiest and most selfish grounds. It was that conviction, and the resentment I felt for being totally cast off, after the fatigues and anxiety I suffered in my Lord's service, and after the services I had rendered him, that made me, as I told you last Sunday,[4] determined never to meddle with his affairs more, though I would always be ready to take care of his person; which now that it is clear that his madness is constitutional and not accidental, I fear will often be my lot as long as I shall live, if my own health permits it.

I forgive my nephew, because I firmly believe that he has not been in his senses for many years: and as actions are the only evidence of forgiveness, my care of him is a proof. Sanity or insanity do not rest on any single man's opinion. The law is, and it is fit it should be, the only judge of that. I am sure we both showed our acquiescence, by setting him at full liberty the moment the physicians pronounced him in his senses; nay even before the month was near expired that Dr Battie[5] had fixed as the term of test, though I believe you, no

3. 'I must always do Sir Edward the honour and justice to say that he does not care a straw about the estate, nor ever thinks of his nephew but when I mention him' (HW to Mann 11 Feb. 1781, MANN ix. 125). Sir Edward was a virtual recluse during Lord Orford's insanity of 1773 and gave HW no help in arranging his affairs (DU DEFFAND iii. 374, n. 8).

4. 20 April, the day before HW set out.

5. William Batty (1703–76), M.D., Cambridge, 1737; fellow of King's College, Cambridge, 1725–39; delivered lectures at Cambridge, which HW attended while at the University; physician to St Luke's in London and proprietor of a private asylum. He attended Lord Orford during his illness in 1773 (COLE i. 298, n. 5; 'Short Notes,' GRAY i. 6, n. 25; OSSORY i. 175, n. 2).

more than I, were of their opinion. The fortnight I passed with him at Houghton on his supposed recovery, would have made me think him distracted, if the idea had never entered into my head before. This relapse with no evident cause, and in such remarkably cold weather, does not tend to make me think I judged rashly.

As there is no authority to control him in his best moments, his relapses will not be unfrequent. He will never be bloodied or take cooling medicines; on the contrary, he takes tar water[6] much, a very hot one. He takes violent exercise, eats voraciously, drinks a good deal of wine, and goes to bed at nine, where he lies till eight the next day. I asked Dr Jebbe if this must not breed too much blood in so strong a man? he said, yes; and that the horizontal posture must throw the blood to his head. I preached to him before on his drinking, and shall now tell him, when he is better, of his sleeping—I suppose with equal effect!

This is too long a letter, but you must allow me to vent myself, when I feel so much, and have nothing to divert my thoughts. I have ever wished to serve and save my nephew. I have wished to save and restore the family. Neither view will be accomplished! I had drowned all such thoughts before and since my Lord's last illness. The present moment revives them—but when I have done all here, that depends on me, I shall drive away these cares and think no more of them, till a new scene of the same nature returns. Indeed I little thought five years ago of passing ten days in the inn at Barton Mills! Adieu! dear brother. Give yourself no concern at anything I have said—Four days will soon be passed;[7] and then I assure you, I shall feel nothing but the joy of being released, and the air and journey will have done me good.

Yours ever

H. Walpole

Saturday night.

The post did not go out this morning, so I can add another day's journal. The fever returned a little last night, but he came down into the garden this morning. However he would not stay there a moment, but said it was too cold and he was weak. He has since talked to himself, and though what he says to Mrs Turke is ra-

6. See Mann ii. 452, 464–5, 505; v. 30, 36.

7. HW left Barton Mills on Wednesday 30 April (see below and Mann viii. 296).

tional, the apothecary[8] thinks only an interval, and even she believes he will have a return. I sat in the parlour under his bedchamber, from two to six, and he did not once stir out of his chair. Mrs Turke told me he said, both the physicians were good, but their medicines would signify nothing: that he did not know what was the matter with him, but he himself must struggle with it. This is very melancholy, and indicates his suspecting his disorder. I have not seen him, and dread it—yet he must know I am there. He one day saw me come in and heard it was I, but took no notice. I shall go tomorrow and dine with an acquaintance[9] near Cambridge, and not go to Eriswell till Monday. You will hear from me no more, but see me on Wednesday night, unless he has any considerable relapse.

From the Duchess of Gloucester, ca Friday 4 July 1777

Missing; answered *post* 22 July 1777; mentioned by HW to Lady Ossory 15 July 1777: 'I had a letter from the Duchess; the Duke had had a tolerable night, and she begins to hope the crisis is over, but he still keeps his bed, and is as weak as possible' (Ossory i. 365). 'Mr Walpole came to Lord Hertford's with a very cheerful countenance, saying he had received a letter from the Duchess of Gloucester to acquaint him the Duke was out of danger; he is at Trent, and was to set out as soon as he was able for England' (Coke, 'MS Journals' 15 July). The Duke had fallen seriously ill at Verona in mid-June (Ossory iii. 247; *Last Journals* ii. 38–9). He reached Trent presumably on 23 June and 'the extremity of the danger was over' by 4 July (HW to Mann 17 July 1777, Mann viii. 313–15; see also Sir Edward Walpole to an unknown correspondent 7 July 1777, ibid. x. 50, Appendix 15).

From the Duchess of Gloucester, Monday 21 July 1777

Missing; mentioned *post* 10 Aug. 1777 and by HW to Mann 11 Aug. 1777: 'I had a letter from the Duchess on Tuesday [5 Aug.], that raised our hopes. Yesterday brought one from Dr Jebbe to my brother that dashed them down again' (Mann viii. 319).

8. Not identified.

9. On Sunday 27 April HW dined with the Rev. William Cole at Milton, 'whither he came on purpose from Barton Mills, where he had been attending on his nephew. . . . It was at least fifty miles to and from dinner' (Cole ii. 43, nn. 1, 2).

To the DUCHESS OF GLOUCESTER, Tuesday 22 July 1777

Missing; mentioned *post* 10 August 1777.

From SIR EDWARD WALPOLE, Saturday 26 July 1777

Printed from the MS now WSL; first printed, Toynbee *Supp.* iii. 244–5. Damer-Waller; for the history of the MS see *ante* 6 July 1758.
Address: To the Honourable Horace Walpole, Strawberry Hill, Twickenham, Middlesex.
Postmark: 26 IY.

Wimpole St,[1] Sat. July 26—77.

Dear Brother,

A LETTER from the Duchess today dated Trent the 15th,[2] speaks of the Duke in very unfavourable terms: and so does a letter from Bryant[3] to Shields the porter[4]—yet the whole to be collected from the two accounts is not so frightful as many of the particulars, and I for my part still think that he will recover. He certainly wastes and grows thinner and is very feeble—yet at times strength returns;[5] and there is a sort of alternate better and worse that indicates a power to struggle for a long time; which as the purging is gone, furnishes good hopes.—Bryant, however, seems to despond and that I do not like—the Duchess does not think him more in danger than for a long time past, but wonders he does not recover his strength faster as the capital complaints cease and indeed so do I. Yet as he is continually falling and rising, I will trust to the latter.

1. Where Sir Edward had his town house from which he refused to stir. He willed it to Lady Dysart for her life, and then to Mrs Keppel (OSSORY ii. 2 and n. 2).

2. Her letter is missing; see her letter of 20 June 1777 printed OSSORY iii. 245–7; Mann to HW 19 July 1777 (MANN viii. 317).

3. Robert Bryant (d. 1788), 'surgeon-page' and page of the presence to the Duke of Gloucester 1777–88 (OSSORY iii. 245; MANN viii. 315; *Last Journals* ii. 39, 52). 'The Duke's page Bryant is dead of a putrid fever' (Charlotte Augusta Keppel to Anne Clement 10 July 1788, MS now WSL).

4. Not further identified.

5. Sir Edward Walpole 'received a very sensible letter [of 18 June] from a very sensible young surgeon who is of his [the Duke's] suite. . . . He thinks the Duke will gather strength by travelling and spirits by his approach to England' (Sir Edward to an unidentified correspondent 7 July 1777, MANN x. 50–1).

The physicians were not arrived but were known to be not far off.[6]

Yours affectionately

E. W.

The Duchess's fatigue would not admit of her writing to you or her sisters,[7] she desired I would for her.

To the DUCHESS OF GLOUCESTER, Friday 1 August 1777

Missing; answered *post* 4 Sept. 1777.

To the DUCHESS OF GLOUCESTER, ca Sunday 3 August 1777

Missing; mentioned *post* 23 Aug. 1777: 'Lord Cholmondeley arrived at seven o'clock this evening, he brought your letter.' Lord Cholmondeley left England ca 3 Aug.; see *post* 10 Aug. 1777 and MANN viii. 319.

From CHARLES CHURCHILL, Thursday 7 August 1777

Printed from the MS now WSL; first printed, Toynbee *Supp.* ii. 155, iii. 245. Damer-Waller; sold Sotheby's 5 Dec. 1921, lot 107, to Harper; bought by WSL from Francis Harper, Cheltenham, 1942.
Address: To the Honourable Horace Walpole Arlington Street London.
Postmark: 8 AV READING FREE.
Franked: Free Cadogan.

Caversham, August 7th 1777.

Dear Sir,

YOUR kindness towards everything that belongs to us, requires my acquainting as *soon* as possible of Mary's[1] marriage; you will wonder at my calling it *soon* when I tell you she is to become

6. Dr Jebb and Dr Adair arrived in Trent 15 July (ibid. viii. 314, nn. 8, 9; 317).

7. Mrs Keppel and Lady Dysart.

1. See *ante* July 1775, n. 1.

Lady Cadogan tomorrow morning;[2] but the whole affair has not been above five days in the transacting. Many objections may be found, but I hope and believe that the good will preponderate. Lord Cadogan's behaviour has been very generous, of which you shall have the particulars when we have the pleasure of seeing you. They all desire their kindest compliments to you. Believe me with great truth

Dear Sir

Your most faithful

CHA. CHURCHILL

From the DUCHESS OF GLOUCESTER, Sunday 10 August 1777[1]

Printed from a photostat of the MS in the possession of Lord Waldegrave; first printed in part in Biddulph 119, 120.

This and the three following letters from the Duchess of Gloucester were wrapped in a separate scrap of paper, apparently torn from her letter of 20 June 1777[2] to Sir Edward; the scrap is inscribed by Sir Edward: 'The Duchess June 20, 1777 from Verona. An exceeding fine letter, most affecting to a feeling mind. Full of sense, goodness, piety and distress'; and by the Duchess: 'These letters are an account of the Duke's illness in the year 1777.'

Address: The Honourable Horace Walpole Strawberry Hill Twickenham Middlesex Angleterre.

Postmark: 22 AV.

Trent,[3] Sunday Aug. 10, 1777.

My dear Sir,

WHEN I wrote you the flattering letter[4] which you acknowledged in yours of July 22d, I really thought we should leave Trent in a few days. I little thought the Duke so ill as he really was

2. They were married 8 August at Caversham Church, Berks. 'She is very pretty, amiable, and eight-and-twenty; he, rich and fifty—It is a great match for her' (HW to Mann 11 Aug. 1777, MANN viii. 320–1; see also OSSORY i. 368).

1. HW describes this letter as 'the most moving I ever read' (HW to Lady OSSORY 24 Aug. 1777, OSSORY i. 373).

2. Printed ibid. iii. 245–7.

3. 'The Duke got to Trent [23 June] and found himself refreshed from the cool air of the mountains; but his dysentery returned with violent pains' (HW to Mann 17 July 1777, MANN viii. 314).

4. *Ante* ca 4 July 1777, missing; HW's reply of 22 July is also missing.

MARIA, LADY WALDEGRAVE   MARIA, DOWAGER LADY WAL-
DEGRAVE, AFTER REYNOLDS

ELIZABETH LAURA, LADY WALDEGRAVE

MARIA, DUCHESS OF GLOUCESTER   THE DUKE OF
GLOUCESTER

—I wrote to you again July 21⁵—and even then I was deceiving myself—however that delusion lasted no longer, for the day after I wrote last he grew so bad, and continued growing worse and worse till he was reduced to the last extremity—and I believe last Sunday evening, if the disorder had not taken a sudden turn, he could not have got through the night: he has been to all appearance so near death within the last three weeks that I should have thought myself happy to have had his life insured to me although it had been with a certainty of his never stirring out of his bed again—he is not much obliged to me for such a compromise, but indeed I have suffered so much, so very much in the last three weeks, that I sometimes think I was at times almost out of my senses. However, I believe *now* I may flatter myself without rashness that he is upon the recovery, for he has been mending ever since last Sunday, but is still so weak, that I do not think we can leave this place for a fortnight to come, and then he must go through the Tirol in a horse-litter. We are indeed most fortunate in our situation at Trent, we are in a house of angels. Never did I know two such men as these two Barons de Cressen.⁶ I hope they will go to England with us, that we may if possible return our obligations to them. They have never seen the Duke, for he was brought into the house too ill, and has remained for seven weeks too bad to see them. I have only seen them the last week, but they are so perfectly well-bred that they leave us their house, and only occupy a small part in it—To the children they devote themselves, and make themselves quite their playfellows; Sophia says 'we do love the two Barons mightily.' William cannot say so much, but he shows that he feels as much, for he runs to them whenever he sees them: indeed all the Trentites are an uncommon race of mortals. They are all good, and all devoted to the Duke's recovery—indeed my sojourn here has done me good, and shown to me that the *few trumpery people* I have reason to complain of in England make a mighty small part of the world, and that there are still very good people existing.⁷

5. This letter is also missing.

6. Not further identified. Sir Edward Walpole wrote an unknown correspondent 7 July 1777, 'The same politeness and hospitality of a nobleman, which he had experienced at the merchant's [at Ala, on the Adige] refreshed and comforted him a second time and he rested well' (MANN x. 50). John Jennings wrote

Lord George Germain 7 Aug. 1777 of 'the romantic generosity of a private gentleman, Baron Cressen, and his brother, who of their own mere motion compelled him in a manner to come into their house' (Hist. MSS Comm., *Stopford-Sackville MSS*, 1904, i. 350).

7. HW wrote Lady Ossory 24 Aug. 1777, 'I must not omit a charming trait of a

Mr Jennings,[8] who is come to see the Duke, brought a gracious (verbal) message to him from the King[9] and I hear from everybody that H.M. expresses great anxiety about his brother: Dr Jebb[10] and Mr Adair[11] write every post to Lord Weymouth.[12] I believe their first letters were not very full of hopes. I desired them also to write to Lord G. Germaine as it is a compliment due to him for his very steady attachment to us.[13] We cannot be in England till October. We have a terrible long journey to take—but think, my dear Sir, what would that journey have been to me following his corpse, as I

little girl in the house. . . . The Duke longed for potatoes. None were to be found. . . . The poor little soul, hearing such a hubbub for potatoes, asked what sort of things they were. On their being described . . . she stole out to a convent . . . begged four, and brought them for the Duke, who ate them all eagerly and desired more. . . . The famous Council that sat at Trent would have given a thousand ducats for a glimpse of inspiration a quarter as big' (OSSORY i. 373). The *London Chronicle* 7–9 Oct., xlii. 350 and *Public Advertiser* 9 Oct. carried reports that the 'Duke . . . was supported by small portions of potatoes and cream beat up together.'

8. John Jennings (d. 1782), Lt-Col., 1758; groom of the Bedchamber to the D. of Cumberland (OSSORY i. 373, n. 8; MANN v. 373, n. 11).

9. 'Colonel Jennings, who was come to visit him, had extorted a decent message from the King after one repulse' (*Last Journals* ii. 55–6; Hist. MSS Comm., *Stopford-Sackville MSS*, i. 350). The Duchess of Gloucester wrote Anne Clement 1 Jan. 1781 of Jennings, 'I love that amiable man. . . . His adoration to the Duke showed itself in more than words: to him my children are obliged for a settlement' (MS now WSL).

10. See *ante* 25 April 1774, n. 4. A courier had arrived in London 5 July 'from the Duchess of Gloucester to fetch Drs Jebbe and Adair to the Duke, though with little probability of their arriving time enough' (HW to Lady Ossory 6 July 1777, OSSORY i. 362; see also *Last Journals* ii. 38, 52); they arrived at Trent 15 July (*Daily Adv.* 7 July, 5 Aug.).

11. Robert Adair (ca 1711–1790), surgeon general of the army 1783; surgeon of

the Royal Hospital at Chelsea 1773; member of the court of assistants of the surgeon's company 1760–89, and of the court of examiners 1761–88; governor of the surgeon's company 1765–8, master 1767–8 (OSSORY i. 153, n. 18).

12. Thomas Thynne (1734–96), 3d Vct Weymouth, 1751; cr. (1789) M. of Bath; lord lieutenant of Ireland, 1765; P.C., 1765; secretary of state for the North, Jan. – Oct. 1768, and for the South 1768–70, 1775–9; K.G., 1778. 'The total indifference, the marked neglect of the Court . . . was so indecent, that Lord Weymouth, so far from expressing even the civility of concern, did not so much as answer one of the constant accounts which Dr Jebbe sent of the Duke's situation' (*Last Journals* ii. 55).

13. Sir Edward Walpole had, without the Duke's knowledge, written Lord George Germain 4 Feb. 1777 requesting 'that some potent man in the House of Commons, would try to get the Duke's debts included in the Bill . . . for the payment of the King's debts' (MS now WSL; Appendix 2). Lord George finally was sympathetic and suggested that the Duke come alone from Italy to see the King (*Last Journals* ii. 47–9; for an account of Lord George's efforts, see ibid. ii. 60–9). It was not until 8 April 1778 that the King requested jointures for the children of the Duke and Duchess of Gloucester (ibid. ii. 156–67; MASON i. 380–1, n. 16; see also *ante* 27 Jan. 1774; Biddulph 131–2; MANN viii. 371, n. 9). George III asked for an annuity of £8,000 for Prince William Frederick, and £4,000 for the Princess Sophia Matilda, 'the annuities . . . to take effect after the death of the Duke of Gloucester' (*Journals of the House of Commons* xxxvi. 896).

certainly should not have sent him by sea: I had for several days no better prospect—yet God was good enough to let me keep my senses —I only wonder how I did—The Duke insists upon my going this evening to take the air, as I have not been downstairs for seven weeks, nevertheless I am upon the whole very well—not in my looks, for I think I am more changed than H.R.H. and could Lord Dalrymple[14] see me now, he would beg Madame du Deffand's[15] pardon for the mistake he had made about my beauty;[16] I wonder he could tell her such a story, for certainly the enervating air of Italy has altered me very much.

My daughters[17] boast much of your goodness to them:[18] the 18th of June I hoped to have been with them some days by the 10th of August. *Mais, l'homme propose, Dieu dispose.*

I am sorry for poor William Tollemache:[19] he was good-natured and obliging, and very much attached to my sister. The innkeeper[20] at Inspruck told Mr Jennings, that the Emperor[21] had lamented that it was not in [his] power to come to Trent to see the Duke of Gloucester, he had talked of the Duke at dinner before many people,

14. John Dalrymple (1749–1821), styled Vct Dalrymple 1768–89; 6th E. of Stair, 1789; served in the American war (87th Foot, captain, 1779); minister plenipotentiary to Poland 1782–4; envoy extraordinary and plenipotentiary to Berlin 1785–7.

15. See *ante* 15 Feb. 1769. She had written HW 17 July 1777 that she hoped the Duchess would pass through Paris on her way back to England (DU DEFFAND iv. 461).

16. 'Nous avons ici Milord Dalrymple qui arrive d'Italie; . . . il a trouvé le Duc dans un état pitoyable pour sa santé, et la Duchesse, la plus belle femme qu'il eût jamais vue' (Mme du Deffand to HW 9 July 1777, DU DEFFAND iv. 456). HW probably repeated Dalrymple's remark to the Duchess in his missing letter of 22 July 1777. On the Duchess's return to England, HW noted that she was 'emaciated and looked older' (*Last Journals* ii. 59). For the Duchess's fabled beauty, see OSSORY i. 123; MANN v. 240, 285.

17. The three daughters of Maria's first marriage to James, 2d E. Waldegrave: Lady Elizabeth Laura, Lady Charlotte

Maria and Lady Anna Horatia Waldegrave (see *post* 27 Sept. 1777).

18. Her daughters lived at Hampton Court during their mother's absence and were partly under HW's care. 'The Duke had said he could not live with another man's children' (*Last Journals* i. 134; see *post* 14, 27 Sept. 1777; MANN viii. 315; COLE ii. 55; Appendix 5).

19. Hon. William Tollemache (1751–76), whose brother, Lord Dysart, had married Charlotte, the Duchess's sister. 'Lord Dysart has lost his youngest brother William, whose ship the *Repulse* with all in it, an hundred and fifty! sunk in a storm on the 26th of *last December*' (HW to Lady Ossory 19 July 1777, OSSORY i. 367). The *Repulse* was lost in a hurricane off the coast of Newfoundland.

20. Not identified.

21. Joseph II (1741–90), German (Holy Roman) Emperor, 'had a great friendship for the Duke. . . . The King had been alarmed with the Emperor's intending, if his Majesty was not reconciled to the Duke, to offer his Royal Highness any establishment at Vienna consistent with the Duke's inclination and religion' (*Last Journals* ii. 51–2).

and expressed great concern at his illness; and although Inspruck is 130 miles from hence, the innkeeper was very anxious about the Duke and said so was everybody upon the road.

I believe when Lord Cowper[22] accepted of the principality, he imagined it would give him rank as an English Duke: he knows the contrary now, and does not intend to be called Prince in England.[23] To be sure it is of little use to him, for I believe he does not intend to live much more in Italy. As this letter cannot go till Tuesday I will keep it to give you (I hope) more good news.

Monday—

The Duke continues better. We expect soon to see Lord Cholmondeley,[24] who was to leave England the third—and as he will not find us at Strasburg will I presume come on.[25]

I am, my dear Sir, ever affectionately yours

MARIA

We shall not go by Paris, or I certainly would see Madame du Deffand. Pray tell her so.

---

22. George Nassau Clavering Cowper (1738–89), 3d E. Cowper, 1764; M.P.; F.R.S.; cr. (1778) by Joseph II, a Prince of the Holy Roman Empire (MANN viii. 38, n. 6; 353, n. 9; 360, n. 12).

23. The *New London Magazine*'s obituary notice, Feb. 1790, held that 'It is *by mistake* that he was called a *Prince of the Holy Roman Empire*, for no man can be a Prince of the Empire who does not possess the *landed territory* in the Empire from which he derives his title, and a seat in the Diet among the Princes. . . . His Lordship therefore was, strictly speaking, a *Prince of Milan* in the Holy Roman Empire' (quoted in GEC iii. 485, n. a).

24. See *ante* 15 March 1769, n. 3.

25. He arrived 23 August (see *post* 23 Aug. 1777).

From SIR EDWARD WALPOLE, Tuesday 19 August 1777

Printed from the MS now WSL; first printed, Toynbee *Supp.* iii. 246. Damer-Waller; for the history of the MS see *ante* 6 July 1758.

Address: To the Honourable Horace Walpole at Strawberry Hill Twickenham Middlesex.

Postmark: 19 AV.

Endorsed (by Sir Edward): Copy of Dr Jebb to Sir E. Walpole dated Trent Aug. 8, 1777—Received this day Aug. 19—77.

Dear Sir etc. etc.

I HOPED to have sent you some real comfort etc. etc. — — — — — — — — — —But although the Duke has not suffered so much by the discharge from his bowels for a few days past, his weakness and languor continue such as to keep us on under the same apprehensions as formerly or indeed increase them; the natural consequence of so much unavailing attempt towards his relief.— — — — — — — —

Dear Horace,

This is wrote in a great hurry being much interrupted—all that is omitted is immaterial—I confess I do not yet think it over but have strong hopes from this very letter.

From the DUCHESS OF GLOUCESTER, Saturday 23 August 1777

Printed for the first time from a photostat of the MS in the possession of Lord Waldegrave.

Trent, August 23, 1777.

My dear Sir,

DR Jebb's letter[1] of last post to my father, was a more comfortable one than has been received of some time by anybody; I dare not flatter myself too much after so many cruel and unexpected re-

---

1. Possibly that of 8 Aug. 1777 enclosed *ante* 19 Aug. 1777.

lapses, but I may say what is true that ever since last Tuesday the Duke has been a little better every day.[2] It is but a little, but that is more than has happened yet: today he was up 40 minutes, which is ten more than he was yesterday, but is gone to bed a little fatigued. However to make up for that he stood an instant when he first got out of bed— if you were here and knew all that I have gone through you would not wonder that I (although with fear) catch at every gleam of hope. Dr Jebb some time past told me I raised my hopes too soon—alas, Dr Jebb has never loved anything as I love the Duke. If he had and had been near losing the person he loved, he would have known, that one *must* catch at every straw or sink under the most cruel of all sufferings, for certainly no bodily torture can equal the anxiety of seven weeks of *terror* expecting almost every hour to lose *forever* all that was dear to me! It is miraculous that I am so well as I am. I am grown frightful and thin and yellow, but my health is quite good. We expect Lord Cholmondeley every day; it is very good of a young gay man like him to seek out the sick and miserable. The Duke says he will make him go to Vienna.[3] Jennings has been with us three weeks. He is another uncommon young man. The Duke wants him to go where he can amuse himself more than he can in this trist place, but he will not leave us till the Duke is *stout*—That is so distant a day that we cannot be in England till November[4]—indeed I think it impossible that I can attain to such felicity—when I think of having the Duke well in England, and *all* my children about me— I *tremble* with the apprehension that such *unbounded happiness* was never meant for me; yet sometimes I flatter myself that as I have gone through a fiery trial to attain it I may be so fortunate.

So, the blooming Grandison[5] is again at liberty to make a third choice—As to poor Sir Charles Montagu, I think he ought to be buried in a crossroad with a stake run through him as a warning to all men of his age who may be tempted to *murder* themselves by becoming the bon ton at 63. I hope Lord C. will bring me a letter from

2. Laura Keppel wrote Jane Clement 9 Sept.: 'I received a letter from the Duchess this morning, dated the 23rd, wrote in great spirits, as the Duke was so much better' (MS now wsl).

3. Lord Cholmondeley left for Venice ca 1 Sept. (see *post* 4 Sept. 1777).

4. They landed at Dover 22 Oct. and reached London 24 Oct. (*post* 23 Oct. 1777; Ossory i. 389).

5. Elizabeth Villiers, Cts Grandison, newly widowed by the death of her second husband, Sir Charles Montagu, Lt-Gen. 1761, K.B. 1771 who died at his house in Grosvenor Square 1 Aug. (*ante* HW to Ds of Gloucester Oct. 1772, n. 3; Ossory i. 369, n. 11; Montagu i. 31, n. 14).

you, Sir. In expectation of one I will leave a space to acknowledge the receipt.

Saturday night.

The Duke is now going to sleep for the night after a better day than he has had yet. Lord Cholmondeley arrived at seven o'clock this evening, he brought your letter,[6] and confirmed all your melancholy accounts in it—indeed, indeed, everything wears a dreadful aspect.[7] The Parliament will have been met long before we get to England, for we cannot be there till the beginning of November. I am much disappointed at having no letters from my daughters either by the post or Lord C. Dr Jebb has received an answer from Lord G. Germaine to the letter he wrote him on his arrival here;[8] at least Lord George has acted like a gentleman as well as treated the doctor as such.

To the DUCHESS OF GLOUCESTER, Sunday 24 August 1777

Missing; answered *post* 14 Sept. 1777. See also HW's letter of 24 Aug. 1777 to Lady Ossory (OSSORY i. 373).

From the DUCHESS OF GLOUCESTER, Thursday 4 September 1777

Printed for the first time from a photostat of the MS in the possession of Lord Waldegrave.

Trent, Sept. 4, 1777.

YOURS of August 1st[1] I received yesterday. It was wrote in low spirits from bad news at that time received, which has been followed by good and bad, good and bad, alternately, but I will now

---

6. Missing.
7. HW was depressed by the war in America and his nephew's increasing insanity (MANN viii. 320).

8. Mentioned in *Last Journals* ii. 55.

1. Missing.

flatter myself that good will still be followed by good—for since those two dreadful days Monday and Tuesday the 25th and 26th of last month, the Duke has continued mending, and today sat up four hours, not without fatigue, but still doing it at all is more than has happened before.—Yet I cannot help still having a dread upon my spirits, still fearing some fresh relapse—for how can I believe it possible for him to be out of danger, when that shocking Tuesday, he had every symptom of death upon him that can be named, and I sat by him twelve hours expecting every moment to be his last. Dr Jebb was so convinced that he could not recover, that he wrote to England and said as much.[2]—They did not pretend to deceive me, for when I said did you *never* see anybody recover as bad as this?— they shook their heads, the tears ran down their cheeks, and they said we *cannot* deceive you, consider this illness has been six months coming which is one of the worst symptoms—When I think of all this and the Duke's deathlike countenance, I cannot believe that it is him now laughing and talking so heartily in the next room. His mind is quite at ease *now*, which is one consolation, for he received a letter from the King[3] by yesterday's post, a very kind one indeed, assuring him that his brotherly affection for him *never has abated* and *never* will, and to promise him that if he dies he will be a protector to his family.—As you may suppose I do not wish you to repeat what was in the letter, but I had rather you should say that the Duke has had a very affectionate letter from the King, because that will make *various* people[4] look about them, and that pleaseth me much.

2. 'If I did not know Dr Jebbe for the most despondent of men, my hopes would be small' (HW to Lady Ossory 8 Aug. 1777, Ossory i. 368).

3. John Jennings wrote Lord George Germain in Sept. 1777, 'In consequence of your Lordship's powerful influence the King wrote a letter to the Duke dated August 18th, which arrived at Trent on the 3d of September. On the 5th . . . his Royal Highness with great difficulty did contrive to write an answer in his own hand to the King' (Hist. MSS Comm., *Stopford-Sackville MSS*, 1904, i. 354). HW wrote in *Last Journals:* 'His Majesty protested "that his affection for his dear brother *had never been altered,* and never should cease; and that . . . his Majesty, in case of a fatal termination, gave his dear brother his royal word that he would

take care of his *Family"* ' (ii. 55). 'This letter was wrung from his Majesty's insensibility—or rather suggested to his hypocrisy' by a strong protest from Col. Jennings (ibid.). 'The Duchess, on her return, . . . disclosed the whole of the royal scandalous machination' (ibid. ii. 57). That the King did not intend to include the Duchess is shown in his letter to Lord North 29 Nov. 1777: 'I should have thought that the very handsome proposal delivered this day by you in my name to the Duke of Gloucester, would have deserved in turn at least the civility of not applying for a public provision for a person who must always be odious to me' (Geo. III's *Corr.,* ed. Fortescue, iii. 499–500).

4. Who were, as HW pointed out, just about everybody. The Duchess wrote Jane

I wish you joy of Lady Cadagon[5]—£1000 is a very small jointure—
I know it to be such, for I have no more for £10,000[6] and I had no
son.—Lord Cadagon has six sons,[7] and I believe Miss Churchill had
no fortune.[8] I think he has chose very well, and although their ages
are not equal,[9] yet the difference is not so great as it would be if they
were both of them ten years younger.

Lord Cholmondeley was here to partake of my sorrows at that
trying time; he is now gone to Venice, but intends to return in about
a fortnight. I hope he will not find us at Trent: he will be in England before us.[10] I think he is grown very large, but looks well.

I am happy that you and your nieces[11] continue so well together.
I do not wish you to lose them yet; they are young enough to remain
unmarried till they find something worth having. Adieu, dear Sir,
I am

ever and ever affectionately yours

MARIA

Friday morning.

The Duke had a very good night—and has been able to answer
the King's letter this morning.—By the crooked lines H.M. will see
how weak his brother is—however I *almost* begin to hope that we
shall begin our journey about the 17th.[12] I am just now unhappy
with thinking what *all* my real friends are to suffer today, as I be-

Clement 4 April 1777, 'It is not debt, which makes us live out of England, it is the Duke's health first, and then the constant persecution we meet with from the King, who will never be at rest whilst one person of quality comes to Gloucester House' (MS now WSL). See Appendix 5.

5. Who was married 8 Aug. (*ante* 7 Aug. 1777). Lady Mary Coke wrote 27 Aug. 1777, 'Lord Cadogan has settled three hundred pounds a year pin money and a thousand pounds a year jointure, which considering she had no fortune, is very handsome' ('MS Journals').

6. 'What was to become of her (should he [the Duke] die), with no jointure from him, liable to his debts, and having nothing but her jointure of £1,000 a year from Lord Waldegrave?' (*Last Journals* i. 138; see also MONTAGU ii. 62).

7. Listed in Burke, *Peerage*, 1928, p. 424: Charles Henry Sloane (1749–1832), 2d

Earl, 1807; William Bromley (1751–97), Thomas (1752–82), George (1754–80), Edward (1758–79), Henry William (1761–74); the last was already dead.

8. Lady Mary Coke thought that 'all Lord Cadogan's fortune is settled upon his children by his first wife, and that he can have little or nothing to give to any he might have by this' ('MS Journals' 8 Aug. 1777, quoted OSSORY i. 368, n. 4). But the second son by this marriage (George, 1783–1864) succeeded as 3d Earl.

9. See *ante* 7 Aug. 1777, n. 2.

10. He returned before the Duke and Duchess and on 8 Oct. 1777 dined with HW at SH (OSSORY i. 388).

11. The Duchess's daughters, HW's great-nieces.

12. The Duke and Duchess set out for England 25 Sept. from Trent (*Daily Adv.* 8 Oct.; OSSORY i. 379, n. 3).

lieve the letters of the 26th will be in town today.—I cannot help flattering myself that two mails may arrive together, as the next post will tell you that he is alive which at that time was *everything*.

From SIR EDWARD WALPOLE, Tuesday 9 September 1777

Printed from the MS now WSL; first printed, Toynbee *Supp.* iii. 246–7. Damer-Waller; for the history of the MS see *ante* 6 July 1758.
Address: To the Honourable Horace Walpole Strawberry Hill.

Tuesday, Sept. 9—77.

Dear Horace,

I COME into your whole reasoning about it, almost against evidence to the contrary; for a letter from Dr Jebb to a friend of his and mine (Mr Browne the merchant)[1] of the 26th,[2] dated 7 o'clock that evening, which followed a letter to me of the same date, wrote in the morning, says, 'tell Sir Edward that I think he is now dying'—nevertheless I reasoned upon it, even against that dreadful sentence, as you do—Today Mr Shield the porter brought me the extract of a letter of the same date (the 26th) from Mr Bryant to Mr Stiel[3] which is gone to the King, and which announces the approach of death, yet says he may possibly hold out three or four days—may he? I think those three days gained will insure three more.

Dr Jebb says that on the 24th[4] he was better than he had been yet; but on the 25th in the morning sunk at once, fell into cold sweats, and was seized with excruciating pain in his leg and thigh attending with great swelling (the diarrhœa then stopped). Why may it not be the King's Evil flung out? Why may it not save him?

1. Not identified.
2. See *ante* 4 Sept. 1777, postscript.
3. Alexander Stiell (d. 1792), page of the back stairs (or page of the bedchamber, or house steward) and clerk of the stables to the Duke of Gloucester 1764–92 (*Court and City Register* and *Royal Kalendar* 1764–92; *European Magazine*, 1792, p. 408; Daniel Lysons, *Historical Account of . . . Parishes in Middlesex Not Described in the Environs of London*, 1800, p. 83; *Last Journals* ii. 39; see also *post* 27 Sept., 23 Oct. 1777).

4. Laura Keppel wrote Jane Clement 9 Sept.: 'Adair says, that H.R.H. had been better for some days, but that on the 24th his face changed very much, and he complained of great pain in his groin, and that his thigh was swelled to his toe. Adair says 'tis not the *matter* that occasions the swelling. So I suppose 'tis mortification. . . . I am under the greatest apprehensions. I suppose news of his death will come this week' (MS now WSL). The Duchess wrote that 25 and 26 Aug. were the two worst days (*ante* 4 Sept. 1777).

It was too late last night when Mr Browne came to me, to send you this information and I too much confused to send.

Yours dear brother of affliction

ED. WALPOLE

From SIR EDWARD WALPOLE, Wednesday 10 September 1777

Printed from the MS now WSL; first printed, Toynbee *Supp.* iii. 248–9. Damer-Waller; for the history of the MS see *ante* 6 July 1758.
Address: To the Honourable Horace Walpole Strawberry Hill Twickenham Middlesex.
Postmark: 10 SE WR.
Heading (in Sir Edward's hand): Copy of a letter to Mr Stiel at Gloucester House from Mr Adair dated as above and received in London this day September 10, 1777.
After Adair's letter Sir Edward has written 'overleaf' before starting his own.

Trente, Aug. 29—77.

Sir,

MR Bryant told me he gave you a perfect account of H.R.H.'s deplorable situation last post[1]—About 12 o'clock on Tuesday night the symptoms of immediate dissolution became less alarming—He took some refreshment and on Wednesday he was kept warm by wine etc. without the aid of bottles filled with boiling water. H.R.H. can now articulate distinctly, though in a low voice, takes nourishment; but is reduced so low in flesh and strength that gives us too little *well grounded* hopes of his recovery.

There is little alteration in the swelling of his right limb unless it is not so painful.

Signed Robert Adair

I think dear Horace, this is a letter of comfort.[2] Be so good as to communicate it to our precious children[3] and the amiable Lady Dysart.

1. Bryant to Stiell 26 Aug. 1777; see *ante* 9 Sept. 1777.
2. 'At seven Mr Stiel, the Duke's chief servant, brought us a letter of the 29th that has put life into us. . . . In short, he had survived for three days after they had thought he would not last for four hours' (HW to Lady Ossory 10 Sept. 1777, OSSORY i. 378).
3. The Duchess's daughters.

I have sent the account to the Bishop and Mrs Keppel.

Yours most affectionately

ED. WALPOLE

PS. On the 12th of last month I took the liberty to suggest to Dr Jebb a medicine to be found in Bates's Dispensatory⁴ prescribed in similar cases by the famous Dr Hoffman,⁵ predecessor of Boerhave⁶— to wit, nothing more (nor less) than mulled wine with yolk of egg, superadding three drops of chemical oil of cinnamon.

He says, 'in animi deliquio, viriumque extremâ debilitate, etiam in moribundis auxilio erit.'⁷

Dr Jebb in his letter to me of the 26th says there was no room for any alteration of medicine—Query whether the warmth procured by wine etc. on Wednesday might not grow out of my letter.

From Sir Edward Walpole, Saturday 13 September 1777

Printed from the MS now wsl; first printed, Toynbee *Supp.* iii. 249–50. Damer-Waller; for the history of the MS see *ante* 6 July 1758.

Address: To the Honourable Horace Walpole Strawberry Hill Twickenham Middlesex.

Postmark: SE WR.

Heading (in Sir Edward's hand): Copy of a letter from Mr Bryant to Mr Stiel, dated September 2—77 Received this morning September 13—77.

Though nothing could be more alarming than my last, yet did it leave you some small ray of hopes: which in truth was all that re-

---

4. *Pharmacopœia Bateana: or, Bate's Dispensatory,* translated by William Salmon, 1694. It included the prescriptions of George Bate (1608–69), M.D., F.R.S., physician to Charles I, Cromwell, and Charles II, first published in 1690 (DNB).

5. Probably Friedrich Hoffmann the elder (1626–75), of Halle, joint author of the *Pharmacopœa Schrodero-Hoffmanniana* (enlarged edn, published at Cologne, 1684, of the original *Clavis Pharmaceutica Schroderiana,* Halle, 1675), in which cinnamon is recommended as 'summum confortativum cordis et cerebri, spiritus vitales, animales et genitales mirifice reficiens' (Toynbee, *Supp.* iii. 249, n. 8).

6. Hermann Boerhaave (1668–1738), professor of medicine, chemistry and botany at Leyden; F.R.S. (A. J. van der Aa, *Biographisch Woordenboek der Nederlanden,* Haarlem, 1852–78, i. 223–6).

7. 'In debility of spirit and in extreme physical weakness, even at the point of death, it will be of help.' Possibly 'tincture of cinnamon,' or 'viper wine,' described by Salmon, op. cit., 2d edn, 1700, pp. 234, 567–8.

mained—a few hours after I wrote that, a happy change took place and H.R.H. grew better: a violent swelling came on from the groin down to the foot, attended with a good deal of pain: which at present seems to have been a crisis to his complaint as his bowels since that time has been more steady than they have been for these four months past.[1] His thigh, leg and foot are much less swelled than they were, his appetite is tolerably good and all things wear a different face from what they did. I should have wrote to you by last post but found Mr Adair saved me that trouble—but with all these things in his favour I can by no means think him out of danger. However, I hope soon to send you better accounts.

From the DUCHESS OF GLOUCESTER, Sunday 14 September 1777

Printed for the first time from a photostat of the MS in the possession of Lord Waldegrave.

Trent, September 14, 1777.

My dear Sir,

YOUR very feeling and affectionate letter of August 24[1] I received last post—and when I read it I grieved to think that you had by that time received the *worst* of accounts—although I still flatter myself that two mails might arrive at the same time and save all my relations and friends the sufferings they would endure by the letters of the 26th.

Dr Jebb owns that he wrote a letter[2] to be shown to my father in which he said he saw the Duke only living from hour to hour, and concluded it would soon be over—thank God the best of physicians can only see as the Almighty permits them. That dreadful day, I did not dare ask anybody to write, yet I wished it, for I knew the post before had carried good news, and I wanted the approaching dreadful event to be broke to you—when those *sad days* were passed I was sorry for the alarm you had received—but why dwell upon a subject which always will make me wretched, as I am not quite sure that a deeply impressed terror and affliction are so soon got over as is

1. HW quotes these details of the Duke's illness in his letter to Mann 18 Sept. 1777 (MANN viii. 325–7).

1. Missing.
2. Dr Jebb to Mr Browne 26 Aug. 1777, mentioned *ante* 9 Sept. 1777.

generally supposed—but I am getting back again; I will now talk of something else—I will talk of Madame du Deffand. Pray tell her that I still hope to see her, for I flatter myself with going to Paris some time or other, although we shall not pass by Paris this time—however I will tell you for your comfort that the Duke has sent to Paris about the horses we shall want upon the road; this looks like moving—and we have some little hopes that he will go out in the coach tomorrow or next day—Now you know after all that has passed I ought to be completely happy with such a change; God knows, that I am *truly grateful,* but I cannot *yet* be gay; nor do I know when [I] shall be quite easy—but I am emerging again—but I must beg of you to be quite easy about my health,[3] for I am very well, and I assure you I dress myself out, and make new caps, and begin again to think of looking *smart.* As to Dr Jebb, he did not bleed me, but both he and Mr Adair took great care of me, by bringing me broth and cooking me up, for they fancied I should starve, but I believe it was eating so little kept me so well, for I do assure you I am very well. They think the travelling will make me ill, as the using so much exercise after leading so confined a life may be too much for me, but I rather think the travelling will be of great service to me, and you will see me arrive as fat as a pig, at present I am thin, but not so thin as I was.[4]

Indeed your manner of speaking of my dear girls makes me quite happy, so happy that it generally makes my eyes run over, they are such good, such affectionate creatures, I do not think that any mother ever was so happy in children as I am.

My poor dear little boy had a great escape today, his nurse tumbled down with him in her arms, he was not hurt but the poor woman was so excessively frightened, that she fainted away and was some time before she recovered.

One better proof I will now give you of the Duke's amendment than you have had yet, the doctors begin to talk of treating them-

---

3. George Selwyn wrote Carlisle in Aug. 1777 of HW's anxieties, 'His *distresses* are, Lord O[rford's] lunacy, and the Duchess of Gloucester's situation if his R. H. dies. . . . I wish these were mine, and I had no other, but we cannot choose our own misfortunes; if we could, there is nobody who would not prefer being concerned for a mad nephew whom they did not care for, or a simple Princess whom they would laugh at, *si l'orgueil ne s'en mêlait pas'* (Hist. MSS Comm., 15th Report, App., pt vi, *Carlisle MSS,* 1897, p. 321; SELWYN 266).

4. See *ante* 10 Aug. 1777, n. 16, and HW to Lady Ossory 28 Oct. 1777, OSSORY i. 389, for descriptions of her appearance.

selves with five days' holidays to go and see Venice and I can affirm that their attention to him is so great, that if they did not think him much improved they would not think of such a thing—Oh! that we were in England.[5]

I think Lord Walpole has acted as all displeased parents should,[6] shown that he is not angry to save his money. A Mrs Bathurst[7] is dead; is it your old love?

The weather is again terribly hot, the peasants are procession*izing* for rain, indeed I wish for a storm to cool the air. I fear it will be bad weather when we begin our journey—

Adieu dear Sir, I am ever affectionately yours

MARIA

Sunday morning—

I have just had a letter from Maria, who tells me that Laura has fretted herself pale[8]—do my dear Sir, comfort her, and assure her that we *are all* very well now; it will indeed be hard to have her ill when I thought my sorrows were over.

From LADY ELIZABETH LAURA WALDEGRAVE, Monday 15 September 1777

Missing; mentioned *post* Sir Edward Walpole to HW 15 Sept. 1777.

---

5. They landed at Dover 22 Oct. (see *ante* 23 Aug. 1777, n. 4; *post* 23 Oct. 1777).

6. Unexplained.

7. See HW's identification, *post* 27 Sept. 1777.

8. HW wrote Lady Ossory 8 Sept. 1777, 'Poor Lady Laura received a favourable letter from her mother of the 21st [Aug.]' followed by unfavourable news; 'I have passed a most terrible evening amidst Lady Dysart and my poor girls: and I doubt it is only the beginning of sorrows' (OSSORY i. 376–7).

From SIR EDWARD WALPOLE, Monday
15 September 1777

Printed from the MS now WSL; first printed, Toynbee *Supp.* iii. 250–1. Damer-Waller; for the history of the MS see *ante* 6 July 1758.

Address: To the Honourable Horace Walpole at Strawberry Hill Twickenham Middlesex.

Postmark: 15 SE.

Memoranda (by HW, in pencil): 13 weeks.[1]

    Col. Jennings's letter.[2]

    Emperor.[3]

    wht Ld Jersey said.[4]

    Hist. of Ld Geo. & his idea

      on Marriage Act.[5]

    Convent of nuns.[6]

Monday September 15, —77.

LADY Laura's letter of today[7] will probably have given you the pleasure which this intends—Two letters to me, one the Duchess, t'other the doctor, say the Duke's recovery looks like reality—he had sat up four hours, he had dined three times at a table out of bed; he gathered strength and *flesh:* he was merry, talking and laughing while she was writing: and they were all happy with appearances—The King had wrote very affectionately to him, promising his protection to his family, should he die.[8] The Duke had strength enough to write an answer (as she calls it, in a waddling hand) and had waddled through it.

The doctor thanks me for my prescription,[9] says it had occurred to him and he had used it. His expression to me upon his having used it is—*Utrumque nostrum incredibili modo, consentit astrum.*[10]

---

1. The Duke's illness and recuperation lasted from mid-June until late September.

2. Jennings's letter to Col. Charles Rainsford about the Duke's miserable condition eventually forced the King to write a sympathetic letter to his brother (*Last Journals* ii. 55–7).

3. Joseph II; see *ante* 10 Aug. 1777, n. 21.

4. George Bussy Villiers (1735–1805), styled Vct Villiers 1742–69; 4th E. of Jersey, 1769; he had urged that the King

see Dr Adair before his departure to treat the Duke in Italy (see *Last Journals* ii. 53).

5. Lord George Germain's attitude is discussed ibid. ii. 48–51, 66–9.

6. The Ursuline nuns who said masses for the Duke's recovery (OSSORY i. 389 and n. 1).

7. Missing.

8. See *ante* 4 Sept. 1777 and HW to Mann 18 Sept. 1777, MANN viii. 326.

9. See *ante* 10 Sept. 1777.

10. 'In an incredible way heaven agrees to both nostrums.'

I think I may now talk like an apothecary—but it must be to *patients*.

The Duchess wishes not to have it mentioned that the King promises his protection, but would have it known that he wrote a kind letter[11]—Private and very particular correspondence inform me (and it must not now be told for the reasons above) that the Emperor (and it is true) did say; if the King would take no notice of him, *he would,* in any shape the Duke should choose,[12] military or other practicable between the two religions and countries.

Yours most affectionately

ED. WALPOLE

PS. The letter before the last from the Duchess you must have a copy of—I never saw such a letter.[13]

To SIR EDWARD WALPOLE, ca Tuesday 16 September 1777

Missing; answered *post* 18 Sept. 1777.

11. See *ante* 4 Sept. 1777, in which the Duchess asks HW not to repeat what was in the King's letter.

12. HW wrote in *Last Journals* (ii. 51–2), 'Sir Edward was told by good authority that the King had been alarmed with the Emperor's intending, if his Majesty was not reconciled to the Duke, to offer his Royal Highness any establishment at Vienna consistent with the Duke's inclination and religion. It might have been written to the King from Germany, as the Emperor did not love the King, and was very capable of having declared such an intention.' See also *ante* 10 Aug. 1777.

13. Missing; probably ca 23 Aug., to Sir Edward.

From SIR EDWARD WALPOLE, Thursday
18 September 1777

Printed from the MS now WSL; first printed, Toynbee *Supp.* ii. 154, iii. 251–2. Damer-Waller; sold Sotheby's 5 Dec. 1921, lot 192, to Dobell. Offered in Maggs catalogues 421 (1922), 445 (1923), 480 (1926), 493 (1927); sold to Henry C. Folger; acquired by WSL 1950 from the Folger Shakespeare Library.

Address: To the Honourable Horace Walpole at Strawberry Hill Twickenham Middlesex.

Postmark: 18 SE.

1

A murm'ring voice at dead of night
Cries Henderson[1] has murder'd sleep
Proud of his guilt he courts the light
And bids the stricken deer go weep.

2

Envy, best friend to rising fame,
Thy labours are true merit's pride:
For flatt'ry dignifies no name
And praise is but a treach'rous guide.

3

The tragic fiction of the stage,
Where, Roscius,[2] thine was sov'reign art,
Is chang'd to real gall and rage:
You now act no fictitious part.

4

Still save your credit; still excel:
Let Roscius cry—, 'This youth's the thing':
Resume those pow'rs that feigned so well:
Feign now and live the stage's king.

It is well for Roscius that I can't write better, for I love him not; and am a volunteer in Henderson's cause, because of the manifold sins of Roscius against him; and indeed against every man that might

---

1. John Henderson (1747–85), Garrick's rival. His first London appearance was on 11 June 1777 at the Haymarket, where he won immediate acclaim. 'In . . . testimony of his success, it is to be remarked that no actor was ever more generally the subject of conversation than Mr Henderson' (*Public Advertiser* 19 June).

2. Garrick; 'Garrick is dying of the yellow jaundice on the success of Henderson a young actor from Bath' (HW to Mason 4 Aug. 1777, MASON i. 326).

prove some check upon his enormous vanity and pride, by any degree of rivalship and the favour of the town; but I will ha' done with Roscius, laying it to your charge that your last letter[3] brought this upon you. Your prejudice in my favour and undeserved partiality to my second-rate and very inferior talents and capacity secures to me your reading these lines with the same indulgence and benignity.

If Roscius gets hold of them he'll trim my jacket for me, for he can write.

Yours most affectionately

Ed. Walpole

PS. We must I think be very cautious of giving Dr Jebb offence by not allowing him the whole extent of his really great abilities and his extraordinary care of the Duke and indefatigable labour in his service—and I have no doubt that he had administered the same sort of medicine himself at the time he mentions in his letter.[4]

I thought what he said to me as far as I was concerned was exceedingly candid and genteel.

To Sir Edward Walpole, ca Friday
19 September 1777

Missing; answered *post* 20 Sept. 1777.

---

3. Missing.

4. See *ante* Sir Edward Walpole to HW 15 Sept. 1777.

From SIR EDWARD WALPOLE, Saturday
20 September 1777

Printed from the MS now WSL; first printed, Toynbee *Supp.* iii. 252. Damer-Waller; sold Sotheby's 5 Dec. 1921, lot 192, to Dobell; offered by Maggs Cat. 459 (1925), and sold to WSL.

Address: To the Honourable Horace Walpole at Strawberry Hill Twickenham Middlesex.

Postmark: 20 SE.

Sat. Sept. 20, —77.

Dear Horace,

I REPLY to your answer[1] so soon, only for the satisfaction of telling you that I have my wish in your liking my verses.[2] I applied to you as a proper judge for your *no* as much as your *aye* and I am glad of your advice in respect to a little deliberation in showing 'em —it would be very unwise not to pass quietly by a hornet's nest, mean you never so well to your fruit.

I have given no copy but to yourself and shall not give another. I am fully satisfied that you like them; I myself like them, but think they are stiff and appear to be laboured, which I assure you they are —nature never made me a poet and no man ever made himself one.

Yours very truly

ED. WALPOLE

To the DUCHESS OF GLOUCESTER, Saturday
27 September 1777

Printed from Toynbee *Supp.* iii. 26–31. Damer-Waller; sold Sotheby's 5 Dec. 1921, lot 19, to Maggs. Offered in their catalogue 421 (1922); present owner unknown.

Memorandum (by HW): To the Dss of Gloucester. N.B. She was set out [from Trent] before it could go away.

Strawberry Hill, Sept. 27, 1777.

I NEED not say, Madam, how much satisfaction your every letter now occasions. We have tasted of the contrary too much lately not to enjoy every step of his R.H.'s amendment. Though his physi-

1. Missing.   2. *Ante* 18 Sept. 1777.

cians have so little of the profession in them, I am sure they would not think of diverting themselves,[1] if they were not sure he was past all danger. As you was not set out, and give so good an account of yourself, Madam, I am far from thinking the journey will hurt you after an interval of repose, and with your mind at peace. I hope the change of air will even restore your looks. You made me tremble for half a paragraph for the little Prince.[2]

You may be perfectly easy about Lady Laura: she has perfectly recovered her spirits and colour, though I own her grief had taken sole possession of her, that when Mr Stiel brought us the first better account, the joy seemed, as I told her, to make no impression on her alone. The truth is, her sensibility is so great, that with her adoration of you and a turn naturally serious, she cannot easily pass from one extreme to the other. As I have nothing new to tell you, Madam, you must allow me to talk a little about your daughters. I have so devoted myself to being of some small use to my family and friends, that I may be permitted to indulge myself to those that are interested in any part. I have studied my nieces as much as possible in the time, and will answer they are all you can wish. They have a veneration and love for you beyond example, and though they all three are very different, there is the most perfect harmony amongst them.

You know Lady Laura best, Madam, and I need not repeat that she has sense, sensibility and tenderness, with a proper pride that will never suffer her to disgrace herself.

Lady Maria has the most uncommon understanding I ever saw at near her age. If one did not know her youth and how very little she has seen of the world, one should take it for strong judgment formed by long experience. She makes me start every day by the quickness of her conception, which is delivered with a truth and precision that are astonishing; and sometimes with dry humour that makes one laugh for half an hour. She has little of our warmth of temper; on the contrary a composure, firmness and penetration into people and things, like her father. In short, I scarce think her understanding even now inferior to his. With this she has a natural unaffected ease, and a tranquillity about the superior beauty of her sisters, that are charming. Her face is very agreeable, and her person very fine.

1. 'With five days' holidays to go and see Venice' (*ante* 14 Sept. 1777). Dr Jebb and Mr Adair accompanied the Duke and Duchess on their return 'as far as France, where it is said their Highnesses will stop two or three days, at which place [they] . . . will leave them and set off for England' (*London Chronicle* 9–11 Oct., xlii. 354).

2. See *ante* 14 Sept. 1777.

Lady Horatia is all life and spirits and cheerfulness, with unbounded good nature, and a great deal of humour. Her vivacity and sweet temper make her the prettiest girl in the world, which she is, though her height makes her look a fine woman. In one thing they are still more surprising, which is their perfect cheerful acquiescence to everything that is proposed to or for them. You are not likely, Madam, to make them unhappy, but I think there is no trial you could put them to, to which they would not submit.

I must not forget Miss Keppel,[3] who is still different, and whom I know a great deal less. She has been here two days with the Bishop and Mrs Keppel, and is not free before them. She is gloriously handsome,[4] but I fear will soon be very large. She seems all modesty and gentleness and sweetness, but having been much more restrained, is far more timid than your daughters. I am much more impatient, and with good reason, to have her married than them.

The Bishop, so far from being changed so as not to be known, as I was told, is not at all more altered than being leaner necessarily occasions. He thinks he has lost his yellowness, though some still remains. He looks upon the whole older than he is and much broken, and is not in spirits; yet he sleeps perfectly well, rides and walks without being fatigued, and has rather too much than too little appetite. I think him in no danger,[5] but if I can guess, the unprovided situation of his family is at his heart. Mrs Keppel looks extremely well and healthy, and thinks the Bishop quite recovered. Pray don't mention anything I say about them, which are only my own fears, and you know I am apt to take alarm easily about those I love.

It is an easy transition, Madam, from your relations to your friends. You have heard the shocking exit of Lord Harcourt,[6] which must affect one. I cannot say I should otherwise have felt for him. He was not fond of so good a son.[7] He has left twenty-five thousand

---

3. Anna Maria Keppel, elder dau. of the Bp of Exeter and Laura (Walpole) Keppel (see *ante* 17 June 1759, n. 1).

4. She was 'handsomer than any of her cousins' (HW to Lady Ossory 29 Sept. 1777, Ossory i. 382).

5. He d. 27 Dec. 1777 of 'a dropsy in the stomach' (*London Chronicle* 30 Dec. 1777 – 1 Jan. 1778, xliii. 8; Ossory i. 410).

6. Simon Harcourt (1714–77), 2d Vct

Harcourt, 1727; cr. (1749) E. Harcourt; Gen., 1772; P.C., 1751; viceroy of Ireland 1772–7. He was 'found suffocated in a well with his head downwards and his dog upon him' (HW to Mann 18 Sept. 1777, Mann viii. 328 and n. 13).

7. George Simon Harcourt (1736–1809), styled Vct Nuneham 1749–77; 2d E. Harcourt, 1777.

THE THREE LADIES WALDEGRAVE,
BY SIR JOSHUA REYNOLDS

pounds to Colonel Harcourt[8] besides five that were settled. Still Lord Nuneham will be very rich, especially as he has never known what it was to be so, and he loves his brother and is too good to grudge him anything. I have sent the present Earl frequent accounts of the Duke,[9] for no man living is more devoted to you.

It is an ancient maiden Mrs Bathurst[10] that is dead and not she that was the lovely Miss Evelyn.[11] The Duke of Norfolk is dead at last at ninety-four.[12] He has left everything with the title but about £3000 a year[13] to Harry Howard,[14] who is next to the new Duke[15] and his son,[16] and about £2000 a year to his great nephew Mr Stourton.[17] To Lady Smith[18] a dirty legacy of fourscore pounds a year.

Since I began to write, I hear Lord Harcourt has left as much to Lady Betty Lee[19] as to Col. Harcourt, but had bought an estate

8. William Harcourt (1743–1830), Lord Harcourt's second son; succeeded his brother as 3d E. in 1809; Col. 16th Light Dragoons; distinguished himself in America while in command of the troop which captured Gen. Lee; Maj.-Gen., 1782; Lt-Gen., 1793; Gen., 1798; Field Marshal, 1821.

9. See HW to Vct Nuncham 7 July, 24 Aug. 1777.

10. Not identified; Lady Selina Shirley (ca 1700 – 14 Dec. 1777), who m. (1720) as 2d wife, Peter Bathurst (1687–1748), had one unmarried daughter, Margaret (Collins, *Peerage*, 1812, v. 88; Sedgwick i. 446; GM 1777, xlvii. 612).

11. Elizabeth Evelyn, m. (1750) Peter Bathurst (1723–1801) (Namier and Brooke ii. 67; MANN iv. 49, n. 24); she was still living in 1787, when Lady Mary Coke reported that she had lost her eyesight ('MS Journals' 28 Sept. 1787). She was celebrated by HW in 'The Beauties,' and her portrait by Eccardt (sold SH xxii. 32) hung in the closet next to HW's bedchamber at SH. HW noted late in life in his extra-illustrated *Des. of SH* 1784 (now WSL), 'In Lord Orford's closet next to his bedchamber in the attic . . . Elizabeth Evelyn with a book and a lamb in small life in oil from a design by Sir Godfrey Kneller by Eckardt' (p. 96). She married General Peter Bathurst' (p. 96).

12. Edward Howard (1686–1777), 9th D. of Norfolk, 1732. He d. 20 Sept.; his ninety-first birthday was 5 June (MANN viii. 283, n. 4).

13. His annual income excluding 'the Sheffield estates,' left to Henry Howard, was to be £32,000 (*London Chronicle* 9–11 Oct., xlii. 354; OssoRY i. 384, n. 17).

14. Henry Howard (1713–87), only son of Bernard Howard of Glossop; grandson of Henry Frederick, 15th E. of Arundel; first cousin once removed of the 10th D. of Norfolk; his son, Bernard Edward became the 12th D. of Norfolk, 1815 (ibid. i. 383–4, n. 13).

15. Charles Howard (1720–86), 10th D. of Norfolk, cousin of the late Duke, son of Henry Charles Howard of Greystock, Cumberland.

16. Charles Howard (1746–1815), styled E. of Surrey 1777–86, succeeded his father as 11th D. of Norfolk, 1786.

17. Charles Philip Stourton (1752–1816), 17th Bn Stourton, 1781; son of Winifred Howard, niece of Edward Howard, 9th D. of Norfolk.

18. Hon. Mary Clifford (1731–97), youngest dau. of Hugh, 4th Bn Clifford; m. (1766) as 2d wife, Sir Edward Smythe, 4th Bt, 1737. Her mother and the Duchess of Norfolk (d. 1773) were sisters (ibid. i. 384, n. 19). 'To Lady Smith, who lived with him twenty years, he gives a trumpery annuity of fourscore pounds a year, as if she were his old coachman' (ibid. i. 384).

19. Lady Elizabeth Harcourt (1739–1811), sister of Col. Harcourt, m. (1763) Sir William Lee, 4th Bt of Hartwell, Bucks (ibid. i. 136, n. 4).

which he designed too for the latter, but had not executed it, of which I am extremely glad.

The suspense about America[20] gives great anxiety and impatience, and no wonder. There is not a word of any other sort of news.

Lady Maria and Lady Horatia go to Windsor[21] tomorrow, and Lady Laura comes to me. I must not certainly repine at the cause, but I shall be very sorry when I am to lose them, though it is so much better for them, than to pass most of their time with an old uncle. I have the honour to be Madam, your R.H.'s

Most faithful humble servant,

Hor. Walpole

From Lady Cadogan, Wednesday 1 October 1777

Printed from the MS now WSL; first printed, Toynbee *Supp.* iii. 253. Damer-Waller; sold Sotheby's 5 Dec. 1921, lot 107 to Harper; acquired May 1942 from Francis Harper, Cheltenham.

Caversham Park, October the 1st 1777.

My dear Sir,

IT is at Lord Cadogan's request as well as to gratify my own inclination that I trouble you with this letter. Hitherto our motions have been so very uncertain, that we were not at all sure how long we might be able to stay here,[1] but I now think we are pretty sure of not stirring from hence for some time except for a few days towards the end of this month. Lord Cadogan has therefore begged me to write to you to say that we expect Papa and Mama here tomorrow for some time, and that he should be very happy if you would be

---

20. Washington had been defeated at Brandywine and Burgoyne had been defeated at Bennington, but dispatches of 30 Aug. from Sir William Howe did not reach London until 28 Oct. (*Daily Adv.* 30 Oct.) and those from Burgoyne of 20 Aug. arrived 31 Oct. (*London Gazette* No. 11818, 28 Oct. – 1 Nov., MANN viii. 331, nn. 1, 2, 4; 334–5).

21. To the Keppels; the Bishop of Exeter was also Dean of Windsor.

1. His estate at Caversham, Berks, from which the 1st Earl's Viscountcy had been taken. He later sold it, apparently in the wake of the divorce: 'in consequence of some unhappy connubial events, the late Earl sold land, house, furniture, wine in the cellar, and, if we are to credit report, the very roast beef on the spit, to Major Marsac, for a sum of money one day before dinner' (*Biographical Index to the House of Lords*, 1808, quoted in GEC).

kind enough to meet them. Or if not convenient to you to come just now, he hopes you will at least promise to let us have the pleasure of seeing you some other time.[2] He also desires me to add how much he wishes that a former acquaintance[3] which he still remembers with infinite pleasure and which he has often lamented having been interrupted of late years, should by *my* means be renewed, as he has all his life had the highest esteem and regard for you.

I trust I need say nothing about myself on this occasion, as I hope you, my dear uncle, are too well convinced of my sentiments in your regard, and that you will ever be persuaded that I am

Your sincerely affectionate and obedient

M. CADOGAN

From SIR EDWARD WALPOLE, Saturday 18 October 1777

Printed from the MS now WSL; first printed, Toynbee *Supp.* iii. 253–5. Damer-Waller; for the history of the MS see *ante* 6 July 1758.

Address: To the Honourable Horace Walpole at Strawberry Hill at Twicken-ham Middlesex.

Postmark: 18 OC.

Wimpole Street, Sat. October 18 —77.

Dear Horace,

SUCH kind inquiries from friends give great pleasure and differ widely from cards—I received no sort of hurt,[1] but had an escape; for I might have broke my neck if I had not broke my fall: and its not proving a windfall for Jenkinson[2] was as good as the best Arquebusade Water[3] I could have used.

---

2. HW dined there 15 Sept. 1778; see Ossory ii. 51.

3. Cadogan was M.P. from Cambridge borough 1749–54, 1755–76, which might account for the acquaintance (Namier and Brooke ii. 169–70; see also *Mem. Geo. III* ii. 301).

---

1. Sir Edward's accident has not been explained.

2. Charles Jenkinson (1729–1808), cr. (1786) Bn Hawkesbury and (1796) E. of Liverpool. He had the reversion of the patent place in the Customs held by Sir Edward, from which HW had an income; it did not prove 'a windfall' for Jenkinson because Sir Edward did not break his neck (MONTAGU ii. 316, nn. 1, 2; MANN x. 54).

3. A lotion regarded as a specific for

I received no bruise of any consequence, or I would have been bled immediately.

I imagine you was alarmed with the nonappearance of our young ladies[4] at 4 o'clock—I was very uneasy both on their and your account, but by your silence today concerning it, I conceive it ended pretty well; in much good humour on your side as soon as your fright was over; in a good dinner spoiled; in a hurried and out-of-glee performance by Mr Tessier;[5] and in the girls going home by moonlight, the dumb silent enjoyment of all girls turned fifteen, not an unpleasing remembrance at seventy and doubly fixed in one's memory by the inimitable description of it in the Castle of Otranto;[6] (I think) the finest portrait of melancholy that ever was drawn.

Very affectionately yours

ED. WALPOLE

PS. I am remarkably well today and my bruises too—*Contusus non ingemisco.*[7] But if I had one of your severe fits of the gout I should talk another language.

---

gunshot and other wounds (OED, *sub* 'harquebusade'). When HW fell in 1789 'the apothecary . . . recommended frequent repetitions of arquebusade, which have certainly alleviated the pain' (HW to Lady OSSORY 22 June 1789, OSSORY iii. 49).

4. Sir Edward's granddaughters, the Ladies Elizabeth Laura, Charlotte Maria and Anna Horatia Waldegrave.

5. A.-A. Le Texier (ca 1737–1814). French actor and reciter, of whom HW wrote Lady Ossory 23 Nov. 1775, 'I cannot decide to which part he did most justice, but I would go to the play every night if I could see it so acted' (ibid. i. 277, 293–4; DU DEFFAND iv. 32, 41 and *passim*; MASON i. 245).

6. Sir Edward probably refers to a scene in the final chapter: 'Isabella, in the mean time, was accompanying the afflicted Hippolita to her apartment; but in the middle of the court they were met by Manfred, who, distracted with his own thoughts, and anxious once more to behold his daughter, was advancing to the chamber where she lay. As the moon was now at its height, he read in the countenances of this unhappy company the event he dreaded. What! is she dead? cried he in wild confusion— A clap of thunder at that instant shook the castle to its foundations; the earth rocked, and the clank of more than mortal armour was heard behind' (*Castle of Otranto*, 1969, p. 108).

7. 'Bruised, I do not groan.'

From SIR EDWARD WALPOLE, Thursday
23 October 1777

Printed from the MS now WSL; first printed, Toynbee *Supp.* iii. 255. Damer-Waller; for the history of the MS see *ante* 6 July 1758.
Address: To the Honourable Horace Walpole at Strawberry Hill Twickenham Middlesex.
Postmark: 23 OC WR.

Wimpole Street, Thursday, October 23 —77.

Dear Horace,

THE Duke landed at Dover[1] yesterday in the packet about 7 in the evening.

They will all be at Gloucester House tomorrow[2] by 3 o'clock, all vastly well.[3]

Princess Sophia I suppose looks upon herself now as a person of knowledge and experience.

When she left England, she was indeed not arrived at months of discretion: but travelling and seeing the world does wonders in a little time with our young nobility.

Yours affectionately,

E. W.

Mr Stiel came to me this morning with this account and I never saw a face so lit up with joy in my life. He is a truly worthy and valuable man.

1. They landed at Dover 22 Oct., and arrived at Gloucester House 24 Oct. (MANN viii. 332, n. 5). 'The Princess Amelia has ordered eight of her finest horses to be ready to set off with the new travelling carriages made for his Royal Highness the Duke of Gloucester, in a few days to Dover, to wait there for the reception of their Royal Highnesses the Duke and Duchess of Gloucester' (*London Chronicle* 9–11 Oct., xlii. 354).

2. HW and Sir Edward called on them, and HW describes the visit in *Last Journals:* 'I was hurt at the Duke's suffering Sir Edward Walpole to kneel and kiss his hand. It was too Royal a reception of a father; but the King himself had not more of the Prince than the Duke had. The Duchess often told me that the Duke . . . had more than once said to her there was a comfort in conversing with Sir Edward and me, for we were gentlemen, and ever treated her with as much respect as him' (ii. 59).

3. The Duke 'was much recovered, and had only a swelled leg and lameness remaining' (ibid.).

TO ANNE CLEMENT,[1] ?Monday 22 December 1777

Printed for the first time from the MS now WSL; acquired in September 1959 from Miss Eleanor Forster of Tynemouth, Northumberland.

The date is conjectural; the letter may be concerned with the illness of the Bishop of Exeter in 1777 (see below nn. 1, 2).

Dear Miss Clement

I AM heartily grieved you may be sure at what you tell me,[2] and fear there is but too much ground for apprehension. I will not come this evening,[3] nor can possibly tomorrow, as it is my day for Princess Amalie;[4] but I will certainly come on Wednesday evening.

I have not seen Mr Suckling[5] which much surprises me. I wish your Aunt[6] could call on me tomorrow morning, for though I dread doing anything to shock my brother,[7] I am still very uneasy at concealing anything from him. If he should be pretty well tomorrow

1. Anne Clement (d. 1813), dau. of Hammond Clement, m. Gen. William Edmestone. In Sir Edward Walpole's will dated 17 May 1782 he left an annuity of £100 to her mother Margaret Clement and the life-use of his house in Ryder Street, London 'now in the possession of Mrs Margaret Clement'; also an annuity of £100 to Anne Clement and the life-use of that house after the death of her mother and aunt (see Appendix 4).

2. Possibly news of the Bishop of Exeter's serious illness, 'a dropsy in the stomach,' from which he died at the Deanery at Windsor on Saturday 27 Dec. 1777 (OSSORY i. 410, n. 2). On 6 July 1777 HW wrote Lady Ossory, 'The distress . . . of my brother with his two sons-in-law so ill, and with his two daughters in so melancholy a situation, calls for all the little comfort I am able to give them, and I dare not think of pleasing myself, when there are such afflictions in my family' (ibid. i. 363 and n. 7). On 29 Sept. 1777 HW wrote Lady Ossory again, 'The Bishop of Exeter, my niece and Miss Keppel have been with me two or three days, and the Dysarts and Waldegraves have come to us all day, so I have been an old patriarch, as far as an uncle can be so' (ibid. i. 382). But Mrs Keppel wrote Jane Clement ca Oct. 1777, 'My dear Lord sat out for Bath last Friday. What we endured all Thursday is not to be described, he was totally overcome, he could not hold up his head. . . . he will send for me and the children, expense, everything must be set aside, for he cannot live without us. . . . we shall stay I suppose all the winter' (MS now WSL).

3. Possibly 22 Dec., since this letter seems to have been written on a Monday. Lady Mary Coke wrote in her 'MS Journals' Wednesday 24 Dec., 'The Bishop of Exeter was said yesterday to be past hopes of recovery; the Duke of Gloucester and his Lady went to Windsor to see him.'

4. Princess Amelia held a weekly card party on Mondays (ibid. *sub* 24 Nov., 1 and 8 Dec. 1777); and HW attended the loo party on 22 Dec. (ibid. *sub* 23 Dec. 1777).

5. Possibly William Suckling (1730–98), whose grandmother was Sir Robert Walpole's sister, Mrs Turner (MANN viii. 178, n. 7); he was deputy collector of Customs London Port Inwards for HW and Sir Edward 1772–98 (ibid. viii. 177, 209).

6. Jane Clement, who would be likely to bring news from Windsor; see Appendix 4.

7. Presumably HW wishes to discuss with Mrs Clement how much Sir Edward is to be told of the Bishop's illness. See OSSORY i. 410, ii. 2.

morning, I do not know whether it would not be prudent to tell him early, that he might have the whole day to recover it before he goes to bed.

I am very sorry to have kept your maid, but the Duchess of Richmond came in before I could answer it.

Yours ever

H.W.

To Sir Edward Walpole, Wednesday 11 February 1778

Printed from the MS now wsl; first printed, Toynbee *Supp.* i. 272–3. For the history of the MS see *ante* 28 April 1769.

Feb. 11, 1778.

Dear Brother,

LORD William Gordon[1] was with me this morning, and brought me Lord North's letter,[2] which being something different from what I expected, I have sent a different answer[3] from that I showed you last night, almost as *civil* in expression, but more intimating my sense of the affront we have received, as his Lordship asserts his being told I had *assented*.[4] I suppose Mr Shirley[5] may have told him so; and yet that is only a possibility, for Shirley told me the letter

1. (1744–1823), 2d son of the 3d D. of Gordon and brother of Lord George Gordon, instigator of the Gordon Riots; M.P. Elginshire 1779–84, Inverness-shire 1784–90, and Horsham 1790–6 (Ossory i. 24, n. 23).

2. Lord North to HW 9 Feb. 1778, concerning Mr Shirley's resignation of the deputy rangership of St James's and Hyde Parks and the appointment of Lord William Gordon in his place. Gordon had obtained the King's consent through North and needed HW's authorization and that of Lord Orford (who was Ranger, and whose deputyship he was to assume). There was an enclosure from North to Lord Orford, necessary to authorize HW to put Gordon in possession of the deputyship.

3. HW to Lord North 11 Feb. 1778; HW expressed 'submission to his Majesty's commands' and anticipated that Lord Orford's servants would 'show all proper obedience to Lord William'; noted that he and Sir Edward '*neither assent nor dissent* . . . from the care of our nephew's affairs' and that 'it was not in my power to give any consent to what in no shape depended on my consent.'

4. North's letter concluded with 'You have, I understand, been already made acquainted with this agreement, and have given your consent thereto.'

5. The Hon. Thomas Shirley (1733–1814), naval officer (Sir Bernard Burke and A. P. Burke, *Peerage*, 1928, p. 926; *Court and City Register*, 1777, p. 75; Collins, *Peerage*, 1812, iv. 102).

was actually written; so they depended on my consent, which I took care not to give.

At Lord William's desire, I gave him a letter to Moone,[6] in which I was as cautious to give *no* orders, but only said I concluded Lord Orford's servants *would* obey Lord William. The latter told me also that Shirley said Lord Orford had formerly allowed him to treat with somebody else for the deputyship—I do not see how that allowed him to treat with everybody. That assertion may have imposed upon Lord North, who, if he gave himself the trouble he ought to do, should at least have asked the family if it was true. His precipitation has established a precedent against himself that he may live to rue, if the King has a mind to give the auditor's place[7] from him.

I hope you will approve my answer, which you will keep if you please. Though I have never yet failed to specify my subordination to you, I have avoided it in this letter, that you may not be implicated in acquiescence; for as no notice has been taken of you, I think upon reflection that it would be below your dignity to involve you in any civility, where you are not called upon to show any.

Yours ever

Hor. Walpole

PS. Lord William showed me the letter to Lord Orford (the first letter, I believe, ever written to a downright madman knowingly) but he took it away with him.

To Sir Edward Walpole, the 2d Lord Walpole of Wolterton, and Lord Cholmondeley, ca Friday 27 March 1778

Three letters, missing. 'I am sending to all my relations and making the recovery [of Lord Orford] as public as I can' (HW to Mann 27 March 1778, Mann viii. 368).

---

6. Lord Orford's steward and also a deputy ranger of the parks 1763–91 (see *ante* 22 April 1777).

7. A valuable patent place in the gift of the prime minister, said to have been worth £8,000 a year (*Mem. Geo. III* i. 165), held at this time by the Duke of Newcastle.

To the Duchess of Gloucester, ca Wednesday
6 May 1778

Missing; mentioned *post* 10 May 1778: 'It was my duty to acquaint you with it.'

From the Duchess of Gloucester, ca Friday
8 May 1778

Missing; answered *post* 10 May 1778.

To the Duchess of Gloucester, Sunday 10 May 1778

Printed from the MS, a draft, now WSL; first printed, Cunningham vii. 60–2; reprinted, Toynbee x. 233–6; an extract is in Biddulph 157–8.

May 10th 1778.

I DO assure you, Madam, your R. H. is totally mistaken[1] about Lord Ch[olmondeley] whom I have not seen this month. I received my account from no relation or friend, but from a gentleman of the strictest honour,[2] who came to me, as not knowing else how to convey the information[3] to you. I will upon no account name him, as I gave him my word I would not. I am extremely happy there is no truth in the idea, though it came to me in so serious a manner and from a man so incapable of an ill meaning, that it was my duty to acquaint you with it; and as I desired to be named to your daughters, they will know how kind my intention is,[4] and that I am, as I have professed to them, as affectionate as if I was their father.

I shall be very glad, Madam, of your brother's picture,[5] and will try to find a place for it[6]—but it is far from being the only near

1. The particular circumstances of this paragraph are unexplained.
2. Not identified.
3. 'Relation' crossed out and 'information' written above in the MS.
4. 'Is' written over 'was.'
5. Col. Edward Walpole (1737–71), natural son of Sir Edward Walpole (MANN v. 240; HW to Conway 28 Sept. 1762; MONTAGU ii. 63). HW was not fond of him (MANN vii. 300).
6. Presumably the portrait, 'Colonel Edward Walpole, only son of Sir Edward Walpole, Knight of the Bath, by Hudson' that hung in HW's bedchamber (*Des. of SH*, 1774, p. 133).

relation of whom I have no portrait—I have none of Lord Dysart, of the Bishop,[7] of Lady Malpas, of Mr and Mrs Cholmondeley, of Lady Cadogan, etc., and therefore the remark of the persons that observed your brother's being wanting, was not very good-natured to him or me. Many of the family pictures I happened to have; others I begged as I wanted them for particular places; and indeed furnished my house to please myself not to please[8] such people as those who have been so obliging as to tell your R.H. that my not having your brother's picture was a mark of contempt. I have no[9] desire of pleasing those who were capable of saying such a thing to you. Your affection for his memory[10] is most amiable, and I shall obey you with pleasure, but allow me to say, Madam, that I hope you will always judge of me by what you know of me, and not from comments of others. I have been taxed with partiality for *you*, long before there was a question of your present rank; nor do I believe you suspect me of attachment to you from that motive. I am too old, too independent, and too contented, to have hopes or fears from anybody: I have the highest respect for his Royal Highness's character and virtues, and always shall have; and am proud of paying my court to him, when it can only flow from personal reverence.[11] Were he in the situation he ought to be, I should be but the less anxious[12] to show it.

Indeed I little expected to be suspected of wanting attachment to any part of my family. I have been laughed at, perhaps deservedly, for family-pride, which certainly is not always a proof of family-affection. I trust I have given proofs that they are not disunited in me; and yet, except from my father, I never received either benefits or

7. Bishop Keppel.
8. 'Others; with great indifference to those' crossed out after 'please'; 'such gossipy people as those' written above cancelled 'those,' then 'gossipy' crossed out.
9. 'Never' crossed out and 'have no' written above.
10. The Duchess of Gloucester admired and loved her brother as her childhood letters to him show (MSS now WSL). Upon his death she wrote an epitaph that was included in a memorial erected to her father at Navestock:
'O my lost brother let me ever mourn
Thy early fate, and too untimely urn;
I saw thee not, when in the pangs of death

Nor did my lips receive thy latest breath
Why held you not to me thy dying hand?
And why received not I, thy last command
Something you would have said had I been there
Which I should still in sad remembrance hear
For never, never, could I words forget
Which night and day, I should with tears repeat'
(MS in the possession of Lord Waldegrave).
11. That is, respectful duty; HW's candid opinion of him is shown in MANN and *Last Journals*.
12. 'Assiduous' crossed out and 'anxious' written above.

favours; and from him only my places, and a small[13] fortune not paid.[14] Thus, whatever I have, except my share of Mr Shorter's[15] fortune that came to me by his leaving no will, and consequently was no obligation, I neither received from my family nor owe to it; it has been saved by my own prudence, is my own to dispose of as I please, and[16] will be a gift, not a claim, however I distribute[17] it, or to whom.[18]

I should not say thus much, Madam, but when any one can think it worth while to make invidious remarks to you on a tender point with you, on what is or is not in my house, you will allow me to justify myself,[19] and even open my heart to you, to whom I desire it should be known, though I certainly owe no account to anybody on so trifling a subject as the furniture of a house which I am master to do what I please with, living or dead. It was from no disregard for your brother, that I had not his picture. I love Lady Cadogan very much, as I do surely your daughters and nieces,[20] yet have not happened to have their pictures: and though I have probably said a great deal too much like an old man, it is always a mark of affection when I submit to justify myself on[21] an unjust accusation: and as tenderness for my family is the duty in which I have in my whole life been the least culpable, though very blameable in a thousand other respects, it is very pardonable to be circumstantial and prolix to her,[22] whose reproach was kind and good, and whom I desire to

13. 'No' crossed out and 'and a small' written above.

14. Sir Robert left HW the lease of his house in Arlington St, a legacy of £5,000, and an additional place in the customs. His income reached £8,000 in 1784. On the death of his brother Edward, he lost his place in the customs worth £1,400. The legacy, of which only £1,000 had been paid, was received in full by HW in 1786 (MANN ix. 637).

15. Erasmus Shorter (d. 1753); see ante 6 Dec. 1753, n. 1.

16. 'Nobody has any claim on it' crossed out after 'and.'

17. 'Dispose of' crossed out and 'distribute' written above.

18. The text of HW's will is printed in SELWYN 344–77 (Appendix 8). The Duchess had written her aunt wishing that HW would leave her £10,000, and SH to her family; both wishes were ultimately granted (Ds of Gloucester to Jane Clement 11 Jan. 1777, MS now WSL).

19. 'And even appeal to you' crossed out after 'myself'; 'to whom I desire to have my heart known' written on opposite page, then crossed out, and 'and even open my heart to you, to whom I desire it should be known' written on opposite page.

20. Anna Maria Keppel (see ante 17 June 1759, n. 1); Laura Keppel (1765–98), m. (1784) George Ferdinand Fitzroy, 2d Bn Southampton, 1797; Charlotte Augusta Keppel (1771 – after 1828), m. (1802) Robert Foote (SELWYN 354, nn. 24–6).

21. 'What I owe no account' crossed out after 'on' and 'an unjust accusation' written above.

22. 'Who is best able to do me justice' crossed out after 'her'; 'whose reproach I take was kind and good, and to whom I desire to prove myself and whom I par-

convince that I have neither[23] wanted affection for my family, nor am unjust to it. I have the honour to be, Madam, your R.H.'s

Most faithful

humble servant

H. WALPOLE

From the 2d LORD WALPOLE OF WOLTERTON, Saturday 18 July 1778

Printed from Toynbee *Supp.* iii. 256. Damer-Waller; sold Sotheby's 5 Dec. 1921, lot 190 to Dobell. Its present whereabouts is unknown.

Bruton Street, July the 18th 1778.

My dear Sir,

BEING named by our late worthy relation Capt. Suckling[1] joint executor to his will with his brother Mr William Suckling,[2] I am to inform you that expressing himself sensible of the obligations he owed to your late worthy father, he bequeaths legacies of £100 each, to the Earl of Orford, Sir Edward Walpole, yourself, and Lady M. Churchill. May I trouble you to notify this to Lady Mary when you have an opportunity.

I am, my dear Sir your most

obliged and obedient humble servant

WALPOLE

---

ticularly desire to know my heart' written on opposite page; then 'I take' crossed out, 'to' before 'whom' crossed out, 'prove . . . heart' crossed out and 'convince' written above.

23. 'Been disregardfull' crossed out after 'neither'; 'wanted family affection for my family' written above, and the first 'family' crossed out.

1. Maurice Suckling (1726 – 14 July 1778), Capt. R.N., 1775; comptroller of the Navy, 1775; grandson of Sir Robert Walpole's sister, Mrs Turner (MANN ii. 152, n. 23); M.P. Portsmouth 1776–8.

2. Younger brother of Maurice Suckling (*ante* ?22 Dec. 1777, n. 5).

From LORD ORFORD, Thursday 1 October 1778

Printed from the MS now WSL; first printed, Cunningham vii. 132, n. 1; reprinted, Toynbee x. 326, n. 1. For the history of the MS see *ante* 15 May 1745 OS.

Address: To the Honourable Hor. Walpole Arlington Street London.
Franked: FREE Orford.
Postmark: 3 OC NEWMARKET.

Eriswell, 1st October 1778.

Sir,

I WRITE one line to thank you for your ready concurrence in the measures I am now pursuing to settle the affairs of the family, and to satisfy Sir Robert Walpole's creditors,[1] and beg leave to trouble you to make my compliments and to return my thanks also to Sir Edward.

If you have a mind to revisit your Penates again, and to see the alterations I am making in both fronts, I will not call them improvements,[2] I shall be extremely glad to have your company at Houghton

---

1. Sir Robert Walpole had left his son a debt of between forty and fifty thousand pounds ('Account of my Conduct,' *Works* ii. 365). His legacy to HW was only partly paid (MANN ix. 637). The second Earl, in turn, left at his death (except for Houghton, which was entailed) little besides debts to his son George, third Earl: 'Indeed, I think his son the most ruined young man in England' (HW to Mann 1 April 1751 OS, MANN iv. 238). The present Earl incurred further debts by gambling and bad management, reducing Houghton to 'half a ruin, though the pictures, the glorious pictures, and furniture are in general admirably well preserved. All the rest is destruction' (HW to Lady Ossory 1 Sept. 1773, OSSORY i. 140-3). Lord Orford was now completing an agreement to sell these pictures to Catherine II of Russia (which HW later discovered he did not need to do) in order to pay the remainder of Sir Robert's debts (HW to Lady Ossory 21 Oct. 1778, ibid. ii. 62 and nn. 5-7). An agreement was signed 13 Oct. 1778 (MASON i. 445) by which HW ('though I do not get a sixpence at present') had

four thousand pounds with interest 'secured to me,' and was 'discharged from paying above three thousands for my house' in Arlington Street, a leasehold bequeathed him by his father, but apparently not entirely paid for at the time of his death. In return for this, HW and Sir Edward renounced their claim to the inheritance of Houghton, leaving Lord Orford free to do with Houghton as he pleased. Eventually, however, HW did inherit it (see OSSORY ii. 62, nn. 7-10).

2. Probably both of the outside stairways were removed at this time (the stone from one set being given to Lord Clermont) and the walls behind the steps were altered to provide doorways to the ground floor (MANN viii. 428, n. 6). 'The mad master has sent his final demand of forty-five thousand pounds for [the pictures at Houghton] . . . to the Empress of Russia, at the same time that he has been what he calls improving the outside of the house—*basta!*—thus end all my visions about Houghton, which I never will *see*, though I must go thither at last' (HW to Mann 18 Dec. 1778, ibid. viii. 427-8).

on Monday fortnight the 19th of October, when I propose staying a week—I am, Sir, with great regard

Your most obedient

and humble servant

ORFORD

From the HON. THOMAS WALPOLE, October 1778

Missing; acknowledged *post* 26 Oct. 1778.

To LORD ORFORD, Monday 5 October 1778

Printed from the MS now WSL; first printed, Cunningham vii. 132–3; reprinted, Toynbee x. 325–6. For the history of the MS see *ante* 15 May 1745 OS.

Endorsed (by Sir Edward): My brother's answer to Lord Orford October 5, 1778.

Strawberry Hill, October 5, 1778.

My dear Lord,

YOUR Lordship is very good in thanking me for what I could not claim any thanks, as in complying with your request and assisting you to settle your affairs, according to my father's will, was not only my duty; but to promote your service and benefit, to reestablish the affairs of my family, and to conform myself to the views of the excellent man, the glory of human nature, who made us all that we are, has been constantly one of the principal objects of my whole life. If my labours and wishes have been crowned with small success, it has been owing to my own inability in the first place, and next to tenderness, and to the dirt and roguery of wretches below my notice. For your Lordship I may presume to say I have spared no thought, industry, solicitude, application, or even health, when I had the care of your affairs—what I did and could have done, and should have done, if you had not thought fit to prefer a most conceited and worthless fellow,[1] I can demonstrate by reams of paper,

1. Probably Carlos Cony, Lord Orford's solicitor ca 1774–91 (*ante* 21 April 1777). HW wrote to Mann that some of Orford's 'old conductors have furnished him with

that may one day or other prove what I say—and which, if I have
not yet done, it proceeds from the same tenderness that I have ever
had for your Lordship's tranquillity and repose. To acquiesce
afterwards in the arrangement you have proposed to me, is small
merit indeed. My honour is much dearer to me than fortune; and to
contribute to your Lordship's enjoying your fortune with credit and
satisfaction, is a point I would have purchased with far greater com-
pliances; for, my Lord, as I flatter myself that I am not thought an
interested man, so all who know me know, that to see the lustre of
my family restored to the consideration to which it was raised by
Sir Robert Walpole, shining in you, and transmitted to his and your
descendants, was the only ambition that ever actuated me. No personal advantage entered into those views; and if I say thus much of
myself with truth, I owe still greater justice to my brother, who has
many more virtues than I can pretend to, and is as incapable of
forming any mean and selfish wishes as any man upon earth. We
are both old men now, and without sons to inspire us with future
visions. We wish to leave your Lordship in as happy and respectable
a situation as you was born to; and we have both given you all the
proof in our power, by acquiescing in your proposal immediately.

For me, my Lord, I should with pleasure accept the honour of
waiting on you at Houghton, at the time you mention, if my lameness
and threats of the gout did not forbid my taking so long a journey at
this time of the year. At sixty-one it would not become me to talk
of another year; perhaps I may never go to Houghton again, till I
go thither for ever—but without affectation of philosophy, even the
path to that journey will be sweetened to me, if I leave Houghton
the flourishing monument of one of the best ministers that ever blest
this once flourishing country.

I am my dear Lord

Yours most affectionately,

Hor. Walpole

a new attorney, who is indecently eager to
riot in what I had gleaned from the ruin'
(HW to Mann 28 March 1774, Mann vii.
560; see also HW to Mann 2 Feb. 1774,
18 June 1777, ibid. vii. 549, viii. 310–11;
'Short Notes,' Gray i. 50).

To the Hon. Thomas Walpole, Monday
26 October 1778

Printed from a photostat of the Holland MS; first printed, Sir Spencer Walpole 12–13; reprinted, Toynbee x. 340–1. For the history of the MS see *ante* 18 July 1766.

Address: To the Honourable Thomas Walpole in Lincoln's Inn Fields.
Postmark: W MO   PENNY POST [another illegible].

Arlington Street Oct. 26, 1778.

Dear Sir,

ON coming to town today I found a most magnificent and beautiful book,[1] and a letter as generous and beautiful.[2] I am ashamed to accept the one, and cannot pretend to answer the other; and when I cannot contend with you in generosity, I am sure I will not in words. Still I am sorry to deprive you of so fine and rare a book, nor can possess it without regret at your expense. All I can do is to give you a thousand thanks; and I owe you still more for your son's[3] visit, which gave me the greatest pleasure. He is so sensible, modest and natural, that I wish Strawberry Hill could have more attractions for him. I shall be in town till Thursday, if you should come this way—I would call on you rather, but must wait here for people of business, being come on the purchase of a house;[4] but I long to thank you in person for all your favours to

Yours most sincerely

Hor. Walpole

1. Probably Franz Michael Regenfuss (1712–80), *Choix de coquillages*, Copenhagen, 1758 (Hazen, *Cat. of HW's Lib.*, No. 3554; Thieme and Becker).
2. Missing.
3. Thomas Walpole the Younger.
4. No. 40 (afterwards No. 11) Berkeley Square, pulled down in 1937. In the autumn of 1778 HW negotiated with the auctioneer to buy the house in Berkeley Square for £4,000 (not including fixtures, 'to be taken at a fair valuation'). There was a delay because of a disagreement among the heirs of the former owner (Sir Cecil Bisshopp, Bt, d. 1778) as to how they should receive and share the purchase money. HW entered a complaint with the Lord Chancellor's office to which the heirs were required to reply. On 21 July the Master of the Rolls heard the case and pronounced in HW's favour. He took possession 14 Oct. 1779 (Mason i. 453; the house is illustrated on the facing page).

From Anna Maria Keppel, Tuesday 13 June 1780

Missing. 'Tuesday last . . . Miss Keppel told me in a postscript that the Duke of Gloucester had asked an audience and been graciously received' (HW to Lady Ossory 16 June 1780, Ossory ii. 198).

From the Duchess of Gloucester, Wednesday 14 or Thursday 15 June 1780

Missing. 'The Duchess of Gloucester wrote to me on the 14th, to desire me to come to town on the 16th, when the Duke would be at Kew[1] and she should be alone, and should have time to tell me all that had passed'[2] (*Last Journals, sub* 10 June 1780, ii. 315–16). 'On Thursday the Duchess herself sent me word of it [the Duke's audience with George III] and desired me to come to town' (HW to Lady Ossory 16 June 1780, Ossory ii. 198).

---

1. To visit the Prince of Wales.
2. The Duke of Gloucester's reconciliation with his brother George III. In HW's entry for 10 June in *Last Journals* (ii. 313): 'The Duke of Gloucester wrote to the King' and 'did beg an audience.' The next day the King responded that 'he should be glad to *see him and his children,* but there must be no mention of the Duchess.' For a long discussion of the Duke's interview with the King on 11 June, the Duke of Cumberland's reconciliation with the King, Gloucester's offer to aid in controlling the Gordon Riots, his meeting with the Queen, the Prince of Wales and Prince Frederick, and the King's continuation of his proscription of the Duchesses of Cumberland and Gloucester, see ibid. ii.

313–19. HW visited the Duchess on the 16th and told her that the King had informed the foreign ministers that he and his brothers were reconciled, but that they might not pay their court to the two duchesses. HW wrote to Lady Ossory: 'When I came away just now, which was past eleven, the Duke was not come back from Kew, where he had been to pass the evening with the Prince of Wales' (Ossory ii. 198; see also *Daily Adv.* 12 June). HW visited the Duke on 18 June, who told him he would not carry his children to Court without their mother. HW advised him to 'keep well with . . . [the King], it will be of the utmost consequence to your children' (*Last Journals* ii. 318; see also Mann ix. 62).

To the Hon. Thomas Walpole, Friday 30 June 1780

Printed from a photostat of the Holland MS; first printed, Sir Spencer Walpole 14–15; reprinted, Toynbee xi. 236. For the history of the MS see *ante* 18 July 1766.

Beginning with this letter, the first pages of HW's letters to Thomas Walpole are numbered in ink in the upper left corner, probably by HW. It was then customary to number letters that were sent to people who were going abroad, in order to trace any letters that failed to arrive.

Address: To the Honourable Thomas Walpole in Lincoln's Inn Fields London.

Postmark: 1 IY [another illegible].

Memoranda (probably Thomas Walpole's):   10
$$\frac{.7}{1.5}$$

Strawberry Hill, June 30, 1780.

Dear Sir,

YOU had better make haste to Paris, or you will have a ship to freight with commissions.[1] Here are a parcel more that I have this moment received from Madame du Deffand for you—not for herself, but your friends. Madame de Mirepoix[2] wants two pounds of tea; Madame de Beauvau[3] *trois serrures*—I suppose you know what sort of locks, I don't: and Monsieur de Caraman[4] wants three *serrures* also. I must send Madame du Deffand some tea and some Stoughton's drops,[5] and I have some tea that the Duchess of Leinster[6] gave me for Madame de Cambis[7] which she begs you would carry; and Lord Harcourt[8] a small deal box with a Wedgwood vase. I will

1. Which are listed by Mme du Deffand to HW, 18 June 1780, DU DEFFAND v. 233.

2. Anne-Marguerite-Gabrielle de Beauvau (1707–91), m. 1 (1721) Jacques-Henri de Lorraine, Prince de Lixin; m. 2 (1739) Gaston-Charles-Pierre de Levis de Lomagne, Marquis (Duc, 1751; Maréchal, 1757) de Mirepoix (MANN ii. 371, n. 2; DU DEFFAND *passim*).

3. Marie-Sylvie de Rohan-Chabot (1729–1807), m. 1 (1749) Jean-Baptiste-Louis de Clermont d'Amboise, Marquis de Renel; m. 2 (1764) Charles-Just de Beauvau, Prince de Beauvau (MANN i. 11, n. 43, vi. 341–2, n. 5).

4. Victor-Maurice de Riquet (1727–

1807), Comte de Caraman (DU DEFFAND *passim*).

5. An 'élixir stomachique,' made chiefly from absinthe, sold by Mr Stoughton of Bath (ibid. iv. 222. n. 4).

6. Lady Emilia Mary Lennox (1731–1814), dau. of Charles Lennox, 2d D. of Richmond, m. 1 (1747) James Fitzgerald, 20th E. of Kildare, cr. (1766) D. of Leinster; m. 2 (1774) William Ogilvie.

7. Gabrielle-Françoise-Charlotte d'Alsace-Hénin-Liétard (1729–1809), m. (1755) Jacques-François-Xavier-Régis-Ignace, Vicomte de Cambis, later Comte de Cambis-Orsan (DU DEFFAND i. 311, n. 9, *et passim*).

8. See *ante* 27 Sept. 1777, n. 8.

swear you are just coming that you may not be more loaded. I believe I shall be in town on Wednesday or Thursday for a night, but had rather see you and your son here whenever you have nothing better to do.

Yours most sincerely

Hor. Walpole

To the Hon. Thomas Walpole, Saturday 15 July 1780

Printed from a photostat of the Holland MS; first printed, Sir Spencer Walpole 15–16; reprinted, Toynbee xi. 245. For the history of the MS see *ante* 18 July 1766.

Address: To the Honourable Thomas Walpole.

Strawberry Hill, July 15, 1780.

Dear Sir,

I TROUBLED you with a few lines at the end of last month,[1] to beg to know when you should set out, and to mention two or three little commissions from Madame de Beauvau: and I warned you that there would be more: I believe they frightened you, and that you would not answer me for fear of them. Your terror, as often happens, increases my courage. I send you a Staffordshire vase in a box for Rousseau's friend,[2] which Lord Harcourt desired me to beg you to carry; and a pound of tea from the Duchess of Leinster; and a pound of tea and two bottles of Stoughton's drops for Madame du Deffand. The Duchess of Leinster has since sent me a small picture and another pound of tea, but they are here; but I must send them to you before you go—so pray let me know when it is to be, for all these parcels together are not considerable. Seriously, I am much more solicitous to see you before you go, and trust I shall.

Yours most sincerely

H. Walpole

1. See *ante* 30 June 1780.
2. Possibly Mme de Boufflers or Mme de Luxembourg, both of whom took Rousseau's part in HW's epistolary controversy with him ('Paris Journals,' Jan. 1766, DU DEFFAND v. 294). Toynbee (xi. 245) identifies the 'friend' as 'probably M. Girardin [René-Louis (1735–1808), Marquis de Girardin]. Rousseau died at Ermenonville, a country place belonging to him.'

From the Hon. Thomas Walpole, Wednesday 30 August 1780

Missing. 'I wrote this on receiving your letter' (*post* 6 Sept. 1780); 'M. Walpole doit vous écrire ce soir' (Wiart to HW 30 Aug. 1780, du Deffand v. 244).

To the Hon. Thomas Walpole, Wednesday 6 September 1780

Printed from a photostat of the Holland MS; first printed, Sir Spencer Walpole 16–20; reprinted, Toynbee xi. 270–2. For the history of the MS see *ante* 18 July 1766.

Address: À Monsieur Monsieur Thomas Walpole chez Messieurs Girardot, Haller et Compagnie à Paris par Ostende.

Postmark: GC DA.

Strawberry Hill, Sept. 6, 1780.

I CANNOT but be infinitely obliged to you, my dear Sir, for the very friendly trouble you have given yourself, though the subject is so exceedingly afflicting to me. My dear old friend's last letter[1] shocked me as much as possible: it was a kind of taking leave of me, when I had no notion of her being ill; for though the preceding letter[2] had talked of her being out of order, she has so often written in the same manner after a restless night, that it had given me no sort of apprehension. You now give me some faint hopes, but my reason gives me none, for all the symptoms that you and Wiart[3] mention, look very ill; and if there are any favourable, her great age forbids my trusting to them. It ought to have prepared me better for the blow; but the distance I am at, the impossibility of going to her, or of being of any use, and the anxiety I must remain under till another post, are much more preponderant than the cold reflections that should comfort me. I am so uncommonly obliged to her, that if I did not admire and love her for her sake, gratitude for my

1. Mme du Deffand to HW 22 Aug. 1780, du Deffand v. 242.
2. Mme du Deffand to HW 17 Aug. 1780, ibid. v. 241.
3. Jean-François Wiart, Mme du Deffand's valet-de-chambre and secretary, who read and wrote all her letters for her; he was in her service before 1758 and remained until her death. He wrote to HW 27 and 30 Aug. and 3 Sept. (ibid. i. 6, n. 25; v. 243, 244, 245).

own would fill me with regret. My only satisfactions are that she does not suffer, and that she is so tranquil—should she be capable of hearing it, when you receive this, I entreat you to tell her—but I do not know how to express, how much I love her and how much I feel. You will judge a little, by the extreme gratitude I feel to you and my cousin[4] for your attention to her. While it is possible, I beseech you to continue it. Nothing is so reasonable or so true, as what you say, dear Sir, about her still having company and suppers—They would kill me, if the distemper did not. But, amazing as it is, that a whole nation should choose to communicate their last moments to a crowd of indifferent wretches, or that the latter should be such wretches as to like to be spectators, or not to care while they can junket, still this is so universally the custom of the French, that I am sure my dear friend would think herself abandoned, if she was treated otherwise—

If I indulged my own feelings, I should write on this sad subject to the end of my paper—but I must not abuse your goodness—only pray tell M. Wiart how very kindly I take his attention to me—I can scarce bear to name it, but should the worst happen, I beg, my dear Sir, that you will get from M. Wiart all my letters, and keep them till you come. After much entreaty my dear friend did I believe burn many, but some I fear she kept.[5] As they all went by the post, and I knew were thoroughly inspected, I should care not who saw them—except a bookseller, and thence, everybody. My bad French ought to be their security even against that chance; but you cannot

4. The younger Thomas Walpole. Wiart wrote to HW, 27 Aug., that 'MM. de Walpole sont très assidus' and that 'M. Walpole père doit vous écrire' (ibid. v. 243).

5. 'M. Thomas Walpole . . . m'a dit qu'en cas du malheur où nous devons nous attendre, quoique pas encore prochain, vous réclamiez vos lettres. Il y a environ six mois qu'elles ont toutes été brûlées, et ce que j'en ai depuis ce temps-là ne paraîtra pas. Je les ai entre les mains, j'en ferai un paquet, et je les remettrai à M. Walpole. Vous devez être sûr, Monsieur, qu'il n'en paraîtra pas une seule' (Wiart to HW 17 Sept. 1780, ibid. v. 248–9). HW's side of the correspondence from its beginning to the end of 1774 had been returned to him at his request; Wiart later returned letters written between March

1780 and Mme du Deffand's death; all of these were eventually turned over to Miss Berry, HW's literary executrix. Mme du Deffand had herself destroyed his letters from Feb. 1775 to Sept. 1778. It is assumed that Miss Berry destroyed almost all of those he turned over to her in accordance with his instructions that she do so after making judicious use of them in editing her edition of Mme du Deffand's letters to him. He was anxious to retrieve them (although he probably had not yet decided on their destruction) because of his 'bad French,' as this letter suggests, but also probably because of his effusions of affection which he feared might, if published, make him appear silly (ibid. i. pp. xxx–xliii).

wonder that I do not desire to run even that, especially as a power of exposing me to ridicule would compensate for the badness of the language.

Your own affairs I hope go on prosperously.[6] Events there have been none since the capture of our fleets.[7] At present I take all the care I can to hear nothing, for I am sure the first thing would be about elections, a subject I abhor. I am much more concerned for the poor post-horses than for the candidates, for the former cannot help being sold. They say there are, or are to be some new peers, but it is indifferent to me who goes out of one stable into another. Geary[8] and Barrington,[9] they say, have both struck their flags.[10]

I wrote this on receiving your letter, but as it could not be in time for the post, I must reserve it to Friday; before which it is possible that I may have another letter from M. Wiart. I shall tremble to open it—but will not finish this till it must go to town.

Thursday night.

I must send this to town tomorrow morning, though I have had no more letters. I don't know that I could, but my impatience and uneasiness increase every hour. Would it be impossible to give James's powder?[11]—if it were but five or six grains? I left some with

6. Thomas Walpole came to Paris to protect his interests (and those of his brother Richard) in Grenada against the Alexanders, former Edinburgh bankers, who had fled to France and had tried to take advantage of the French capture of Grenada by evading the Walpoles' claims on their property there (DU DEF-FAND v. 180, n. 1). MS abstracts of a memoir and several letters by Thomas Walpole regarding this case are now WSL. See *post* 11 Nov. 1781, n. 2.

7. The outward-bound West India and East India fleets which left Portsmouth 28 July had encountered a squadron of Spanish and French men-of-war on 9 Aug. (OSSORY ii. 216, n. 1); for reports on the number of ships lost see MANN ix. 78, n. 3; MASON ii. 75–7 and n. 3.

8. Sir Francis Geary (1709–96), 1st Bt, 1782; Rear-Adm., 1758; Vice-Adm., 1762; Adm., 1775.

9. Hon. Samuel Barrington (1729–1800); Rear-Adm., 1778; Vice-Adm., 1779; Adm., 1787.

10. When Sir Charles Hardy died suddenly (17 May), command of the fleet was first offered to Barrington, who refused the command on the grounds that it should go to Keppel, and that he did not personally feel able to overcome the difficulties produced by bad administration, poor training, and lack of discipline (MASON ii. 47, n. 31). Command was then given to Geary, who resigned in early Sept. 1780. 'It was said he was disgusted at not having had frigates enough to watch the Brest fleet, and that the Admiralty had not answered his demands of many articles' (*Last Journals* ii. 329). The fleet was again offered to Barrington; he agreed to take it only if given full powers, and made independent of Lord Sandwich; or else he would serve under any other Admiral. Neither of these conditions was granted, so he 'struck his flag and retired' (ibid.).

11. 'J'ai fait voir aussi, Monsieur, à M. Bouvart l'article de la poudre du Docteur James. Il m'a dit que s'il lui en don-

her, and I conclude you have some. I would give the universe to have her try it. I earnestly beg you to recommend it.

PS. The new peers are Fitzroy,[12] Lord Gage,[13] Lord Chief Justice De Grey,[14] and Sir W[illiam] Bagot.[15]

To the Hon. Thomas Walpole, Tuesday 19 September 1780

Printed from a photostat of the Holland MS; first printed, Sir Spencer Walpole 21–3; reprinted, Toynbee xi. 275–6. For the history of the MS see *ante* 18 July 1766.
Address: À Monsieur Monsieur Thomas Walpole chez Madame la Marquise du Deffand à la communauté de St-Joseph rue St-Dominique à Paris par Ostende.
Postmark: 19 SE.

Berkeley Square, Sept. 19, 1780.

THE note I have this moment received from Wiart of the 10th[1] renews my alarms, which his three last bulletins[2] had almost quieted. He says it is the 20th day, and the fever not gone.[3] Indeed, her *not* dictating one word herself[4] has to me a still worse aspect. Your silence too has the same—I shall dread every post. I know how much her great age and weakness are against her—yet I should hope, if she had taken James's powder; though I did not press it, so much as I wished to do, because I am at a distance and cannot be a perfect judge. All I can say, is to give you and your son a million of thanks for your extreme attention to her. Though I must not impute it all to myself, I take it as kindly as if you could have no other motive.

You know, you must know, how occupied all the world here is

nait il lui procurerait des douleurs cruelles' (Wiart to HW 17 Sept. 1780, DU DEFFAND v. 248; see also *ante* 27 March 1764, n. 19, *post* 19 Sept., 8 Oct. 1780).

12. Charles Fitzroy (1737–97), brother of the 3d D. of Grafton, cr. (1780) Bn Southampton; M.P.

13. William Hall Gage (1718–91), 2d Vct Gage of Castle Island (I.), 1754; cr. (17 Oct. 1780) Bn Gage of Firle (G.B.); M.P.

14. William De Grey (1719–81), lord chief justice of the Common Pleas 1771–80, cr. (1780) Bn Walsingham; M.P.

15. (1728–98), 6th Bt, 1768; cr. (17 Oct. 1780) Bn Bagot; M.P.

———

1. See DU DEFFAND v. 246.

2. Of 30 Aug., 3 and 6 Sept. (ibid. v. 244–6).

3. 'C'est aujourd'hui le vingtième jour de la maladie' (Wiart to HW 10 Sept. 1780, ibid. v. 246).

4. Her last letter to HW was dictated 22 Aug. 1780 (ibid. v. 242).

with elections; and you may judge how singular I am who do not care a straw about them. The Court seems likely to be no gainer by the dissolution;[5] and it['s] said will lose, particularly in the county elections. Burke[6] has given up Bristol; Sawbridge[7] was rejected in London, but Kirkman[8] being dead a few hours before the poll was closed, there will be much squabbling about it. The authority employed to depose Keppel[9] at Windsor, has been returned with interest: Suffolk and Surry offered to choose him: he preferred the latter, and will throw out Lord Onslow's son,[10] who has been jockeyed at Guilford by his cousin the Colonel.[11] Charles Fox[12] is likely to succeed in Westminster. The seven new peers, are Earl Talbot (for Rice's son),[13] Lord Gage, Sir W. De Grey, Sir W. Bagot, Fitzroy, old James Brudenel,[14] and Mr Herbert of High Clear.[15] I

5. Parliament was suddenly dissolved 1 Sept. 'It was said that the Ministers consulted Lord Loughborough . . . and he advised it, as he said he found the Court was losing ground again every day' (*Last Journals* ii. 329; HW to Mann 19 Sept. 1780, MANN ix. 85 and n. 1).

6. Edmund Burke (1729–97); M.P. Wendover, 1765–74; Bristol, 1774–80; Malton, 1780–94. His support of the proposals for relaxing the restrictions on the trade of Ireland with Great Britain and for Catholic tolerance cost him the seat at Bristol.

7. John Sawbridge (1732–95), M.P. Hythe 1768–74, London 1774–80, 1780–95. Sawbridge, too, was defeated for having supported 'toleration of popery' (*Last Journals* ii. 329); however, at the by-election 28 Nov. for the vacancy created by the death of his opponent, John Kirkman (see below) he was returned again.

8. John Kirkman (1741–80); M.P. London 1780.

9. Hon. Augustus Keppel (1725–86), cr. (1782) Vct Keppel; M.P. Chichester 1755–61, Windsor 1761–80, Surrey 1780–2. 'Admiral Keppel has been thrown out at Windsor, and it is pretended by the personal veto of the first inhabitant of the castle—the consequence already has been that the counties of Surrey and Suffolk solicited the honour of electing the Admiral, who has accepted the offer from the former' (HW to Mann 19 Sept. 1780, MANN ix. 86; see also OSSORY ii.

225–6, nn. 5–6, 8; 228, nn. 8, 10). He was defeated at Westminster by the Hon. John Montagu (Hussey Montagu) and Penyston Portlock Powney.

10. Thomas Onslow (1754–1827), 2d E. of Onslow, 1814, was M.P. for Rye 1775–84, Guildford 1784–1806. He was a candidate for Surrey but, out-distanced, withdrew before the end of the poll, having already been re-elected at Rye (Namier and Brooke iii. 231).

11. George Onslow (1731–92), M.P. Guildford 1760–84.

12. Charles James Fox (1749–1806); M.P. Midhurst 1768–74, Malmesbury 1774–80, Westminster 1780–4, Tain Burghs 1784–5, Westminster 1785–1806. He was returned for Westminster 22 Sept. (*Last Journals* ii. 330).

13. William Talbot (1710–82), 2d Bn Talbot of Hensol, 1737; M.P.; cr. (1761) E. Talbot, (17 Oct. 1780) Bn Dinevor with a specific remainder of that dignity to his daughter, Lady Cecil Rice (widow of George Rice) and her heirs male. She became Bns Dinevor in her own right, and on her death in 1793 the Dinevor title passed to George Talbot Rice (1765–1852), afterwards De Cardonnel, and finally Rice (GEC).

14. Hon. James Brudenell (1725–1811), cr. (17 Oct. 1780) Bn Brudenell; 5th E. of Cardigan, 1790; M.P.

15. Henry Herbert (1741–1811), cr. (17 Oct. 1780) Bn Porchester of High Clere, (1793) E. of Carnarvon; M.P.

believe there is nothing else new; if there is, I know it now [*sic*]. Your nephew,[16] I see, is chosen at Wigan, and you and your brother[17] as usual—and Macreth[18]—as if one of the family—and so he is I believe as much as he that chooses him.[19] Adieu! my dear Sir; I am most anxious, but with little hope—Thank God, she does not suffer!—Tell her, I have written to you—if she is capable of knowing it.

PS. I am forced to direct this to you at Madame du D.'s for I left your direction at Strawberry and forgot it.

From the Hon. Thomas Walpole, ca Thursday 21 September 1780

Missing; referred to *post* 28 Sept. 1780.

From the Hon. Thomas Walpole, ca Wednesday 27 September 1780

Missing; mentioned *post* 8 Oct. 1780. Mme du Deffand died 23 Sept. and Wiart's letter informing HW (which arrived in the same post as the missing letter) was dated 27 Sept.

16. Hon. Horatio Walpole (1752–1822), 2d E. of Orford, n.c., 1809; M.P. Wigan 1780–4, Lynn 1784–1809.

17. Richard Walpole; M.P. Great Yarmouth 1768–84. Thomas Walpole at this time held the seat at Lynn.

18. Sir Robert Mackreth (?1725–1819), Kt, 1795; M.P. Castle Rising 1774–84, Ashburton 1784–1802.

19. Lord Orford, HW's nephew, whose paternity HW considered doubtful (MANN vii. 548–9, ix. 132).

To the HON. THOMAS WALPOLE, Thursday
28 September 1780

Printed from a photostat of the Holland MS; first printed, Sir Spencer Walpole 23–7; reprinted, Toynbee xi. 286–8. For the history of the MS see *ante* 18 July 1766.

Address: À Monsieur Monsieur Thomas Walpole chez Messieurs Girardot, Haller, et Compagnie ['Hôtel Lachine' inserted in another hand] à Paris par Ostende.

Postmark: GC.

Strawberry Hill, Sept. 28, 1780.

I DID fear, and for the last ten days did expect the unhappy event[1] for which you bid me now prepare, dear Sir. I own it afflicts me more than I thought it would, considering her great age, and the constant dread I have lived in for some time of her growing deaf. The cruel obstinacy of Bouvard[2] augments my concern. It is very probable that James's powder[3] would not have saved her—but what absurd reason to say it would kill her by vomiting—when he has not the smallest hope, and gives her nothing, what does he but say, that *he* will prescribe the precise mode in which she shall die? Nothing could have given me a more happy transport than to have prolonged her life, if but for six months—can I help suspecting that he thinks she will be longer dying, and that he shall have a few more fees?—how I abhor all professions!

Her silence and *assoupissement* make me hope she is almost insensible. Indeed I dreaded her dictating some letter to me, which I could not stand. I loved her most affectionately and sincerely, and my gratitude to her is without bounds. I admired her too infinitely; her understanding, I am sure till within these three months was astonishing. I received one instance of her affection, that I never can forget while I have a grain of memory left, and which I have never had an opportunity of telling her how deeply I felt—but I am sure when you hear it, you will think it justifies all the sorrow I feel for losing her—for alas! by this time I doubt I have lost her! If she still exists, and you can show her any mark of kindness, it will be the highest obligation to me. I feel thoroughly all you have done.

---

1. Mme du Deffand's approaching death; see *post* 8 Oct. 1780.
2. Michel-Philippe Bouvart (1717–87),
Mme du Deffand's physician (DU DEFFAND v. 243–6, 248).
3. See *ante* 6 Sept. 1780 and n. 11.

Yesterday I received another shock. General Conway has had a fall, I know not how, and broken his arm.[4] Lady Ailesbury assures me he is in no danger, and has even no fever—but I shall go to him myself tomorrow, after the post is come. I tremble for letters from Paris, yet must wait for them!

We have little new. The papers say that General Dalrymple[5] is arrived with bad accounts from New York—it is probable, for nothing is told—but I credit little on any side for some time. From Glasgow we are told of revolts in five Spanish-American provinces—but it is from *Glasgow*, whence I am still longer before I believe. Can any truth come out of Nazareth?

Charles Fox is returned for Westminster, but Lord Lincoln[6] has demanded a scrutiny. Lord Ongley[7] and Lascelles[8] have been forced to give up Bedfordshire and Yorkshire. Today ends the election for Surry. I am going to Ditton this evening, and if I learn the event, will add it, as this does not go to London till tomorrow.

I am truly sorry your business moves so slowly.[9] I was in hopes M. Necker's[10] good sense would have been able to do Justice, justice, and give rapidity to her motions, though he cannot take off her bandage.

I beg you, dear Sir, to thank Wiart for his attentions to me. I thank him ten thousand times for those he has to his dear mistress —Oh! if it were not too late to give her James's powder!

4. See OSSORY ii. 231, n. 11; MANN ix. 89.

5. John Dalrymple (1749–1821), styled Vct Dalrymple 1768–89; 6th E. of Stair, 1789; Capt. in the 87th Foot, taking part in the attack on New London and Fort Griswold. 'General Dalrymple arrived [in London 25 Sept.] from Sir H. Clinton with an account of the capture of the greatest part of the fleet going to Quebec with supplies, of the great distress at New York, and the superiority of the Americans' (*Last Journals* ii. 330). See also HW to Mann 4 Oct. 1780 (MANN ix. 88).

6. Thomas Pelham Clinton (1752–95), styled E. of Lincoln 1779–94; 3d D. of Newcastle-under-Lyme, 1794; M.P. Westminster 1774–80, East Redford 1781–94. On his defeat at Westminster by Charles Fox and Sir George Brydges Rodney, he demanded a scrutiny, to begin 10 Oct., but on that date declined to poll (OSSORY ii. 227 and n. 5).

7. Robert Henley Ongley (ca 1721–85), formerly Henley; cr. (1776) Bn Ongley;

M.P. Bedford 1754–61, Bedfordshire 1761–80, 1784–5.

8. Edwin Lascelles (1713–95); cr. (1790) Bn of Harewood; M.P. Scarborough 1744–54, Northallerton 1754–61, 1780–90, Yorkshire, 1761–80.

9. See *ante* 6 Sept. 1780, n. 6. The affair was delayed by the death of Thomas Walpole's lawyer, M. Bontour (MS abstract of a letter by Thomas Walpole to Turpin, 4 Aug., now WSL).

10. Jacques Necker (1732–1804), banker and statesman; director of the treasury in France, 1776; director-general of finance 1777–81; the father of Mme de Staël. He was Thomas Walpole's friend and had taken a personal interest in his legal actions against the Alexanders of Edinburgh (Mme du Deffand to HW 11, 20 May, 13 June 1780, DU DEFFAND v. 228, 229, 231). Necker had suggested the lawyer Turpin as a replacement for Thomas Walpole's deceased lawyer (Thomas Walpole to Turpin, 4 Aug.).

PS. As I went through Kingston I saw the union flag displayed at an inn, and the windows illuminated, so I knew the Admiral[11] had succeeded. He had a majority of 700, on which Onslow gave out. As I came home, I saw at a distance a great bonfire, that must be at Hampton Court or Hampton, and I hear there are to be illuminations at Windsor, when the account arrives there. What happened there is to be a capital episode, they say, when the Parliament[12] meets. Adieu!

Yours most sincerely

H. W.

To the Hon. Thomas Walpole, Sunday 8 October 1780

Printed from a photostat of the Holland MS; first printed, Sir Spencer Walpole 27–31; reprinted, Toynbee xi. 296–7. For the history of the MS see *ante* 18 July 1766.

Address: À Monsieur Monsieur Thomas Walpole chez Messieurs Girardot, Haller, et Compagnie à Paris par Ostende.

Postmark: EK   DA ?B.

Strawberry Hill, Oct. 8th 1780.

I DID not receive your letter[1] with the fatal news, dear Sir, till yesterday morning, with two from Wiart[2] at the same time, so that I had remained twelve days in the most cruel suspense!

Complain I must not: I had been happy in her living longer than could be expected; and my dread of her becoming deaf, had constantly mixed anxiety with the satisfaction of preserving her. With these reflections I endeavour to console myself—and yet, and though prepared as I was by your foresight, I was greatly shocked at the sight of Wiart's black wax—and the melancholy contents. Bouvart's refusal of James's powder I own has much contributed to the impres-

---

11. Keppel, in gaining the seat for Surrey (see *ante* 19 Sept. 1780). 'Keppel chosen for Surrey by a majority of 700, on which Onslow declined, and Keppel and Sir Joseph Mawbey were returned' (*Last Journals* ii. 330, *sub* Sept. 1780).

12. 'Parliaments' in MS.

1. Missing.

2. Wiart wrote HW 13, 17, 20 and 27 Sept. (DU DEFFAND v. 247–50). This probably refers to the latter two letters, since that of 27 Sept. would have carried the 'black wax' of mourning.

sion, and I cannot forgive it—though most probably it would not have saved her—but it is not fair to weary you with my regrets.

Wiart promises me to deliver my letters to you, and a number of the *Voyage pittoresque*.[3] It is the last thing I shall receive thence. I have great regard for some persons at Paris—but I have done with France! It was for my dearest friend alone that I kept up any connection there.

In the midst of all my anxiety for her, I received another terrible alarm. General Conway broke his left arm just below the shoulder, by a fall on one of his own steep hills. I went to him immediately, and shall go again tomorrow; but he is in the fairest way possible, and has not had the least symptom of fever.

I know nothing new but what I see in the papers, that Laurence,[4] President of the Congress, has been taken going to Holland, brought over and committed to the Tower. By the last cargo of news from New York,[5] I should think his papers[6] are taken a little too late.

The elections, they say, have turned out less favourable for the Court[7] than was expected—but I know scarce any particulars. The new Parliament is to meet only to be sworn,[8] but will not sit till

3. *Voyage pittoresque de la Grèce*, by Marie-Gabriel-Florent-Auguste (1752–1817), Comte de Choiseul-Beaupré. Mme du Deffand sent the prospectus to HW 12 Oct. 1778 (ibid. v. 75). 'Je remettrai encore à M. Walpole un cahier du *Voyage pittoresque*' (Wiart to HW 27 Sept. 1780, ibid. v. 250). Vol. I was completed, 1782; HW had one folio volume of it, sold SH viii. 55 (Hazen, *Cat. of HW's Lib.*, No. 3586).

4. Henry Laurens (1724–92), president of the Continental Congress 1777–8; he sailed from Philadelphia 13 Aug., was captured 3 Sept. and taken, 12 Sept., to St John's, Newfoundland. He was brought to the Admiralty 5 Oct., and after a night in Scotland Yard was taken to Whitehall for a 'long examination, which lasted till near six o'clock, when a warrant of commitment was made out . . . committing him a close prisoner to the Tower' charged with 'high treason' (*Daily Adv.* 9 Oct.; MANN ix. 91, nn. 6, 9). He had been commissioned by Congress 30 Oct. 1779, to negotiate a loan 'not exceeding ten million dollars' in Holland at 6% or less, and 'to treat . . . and conclude . . . a treaty of amity and commerce' with Holland. The latter commission was suspended by Congress 7 July 1780, pending a report from Laurens on affairs in Holland (ibid. ix. 91, n. 10).

5. The bad news brought by Lord Dalrymple (see *ante* 28 Sept. 1780, n. 5).

6. A 'packet of letters . . . thrown overboard [at his capture] . . . great part of them . . . recovered [by a 'daring tar']' (*Daily Adv.* 4 Oct.). Laurens called them papers of 'no consequence . . . for arranging of which the British ministry gave Mr [Joseph] Galloway, according to report £500 sterling, and were at a farther expense to bind [them] in rough calf, gild and letter them in 18 folio volumes, and afterwards returned . . . to Mr Laurens again' (Laurens's 'Narrative,' *Collections of the South Carolina Historical Society*, 1857, i. 20; MANN ix. 91, n. 11).

7. Cf. HW to Mann 2 Nov. 1780, MANN ix. 95, and nn. 2, 3.

8. It met 31 Oct. (ibid. ix. 95, n. 1).

about the 15th of next month. I wish it may bring you, and consequently your son too, back.

You will excuse my brevity just now; you see, as you might conclude, that I know nothing, and my mind, if I indulged my pen, is so full of my poor lost friend, that I should talk of nothing else. If before your return, you should happen to see the Prince of Bauffremont,[9] I should be obliged if you would ask him in what way he wishes a Chevalier de St Sauveur,[10] whom he has recommended to me, should be served. I have told both the Prince and him that I have no kind of interest or credit, and can only direct the latter where to apply. He is a Protestant, and yet it seems odd for a Frenchman to desire to come into our service at present. I know nothing of his history—perhaps he has had a duel—The Prince recommended him too to my Lord Courtney[11]—not a much better channel!—and he is gone into Devonshire to learn English—which he must learn again when he has learnt Devonshire. I don't know what to do with him, and yet I received so many civilities in France, that I will not neglect him—and besides the Prince was a friend of my poor dear friend, and I would do anything upon earth to show my regard for and remembrance of her!—you see I am returning again to that chapter!

Yours most sincerely

H. W.

9. Charles-Roger de Bauffremont (1713–95), Chevalier de Listenois; Prince de Bauffremont, 1769.

10. HW had already had this question conveyed to Mme du Deffand in his letter of 27 August 1780 (missing, but the request is acknowledged by Wiart to HW 6 Sept. 1780, DU DEFFAND v. 246). The Chevalier de Saint-Sauveur may have been Hyacinthe-Philémon de Grégoire (d. 1784), Chevalier (later Comte) de Saint-Sauveur (Bauffremont to HW 5 Aug. 1780, ibid. v. 246, n. 1).

11. William Courtenay (1742–88), 2d Vct Courtenay.

To the Hon. Thomas Walpole, Thursday 26 October 1780

Printed from a photostat of the Holland MS; first printed, Sir Spencer Walpole 31–7; reprinted, Toynbee xi. 302–5. For the history of the MS see *ante* 18 July 1766.

Address: À Monsieur Monsieur Thomas Walpole chez Messieurs Girardot et Compagnie à Paris par Ostende.

Postmark: EK.

Strawberry Hill, Oct. 26, 1780.

I HAD heard of my dear friend's legacy,[1] dear Sir. Madame de Cambis had wrote word of it to the Duke of R[ichmond].[2] Indeed even that notice was no novelty. Several years ago my dear old friend told me she should leave me her *porcelaine and other things.*[3] I assured her that if she did not promise me in the most solemn manner *not* to do any such thing, I would never set my foot in France again, for that, considering her age, I should be thought to have paid court to her with that view: and I protested that if she left me anything of value, I would immediately give up all to her family, and then perhaps what she left would not be distributed just in the manner she would have wished. After some contest, and various requests from her to name what I would accept, as her books etc. all which I positively refused, she said, would I at least take her papers? To satisfy her, and as there would be nothing mercenary in that acceptance, I did consent[4]—This was during the life of Monsieur de Pontdeveylle,[5] who was to have been her executor. The last time I was at Paris she pressed me to choose and then take some of her

1. She had left to HW 'mes brochures, feuilles volantes et manuscrits' and her gold snuff-box with Tonton's portrait (DU DEFFAND vi. 7). The box and most of the MSS are now WSL.

2. See *ante* 27 Jan. 1774.

3. They are not mentioned in Mme du Deffand's will (DU DEFFAND vi. 7, 26), dated 30 August 1780. Probably HW refers to a conversation with her some time before 1771 (see following note).

4. 'Je désire de vous confier tous mes manuscrits; je suis décidée à ne pas vouloir qu'ils soient en d'autres mains que les vôtres. Il n'y a certainement rien de

précieux, et si vous ne les acceptez pas, je les jetterai tous au feu sans aucun regret. Vous comprenez bien dans quelle occasion ils vous seront remis' (Mme du Deffand to HW 2 Jan. 1771, DU DEFFAND iii. 1–2). Her bequest to HW is discussed (and excerpts from catalogues relating to subsequent sales of the MSS are printed) ibid. i. pp. xliii–xlviii. Her will and an inventory of her effects remaining after her death are printed ibid. vi. 5–10, 10–49.

5. Antoine Ferriol, Comte de Pont-de-Veyle; see *ante* 16 July 1774.

porcelaine. I refused—She persisted—at last to pacify her, I took one of the cheapest cups and saucers, and pretended I preferred it because it had *strawberries* on it[6]—and it is now in this room. I believe Monsieur Wiart must remember that transaction, and probably all the rest I have been telling you. I am not sure, but I think I recollect her desiring me to accept the box with her dog's picture—and as it is I believe a trifle, I shall not decline it.[7]

The papers, as there are many of her own writing, will be infinitely dear to me. I know them all well. There are letters and characters and portraits[8] etc. and her correspondence with Voltaire,[9] and a volume or two of miscellaneous verses,[10] and much of the Chev. de Boufflers.[11] They will all be in very safe hands. I not only revere Madame du Deffand's memory, but her friends may be assured that *she* shall not be blamed for having bequeathed them to an Englishman. I will show that I deserved her confidence, and that I am not unworthy of the civilities I received in France. I mean, that though her papers are and could be only trifles of society, they will remain as secret as if they were of the highest importance. It will be a melancholy pleasure in my solitude to read what I have often perused with her and in her room—but I shall not communicate what—indeed few here would understand. In one word, I can[12] have no greater satisfaction than in paying every positive or negative mark of respect to her dear memory. I beg your pardon for troubling

6. 'A cup and saucer of Sève china, all over strawberries, a present from Mme du Deffand' (*Des. of SH,* 1784, p. 14). It was sold SH xii. 96 and in 1968 belonged to Miss D. W. Pears, Heddington, Dorset.

7. 'Je fis hier mon testament, j'en avais déjà fait plusieurs, je compte que celui-ci sera le dernier. J'y parle de vous comme vous me l'avez permis. Je joins à votre article une boîte sur laquelle est le portrait de mon petit chien, je voudrais vous le laisser lui-même, je suis sûre que vous l'aimeriez et en auriez grand soin. Si cela pouvait être possible, faites-vous l'apporter' (Mme du Deffand to HW 25 Jan. 1780, ibid. v. 201). HW adds in a note: 'M. Walpole l'eut, et en eut tous les soins possible.' The box (now WSL) was sold SH xv. 20: 'A circular shaped gold snuff-box, engine turned, with the image

in wax of Madame la Marquise du Deffand's dog, Tonton, which she bequeathed, with the snuff-box and her manuscripts, to Horace Walpole.'

8. The 'portraits' are printed as appendices in DU DEFFAND vi.

9. One folio volume bound in calf and another in blue paper (sold SH vi. 107, No. III) and scattered letters in a packet (No. XI; ibid. i. pp. xlvi–xlvii); now in the Bibliothèque Nationale.

10. Five packets of these were sold SH vi. 107 (Nos VI–X).

11. Stanislas-Jean de Boufflers (1737–1815), Chevalier de Boufflers, Marquis de Remiencourt (DU DEFFAND i. 13, n. 21). 'A large folio vol., bound in green vellum, *Œuvres de M. le Chevalier de Boufflers,* in prose and verse' (sold SH vi. 107, No. I); now WSL.

12. 'Not' crossed out after 'can' in MS.

you with this detail, but it was necessary; and I must entreat you, dear sir, to repeat as much of it, or all, as may be necessary, to Madame du Deffand's friends—in particular to the Prince de Beauvau,[13] to whom I beg you will make my compliments, and tell him that though I value most exceedingly the Chev. de Boufflers's letters, yet if there are any which the Prince may wish not to be sent to me, I consent to his retaining them. It is an attention I should wish to receive, and therefore ought to pay. Madame du Deffand always expressed the utmost gratitude for the Prince's unaltered friendship, and I think I do not violate her last will by paying that compliment to her friend. I shall beg you to receive whatever he delivers to you. I will write to Monsieur d'Aulan[14] the nephew on Tuesday,[15] but it is impossible tonight, as I beg you will tell him; and then I will authorize him to entrust you with everything; which I shall beg you to keep till you come.

I have scarce anything to tell you, for I have not been in town this month; and here I see none but old women. The Parliament is to meet on Tuesday, and go on business as soon as the members are sworn. I have heard that the Opposition intend to propose Sir Fl[etcher] Norton[16] for speaker (for Fred[erick] Montagu's[17] health will not let him undertake it) and that the Court will set up somebody else whom I do not know. Lord Cornwallis's victory[18] revived

13. Charles-Just de Beauvau (1720–93), Prince de Beauvau; son of the Princesse de Craon; HW's correspondent; Maréchal de France, 1783 (MANN i. 11, n. 43). The Prince de Beauvau later suggested that HW withdraw any of the 'portraits' which might compromise living people. HW (through Thomas Walpole; see post, 29 Nov., 29 Dec. 1780; 13 March, 30 April, 31 July 1781) asked to have them all, and assured Beauvau that they would be kept private. The dispute over the papers continued until Sept. 1781 (DU DEFFAND i. pp. xliv–xlv).

14. Denis-François-Marie-Jean de Suarez (1729–90), Marquis d'Aulan, son of Mme du Deffand's sister. He was Mme du Deffand's executor (DU DEFFAND vi. 5, 8, 11, 47).

15. The 31st. The letter is missing.

16. Sir Fletcher Norton (1716–89), Kt, 1762; cr. (1782) Bn Grantley; M.P. Appleby 1756–61, Wigan 1761–8, Guildford

1768–82; Speaker of the House of Commons 1770–80. 'The Court . . . has nominated a new Speaker, Mr [Charles Wolfran] Cornwall. Sir Fletcher . . . declared he had been laid aside without notice' (HW to Mann 2 Nov. 1780, MANN ix. 95). 'Though he had been in town three days, he had never been asked whether his health would enable him to continue in the chair . . . nor had he been applied to, either directly or indirectly, on the subject of choosing a new Speaker' (Sir Fletcher Norton's speech, 31 Oct., in Cobbett, Parl. Hist. xxi. 799, 800, quoted ibid.).

17. (1733–1800); M.P. Northampton borough 1759–68, Higham Ferrers 1768–90.

18. At Camden. Charles Cornwallis (1738–1805), 2d E. Cornwallis, 1762; cr. (1792) M. Cornwallis; M.P. 'An express from Lord Cornwallis in Carolina, that with only 2000 men he had attacked General Gates at the head of 7000, and totally

our martial ardour at first, but it rather seems to cool again—last week the stocks imagined peace with Spain was near—but that seems blown over too—however I only talk from newspapers and their echoes. Lord Carlisle[19] and Eden [20] certainly go to Ireland. Sir John Mordaunt[21] is dead, as I heard this evening. General Conway I hope is out of bed by this time: he has not had the least fever. Lord Maccartney[22] has carried his point of going to India. Lord Bute and Mackinsy[23] are both out of Parliament.

This is the sum total of my knowledge, for in truth I do not go a step out of my way to inquire after news; and seldom learn any till it has been in print. I wrote a long letter to Wiart[24] with some questions about my dear old friend, which I hope he received and will answer. He told me she had acted kindly by him. I knew her intentions on that head, and towards all her servants. When you return, which I should hope would be soon and with satisfaction, you must allow me to talk a little about her, which I will not do now, though I can scarce refrain. I hope not a line of hers will be detained from me; especially the written portraits. She had many most entertaining letters from the Abbé Barthélemi,[25] of which I was very fond too. I repeat how careful I shall be of everything. As I outlive my friends, my greatest pleasure is thinking and talking of them. What is past is much more dear to me than anything that is passing now—and begging the present time's pardon, I cannot think

defeated him, with little loss of Royalists, and had killed 900 and taken 1500 prisoners' (*Last Journals* ii. 331). The news reached London 9 Oct. (*Daily Adv.* 10 Oct.; MANN ix. 92; MASON ii. 84).

19. Frederick Howard (1748–1825), 5th E. of Carlisle, 1758, kissed hands as lord lieutenant of Ireland, 18 Oct. 1780 (OSSORY ii. 243, n. 16).

20. William Eden (1744–1814), cr. (1789) Bn Auckland (I.) and (1793) Bn Auckland of West Auckland (G.B.); M.P. Woodstock 1774–84, Heytesbury 1784–93; accompanied the E. of Carlisle to Ireland as chief secretary (see Namier and Brooke ii. 377).

21. (1697–1780), K.B. 1749; Gen. 1770; M.P.

22. George Macartney (1737–1806), cr. (1776) Bn, (1792) Vct, and (1794) E. Macartney; M.P.; Gov. of Madras, June 1781 – June 1785.

23. Lord Bute's brother, James Stuart Mackenzie (?1719–1800), who had been M.P. Ross-shire 1761–80. Lord Bute had been representative peer for Scotland.

24. ?October 1780, missing. 'Votre lettre m'a fait pleurer; votre attachement y est peint d'une manière si vraie, si naturelle, qu'il est impossible de s'y méprendre. . . . Vous me demandez, Monsieur, des détails de la maladie et de la mort de votre digne amie' (Wiart to HW 22 Oct. 1780, DU DEFFAND v. 251).

25. Jean-Jacques Barthélemy, a devoted friend of Mme de Choiseul, and Mme du Deffand's correspondent. HW particularly wanted his letters from Mme du Deffand's bequest, but later decided to return them to him, only to discover that he had already withdrawn his letters from the bequest before he had HW's permission to do so (ibid. i. 21, vi. 236; see also *post* 29 Dec. 1780, 25 March 1781, 3 Jan. 1784).

I am much in the wrong! your son is one of the very few that could replace any of those that I loved and are gone; but I shall not make him so bad a compliment as to offer him the friendship of a superannuated man.

From the HON. THOMAS WALPOLE, Sunday 12 November 1780

Missing; answered *post* 24 Nov. 1780.

To the HON. THOMAS WALPOLE, Friday 24 November 1780

Printed from a photostat of the Holland MS; first printed, Sir Spencer Walpole 37–41; reprinted, Toynbee xi. 325–7. For the history of the MS see *ante* 18 July 1766.

Address: À Monsieur Monsieur Thomas Walpole chez Monsieur Girardot et Compagnie à Paris par Ostende.

Postmark: [Illegible].

Berkeley Square, Nov. 24, 1780.

I WAS most agreeably surprised the other day, dear Sir, by a visit from your son,[1] whom I little expected. He tells me you will be here too at the beginning of the year; but I fear his arrival is no omen of your coming soon. I have since received yours of the 12th[2] with one enclosed from the Prince of Beauvau,[3] with which I am not at all pleased. There are mighty fine compliments, but those are not what I want. He says, 'if there are any portraits or characters *qui paraissent compromettre quelqu'un, et qui pourraient par conséquence blesser la mémoire de notre amie,*' he shall '*les mettre à part.*' *That* I by no means consent to. I told him I desired to have every scrap of her writing or dictating; and when I so readily relinquished all letters of living persons, he might be sure I should show nothing that would hurt anybody, and am as little likely to occasion any reflection on my dear friend for having left them to me. I beg you

1. Thomas Walpole the Younger.　　　3. Missing.
2. Missing.

will mention this civilly to the Prince, and that I should be hurt at having it supposed with my extreme regard for Madame du Deffand, that I should let any such thing appear. I do not care to write to him myself, as I should conceal but ill how much such a paragraph wounds me. I pique myself on my tenderness for her, and the Prince affects to act it for me, and sends back my own words, as a sop to quiet me. I have seen the portraits and characters over and over; and as she chose I should have them, I shall never give my consent to relinquishing them; and they are certainly less liable to be seen in England, where they would excite no curiosity, than in France. He says too, that she gave him leave to have copies of what he pleased— In that case, I may bid adieu to your bringing them over!—you may guess what I think of all this! My idea of wills is perhaps particular —indeed I have seen by other instances that it is so.[4]

I received from Wiart one of the most touching and sensible letters[5] I ever saw, indeed the most simply eloquent; it shows how he had imbibed his dear mistress's natural style. But he mistook me in one point, and thence occasioned your doing, dear Sir, what I by no means meant. In his first letter[6] he made many humble apologies for writing to me. In answer, I told him that I was very far from having any such foolish pride, and that his attachment to his mistress levelled all distinction; that I should always be glad to hear from him and of his welfare, and that he needed not make any secret of my writing to him. He understood this, as a desire in me that he should show my letter,[7] as a proof of my grief, which was not at all my meaning, and I suppose it will be thought ostentation, which I despise. I had infinite reason to love my dearest old friend: I would do anything to show regard and respect to her memory; but I have lived too long, and am too near going myself, to value vainglory—and as the late Duke of Cumberland said wisely, when he became unpopular,[8] 'I recollected in the height of my popularity, that Admiral Vernon[9] had been popular too!'

4. Probably a reference to the dispute with 'Old Horace,' Thomas Walpole's father, over the mutual entail (see *ante* 13 April 1756).

5. 22 Oct. 1780 (du Deffand v. 251).

6. Wiart first wrote HW 24 Sept. 1766: 'Je vous demande mille pardons, Monsieur, de la liberté que je prends; mais j'ai cru qu'il était de mon devoir de vous informer de l'inquiétude où est Madame de votre santé; cela me donne occasion,

Monsieur, de vous remercier des bontés que vous daignez avoir pour moi' (ibid. i. 141). HW's reply is missing.

7. 'Je la montrerai à tous les véritables amis de votre amie' (Wiart to HW 22 Oct. 1780, ibid. v. 251).

8. The Duke's early popularity for his military victories had been succeeded by criticism and satire of him as a 'butcher.'

9. Edward Vernon (1684–1757), Vice-Adm. 1739, Adm. 1745; M.P. He attained

I told you, on misinformation at Richmond, that Lord Maccartney had got the government[10] of Madras—the election is not over yet.

I cannot tell you a syllable more than you see in the public papers. We are thanking or accusing or abusing with our usual judgment. I say, as was the way formerly, the accused should cry, 'I appeal to a general council.'

I was diverted with the French astonishment at Lord Pomfret's[11] being of the Bedchamber—in truth, he had resigned, but Lord O[rford] has not, nor Lord Bolinbroke;[12] two names that were not formerly worn by lunatics. I proposed last year, but it was too reasonable and too cheap a plan to be adopted, that the few who remain in their senses should be shut up in Bedlam, and all the rest be at liberty—perhaps it was not accepted, because the majority do not like liberty. Accordingly, they are now humoured, and sent to the Tower, instead of to Moorfields.[13] Adieu!

tremendous popularity with his victory at Porto Bello, 1740, and in the '45, but after his retirement from active service in the navy he became unpopular with the government because of pamphleteering on the management of the navy; he was called upon for an explanation and his name was struck off the list of flag officers in 1746.

10. 'Election' crossed out and 'government' written above. See *ante* 26 Oct. 1780; in *Last Journals* HW recorded the appointment 20 Dec. (ii. 340).

11. George Fermor (1722–85), styled Bn Lempster (Leominster); 2d E. of Pomfret, 1753; lord of the Bedchamber 1763–81. 'Lord Pomfret, half a madman, was committed to the Tower by the House of Lords, for challenging and grossly insult-

ing the Duke of Grafton without any provocation' (ibid. ii. 334). He was imprisoned from 6 to 17 Nov.

12. Frederick St John (1734–87), 2d Vct Bolingbroke, 1751. For the last six years of his life he was in a madhouse (GEC). 'Were I on the throne, I would make Dr Monroe a groom of my Bedchamber—indeed it has been necessary for some time, for of the King's lords, Lord Bolingbroke is in a madhouse, and Lord Pomfret and my nephew, ought to be there' (HW to Mann 6 Feb. 1780, MANN ix. 11).

13. Bedlam was located in Moorfields from 1676 until 1814–15 (Henry B. Wheatley and Peter Cunningham, *London Past and Present*, 1891, i. 173; see also Edward G. O'Donoghue, *The Story of Bethlehem Hospital from its Foundation in 1247*, 1914).

From SIR EDWARD WALPOLE, Friday
29 December 1780

Printed from the MS now wsl; first printed, Toynbee *Supp.* iii. 282. Damer-Waller; for the history of the MS see *ante* 6 July 1758.
Address: To the Honourable Horace Walpole Berkley Square.

December 29, 1780.

Dear H.,

I SEND you the scribble[1] which I read to you t'other day—it is altered in some places a good [deal] for the better—such as it is I beg your acceptance of it—It was false printed in the papers: for which reason and that of my friends wanted copies of it, I printed off a parcel to save the trouble of writing.

Yours affectionately

E. W.

PS. I was desired by a friend to write a short *Spectator*[2] upon the subject, for the public papers—and I have done it as well as I can. I know where it would have been in better hands.

To the HON. THOMAS WALPOLE, Friday
29 December 1780

Printed from a photostat of the Holland MS; first printed, Sir Spencer Walpole 41–5; reprinted, Toynbee xi. 346–8. For the history of the MS see *ante* 18 July 1766.
Address: À Monsieur Monsieur Thomas Walpole chez Messieurs Girardot et Compagnie à Paris par Ostende.
Postmark: GC [another illegible].

Dec. 29, 1780.

I AM ashamed and sick, dear Sir, of the chicaneries I meet with about my poor friend's papers, though I never expected to get any worth a straw. Since I wrote to you last, I received a mighty

1. Missing.
2. Not identified. The Duchess of Gloucester wrote Sir Edward 16 Jan. 1781, 'I assure you I did admire that *Spectator* very much but I cannot think it better than many things I have seen of your writing' (MS now wsl).

zealous letter from the Prince[1] vaunting his having insisted on having for me the MS books, which the executor[2] would have withheld. I took that opportunity of writing him a mighty grateful letter,[3] which I showed to your son, in hopes of peeking [piquing] his generosity—*à la bonne heure!* He now, *he* who was so afraid of the characters being printed, desires me to print such as he shall mark to me, to save him the trouble of having them copied!—In that letter too he proposed to me to give the correspondence with Voltaire[4] to be printed with the latter's works; adding, that as far as he had gone, he found they would do her honour. To that I consented. Now again, in the letter you enclosed from him,[5] he says he finds very few of Voltaire's original letters! All this is so shuffling, that to save myself and you, dear Sir, any farther trouble, I will add a note which you will be so good as to translate to him, that I hope will prevent any more messages backwards and forwards.

I forgot another trait. He says that amongst what is left to me are many brochures,[6] chiefly things of Voltaire that are or will be in the new edition, and which he supposes I should not desire to have. I certainly did desire nothing—but being thus treated, I cannot be such a fool as to acquiesce blindly—and if I am wronged, it shall not be with my own consent. I will therefore beg you very civilly, dear Sir, to make my compliments to the Prince and tell him, that as he is not well, I do not write myself, not to put him to the trouble of answering it. That as to printing any of the portraits or characters, I am sure that upon reflection he will not wish it, for as it is impossible for me to be secure that my printer would not reserve a copy or copies for himself,[7] it must risk what the Prince himself apprehended, their being published; and that nothing could induce me to run a hazard of that kind. That if the Prince will mark those of which he desires copies, I can have them transcribed in my own room without any danger. That as to the letters of Voltaire, my dear friend had his and her own letters all transcribed into a folio,

1. Prince de Beauvau to HW, ?Dec. 1780, missing.

2. Aulan (*ante* 26 Oct. 1780, n. 14).

3. Missing.

4. See *ante* 26 Oct. 1780 and DU DEFFAND i. pp. xliii–xlviii.

5. With Thomas Walpole to HW, ?Dec. 1780, missing.

6. 'Five bundles or packets of printed works, pamphlets, tracts, plays, poems, etc.

many of which are extremely rare and curious' (sold SH vi. 107, No. XIII).

7. HW's distrust of his printer, Thomas Kirgate, was justified, since Kirgate surreptitiously reprinted some of the SH imprints, and also made a copy for himself, of suppressed passages from HW's correspondence with Sir Horace Mann (MANN i. p. xlii, n. 4; Hazen, *SH Bibl.* 12–14).

which may have occasioned the neglect of the originals; but such a book there was and ought to be. That as to the brochures, they will be very valuable to me, as I may not be able to get them in England, and in France they must be common, and therefore I should wish to have them.

This, dear Sir, is with the reserve of their not being too bulky to trouble you with, but I had rather you should leave behind you what you do not think worth bringing, than comply with a request that I do not at all admire. I am very sorry you have so much trouble; but I flatter myself you approve me and do not think that I have insisted on too much; perhaps I have on too little. I received the snuff-box,[8] and 'tis most precious to me. I own I wish to have the dog[9] itself, that I may make it as happy as my poor friend did. She is if possible more dear to me, by comparing her with others.

I do not pretend to send you news, as your son is here.

If you see the Duchesse de Choiseul or the Abbé Bartélemi, I will beg you to let them know that I had ordered their letters to be restored, *before* they asked for them.

I have barely time to seal my letter, and am dear Sir

> infinitely ashamed of and grateful
>
> for the trouble you have for
>
> yours most affectionately
>
> H. W.

To Lord Orford, Tuesday 6 February 1781

Missing. 'I have this minute written to her son, and sent him the individual copy of her will that I have received from you, and the few particulars you have told me. I am sorry that when you first gave me notice of her illness, I did not beg you, in case of her death, to write to her son, which would have saved me the disagreeable necessity of writing to him, *which* I had totally left off, as he has so totally shaken off *me*' (HW to Mann 6 Feb. 1781, Mann ix. 121). 'I then spoke, and called on Lucas to acknowledge that I had at first declared in writing to my Lord that I would not undertake the office of umpire, unless I were allowed to act as a gentleman, and not as a lawyer' (HW to Mann 21 Nov. 1783, ibid. ix. 445).

8. See *ante* 26 Oct. 1780.   9. Tonton arrived in 1781.

From Lord Orford, ca Friday 9 February 1781

Missing. 'This morning I received a letter from himself, in answer to my notification, in which he repeats the same, though, he says, he has *for precaution* entered a caveat. . . . His letter to me is as cold and formal as it could be to you, if you had written directly to him; nor is there the most slight implication of any relation between us. It is evidently drawn up for him, and no doubt with the intention of giving me to understand that he has no thoughts of ever remembering that I am his uncle. . . . There is one aim at propriety that is not likely to have been my Lord's own, as it is too vulgar. He says he shall send Sir Edward and me *rings*—not because brothers-in-law to his mother, but because we were formerly acquainted with her' (HW to Mann 11 Feb. 1781, Mann ix. 124).

To the Hon. Thomas Walpole, Tuesday 13 March 1781

Printed from a photostat of the Holland MS; first printed, Sir Spencer Walpole 45–7; reprinted, Toynbee xi. 415–16. For the history of the MS see *ante* 18 July 1766.
Address: À Monsieur Monsieur Thomas Walpole.

Berkeley Square, March 13, 1781.

Dear Sir,

YOUR son has just sent me the Prince of Beauvau's letter to you,[1] but it by no means satisfies me. He talks of sending you *only* two more folios of transcribed letters; but what I want, is, *the volume of portraits and characters, written by my dear friend herself, and another of miscellaneous verses, songs, epigrams, etc.* The former are what she particularly wished me to have; and I beg you will look whether they are amongst what he has already sent you; and if not, I beg you will tell him, when you see him, that it is those I am most anxious about.[2] He cannot well deny having them, for they are what he first begged to retain, and then, when I refused, what he desired me to print for him, which I also refused.

1. Missing.
2. The Prince in the end withheld some MSS of which HW received no copies. Pages 254–61 and 288–9 were cut out of the *Recueil de lettres choisies de différ-* *entes personnes* (sold SH vi. 107, No. II), including (according to the index) two letters from Beauvau himself, a letter from the Chevalier de Boufflers, a letter from the Comte de Broglie, and part of a

I am very sorry you do not mention your own return. I am perfectly easy about whatever is in your hands. For the brochures and indifferent things, you will have an opportunity of sending them. Lord Lucan[3] set out this morning for Paris to see his son[4] who has the measles there, and would take charge of them. But if you should have the portraits, etc., I should not venture to trust them to an Irish head.

I have desired Lord Lucan to inquire of Le Duc the tailor,[5] whether he has not several suits of clothes (I know he has) belonging to the late Mr Beauclerc,[6] and which he left to his servant. Wiart, if anybody, could get them, and would keep them, till the poor man could get them over, which he will soon have an opportunity of doing. Will you permit your own servant to speak to Wiart on that subject?—but I do not suppose they will be recovered—When a French will is so ill observed, can one expect that a tailor, though a great prince too,[7] should respect an English one?

The Park and Tower guns have been firing today for the conquest of St Eustathia[8]—They were almost ready to go off last week for a peace that the Emperor and Czarina were to get for us[9]—but I conclude your son tells you all our news, and I should only repeat him. I wish very much to see you—I hope you will not stay till the peace is made.

Your much obliged and very humble servant

Hor. Walpole

letter from Broglie to Beauvau (DU DEFFAND i. pp. xlv–xlvi).

3. Sir Charles Bingham (1735–99), 7th Bt; cr. (1776) Bn and (1795) E. of Lucan; M.P.

4. Hon. Richard Bingham (1764–1839), styled (1795) Lord Bingham; 2d E. of Lucan, 1799.

5. Referred to also by Mme du Deffand to HW ?18 July 1766, DU DEFFAND iv. 341.

6. Topham Beauclerk (1739 – 11 March 1780).

7. Word play on the tailor's name.

8. One of the Dutch West Indies. On 3 February Admiral Rodney and Maj.-Gen. Vaughan gave the governor 'one hour' for the 'instant surrender of the island' and he complied (London Gazette Extraordinary 13 March; HW to Mann 13 March 1781, MANN ix. 139).

9. 'Last week the stocks rose six per cent in two days. It was given out that the Emperor and the Empress had offered their mediation, and that all parties had accepted it, and that Sir Joseph Yorke was to depart on wings of winds to Vienna and conclude the peace. Much of this cargo of propitious news is fallen off as well as the stocks' (ibid.). 'It appeared to be at least a very exaggerated account. . . . The two Imperial Powers [Emperor Joseph II and Catherine II of Russia], had indeed made a defensive alliance, as if to enforce peace, and had offered us their mediation, but it did not appear that either France or Spain had accepted it' (Last Journals ii. 355).

To the Hon. Thomas Walpole, Sunday
25 March 1781

Printed from a photostat of the Holland MS; first printed, Sir Spencer Walpole 48–51; reprinted, Toynbee xi. 416–18. For the history of the MS see *ante* 18 July 1766.

Berkeley Square, March 25, 1781.

DR Warner,[1] who is going to Aix to conduct home the Dowager Carlisle,[2] will bring you this, dear Sir.

I have received a letter from the Duc de Guines,[3] recommending to me an Italian abbé,[4] in which he tells me (and I do not know how he came to do so, as we have had no correspondence) that Madame du D. left me only such papers as were specified in an inventory, and that there remain a great many, not inserted there, and perhaps not the least precious, which he laments not coming to me. I do not know whether this is a fact, or a mistake arising from what the Marquis d'Aulan disputed at first and then gave up; or to sound me by *somebody's* desire, or in consequence of having heard anything of the treatment I have received. I have answered very guardedly,[5] told him the heads of my story without complaint, and concluded by saying, that having had no pretensions to anything, I certainly can claim nothing but what was left to me.

I should be much obliged to you however, if you could indirectly inform yourself whether this relation is well founded. You may, if you please, mention it to the Duc de Guines himself, and say how much I am obliged to him for the information, and for the part he takes in what relates to me. This may lead to his telling you more. I certainly do not mean to ask for anything to which I have not the most strict right—I wish I could get that—though indeed I have

1. Rev. John Warner (1736–1800), rector of Stourton in Wiltshire, an intimate friend of George Selwyn (J. H. Jesse, *George Selwyn and his Contemporaries*, 1882, iii. 306).

2. Isabella Byron (1721–95), dau. of William, 4th Bn Byron, m. 1 (1743) Henry Howard, 4th E. of Carlisle; m. 2 (1759) Sir William Musgrave, 6th Bt (MANN vii. 447, n. 29). Warner had been sending news of her to Selwyn (Warren H. Smith, *Orig-*

inals *Abroad*, New Haven, 1952, pp. 103–12).

3. Of 12 Feb. 1781, from Adrien-Louis de Bonnières (1735–1806), Comte and (1776) Duc de Guines; French ambassador to England, 1770 (DU DEFFAND ii. 416, n. 18).

4. 'M. l'abbé Pizzaná, chargé de faire exécuter une édition complète des œuvres de Metastase' (Guines to HW 12 Feb. 1781).

5. HW to Guines 23 March 1781.

never expected to get a scrap of paper that is worth reading! I have hitherto forborn complaining, because I dread the suspicion of having wished to have anything left to me—but having gone so far as to make my dear old friend very angry with me, by positive refusals of everything; they who defraud me, will not act very honourably, if they deprive me of a parcel of manuscripts.

Though I write securely, I can tell you nothing but general topics. The nation is more besotted and the ministers more popular than ever. Were it only that the Opposition is more unpopular, I should not wonder, nor think people so much to blame. The enormous jobs given in the loan[6] have made a little noise; indeed so much, that the Court has taken pains to spread reports of invasion[7] to lower the premiums; and have succeeded. Perhaps they believe these reports, for troops are dispatched to all the important posts on the coast, and last night the grand fleet was said to be recalled.[8] It is positively said too that the negotiations of peace are broken off,[9] which I expected, though not so soon.

General Conway is gone to Jersey[10] with strong additional force, which he obtained only by dint of perseverence.

If you stay much longer, I believe you will find new *embarras* from a *new* quarter. The youngest uncle[11] has got possession of the eldest

6. Lord North declared that in order to raise the necessary revenue for the budget he had negotiated a loan for twelve million pounds and 'was obliged to avow, that the complexion of the times made it impossible to procure money but on terms extremely disadvantageous to the public' (*London Chronicle* 6–8 March, xlix. 230). The terms of the loan were severely attacked, and Lord North was accused of partiality and corruption in disposing the loan to members of Parliament and favourites: 'Sir George Saville moved for an inquiry into Lord North's behaviour on the Loan. Mr Byng produced numberless instances of his partiality in that affair. . . . Charles Fox most severe on Lord North' (*Last Journals*, ii. 357–8).

7. 'The grand fleet . . . sailed this week to relieve Gibraltar. . . . This was a most desperate stroke; as a large French fleet was at Brest, and another Spanish as large at Cadiz. If they joined or enclosed ours,

the odds were great; if they did not, the Channel was open to the French: we had no ships at home, nor a camp formed; and Portsmouth, Plymouth again, Newcastle, and many other parts of the island, were exposed to invasion' (ibid. ii. 356).

8. Admiral Darby's fleet sailed from St Helen's 13 March, and from Cork 26 March; he arrived off Gibraltar 12 April (MANN ix. 139, n. 5; 142, n. 8).

9. See *ante* 13 March 1781.

10. Conway had taken office as governor of Jersey in 1772. In January of this year the island had been invaded by the French who were repulsed. Conway had been in London negotiating with Lord Hillsborough for constant naval assistance and reinforcements; he embarked for Jersey 24 March and arrived there 26 March (Conway to Hillsborough 21 Feb., 17, 27 March 1781, S.P. 47/9; MANN ix. 110–11).

11. The Duke of Cumberland,

nephew,[12] and sets the father[13] at defiance. A moppet[14] in Grosvenor Square has conceived hopes from this rising storm, which are about as well founded as any of his pretensions have ever been. This is a slight sketch, which you will be able to detail in your own mind, as no material change has happened anywhere.

If Dr Warner returns from Aix, where he will stay very little, before you set out for England, you may write safely to me by him, and send me any of the papers, if you should receive them; and the *Voyage pittoresque de la Grèce* and the tomes of the *Bibliothèque de romans*,[15] both which Wiart has for me, and for which I will beg you to pay him.

Yours most sincerely

H.W.

From the Hon. Thomas Walpole, ca Monday 23 April 1781

Missing; referred to *post* 30 April 1781.

To the Hon. Thomas Walpole, Monday 30 April 1781

Printed from a photostat of the Holland MS; first printed, Sir Spencer Walpole 51–3; reprinted, Toynbee xi. 435–6. For the history of the MS see *ante* 18 July 1766.

Address: À Monsieur Monsieur Thomas Walpole chez Monsieur Magon de la Balue à Paris.

April 30, 1781.

I CANNOT express, dear Sir, how my heart bleeds at what you said in your last[1]—but I will not say anything on that subject now; as I shall refer myself to your son when you see him. He is

12. The Prince of Wales.
13. George III.
14. The Marquis of Rockingham; see *post* 14 May 1781.
15. The *Bibliothèque universelle des romans,* published 1775–89, of which HW

had 8 volumes, sold SH v. 116. The Hon. Thomas Walpole obtained four of them for him (see DU DEFFAND, *passim,* and *post* 3 Jan. 1784).

———

1. Missing.

indeed one of the most meritorious and amiable young men in the world. I wish the great affection I have for him could be of any value to him!

He delivered me the *Voyage pittoresque,* the dear little dog[2] of my poor friend, and a box of papers—but I was surprised at not finding one miscellaneous volume, and more particularly the volume of portraits and characters, which I should think might easily have been copied before now. I beg you will make my compliments to the Prince of Beauvau, and acknowledge the rest, but say that I am anxious to have the two others, as it was what my dear friend particularly recommended to me often and often, and that I hope he will have it finished as soon as he can that I may have it in my possession.

Le Duc is a great rogue; Mr Beauclerc certainly left several suits in his possession—if he has sold them, it is no wonder he has none of them these eight years.

I begged your son to mention to you a little volume of the works of the Chevalier de Boufflers, lately printed,[3] which Madame de Cambis has sent a copy of to the Duke of Richmond. If it is to be bought, I should be glad to have one.

There is nothing at all new here of any sort. Whatever I hear before he sets out, you shall know by him.

I am with far more earnestness than what is said for the conclusion of a letter, and with the sincere friendship that I have long professed to you

Yours most affectionately

Hor. Walpole

---

2. Tonton.

3. At The Hague, 1780: *Œuvres du Chevalier de Boufflers* (Bibliothèque Nationale catalogue). HW had Mme du Deffand's MS volume of Boufflers's *Œuvres* (see *ante* 26 Oct. 1780, n. 11), but no printed copy appears in his library.

To the Hon. Thomas Walpole, Monday
14 May 1781

Printed from a photostat of the Holland MS; first printed, Sir Spencer Walpole 53–8; reprinted, Toynbee xi. 444–7. For the history of the MS see *ante* 18 July 1766.

May 14, 1781.

IT is impossible in a letter, my dear Sir, to tell you the concern I feel for your situation,[1] because compliment has so abused all terms, that none are left appropriated to sincerity. I can only appeal to my character, which is not that of a flatterer, and to that of mankind, who are not apt to flatter the unprosperous. I must not mention my own share, though I assure you your absence adds very considerably to my concern. Yet, were you not so tender a father, you yourself would have little reason to regret this country, which is so degraded, that the *Amor Patriæ* is little more justifiable than a man who falls in love with a common whore. Your son deserves every kind of esteem: his courage, his patience, his temper, his reason are beyond description. Had I any prospect of being useful to him, it would give me the greatest satisfaction—but neither the present moment, nor the future, should my life be longer than it probably will, offer any views on which an honest man would build—but while I do live, he will have a sincere friend, and a home to which he will always be most welcome.

I can add nothing to all you know. Lord Cornwallis's late success over Greene[2] will certainly make us more obstinate against any pacification in favour of America—and Darby's[3] relief of Gibraltar[4] without the slightest opposition from France or Spain,[5] will confirm *entêtement* in the opinion of its own wisdom; though all it proves, is, that France and Spain are still more contemptible than England. An Opposition that could muster *134* on Sir George Saville's late motion[6] for hearing the delegates, shows how strong the Opposition

1. Unexplained.
2. Nathanael Greene (1742–86), Maj.-Gen. in the American army, defeated by Cornwallis at Guilford, North Carolina on 15 March, the news of which reached London 11 May (Mann ix. 151–2, n. 1).
3. Adm. George Darby (d. 1790), com-

mander-in-chief of the Channel Fleet (see Mason ii. 122).
4. See ibid ii. 138.
5. See Mann ix. 147.
6. On 3 March 1781 the deputies of several local associations for Parliamentary reform met in London to consider an

might be, had they any union or conduct,—but neither is to be expected—and as folly and chance seem to be the only managers on this side of Europe, it is impossible to guess what will happen; for penetration cannot calculate on such data.

You talked very sensibly on the sensations occasioned by the wild behaviour of a certain young person[7]—and yet, though the elder[8] no doubt at first comforted himself with the *favourable* comparison that would be made in preference to hypocrisy over debauchery, yet as insults are more felt than reflections, I should think provocations would have more effect than the cool deliberations of envy—and yet timidity will strengthen the latter. I confess I am angry at the younger for giving these advantages to the elder—but what good could come out of Nazareth? *Ætas parentum* peior avis *tulit æquiores!*[9]

16th.

La Mothe Picquet's[10] capture of several of the Eustatia ships[11] arrived yesterday noon. In the City it occasioned rage against Lord Sandwich,[12] who had been applied to for convoy—but by night the word given out at this end of the town, and which will be echoed,

application to Parliament 'for correcting the gross abuses in expenditure of public money, and for reducing the . . . influence of the Crown' (Christopher Wyvill, *Political Papers, Chiefly Respecting the Attempt of the County of York . . . To Effect a Reformation of the Parliament of Great Britain*, York, 1794, i. 385). 'Sir George Saville [8th Bt (1726–84)] moved to hear the petition of the delegates of counties. It was rejected on pretence that delegates were not authorized persons, by 215 to 135. So large a minority on a topic no longer popular, showed what they might have done had not the Opposition been disunited' (*Last Journals* ii. 362).

7. The Prince of Wales (see ibid. ii. 360–2 for details of this 'wild behaviour').

8. George III.

9. Horace, *Carmina* Bk III, Ode 6, ll. 46–7: '*Ætas parentum, peior avis, tulit nos nequiores*' ('Our parents' age, worse than our grandparents', has raised us even worse').

10. Toussaint-Guillaume Picquet de la Motte (1720–91), Comte de la Motte

Picquet, chef d'escadre, 1778; Lt-Gen., 1782 (Mann ix. 152, n. 4).

11. 'An express arrived on Monday night . . . with an account that Commodore Hotham, who had the conduct of the St Eustatia fleet, consisting of thirty-two sail to this country, has put into Beerhaven in Ireland, accompanied by four ships of the line; that in his passage here, just off Scilly, he met with the squadron under the command of Mons. La Motte Piquet, consisting of six ships of the line and four frigates; that the Commodore finding this squadron too numerous for him to engage with any chance of success, made a general signal for all the trade to disperse, which was accordingly obeyed' (*Public Advertiser* 16 May). The *Gazette de France* 18 May reported La Motte Picquet's return to Brest 'avec les 22 bâtiments qu'il a pris aux Anglais, dont 21 marchands et un corsaire' (Mann ix. 152, n. 5).

12. John Montagu (1718–92), 4th E. of Sandwich; lord of the Admiralty 1771–82.

was, that it was a blow that would fall only on some underwriters[13] —and for convoy, how should it be sent? our ships not being half-manned?—in short, we desire nothing but to be imposed on, and the worst reasons satisfy—on Monday on Burke's motion[14] for inquiry into the transactions at St Eustatia,[15] the Opposition were treated with the utmost scorn, for impudence is accepted by the nation for spirit, and unfair war for policy—to be sure, unfair war, when we are inferior, is spirit—but then it is not policy.

22d.

My letter, as you see by the date, has been long written, but waited for your son's departing. He called this morning when I was abroad, and left word he would call again after dinner, so I finish it for him.

I have nothing material to add, for any new folly of Lord Rockingham is certainly not important. In his panic on the riots last June,[16] he went to Gloucester House one morning, when the Duke, from his having done so once before four or five years ago, and from his never having been since nor to the Duchess, would not see him. On this he has turned drummer and trumpeter for the Cumberlands, made all his friends go thither, and has kept Lord John and Burke entirely from Gloucester House. On Saturday the Duke of Cumberland gave a great dinner to this moppet of chieftain, and to the Duke of Portland and others—but as Lord Rockingham

13. HW wrote in *Last Journals:* 'Account of La Mothe Picquet, with ten ships, having waited at the mouth of the Channel for Commodore Hotham, who, with four men of war, was convoying home thirty transports laden with the plunder of St Eustatia. La Mothe had taken about twenty-one; nine more and the men of war escaped into a port in Ireland. Great clamours rose amongst merchants and insurers, who had demanded a large convoy to meet them from Lord Sandwich. It was now pleaded in his defence that we had but twelve ships at home, and those not half manned' (ii. 363).

14. 'Burke moved for an inquiry into the conduct of Sir George Rodney and General Vaughan, at St Eustatia, and of their forfeitures and expulsions there; rejected by 160 to 56' (ibid. ii. 362).

15. 'Lord Sandwich, to captivate the Navy, persuaded the King to give the private property at St Eustatia to the captors. . . . The West India merchants were alarmed at this savage and dangerous precedent, and remonstrated to Lord George Germaine' (ibid. ii. 358). In his speech on the motion Burke stressed the contrast of this to the earlier treatment of English landowners when the French captured Grenada in July 1779; the French had seized no property, and British inhabitants were put on the same footing with French subjects on the island (Mason ii. 124–5, n. 16).

16. The Gordon Riots, 2–7 June 1780 (see *Last Journals* ii. 306–12). 'Lord Rockingham did not wait on the Duke and Duchess [of Gloucester], on pretence that it would look too like a system of opposition' (ibid. i. 175).

never despairs of being minister, nor is delicate about the means, I
believe the influence the Duke of Cumberland has over his nephew,[17]
is a great ingredient in Lord Rockingham's views—and he who
shunned Wilkes, will crouch to the Lutterels—but what signify
the views of such a gang of fools, who have no spirit but what pride
and a bottle of hartshorn can infuse into their leader?—somebody
knocks, and I must finish—I shall be ever

most truly and affectionately

yours

H. W.

From the HON. THOMAS WALPOLE, ca Saturday 19 May 1781

Missing. 'At the same time with yours I received a letter from another cousin
at Paris, who tells me Necker is on the verge; and in the postscript says, he has
actually resigned' (HW to Conway 28 May 1781).

From SIR EDWARD WALPOLE, ca June 1781

Missing; answered *post* 4 July 1781.

From SIR EDWARD WALPOLE, Wednesday 4 July 1781

Printed from the MS now WSL; first printed, Toynbee *Supp.* iii. 283. Damer-
Waller; for the history of the MS see *ante* 6 July 1758.
Address: To the Honourable Hor. Walpole Strawberry Hill Twickenham
Middlesex.
Postmark: 4 IY.

Wednesday, July 4, 1781.

Dear Horace,

I FIND by Lady Maria[1] that my letter[2] was not so clear as it should
have been. Therefore that I may not keep you in suspense, you

17. The Prince of Wales.

1. Lady Charlotte Maria Waldegrave.
2. Missing.

will understand by this that I can not yet make use of your kind offer³—when I am got a little farther in the process of my negotiation,⁴ if I find that I can not step into my own house to finish my matters and give my orders, I will inquire you out and if you are at the Hill, will very kindly and indulgently to myself, comply with your request.

Your etc.

E. W.

PS. I intend to christen my place, Raspberry Plain, not expecting it to be famous but {Strawberry Hill and its companion.

To the HON. THOMAS WALPOLE, Tuesday 31 July 1781

Printed from a photostat of the Holland MS; first printed, Sir Spencer Walpole 58–60; reprinted, Toynbee xii. 33–4. For the history of the MS see *ante* 18 July 1766.

Address: To the Honourable Thomas Walpole at Paris. [In another hand] Rue basse du Rempart No. 4.

Berkeley Square, July 31st 1781.

I DON'T know when you will receive this letter, perhaps not under three weeks; but I could not let slip the opportunity of writing to you, dear Sir, by Dr Gem,¹ whom I still found here, and who hopes to set out at the end of this week. I have nothing to tell

3. Probably of assistance in the purchase of a house (see the following note).

4. On 20 July 1781 Sir Edward purchased a house at Isleworth from the 'trustees in the settlement made on the marriage of Willoughby Lacy Esquire with Maria Ann Lacy his now wife.' The house was 'by the waterside,' built about 1750 by James Lacey, Esq., patentee of Drury Lane Theatre. Sir Edward bequeathed the house and 'five acres of customary land at the Rails Head in Isleworth' to his daughter Mrs Keppel. It was pulled down some years before 1840 (Dan-

iel Lysons, *Environs of London*, 1795, iii. 100; Sir Edward Walpole's will, 57 Rockingham; BERRY i. 320–1 and n. 15; George James Aungier, *History and Antiquities of Syon Monastery, the Parish of Isleworth*, 1840, pp. 232–3). 'This country house will I hope add many years to his life' (Lady Elizabeth Laura Waldegrave to Anne Clement 7 Sept. 1781, MS now WSL).

1. Dr Richard Gem (ca 1717–1800), physician to the British embassy; he had the 'practice of the sick English at Paris' (MANN vii. 158, n. 8).

you, but that I am and always shall be affectionately yours and your
son's—here my letter ought to end, and I hope it was not necessary
even to say so much—but I own I am disappointed. I expected to
see your son before now. Last night I came to town to see and wish
joy to our again united families,[2] which is great joy to me too. I
asked Lord Walpole[3] about you both, and he said you cannot part
with your son, which in truth I do not wonder at: his virtues deserve all your affection. I do not desire either of you to write when
it is inconvenient or disagreeable to you; but be assured that it will
always give me pleasure to hear of you, and more to hear anything
that is fortunate to you.

In politics I know nothing new—nor inquire, nor—had almost
said, care; which is natural, when both belief and hope are tired out.

Of the Prince of Beauvau I find I am to hear no more!—I should
blush if I had executed my dear old friend's will no better than he
has!—her poor little dog has all my care—I am happy the Prince
did not want the copy of him, for then I should never have seen the
original.[4]

My nephew,[5] who has more excuse, for at least *he* has been mad,
is much such an executor, only a little more fairly as more openly,
for he contests part of what his mother left to her paramour,[6] though
he declared he would not—however, he offers to compromise, and has
desired me to be referee, and Mozzi has named Mr Morrice[7] for the
other. I accepted[8]—on the express condition that I should be allowed
to act as a gentleman, not as a lawyer. This office has brought to my
sight a letter[9] that he wrote to his mother on his first recovery in
which he states the great improvement of his and her estates, and
attributes all to my care. This is a satisfaction I never expected to
see under his hand—but I beg your pardon for troubling you with

2. Hon. Horatio Walpole (*ante* 19 Sept.
1780, n. 16) m. (27 July 1781) Sophia
Churchill (d. 1797), dau. of Charles
Churchill and Lady Maria Walpole, thus
uniting the descendants of Sir Robert and
his brother Horatio ('Old Horace'),
Thomas Walpole's father.

3. The 2d Bn Walpole of Wolterton,
'Pigwiggin' (*ante* 7 May 1745, n. 4).

4. Mme du Deffand's bequest of MSS to
HW had not been delivered because the
Prince de Beauvau was requiring copies

of them for himself (see *ante* 26 Oct., 24
Nov., 29 Dec. 1780).

5. Lord Orford.

6. Cavaliere Giulio Giuseppe Mozzi
(1730–1813), poet and mathematician; sen-
ator; president of the Accademia della
Crusca; minister of foreign affairs, 1801
(Mann v. 70).

7. Humphrey Morice (?1723–85); M.P.
Launceston 1750–80.

8. See HW to Mann 8 June 1781, Mann
ix. 157–8.

9. Missing (ibid. ix. 171).

my personal concerns—and yet I have nothing better to send you, and therefore conclude

yours most affectionately

and sincerely

H. Walpole

From and to Lord Orford, October 1781

Two letters, missing. 'He is going to set up *at Leghorn* a monument for his mother and has sent me the epitaph for my opinion. It says, she died *universally lamented.* Oh! that he would translate it into Greek or Coptic, or any *lingo* that every English sailor could not understand! I have answered very respectfully, as becomes a dutiful uncle without giving any opinion or advice at all, for to contradict a madman is to persuade him. If he thinks I approve, he may change his mind' (HW to Lady Ossory 26 Oct. 1781, Ossory ii. 300).

From the Duchess of Gloucester, ca Monday 29 October 1781

Missing. 'The Duchess of Gloucester has ordered me to thank you very particularly for a very obliging letter that she has received from you—she does not say on what occasion. They are at Weymouth, and greatly happy at having lately inoculated Prince William as successfully as they could possibly wish' (HW to Mann 29 Oct. 1781, Mann ix. 202–3).

To the Hon. Thomas Walpole, Sunday 11 November 1781

Printed from a photostat of the Holland MS; first printed, Sir Spencer Walpole 61–4; reprinted, Toynbee xii. 88–90. For the history of the MS see *ante* 18 July 1766.
Address: À Monsieur Monsieur Thomas Walpole.

Nov. 11, 1781.

I HAVE seldom in my life been so delightfully surprised, as I was on Wednesday last[1] by a visit from your son. It is not to reproach

1. 7 November.

your silence, dear Sir, for I allowed for the numerous reasons that might occasion it—but I own I was very unhappy at it, and feared you did not know how cordially and sincerely I took part in your cares. The Duke of Richmond told me Madame de Cambis had mentioned the decree in your favour;[2] but hearing no more of it, nor being able to learn the truth, I did fear it was not so propitious as your son tells me. I do most heartily congratulate you and your family, and believe few but they have more real pleasure in your good fortune. Your son speaks modestly of it, as he does of everything; but Mr Suckling,[3] whom I saw yesterday, was much more sanguine, and made me hope such a reestablishment as I wish. Do not talk of philosophy—you have such very meritorious children, and have so much courage yourself, that I hope you will again be active, and make them as considerable as they ought and deserve to be. For your son, if my affection is any present, he is very sure of it. Nothing can be more insipid than my life, but whenever he will partake of it, he will make me happy, and as often and for as long as he pleases, though a lame old man is poor company.

You are sensible I can tell you nothing but what everybody knows; nor is it pleasant to write that, if one speaks truth: nor is France the spot to which I would send what I think.

I have received all the papers of my old friend—that I ever shall receive. I will tire you no more on that subject—though I hear you have not more reason to be pleased, than I am, with certain persons.[4]

As I hear you see Madame de Guerchy[5] sometimes, I beg my sincere respects to her, and to the Duchesse de la Valière du Carousel,[6] if her you should see too. Those two ladies have always been equally and constantly good to me. There is another, whom I will not name,[7] who I own has surprised me—but I will remember the kindness, and forget the neglect.

2. Thomas Walpole had won his lawsuit, but costs had depleted his fortune. He was obliged to appeal to the Governors of the Bank of England (which held unsatisfied claims upon him) for an allowance for himself and his children. HW printed the appeal at SH in Aug. 1781: *A Letter from the Honourable Thomas Walpole, to the Governor and Committee of the Treasury of the Bank of England* (Hazen, *SH Bibl.* 121–3).

3. William Suckling (*ante* ?22 Dec. 1777, n. 4).

4. The Prince de Beauvau and others involved in the execution of Mme du Deffand's estate.

5. See *ante* 27 March 1764.

6. Anne-Julie-Françoise de Crussol, m. Louis-César de la Baume le Blanc, Duc de la Vallière (*ante* 15 Oct. 1769, n. 9).

7. Probably Mme de Choiseul.

Your niece Mrs Walpole[8] is breeding. There was a time when I should have thought that a felicity!

Sir Edward has bought a house at Isleworth,[9] has been there these three months, nay, has been here twice, and made a few other visits. He is amazingly well, and better for the air; nay, it gave him a little gout in his foot for two or three days.

Tonton is perfectly well, and does not bite anybody once in a month. I imitate George Selwyn about Mimy,[10] and do not try to convert him, but let him go to mass every Sunday. Perhaps that may not be a great merit in France now. Perhaps it is a greater merit here.

Old Lord George Cavendish[11] comes into Parliament again in the room of his nephew Lord Richard,[12] to prevent a contest in Derbyshire. Lord Richard, I suppose, you know, left what money he had to his sister.[13]

Lord Despencer,[14] and Lord Falmouth[15] are past recovery. Lord Aylesford marries Miss Thynne,[16] or rather her father,[17] for I fancy Bacchus will be better served than Venus.

Adieu! my dear Sir. Do not write but when you like it. I shall have the pleasure of hearing of you from your son; and in the present situation of things, our correspondence is too much *genée* to afford us much satisfaction.

8. Sophia Churchill, wife of Lord Walpole's son (*ante* 31 July 1781, n. 2).

9. See *ante* 4 July 1781.

10. Maria Emily Fagnani (1771–1856) m. (1798) Francis Charles Seymour-Conway (1777–1842), styled E. of Yarmouth, 3d M. of Hertford, 1822. Legally the dau. of Giacomo, Marchese Fagnani and Costanza Brusati, 'Mie Mie' was probably the natural daughter of the Marchesa and William Douglas, Earl of March and later D. of Queensberry, Selwyn's friend. George Selwyn virtually adopted her from her birth (except for a brief period, 1778–9, when her mother reclaimed her) and made her his heir (SELWYN 263, 268; Ossory ii. 236).

11. Lord George Augustus Cavendish (ca 1727–94), M.P. Weymouth and Melcombe Regis 1751–4, Derbyshire 1754–80, 1781–94.

12. Lord Richard Cavendish (1751–81),

M.P. Lancaster borough 1773–80, Derbyshire 1780–1.

13. Dorothy Cavendish (1750–94), m. (1766) William Henry Cavendish (1738–1809), 3d D. of Portland.

14. Francis Dashwood (1708 – 11 Dec. 1781), 11th Bn Le Despenser, 1763; M.P., chancellor of the Exchequer 1762–3.

15. Hugh Boscawen (1707 – 4 Feb. 1782), 2d Vct Falmouth, 1734, M.P.

16. Heneage Finch (1751–1812), 4th E. of Aylesford 1777, m. (18 Nov. 1781) Lady Louisa Thynne (1760–1832).

17. Thomas Thynne, 3d Vct Weymouth (*ante* 10 Aug. 1777, n. 12). 'The love of gaming and of wine lately absorbed his attention and faculties, and having absorbed his estate into the bargain, necessity in some degree restored him to himself' (*Royal Register* ii. 62, quoted in GEC ii. 25, n.*b*.).

From Lord Orford, February 1782

Missing. 'I was . . . surprised the other day by a letter from his Lordship. It was to desire the favour of me to go and see a large picture that Cipriani has painted for him for the salon at Houghton' (HW to Mann 25 Feb. 1782, Mann ix. 247).

From Thomas Walpole the Younger, ca Wednesday 4 September 1782

Missing; answered in the following letter.

To Thomas Walpole the Younger, Friday 6 September 1782

Printed from a photostat of the Holland MS; first printed, Sir Spencer Walpole 64–5; reprinted, Toynbee xii. 326. For the history of the MS see *ante* 18 July 1766.

Address: To Thomas Walpole Esq. in Lincoln's Inn London ['White 49 Holbourn' added in another hand].

Postmark: 7 SE.

Strawberry Hill, Sept. 6, 1782.

My dear Sir,

THOUGH I shall lose your company, which I expected again with great pleasure, I must not lament your journey to Paris, as it will make your father and sisters[1] so happy. Whenever you can make me amends, be assured I shall always be very thankful, and that you have no friend who more cordially wishes you well. I wish I had more power of showing you my regard—but though it is a barren friendship, it is a very sincere one, and not offered but to the very few whom I love and esteem.

I will trouble you with no commissions, but to tell your father how happy I should be to see *him* again, and how much I value *you;* and to beg you to bring me the residue of the *Voyage de la Grèce*[2] that

1. Catherine (1756–1816) and Elizabeth (1759–1842).

2. See *ante* 8 Oct. 1780, n. 3. Vol. I was completed in 1782.

is published, the continuation of the *Bibliothèque des romans;*[3] and one cup, or a cup and saucer of the Sève china in imitation of lapis lazuli.[4]

I was in town on Wednesday[5] for one night, and should certainly have contrived to see you if I had known of your going so soon, but I only found your letter[6] here at my return. If you see poor Wiart, pray tell him how well Tonton is, and what care I take of him.

Yours most affectionately

Hor. Walpole

From Lady Charlotte Maria Waldegrave, November 1782

Missing. 'I have just received a most kind and pleasing letter from Lady Maria, who is . . . charmed with the improvements at Nuneham. . . . I beg your Lordship to tell her that I will write to her as soon as I am able, but I cannot even dictate now for any time' (HW to Lord Harcourt 28 Nov. 1782).

From Lady Chewton,[1] ca Thursday 28 November 1782

Missing. 'I had a note from her [Lady Chewton] this morning, and expect to see her, and I hope Lord Chewton, tomorrow' (HW to Lady Ossory 29 Nov. 1782, Ossory ii. 374).

To the Duchess of Gloucester, after Monday 24 February 1783

Missing; referred to *post* 13 March 1783.

---

3. See *ante* 25 March 1781, n. 15.
4. HW lists 'a cup to hold an egg, imitating lapis lazuli, porcelaine de Sève' in 'Des. of SH,' *Works* ii. 416.

5. 4 Sept.
6. Missing.

———

1. See *ante* 25 May 1776, n. 2.

To the Duchess of Gloucester, Thursday 13 March 1783

Printed from the MS now wsl; first printed, Toynbee xii. 426–8. For the history of the MS see *ante* 15 May 1745 OS.

Endorsed (by HW): To the Dss of Gl. but not finished nor sent.

Thursday March 13th 1783.

YOUR R.H. may be surprised, Madam, that after announcing the fall of Lord Shelburne,[1] I should not have told you who was his successor. I had more reasons than one, like the Mayor of Orléans;[2] though that one were sufficient, viz. his having no successor till yesterday. I know Lord Cholmondeley had written to the Duke;[3] and in truth I did not care to tell foreign post offices,[4] though no secret, the confusion we were in. I had rather anybody should publish our disgraces than I. Nay, I should perhaps have sent false news, for several appointments of premiers were believed, each for a day, and proved false the next. The post was certainly offered to and declined by young Mr Pitt,[5] to Lord North,[6] Lord Gower,[7] and it was said to

1. William Petty (1737–1805), 2d E. of Shelburne, 1761; cr. (1784) M. of Lansdowne; army officer; M.P.; secretary of state for the South 1766–8; foreign secretary March–July 1782; first lord of the Treasury (prime minister) 13 July 1782–5 April 1783. Upon the fall of Lord North's ministry in 1782, Shelburne declined to form a government, but became secretary of state under Rockingham. Upon Rockingham's death the same year, the King offered Shelburne the Treasury. Fox resigned and Shelburne introduced William Pitt into office as his chancellor of the Exchequer. This ministry resigned when outvoted by the coalition of Fox and North in Feb. 1783 (*Last Journals* ii. 479–505; Mann ix. 371–2; Ossory ii. 390–5).

2. Unexplained.

3. Of Gloucester.

4. The Duke and Duchess of Gloucester travelled about in Europe from July 1782 to Nov. 1787.

5. William Pitt (1759–1806), the future prime minister. 'The Lord Advocate . . .

proposed to the King to send for the very young chancellor of the Exchequer William Pitt, not yet past twenty-three. The offer was no doubt dazzling . . . to one so ambitious, it was placing him at the head of a party. . . . The young man had the discretion, however, to ask time to consider' (*Last Journals* ii. 489, *sub* 24 Feb. 1783). On 27 Feb. 'Mr W. Pitt excused himself to the King' (ibid.). See also Ossory ii. 390, n. 1.

6. Frederick North (1732–92), styled Lord North; 2d E. of Guilford 1790; prime minister. 'The overtures made to North gave him an opportunity of vaunting his fidelity to his new allies.' The King sent for Lord North, 'but repenting before his arrival, dismissed him immediately, saying he had not yet resolved what he would do' (*Last Journals* ii. 496).

7. Granville Leveson Gower (1721–1803), 2d E. Gower, 1754; cr. (1786) M. of Stafford. He 'had not resolution enough to accept' (HW to Mann 2 March 1783, Mann ix. 379; see also *Last Journals* ii. 489). On 7 March Gower was summoned

Lord Thurlow.[8] At last, after a vacancy of 17 days, Lord North was summoned yesterday, and ordered to make his proposed arrangement;[9] in consequence of which the Duke of Portland[10] was sent for next, and is first lord of the Treasury. I have not yet heard the other changes or dispositions, but suppose we shall know the principal before this shall set out tomorrow.

There have been cartloads of abuse, satiric prints, and some little humour on the coalition of Lord North and Mr Fox;[11] nor has Lord Shelburne been spared before or since his exit. It is remarkable that the counties and towns are addressing thanks for the peace, which their representatives have condemned. George Selwyn has been happiest, as usual, in his bons mots; he calls Mr Fox and Mr Pitt the Idle and Industrious Apprentices.[12] It is a coarser and much poorer piece of wit, I don't know whose, that the Duke of Portland is a fit *block* to hang *Whigs* on. You have seen in the papers, Madam, the new peerages and pensions,[13] and therefore I do not mention them. I very likely repeat what you hear from your daughters and others—but what can I tell, but what everybody knows?

My aunt Lady Walpole[14] is dead, and they say, has left but little,

by George III 'to form an administration' (George III's *Corr.*, ed. Fortescue, vi. 265).

8. Edward Thurlow (1731–1806), cr. (1778) Bn Thurlow; M.P.; solicitor-general 1770–1; attorney-general 1771–8; lord chancellor 1778–83, 1783–92. He was employed as negotiator (Fortescue, op. cit. vi. 263–72).

9. On 12 March ('this morning and not before') the King 'sent for Lord North, and desired him to acquaint the Duke of Portland that he was desirous of forming an administration, and had no objection to his being at the head of it' (Ossory ii. 391, n. 2). The immediate object was to form 'an administration . . . on a broad basis,' with the 'Duke of Portland, being at the head of the Treasury' (George III's memorandum dated 12 March, Fortescue, op. cit. vi. 323; see also Mann ix. 380).

10. The King had agreed on 12 March to accept Portland, but many difficulties had to be resolved before the official appointment on 2 April (Ossory ii. 393–4, n. 1; see also *Last Journals* ii. 494–5, 499–500).

11. For instance, 'The Subtle Fox,' in *London Chronicle*, 1–4 March 1783, liii. 216; and 'The Wonders,' ibid. 8–11 March, liii. 235.

12. HW repeated this in his letter to Lady Ossory 11 March 1783 (Ossory ii. 393).

13. See *London Chronicle* 4–6 March 1783, liii. 217–18, for a list of new dignities and ibid. liii. 220 for a list of 'useless' offices in the Customs to be abolished, 'in compensation for which, an annual value is to be paid to the grantees during their lives.'

14. Mary Magdelaine Lombard, Lady Walpole of Wolterton, wife of 'Old Horace' (see *ante* 7 May 1745 OS). She d. 9 March in Whitehall (*London Chronicle*, 8–11 March, liii. 234; Mann ii. 47, n. 2). 'Lady Walpole died yesterday morning at past eight-seven. She has been quite blind for some years. . . . I sat with her three weeks ago, and never saw her look better, nor possess her senses more' (HW to Mann 10 March 1783, ibid. ix. 385).

and that little to her two daughters.[15] Mr Skrine[16] has shot himself, it is supposed, from excruciating illnesses. Old Lady Jerningham[17] is recovering from a most violent palsy. General Conway has had as violent a St Antony's fire, but is well again. I will reserve the rest of my paper for new promotions.

I never deal in scandal, Madam, but one may make use of it as an antidote to itself. You must have seen in the papers much gross abuse on a pretty ingenious friend[18] of mine for a low amour with one of her own servants, for which I seriously believe there was not the smallest foundation. The charge is now removed to much higher quarters, which at least are more creditable. The town has for these ten days affirmed that the Lord Husband was going to cite into the *spiritual* court the head of the *temporal* one[19]—nay, and the third chief of the common law[20]—nay, and the second of the spiritual one too.[21] Such conquests would be very honourable in the records of love, and the first very diverting, as the hero has so much distinguished himself by severity on bills of divorce. I do not warrant any of these stories, but totally discredit that of the domestic. A prude may begin with a footman, and a gallant woman may end with one, but a pretty woman who has so many slaves in high life, does not think of a livery, especially where vanity is the principal ingredient in her composition.

15. Henrietta Louisa (1731–1824) and Anne (1733–97); three other daughters, Mary, Susan and Caroline, predeceased her.

16. William Skrine (?1721–83), M.P. Callington 1771–80 (Ossory i. 212, n. 4; Mann iv. 145, n. 15; ix. 385–6). According to Namier and Brooke, he 'blew out his brains in a tavern on Newgate Street,' having lost heavily at cards at Brooks's (iii. 443).

17. Mary Plowden (ca 1703–85), m. (1733) Sir George Jerningham (1680–1774), 5th Bt; mother of Edward Jerningham (1737–1812), the poet and HW's correspondent (B. M. P[lowden], *Records of the Pelham Family*, privately printed, 1887).

18. Not identified, but possibly Lady Elizabeth Berkeley (1750–1828), m. (1767) William, 6th Bn Craven. She had separated from him, after various amours, and in 1783 went abroad to live, eventu-

ally (in 1791) marrying the Margrave of Brandenburg-Ansbach (A. M. Broadley and Lewis Melville, *The Beautiful Lady Craven*, 1914, i. pp. xxiv–xxvii, 47–53 *et passim*).

19. Lord Thurlow, the lord chancellor, who, according to Lady Craven 'had always shown me the greatest partiality' (ibid. i. 48).

20. Alexander Wedderburn (1733–1805), cr. (1780) Bn Loughborough, (1801) E. of Rosslyn; lord chief justice of Common Pleas 1780–93; also mentioned by Lady Craven as one of her advisers (ibid. i. 48–9).

21. The second member of the 'college of doctors of law, exercent in the Ecclesiastical and Admiralty Courts' (as listed in the *Court and City Register*, 1783, p. 107), is Sir James Marriott (?1730–1803), Kt, 1778; M.P.

From Lord Chewton, July 1783

Missing. 'With your letter, I received one from Lord Chewton, to tell me of the birth of his daughter' (HW to Lady Ossory 15 July 1783, Ossory ii. 405).

To the Hon. Thomas Walpole, Wednesday 23 July 1783

Printed from a photostat of the Holland MS; first printed, Sir Spencer Walpole 66–70; reprinted, Toynbee xiii. 23–6. For the history of the MS see *ante* 18 July 1766.

Strawberry Hill, July 23d 1783.

I AM much obliged to you, dear Sir, for your goodness to Madame de la Villebague,[1] of which she herself has told me too; she says she is trying to make interest in the way you recommended to her. I am extremely concerned that it is totally out of my power to return your kindness; nor did I want the addition of gratitude to excite me to serve you or any child of yours. Your son Thomas will have explained to you that it is not even in General Conway's power[2] to replace your son[3] yet, as he would have been happy to do when he knew it would so much oblige me; but the late regulations of the Army have not left it at his disposition. Should I by any unexpected chance be able to be useful to my cousin Thomas, I shall seize it eagerly. He has every quality of head and heart that can endear him to me—but I am so useless and of so little consequence to ministers, that it is not very likely; nor are there many from whom I would ask a favour.

1. Evidently a friend of the Mme de Villegagnon who later became the Hon. Thomas Walpole's second wife; Mme de la Villebague visited SH in 1788 and 1791, and was with Mrs Thomas Walpole and HW in 1790 (Berry i. 96, 176, ii. 230). The suffix 'de la Villebague' was used by the d'Éon family (Henri Jougla de Morenas, *Grand Armorial de France*, 1935, iii. 273).

2. Conway was made commander-in-chief of the Army in March 1782 on the formation of the Rockingham ministry, and held the post until Dec. 1783 (*Last Journals* ii. 431).

3. Thomas Walpole's second son, Lambert Theodore (1757–98), was later Lt-Col. and deputy adjutant-general in Ireland where he was killed in action; 'an officer of distinguished abilities' (GM 1798, lxviii. 540).

Your son and I have been together at Lord Dacre's,[4] where I assure you he is a great favourite. Next week I hope to see him here.

I believe your political prospectus was a very just one; but I now live so much out of the world and in so narrow a circle, that I am entirely ignorant both of what is going on, and of what is to be done. I have, you know, a very high opinion of Mr Fox's abilities,[5] and believe him much more capable than any man of restoring this country to some credit—but I know various reasons,[5a] and you can guess them, why he may not have it in his power. Conjectures on futurity are very idle. For sagacity, I pretend to none, nor much depend on it in those that have most—for this reason: the wisest penetration does not condescend to calculate the thousand foolish reasons that weigh in and determine political events. It may know what ought to be the consequence of such or such measures; but the collateral decisions of chance or absurdity produce such rubs or give a wrong bias, that a foreseer is seldom a true prophet.

It would be still more idle in me, whose life is drawn to the dregs, to busy myself with speculations on future scenes, of which I shall probably have but a glimpse. There is little merit in loving one's country and wishing its prosperity, for it is as natural as to love individuals. But when one totters on the verge of quitting it, the passion is weakened by its extensiveness. One regards the state of one's country always with some reference to self, to one's posterity, one's family or one's friends—when one is to bid it adieu, one wishes one's country may be happy while those connections shall last; and by the preference for what one has loved, one wishes one's country may always be prosperous—but that *always* is so vague and indefinite a desire, the impossibility of any one country always prospering is so certain, that however fervent Father Paul's[6] ejaculation 'Esto perpetua!'[7] might be at the moment of utterance, he would not have

4. Thomas Barrett Lennard (1717–86), 17th Bn Dacre of the South, 1755. His seat was Belhus in Essex.

5. See HW to Conway 15 Aug. 1783.

5a. The chief reason was the King's distrust of Fox, who in May and June of 1783 had supported the Prince of Wales against the King in the Prince's request for an increase of his establishment; see John Brooke, *King George III*, New York, 1972, pp. 241–2, 248–9; *post* 16 Jan. 1784; Mann ix. 406–7, 418.

6. Pietro Sarpi (1552–1623), known as Fra Paolo, the historian of the Council of Trent. HW had his *Histoire du Concile de Trente*, tr. Pierre-François Le Courayer, Amsterdam, 1736, 2 vols (Hazen, *Cat. of HW's Lib.*, No. 933), now wsl.

7. His dying words, 'Ce que l'on interpréta d'une prière qu'il faisait pour la conservation de la République' of Venice (Ossory i. 273).

found that it had much meaning, if he had analysed it. When one wishes what is impossible, there is more piety than sense in the effusion.

Having lived so long and seen so much, I could still with more facility moralize backwards than forwards; but you and I, dear Sir, have so many parallel reasons for making many of the same reflections, that I should only be wording your own thoughts. Besides, I am writing a letter, and not a dissertation—and yet perhaps one who has been a silent spectator of the *whole* change of scene, could suggest many observations that have not been made by the actors, nor by those who have come upon the stage in the middle of the drama, and will still less occur to posterity—but you, though much younger, have seen almost all that has operated our present situation. I say *almost* because I throw the date farther back than most men, and should make some stare who are little aware of what I mean—yet you I believe want no key to my hypothesis.[8]

I do not pretend to send you news. At present I actually know none. Your son is I believe a most punctual correspondent; and as I have the satisfaction of seeing him often, he very seldom but knows whatever I happen to know. Nor will I make professions to you. They would probably be vain as to effects; and of their sincerity in intention, I trust you have no doubt. What then remains but to repeat that I am

Most cordially yours

H. W.

Aug. 7th.

This letter has been written this fortnight, as you will perceive; but I waited for your son to send it to you. He has now been here for two or three days, but leaves me tomorrow, to my concern; I wish I could make such a dull life as mine more entertaining to him: I do think it great condescension when he gives any time to such an antiquated relation.

---

8. HW is presumably referring to his theory of the baleful influence exerted by Bute and the Princess Dowager of Wales upon the King; in fact Bute's influence may have declined after 1762, when he had supported Henry Fox as leader of the House of Commons (Brooke, op. cit. 95; *Last Journals* ii. 526–7).

From the HON. THOMAS WALPOLE, ca Monday
29 December 1783

Missing; answered *post* 3 Jan. 1784.

To the HON. THOMAS WALPOLE, Saturday
3 January 1784

Printed from a photostat of the Holland MS; first printed, Sir Spencer Walpole 70–5; reprinted, Toynbee xiii. 110–12. For the history of the MS see *ante* 18 July 1766.

Berkeley Square, Jan. 3d 1784.

I HAVE received your letter,[1] dear Sir, and the four *Bibliothèques,* which, since I have so many, I wish to continue, though so many are most indifferent; and I will pay your son. I am very happy to have contributed in any degree to his establishment;[1a] and I may agree with you in rejoicing that he will be removed from the disagreeable scenes here. This last revolution[2] was the wildest and most indigested scheme possible; for though long premeditated by, I believe, the *sole author,*[3] no preparatory measures had been taken, nor scarce anybody consulted till very few days before the execution; the definitive resolution having been taken probably from the very *local* unpopularity of the India bill[4] with the persons interested here in town, and here only. The consequence is, that rebuffed in all decent offers, so contemptible and ridiculous a set have been picked up, that they would be laughed out again, had they any real strength— but you will see by the list[5] how very slender a portion of abilities

1. Of ca Monday 29 Dec. 1783, missing.
1a. See *post* 16 Jan. 1784, n. 5.
2. George III had dissolved the North-Fox coalition ministry, after the House of Lords defeated Fox's East India Bill.
3. George III, who exerted his influence to get the Lords to reject the bill (MANN ix. 458–9, n. 1).
4. Fox's bill (probably planned by Burke) provided for a commission of seven members to be nominated in the Act for terms of at least four years, to sit in England with power over the gov-

ernor and council in India. Assistant commissioners were to manage the East India Company's commerce. The King and his faction feared the patronage this would give the Whigs, even when the latter were no longer in power; others opposed the bill as a violation of the East India Company's charter (L. S. Sutherland, *The East India Company in Eighteenth-Century Politics,* Oxford, 1952, pp. 395–405).
5. William Pitt, not yet twenty-five, was made first lord of the Treasury and

lies amongst them. Do but think of the two ambassadors![6] nor have they acquired one convert, nor made even an inconsiderable breach yet in the House of Commons. In short, this system can only last ten days more—What will happen next, I do not pretend to guess— perhaps, what the person guessed who was asked about a certain road—[6a]

Such are the present consequences of that absurd rogue Lord Sh[elburne]'s finesses![7] They soon blew up himself—no great harm —but he drew others after him, who are more to be lamented, and who will get into almost inextricable difficulties. Lord T[emple][8] one of his dupes, and not much more estimable, has already made a preposterous figure—and all their manœuvres together have com- pacted a body together that possesses almost all the abilities of this country—and you may guess what will be the success of rashness founded on weakness!

I should write a history not a letter, were I to repeat half the extravagancies of the last three weeks—some indeed are too strong to be trusted to paper! It is my opinion that the accomplices, or acces- sories, will be frightened and desert—I know that they who used to move the occasional puppets, *are* alarmed.

I am glad of the Duchess of Choiseul's recovery. In my own par- ticular indeed I have no great reason to interest myself about her, or the Abbé Bartélemi, for though out of civility to you, dear Sir, he may inquire after me, I have little opinion of his or the Duchess's

chancellor of the Exchequer; Earl Gower became lord president of the Council; the Duke of Rutland took over the privy seal; the Marquess of Carmarthen and Lord Sydney became the secretaries of state; Lord Thurlow, lord chancellor; Lord Howe was made first lord of the Ad- miralty; Dundas became treasurer of the Navy; the Duke of Richmond, master- general of the Ordnance (MANN ix. 460 and n. 5).

6. John Frederick Sackville (1745–99), 3d D. of Dorset, was ambassador to Paris 1783–9; and Philip Stanhope (1755–1815), 5th E. of Chesterfield, ambassador to Spain 1784–7. Neither man was well quali- fied for his position. In the case of Lord Chesterfield, the appointment was nom- inal since he never went to Madrid. Dor- set, however, went to Paris, where 'under his roof fiddlers and buffoons, w—res

and parasites, sharpers and knaves were always welcome . . . Billiards and hazard engrossed almost the whole time of our A-b-r, unless when he relaxed from the fatigues of gaming in the arms of beauty' (quoted from *The Jockey Club*, 1792, in GEC, iv. 428).

6a. This anecdote has not been found.

7. HW had an extremely low opinion of Lord Shelburne, primarily because he had succeeded in dividing Rockingham's Whig ministry, and, on the death of Rock- ingham, formed a ministry subservient to George III. Shelburne's policies had re- sulted in the North-Fox coalition (*Last Journals* ii. 443, 520–22).

8. Temple, who had acted as the King's agent on the East India Bill, was made secretary of state. He resigned the ap- pointment a few days later (22 Dec.).

regard for me. Though they both *seized* their letters before I could have any notice, yet as I had ordered them to be restored, without being acquainted with that proceeding, they at least owed me, either an excuse, or thanks—I never received a word from either. In the Abbé, it was impertinence—a great lady cannot be in the wrong, though she had professed so much friendship for me, and still more for my late dear friend. Indeed the treatment I received from all concerned in her papers, has given me no high opinion of French honour or French friendship! I should blush if my conduct had not been the very reverse—and had they any delicacy, it would have taught them how to act.

Mr White[9] who brings you this is a bookseller with whom your son is well acquainted, as I believe you are too. He goes to purchase books at the Duc de la Valière's sale.[10] I have given him some commissions at a very high rate, and yet do not expect, indeed almost hope not, to obtain the articles, especially as I have never seen them and may be much disappointed when I do. But as the occasion is unique, and as I should be vexed not to have bought them, should the articles I wish for go cheap, I have run the risk; though contrary to my late rule, for I reckon everything much dearer now, as I have so little time left to enjoy what I purchase. I will be obliged to you if you could give Mr White any assistance in my commission. The Duke of Bedford's book[11] I do not expect to get. The one[12] I wish for most you will know by the largeness of my commission. I have long thought of writing a life of René of Anjou,[13] father of our Margaret[14] (though I probably shall not now) and as he was a royal painter as

9. Joseph White (d. 1791), bookseller in Serle St, Lincoln's Inn Fields (GM 1791, lxi pt ii. 1161); probably the Mr White in whose care the letter of *ante* 6 Sept. 1782 was sent.

10. Louis-César de la Baume le Blanc (1708–80), Duc de la Vallière (DU DEFFAND ii. 472, n. 18); the sale of his books and MSS took place 12 Jan. to 5 May 1784. HW had the *Catalogue des livres de la bibliothèque de feu M. le duc de la Vallière*, compiled by Guillaume de Bure, 1783 (Hazen, *Cat. of HW's Lib.*, No. 3335). The Duc de la Vallière's paintings had been sold in 1781 (Frits Lugt, *Répertoire des catalogues de ventes*, The Hague, 1938–64, i. No. 3221).

11. The 'Sarum Breviary,' a 15th-century illuminated MS executed for John,

D. of Bedford, and sold as lot 273 for 5000 livres to Louis XVI (White to HW 11 March 1784). It is now in the Bibliothèque Nationale.

12. The 'Anjou Hours,' an illuminated 15th-century book of hours executed for René d'Anjou. It was sold as lot 285 to Louis XVI for 1200 livres and is also in the Bibliothèque Nationale (ibid.).

13. René d'Anjou (1409–80), Duc d'Anjou, 1435; K. of Sicily 1435–42. HW on 1 Feb. 1779 wrote a sketch of him (MORE 438–9, Appendix 10; see also ibid. 143, n. 6). HW's continuing interest in René is shown by two notes in his unpublished 'Miscellany, 1786,' now WSL, pp. 4 and 40.

14. Margaret of Anjou (1429–82), m. (1445) Henry VI of England.

well as royal author, I am doubly interested about him—though I have very few *royal* passions!—and they do not increase!

I forgot to tell you that I do not believe the Parliament will be dissolved[15]—not from scruples about promises—but as it would produce infinite mischiefs at present, and probably not mend the matter by a re-election: and if it did not, the recoil would be tremendous! In short I hope and believe that this interlude will prove to have been only a very silly one. Adieu!

Yours most cordially

H. W.

To the Hon. Thomas Walpole, Tuesday 6 January 1784

Printed for the first time from a photostat of the Holland MS; for the history of the MSS see *ante* 18 July 1766.

Address: À Monsieur Monsieur Thomas Walpole, rue basse du Rempart à Paris.

Postmark: ANGLETERRE.

Berkeley Square, Jan. 6, 1784.

Dear Sir,

SINCE I wrote to you last, I have changed my mind, for reasons that I have not time to tell you now,[1] about purchasing some MSS at the Duc de la Valière's sale; and therefore I entreat you to tell Mr White the bookseller that I beg he will not bid for any one of those for which I gave him commissions. If you do not know where he lodges, I beseech you to employ somebody to find him out at the sale as soon as ever it begins, and forbid his buying anything for me. Excuse my haste, I am going to dine and pass the whole day at Princess Amelie's[2] and have barely time to scribble these few lines.

Yours ever

H. Walpole

---

15. It was dissolved 25 March 1784 (Namier and Brooke i. 536).

1. His reasons were financial; see *post* 1 Feb. 1784.

2. Amelia Sophia Eleanora (1711–86), daughter of George II. Her house was in Cavendish Square, at the corner of Harley Street (Ossory ii. 535, n. 20).

To the DUKE OF GLOUCESTER, ca Monday
12 January 1784

Missing; answered *post* 4 Feb. 1784.

From the HON. THOMAS WALPOLE, Friday
16 January 1784

Printed for the first time from the MS now WSL. For the history of the MS see
ante 15 May 1745 OS.

Paris, 16 January 1784.

My dear Sir,

I TAKE the first opportunity that offers of writing you a few
lines by a person who is going to England[1] to thank you for your
letter of the 3d by White the bookseller, and acquaint you that
your letter by the post arrived time enough to prevent his buying
any books for you at the Duc de la Valière's sale, although I am sorry
you seem to have given over the agreeable employment you had
proposed to yourself of writing a history of René d'Anjou, for such
an occupation is become almost a necessary relief to a thinking man
amidst the endless disquietudes which lawless *ambition* has given
rise to or rather lack of power and influence for the other is a word of
a much more noble signification to be applied to those who have
now defeated all possibility of regular and systematic government.
I am much concerned for one[2] I love and esteem having taken a part
which his professional knowledge and the facility with which he re-
signs himself to those who are much about him prevented his considering upon a more large view, he writes me a long letter which
makes me regret much my absence. I think I could have tempered his
imagination, since the lively and forcible manner in which he repre-

1. Monsieur de Germany (see below).
2. 'Lord Camden' added by HW. Camden opposed Fox's East India Bill on the
ground that the patronage given to the
Whigs would be dangerous to the nation;
he wrote his son-in-law 19 Dec. 1783, 'Mr
Fox . . . formed a plan . . . to get possession of the East India patronage by

vesting it in seven of his own friends, by
which means the Parliamentary influence
of a private man would have been almost
equal to the great power of the prerogative' (quoted in Namier and Brooke ii.
460). He also felt that the bill was
dangerous because it violated the Company's charter.

sents to me the reasons for what has happened do not convince me nor satisfy me that he has not too uneasily helped to undo that which never will be done again, and the pains he takes make me see he doubts—as for the East India Company and their charter—it is a rotten company supported by a broken charter, and with regard to the refined reasoning of the influence of the minister[3] overbearing that of the Crown and the public it is quite unintelligible to me. I see nothing but that the ———[4] being convinced that a sessions of Parliament conducted by the ablest in the country would establish their administration whose person he most disliked beyond the power of his private cabal and therefore the first opportunity was to be taken at all hazards to obstruct their progress and success. The blow is struck and notwithstanding the apparent folly of it as you will describe, I am very apprehensive that the unfortunate state of the nation will raise in short time a clamour against the present Opposition amongst the moneyed interest which may give apparent popular grounds for dissolving the Parliament—if the ministers should take sufficient courage from such a circumstance to adhere to the [King]. At all events, my dear Sir, the peace of individuals is destroyed for ever and every means of recovering the credit and dignity of the nation totally annihilated. Under these considerations I should not think myself very unhappy at being here if I had a moderate and secure means of subsisting and I must be very glad that my most excellent son has got a provision[5] which I trust his abilities and diligence will make permanent.[6] You may well imagine that the ministers here rejoice in your weakness and folly. They may perhaps overrate them, and yet that is but a forlorn hope, for they

3. Lord North warned Fox in a letter of ca 21 Nov. 1783, 'Influence of the Crown and influence of Party against Crown and People are two of the many topics which will be argued against your plan. The latter of the two objections will not be sounded so high and loudly in the House of Commons but it may be one of the most fatal objections to your measure. It certainly ought to be obviated as much as possible' (BM Add. MS 47561, f. 23, quoted by L. G. Mitchell, *Charles James Fox and the Disintegration of the Whig Party 1782–1794*, 1971, p. 68).

4. 'King' added by HW. George III's hatred of Fox and interference in the vote on the East India Bill in the House of Lords led to the downfall of the coalition (John Brooke, *King George III*, New York, 1972, pp. 250–4).

5. As minister plenipotentiary to the Elector Palatine, and minister to the Imperial Diet at Ratisbon; his credentials were dated 31 Jan. (D.B. Horn, *British Diplomatic Representatives 1689–1789*, 1932, pp. 43, 62–3).

6. He was made envoy extraordinary and plenipotentiary to the Elector Palatine in 1788, remaining until 1796 (ibid. 62–3).

have, I verily believe, taken possession of the Morea and Candia[7] and are assembling a large combined fleet of their own, Dutch and Spanish ships in those parts which may, however, draw upon them the Emperor's resentment. In the meanwhile they are also intriguing and quarrelling here about the arrangements of office and promotions. The Comtesse d'Artois[8] has had the misfortune to have had intrigue with a friend of her femme-de-chambre which by awkward management has been made too public. The gentleman has been sent to prison, the R.H. did not appear at Court for some time, but she is returned again they say with a five months' burden. At her first interview with the King and her husband on this subject she told them boldly it was the latter's fault, who had twice used her *ill* and then abandoned, and nature would have its dues.

I shall endeavour to prevail on Monsieur de Germany[9] who takes this letter to charge himself with four *romans*. If you want any other books and will give me your limits I may probably be able to pick them up reasonably as I have a very honest little fellow who is my runner on those occasions and I shall be happy to do you any service particularly in a way that may contribute to your amusement, for I am with the sincerest affection and attachment

Most entirely yours

Thomas Walpole

To the Hon. Thomas Walpole, Sunday 1 February 1784

Printed from a photostat of the Holland MS; previously printed, Sir Spencer Walpole 75–82; reprinted, Toynbee xiii. 118–21. For the history of the MS see *ante* 18 July 1766.

Memorandum (in an unidentified hand): The latter part refers entirely to the King—*vide* Junius.

Berkeley Square, Feb. 1st 1784.

I AM much obliged to you, dear sir, for two parcels of *Bibliothèques,* and for your very sensible and judicious letter of Jan. 16 which came in one of them. Your reasoning on poor Lord C[am-

7. The Peleponnesus and Crete. French seizure of them was only rumour.

8. Marie-Thérèse (1756–1805) of Savoy,

m. (1773) Charles-Philippe, Comte d'Artois, later (1824–30) Charles X.

9. Not identified.

den] and on our situation, is perfectly just. The former has certainly
been swayed against his own opinion by his son,[1] and has betrayed a
want of firmness, which I have more than once perceived in his
character. If charters can authorize the most shocking inhumanities
that ever were exercised, not excepting those in Peru and Mexico;
so far from being sacred, they would be the most execrable instru-
ments imaginable—and Lord C. would be better founded in main-
taining the charter of the Inquisition, which has to this day scarce
murdered so many thousands, as were swept away at once by the
monopoly of rice and betel in India. Mr Burke's speech[2] on Mr
Fox's bill, which he has published, and which makes no impression
here, touches on many other of our dreadful excesses, and will no
doubt make us the horror of Europe, as we are of the Eastern world.
Mr Fox felt and had genius enough to have put a stop to and cor-
rected those crying grievances—and consequently has been rendered
odious by the interested villains of the Company and by the tools of
Mr Hastings;[3] and is proscribed, literally and personally, by the
father of his people,[4] who became popular the moment he had *out-
done his former outdoings*[5]—but France is going to, as you say, and
no doubt, will, punish our abominations—nay, I shall not be surprised, if the present inundation of zeal should ensure punishment
to this country itself and its posterity, and should think the sacrifice
of our liberties not too great a compliment in return for the dismission of the coalition! The Church, the old women, and the country
gentlemen (who as I have often heard you say justly, would like
despotism, provided they could be assured of a low land tax, a good
price for corn, and the Game Act)[6] are all running headlong to support good King Charles the First,[7] and the immaculate Master Billy[8]
has already taken a giant's step toward imitation of Lord Strafford;[9]

1. John Jeffreys Pratt (1759–1840), 2d E.
Camden, 1794; cr. (1812) M. Camden; M.P.
Bath 1780–94; lord of the Admiralty in
Shelburne's ministry (July 1782 – April
1783) and again under Pitt (Dec. 1783 –
Aug. 1789).

2. *Mr Burke's speech, on the 1st December 1783 . . . on Mr Fox's East India
Bill,* 1784. HW's copy, with markings
and an identification, is now WSL (Hazen,
Cat. of HW's Lib., No. 1609:46:9).

3. Warren Hastings (1732–1818), gov-
ernor-general of India 1773–85.

4. George III.

5. Cibber's remark about Mrs Oldfield
(MANN vi. 46, n. 2).

6. 'An act for better preservation of . . .
game' (10 Geo. III c. 19) was superseded
by a more severe act of 13 Geo. III c. 80,
imposing penalties for poaching etc.
(Owen Ruffhead, *Statutes at Large,* 1763–
1800, x. 669, xi. 882).

7. George III.

8. William Pitt.

9. Thomas Wentworth (1593–1641), cr.
(1640) E. of Strafford; upholder of Charles
I's prerogative; executed by the Commons
for treason.

yet finding that the torrent of words which he inherited, cannot combat Mr Fox's invincible powers of reasoning, and that equivocation was still less a match for them, he has prudently adopted an arrogant sullenness, and literally finds that contemptuous silence will govern the House of Commons better than paying court to them. Indeed he does not omit more solid methods. *Three* Scotch Dukes were yesterday made peers of England,[10] to purchase only *four* votes for tomorrow! You will say, 'a very dear bargain indeed!'—and will perhaps conclude that there is a little want of specie, when paper and parchment are substituted at such high rates—it may be so—but at least it shows how large the object is, and how desperate the resolution of not being foiled!

It is true that on the other hand there is all the good sense of both Houses of Parliament. Excepting the Chancellor,[11] Lord Gower, Dundas,[12] Pepper Arden,[13] the Duke of Richmond, and the premature boy's[14] parts, such as they are, nothing is so despicable as all the rest of the administration, of which you have a sample before your eyes. Nay, in those I have quoted, I do not believe you will discover much of solid abilities. There is not the least knowledge of the world in any but the second—and he knows nothing else. Nor has he or the Chancellor, any true courage—the latter, a real bully. The Duke has just that sort of spirit that involves him in scrapes with more facility than it extricates him. On his being enrolled of the Cabinet a few days ago, G. Selwyn, though of the same side, said, 'Why, it is turning a monkey into a china shop to break everything to pieces!'

Upon the whole, the best that I expect is, that there will be a strong manly Opposition remaining (if they are beaten tomorrow, as I apprehend—or as I conclude they will be soon) who will be able to prevent some mischief, and may, as happened at last in the American War, force (in concert with the blunders and misfortunes that will be committed) the nation to open its unwilling eyes—but that time I probably shall not live to see—nor will it avail when it comes—We

10. In July the Duke of Gordon, a Scottish duke, was made an English peer, but the creations in January were not of those who had been peers in Scotland. The Duke of Northumberland was made Bn Lovaine in the English peerage; Henry Thynne (afterwards Carteret) was made Bn Carteret; and Edward Eliot (later Craggs-Eliot) was made Bn Eliot (GM 1784, liv pt i. 154, *sub* 31 Jan.).

11. Edward Thurlow (*ante* 13 March 1783).

12. Henry Dundas (1742–1811), cr. (1802) Vct Melville; treasurer of the Navy; M.P.

13. Richard Pepper Arden (1744–1804), cr. (1801) Bn Alvanley; attorney-general; M.P.

14. Pitt.

shall be undone before that moment arrives! Mr Fox, the only man upon earth who could have restored us to any tolerable state, and who has displayed as consummate temper as genius, is not allowed to save us while the opportunity was within our reach!

I admire the rational defence of Madame d'A[rtois] and I admire too its being admitted. I wish they were as equitable to the poor lover, who is punished *for* consenting, as, considering the lady, he was *by* consenting.

You are very obliging in offering to execute commissions for me; but, excepting the *Bibliothèques* and the *Voyage de Grèce,* I will not trouble you. I must be more economic now than formerly: I have lost £1400 a year by my brother's death,[15] the foresight of which made me recall my commissions at the Duc de la Valière's sale. My place in the Exchequer is much sunk too by our reforms and the peace—and what worse may happen, who can tell? All I do know is, that having kept myself (without ambitious views) as incorrupt as the *Immaculate* Idol[16] of the moment, I will not disgrace the small remains of life—I do not mean that a high price would be offered for so insignificant man as I am—but when such a dumb beggar as Mr Carteret,[17] and such a poltroon as his brother Weymouth[18] are thought worth a second peerage, who needs despair that wished to sell himself? I do feel your situation sensibly—and it is one of the few points which would make me desire what I never shall have, power, that I might be useful to you and your family. In fact, I question whether any man will long have opportunities of serving anybody—No—the French do not overrate our folly; it is *au comble!* it is as great as they could wish! and Mr Pitt's ambition lending itself to the [King]'s views, will revenge France for the mortifications she received from his father, Chatham.

3d.

The three Scotch Baronies are now denied; yet I don't quite disbelieve at least two of them. Mr Fox last night recovered a majority of nineteen, and has by his temper and address gained several of

15. Sir Edward Walpole d. 12 Jan. 1784. HW had been receiving an income from the patent place of Collector of Customs, given by George I to Sir Robert Walpole, passing to Sir Edward, and expiring on his death. From the place HW had received £1000 a year, plus a surplus of £800 which he divided with Sir Edward (MANN x. 52–4, Appendix 16).

16. Presumably Pitt.

17. Hon. Henry Frederick Thynne (1735–1826), cr. (1784) Bn Carteret; M.P.

18. Thomas Thynne, 3d Vct Weymouth (*ante* 10 Aug. 1777, n. 12).

the country gentlemen from Mr Pitt—yet we are far from any settlement; but expect farther obstinacy from *the Park,*[19] and hostile counter-resolutions from the Lords. Your son, whom I expect every minute, as he talked of setting out tomorrow, must explain details, for which I have not time. Adieu! dear Sir—you may guess more easily than I can describe our situation—even private life is grown unpleasant from the violent divisions sown in families, friendships, connections—in *that* art we have an able master!

From the Duke of Gloucester, Wednesday 4 February 1784

Printed for the first time from the MS now WSL. For the history of the MS see *ante* 15 May 1745 OS.

Address: Honourable Horace Walpole Berkley Square London Angleterre.
Postmark: FE 20 NICE.

Nice, February 4th 1784.

Sir,

SATURDAY'S post brought me your letter[1] with the melancholy account of Sir Edward Walpole['s] death;[2] which I acquainted the Duchess with as tenderly as possible. Though her great attachment to Sir Edward made her feel most deeply this event, yet I found her more prepared, and resigned than I expected.[3] I took it very kind of you Sir, that you took this manner of informing the Duchess.

Yours

William Henry

19. St James's Park, i.e. the King.

1. Missing.
2. See *ante* 1 Feb. 1784, n. 15; Mann ix. 462–3, 466.
3. Before she received the news of Sir Edward's death, the Duchess wrote Anne Clement 26 Jan. 1784, 'I see but too plainly that I shall never see my father again; it is not probable that at his age and without proper care, he should recover from a decline' (MS now WSL).

To LADY CHARLOTTE MARIA WALDEGRAVE, ?Monday 21 June 1784

Missing. 'Mr W. gave to my charge a letter for his niece, Lady Maria Walde-grave, which I was to send to Gloucester House' (*Mary Hamilton*, ed. E. and F. Anson, 1925, p. 210, *sub* 21 June 1784).

From LADY CHEWTON, ca Saturday 3 July 1784

Printed for the first time from a photostat of the MS in the possession of Lord Waldegrave.

Probably written after 28 June 1784, when Laura Keppel and George Ferdinand Fitzroy were married at her mother's house in Pall Mall.

Address: The Honourable Horace Walpole Strawberry Hill near Twickenham.

Saturday morn.

My dearest Sir,

LORD Waldegrave has just called in Berkeley Square to inform you that through Lord Cornwallis's most friendly interposition Lord and Lady Southampton[1] are to receive Mr and Mrs Fitzroy this evening—Lord Cornwallis has been out of town but came up on purpose to see what he had so kindly undertaken[2] brought to a conclusion, and he is to accompany them to Stanhope Street[3] this evening.—We are just going to Navestock,[4] therefore I have only time to assure you that I am most affectionately your

dutiful niece

E. LAURA WALDEGRAVE

1. Lord Southampton (*ante* 6 Sept. 1780, n. 12) m. (1758) Anne Warren (d. 1807).
2. The account of the elopement with George Ferdinand Fitzroy (1761–1810), later (1797) 2d Bn Southampton is in HW to Mann 8 July 1784 (MANN ix. 508). Cornwallis had undertaken to effect a reconciliation between Fitzroy and his parents. The Prince of Wales had earlier effected a reconciliation with Mrs Keppel: 'His Royal Highness on his return to Carlton House dispatched an express to the fugitives, and on their arrival in town accompanied them to Mrs Keppel's, where they were married' (*London Chronicle* 1–3 July, lvi. 12).
3. Residence of the Southamptons; the first Baron died there in 1797.
4. The residence of the Waldegraves. Upon the death of his father 22 Oct. 1784 the 4th Lord Waldegrave moved his family there.

From LORD ORFORD, ca July 1784

Missing. 'My nephew, from whom I have (to *my* great surprise) received a letter of thanks; but saying that Cav. Mozzi must be satisfied, as many points had been given up' (HW to Mann 9 Aug. 1784, MANN ix. 516).

To LORD ORFORD, ca August 1784

Missing. 'I replied "that I had done but my duty in undertaking the arbitration, to prevent a very disagreeable discussion in a public court—(on *that* head you will not lay much stress to Mozzi) that I confessed I had favoured Mozzi to the utmost of my power as far as I thought I might, that *he,* a stranger, and not acquainted with even his own lawyer or referee, might not think himself betrayed: and that I had done it the rather lest he should suspect me of partiality too. That for thanks, his Lordship owed me none, as I owned, that if Mr Duane had not given his opinion so much in favour of his Lordship, I should have been inclined to have allowed him less; and consequently I could not agree that any rights had been ceded on that side"' (HW to Mann 9 Aug. 1784, MANN ix. 516).

To and from the DUCHESS OF GLOUCESTER, ca September 1784

At least two letters are missing to her and one from her. 'The Duchess of Gloucester in her last to me told me that my letters contain nothing but excuses for having nothing to say' (HW to Mann 30 Sept. 1784, MANN ix. 527). 'The Duchess of Gloucester tells me that my letters are composed of nothing but excuses for having nothing to tell her' (*post* 2 Dec. 1784).

From LADY WALDEGRAVE, Tuesday 16 November 1784

Missing; mentioned by HW to Lady Ossory 17 Nov. 1784: 'A letter from Lady Waldegrave this morning acquainted me that the marriage [of Lady Charlotte Maria Waldegrave to Lord Euston] was solemnized yesterday' (OSSORY ii. 452).

From Thomas Walpole the Younger,
late November 1784

Missing; implied *post* 2 Dec. 1784.

To Thomas Walpole the Younger, Thursday
2 December 1784

Printed from a photostat of the Holland MS; first printed, Sir Spencer Walpole 82–6; reprinted, Toynbee xiii. 222–4. For the history of the MS see *ante* 18 July 1766.

Address: À Monsieur Monsieur Thomas Walpole Ministre Plénipotentiaire de sa Majesté Britannique à Munich p[ar] Ostende.

Strawberry Hill, Dec. 2, 1784.

I WAS a little surprised, I confess, dear Sir, at not hearing a word from you since your arrival[1] in Germany,[2] not even to tell me how you liked your situation. I was more surprised when your cousin[3] told me you did not know whether you *might* write to me. That sounded a strange expression to so near a relation, to one who flattered himself that he had always shown the warmest disposition to be your friend, to one with whom you had corresponded familiarly, and to one who is a most insignificant old man, and who can have no pretensions to respect, unless from the trist precedence of great age. I am no Aulic counsellor, and have not a quarter in my coat of arms more than you—but there is an end of etiquette: my answer to your cousin showed my perfect good humour: we will never say a word more on the subject, but write as we used to do, when we have anything to say.

That condition indeed seems to admit of difficulties. I have been here these six months in utter ignorance, living in a small neighbourhood composed chiefly of gossiping old women, to whom I do not listen, and seeing neither politicians nor fashionable people, so I neither know what passes in the grave world or in the gay one. The

---

1. 19 April 1784 (D.B. Horn, *British Diplomatic Representatives 1689–1789*, 1932, pp. 62–3).
2. As minister to the Imperial Diet and the Elector Palatine (*ante* 16 Jan. 1784, n. 5).
3. Not identified.

Duchess of Gloucester tells me that my letters are composed of nothing but excuses for having nothing to tell her. She and you should recollect that sixty-seven is no very amusing age.

I am sorry that your time at a very different period is not better diverted. Not being very diplomatic, I am ashamed I know nothing of your Elector[4] but the good you tell me of him—but I will consult Lady Mary Coke who is better acquainted than the Heralds' Office with Europe *vivante et mourante*. I should think you might ask leave to make little jaunts to different courts—you are not likely, I trust, to be employed in hiring mercenaries—at least you have an auctioneer[5] in the neighbourhood, who, though bidding less, may leave you no business of that sort. As one at least of his aquiline beaks is always prowling for prey, our coffee-houses are in expectation of hearing he has begun his breakfast. Lord George Gordon would fain go fowling against him—but as his Lordship's sole skill lies in raising a conflagration, I imagine an inundation[6] will be more serviceable.

If you make any tours, your pencil will add to your pleasure. If you would send me a slight drawing of your Elector, I should be glad. Keep a journal of all you hear and see, I speak very disinterestedly, God knows—but if you live, as I hope you will, to my age, it will be a kind of recall of youth, and bring back a thousand passages you would else forget, but be glad to remember. Your brother's[6a] company, which I am glad you have, though sorry he has leisure to give it, would make little jaunts doubly agreeable.

Pray don't give yourself any particular trouble about the amber box.[7] Though in my second childhood, I am no longer very eager about toys, with which I have little time left to play. I am in no haste, and whenever the box comes, I shall be equally obliged to you.

This letter would have set out sooner, but you are in one respect so little yet of a minister in a German Court, that you had omitted all dates of place and time, and I was forced to write to your cousin for a direction. Or perhaps though being so old-fashioned myself, our Maccaronic omission of all useless usages may have penetrated into

4. Karl Theodor (1724–99), Count Palatine of Sulzbach, 1733; Elector Palatine, 1742; Elector of Bavaria, 1777.

5. Joseph II had raised an army of 60,000 to march against Holland in an attempt to open the Scheldt and give himself access to the East and West Indies (Mann ix. 541, n. 6; 545, n. 22).

6. The Dutch met the attack by breaking down the dikes around the fort of Lillo which the Austrians had threatened (ibid. ix. 543, n. 8).

6a. Lambert Theodore, who had requested a place in the army from Conway; see *ante* 23 July 1783, n. 3.

7. Not identified.

the Holy Roman Empire. I dare not send my compliments to your brother, lest it should look formal to remember anybody—and this shall be the last time I will make a ceremonious conclusion to my letter, if Ratisbon[8] has adopted the contrary practice. Till you tell me so, I will beg leave to be, dear Sir,

Yours most affectionately

HOR. WALPOLE

From THOMAS WALPOLE THE YOUNGER, January 1785

Two letters, missing; referred to, *post* 19 Feb. 1785.

To LADY WALDEGRAVE, ca Tuesday 1 February 1785

Missing; answered *post* 7 Feb. 1785.

From LADY WALDEGRAVE, Monday 7 February 1785

Printed for the first time from a photostat of the MS in the possession of Lord Waldegrave.
Address: The Honourable Horace Walpole Berkeley Square London.
Postmark: 8 FE 19 BRENTWOOD.
Memoranda: 1.10
                  14
                ─────

Navestock, Feb. 7, 1785.

My dearest Sir,

I FOUND my two little babes[1] in perfect health and Maria much advanced in conversation when I returned here on Monday. The number of complaints that she has to make of her brother is astonish-

---

8. Seat of the court of the Imperial Diet. Thomas Walpole did not go there until 1789, residing chiefly in Munich (Horn, op. cit. 43).

1. George Waldegrave (1784–94), styled Vct Chewton 1784–9; 5th E. Waldegrave, 1789; and Lady Maria Wilhelmina Waldegrave (1783–1805), m. (1804) Nathaniel Micklethwait (OSSORY ii. 405, n. 5; 416).

ing and I cannot help acknowledging he gives too much reason for them, snatching her cap off, taking her doll from her are the smallest provocations she receives, and I fear there is not much chance of amendment as he looks at her with a stern steady countenance when she flies for redress to Lord Waldegrave or myself, and is perfectly unmoved when she urges with vehemence 'Cap, cap,' or 'Doll, doll,' which are the only arguments she can make use of—

I am much obliged to you for your inquiries after Lord Waldegrave who only suffered just at the time he returned from the supper and has been very well ever since—We rejoice very much at your being so well; the badness of the weather will prevent your going out some time, but the warmer you keep yourself at present must be best for you—I do not pretend to the gift of prophecy like Mrs Keppel,[2] but feel great satisfaction in not having been mistaken in the opinion that I formed from the instant I saw you that your gout was more upon your spirits than elsewhere, and that you would do well.

Adieu, my dear Sir

Your affectionate and dutiful

E. LAURA WALDEGRAVE

2. 'I have expected this bad news [the serious illness of the D. of Gloucester], for t'other night I dreamed I saw his funeral, and the night before last, I dreamed Mr Walpole told me H.R.H. had broke a tubercle upon his lungs and was suffocated' (Laura Keppel to Jane Clement 9 Sept. 1777). 'By my dreams and my eyes itching, I'm sure there will be a pretty piece of work about it' (Laura Keppel to Jane Clement ca 18 Feb. 1776, MSS now wsl).

To Thomas Walpole the Younger, Saturday 19 February 1785

Printed from a photostat of the Holland MS; first printed, Sir Spencer Walpole 86–90; reprinted, Toynbee xiii. 249–51. For the history of the MS see *ante* 18 July 1766.

Address: À Monsieur Monsieur Thomas Walpole Ministre Plénipotentiaire de sa Majesté Britannique à Munich.

Berkeley Square, Feb. 19, 1785.

Dear Sir,

I HAVE been so very ill[1] for near three months, that I could neither answer your former letter, nor that which I had the pleasure of receiving by your brother;[2] as I begged him to tell you. I have yet but one hand quite free, which will prevent my saying much, as I write uneasily. I give you many thanks for the drawing;[3] it is an amiable countenance.

Were I to talk of what is uppermost in my thoughts, it would be of the severity of the weather, which checks my recovery: I call it *the year of forty winters.* The snow first appeared on the first of October, a circumstance that in my long life I never knew before. Every day almost since has been remarkable for two or three changes, all bad, but I do not imagine that you want a diary of the weather. Topics there are enough at last of various sorts, but rather subjects of discussion than events, and consequently not easily detailed, were I able. The chief themes are India,[4] Ireland[5] and the Westminster Scrutiny.[6] I understand nothing of the two former, and elections

1. With the gout. HW wrote Mann 5 March 1785, 'I am still a prisoner and have been so above three entire months, the longest fit I ever had, but one' (MANN ix. 561).

2. Both letters are missing.

3. Of Karl Theodor, Elector Palatine (see *ante* 2 Dec. 1784).

4. Continuing debate on the East India Company (see *ante* 1 Feb. 1784; HW to Mann 5 March 1785, MANN ix. 566).

5. Propositions for equal trade with Ireland (ibid. ix. 564–5).

6. On Rodney's elevation to the peerage, Sir Cecil Wray (1734–1805), through Fox's influence, was nominated to fill the vacancy in the representation of Westminster, and held the seat from 12 June 1782 to 1784. Wray denounced the Fox-North coalition and opposed Fox's East India bill. In 1784 he stood for Westminster with Tory support, in the hope of ousting Fox from the representation. When he came in third (after Hood and Fox) he demanded a scrutiny and was granted it by the high bailiff, a tool of the Tories. It was abandoned 3 March when Hood was declared to have received 6,588, Fox 6,126 and Wray 5,895 votes (ibid. ix. 565 and n. 16; Namier and Brooke i. 337, iii. 664).

I never in my life would attend to, having no notion of loading my head with what I should certainly mean to forget the moment the business was over.

The gay world has its affairs too as well as the grave: but I have still less to do if possible with what the young are doing, than with settling what is to be when I shall be gone! I will only tell you what I cannot avoid hearing, that the Prince of Wales had given to him and gave five balls running last week; and it was well said, that there was to be a sixth, or *Tontine,* to consist of those that should survive from the five preceding.

Poor Lady Strafford[7] is dead after nine weeks of dreadful sufferings from falling into the fire in a fit; and the old Lady Gower is probably dead by this time by a similar accident, that is, by setting her gown in flames.[8]

Lord Graham's intended match with Lady Jemima Ashburnham[9] is declared. It makes my poor old friends the Duke and Duchess of Montrose[10] very happy.

Your brother will probably pick up more news for you. The Duc de Chartres[11] is again here, which may furnish some, which I am not likely to know, but told with twenty lies by the newspapers.

Two days ago there was a report that your Emperor was besieging Maestricht,[12] but it is not believed—We had just been believing that he was exchanging countries,[13] and like ancient Cæsars, conferring new crowns.

I must now rest; I am forced to begin my letter *d'avance,* as I cannot be sure my hand will hold out, if I wait for the post day —so I have two days in bank before my letter will set out.

7. Lady Anne Campbell (ca 1720–85) m. (1741) William Wentworth, 2d E. of Strafford, HW's correspondent. She d. 7 Feb.

8. Lady Mary Tufton (1701–12 Feb. 1785), m. 1 (1718) Anthony Grey, Lord Lucas, styled E. of Harold; m. 2 (1736) as his third wife, John Leveson Gower (1694–1754), 2d Bn Gower, 1709, cr. (1746) E. Gower. She did die from the accident.

9. Lady Jemima Elizabeth Ashburnham (1762–86) dau. of the 2d E. of Ashburnham, m. (1785) James Graham, styled M. of Graham, 3d D. of Montrose, 1790.

10. William Graham (1712–90), 2d D. of Montrose, m. (1742) Lady Lucy Manners (ca 1717–88), dau. of the 2d D. of Rutland.

11. Louis-Philippe-Joseph de Bourbon (1747–93), Duc de Chartres; Duc d'Orléans, 18 Nov. 1785.

12. Joseph II, in an effort to force the Dutch to open the Scheldt for navigation to Austria for her India trade, threatened to seize Maestricht. There were reports of 'treasonable practices' designed to deliver the city without a siege (MANN ix. 566, n. 21), and the Emperor sent troops to march against the city, but it was never besieged. Peaceful negotiations gave the Emperor ten million florins in exchange for the sovereignty of Maestricht (ibid. ix. 608, n. 3).

13. He desired to acquire Bavaria, and presumably was willing to give up the Austrian Netherlands, difficult to defend.

Sunday night 21st.

Lady Gower is dead, and puts 132 persons into close mourning; some indeed will only wear black strings to their corals. The Duchess of Devonshire[14] is once more breeding.

22d. My letter must set out without any more provender in its knapsack. The town, I hear, seems to be expecting some crisis; but prognostics do not always prove prophecies—at least, the wisest prophets make sure of the event first—and I will imitate them.

If your Elector becomes King of *Austrasia,* as foreign letters announce, you will at least approach nearer home. I hope he will, like the Popes, take a new name too, and call himself *Childebert* or *Clotaire.*[15] I shall feel at home too, when such titles are revived—they will accord with *my* old lore. Adieu, dear Sir,

Yours most cordially

H. W.

From George, 4th Earl Waldegrave, Sunday 14 August 1785

Printed for the first time from a photostat of the MS in the possession of Lord Waldegrave.

Navestock, August 14th 1785.

My dear Sir,

LADY Waldegrave and myself request the favour of you to be godfather to our son.[1] As the christening is to be in the country, I am afraid we shall not have the pleasure of your company. I need not add how happy it would make Lady Waldegrave and myself if

14. Lady Georgiana Spencer (1757–1806), m. (1774) William Cavendish, 5th D. of Devonshire, 1764. Lady Mary Coke wrote in her 'MS Journals,' 25 Feb. 1785, 'The Duchess of Devonshire is with child and though she has gone to all the balls has not danced and gone home before twelve o'clock.'

15. Childebert (d. 558) and Clotaire (or Chlotar, d. 561), sons of Clovis, King of the Franks. They murdered the children of their brother Clodomir in 524 in order to divide up his kingdom. Austrasia, which included the Dutch and Austrian Netherlands and the lower Rhine valley, was part of the old Frankish kingdom, and was nearer to England than the Elector's present dominions in Bavaria and the Palatinate.

1. Their second son, John James Waldegrave (31 July 1785 – 1835), 6th E. Waldegrave, 1794; he was baptized 25 Aug. (Ossory ii. 495, n. 25).

you would pass a few days with us at Navestock, either then or at any other time that would be convenient to you.

We propose being in town for a few days the end of next month or in the beginning of October, when if you will permit us we will wait upon you at Strawberry Hill.[2] We hope before this time you have been able to negotiate a peace between Ham and Isleworth.[3] I am, dear Sir,

Very sincerely yours

WALDEGRAVE

To LADY WALDEGRAVE, ca Friday 2 December 1785

Missing; mentioned *post* 4 Dec. 1785.

From GEORGE, 4TH EARL WALDEGRAVE, Sunday 4 December 1785

Printed for the first time from a photostat of the MS in the possession of Lord Waldegrave.

Dated by Waldegrave's accession to the title (after 22 Oct. 1784) and HW's gout (HW to Mann 4 Dec. 1785, MANN ix. 615).

Navestock, Dec. 4th.

My dear Sir,

I AM extremely sorry to find by a letter[1] Lady Waldegrave has received this morning from you that you are confined with the gout.[2] I hope it will be but a slight fit. I have had a return of my rheumatic complaint which prevented my waiting upon you last week as I intended. I propose being in town Wednesday, or Thurs-

2. HW wrote Conway 6 Oct. 1785, 'I expect Lord and Lady W. tomorrow, who are to pass a few days with me.'

3. Between the Dysarts at Ham and Mrs Keppel, who had inherited the Isleworth house from Sir Edward.

1. Missing.

2. This attack confined him 'above six weeks, and for a few days was very near being quite serious' (HW to Mann 4 Dec. 1785, 8 Jan. 1786, MANN ix. 615, 617).

eight that exhibit anything but shells, ores, fossils, birds' eggs and natural history—and in the eight days there are hundreds of old-fashioned snuff-boxes that were her mother's,[7] who wore three different every week; and they probably will sell for little more than the weight of the gold. I once asked the Duchess to let me see them—and after two drawers full, I begged to see no more, they were so ugly. Madame de Luxembourg[8] has as many, but much finer and beautiful. The Hamilton Vase[9] is in the last day's sale—it will not, I conclude, produce half of what it cost the Duchess,[10] unless it is sent for to the Houghton Collection in the North. The *vendor*[11] of the latter has been giving extravagant prices for Cipriani's trumpery drawings, who is dead—and *the purchaser*[12] has bespoken a large picture by Sir Joshua Reynolds. He was to choose the subject, size and price. He told me, he had pitched on the Infant Hercules and the Serpents —'Lord!' said I, 'people will say she is strangling the two Emperors!'[13]

Monsieur Adhémar[14] is returned to us and Mlle Déon[15] has been here all the winter, and much in request. I have met her twice, but would not visit her out of regard to Madame de Guerchy.[16] The Duc de Nivernois has made an incomparable translation of my history of modern gardening,[17] as I suppose your sisters,[18] to whom I gave

7. Henrietta Cavendish Holles (1694–1755), m. (1713) Edward Harley (1689–1741), 2d E. of Oxford, 1724.

8. Madeleine-Angélique de Neufville (1707–87) m. 1 (1721) Joseph-Marie, Duc de Boufflers; m. 2 (1750) Charles-François-Frédéric de Montmorency-Luxembourg, Duc de Luxembourg, Maréchal de France.

9. The Portland Vase, as it has since been called: 'Some few months before her death . . . [the Duchess] was tempted by the celebrated Barberini Vase, imported by the noted virtuoso Sir William Hamilton, minister at Naples' (HW's note in the catalogue). The vase has been in the British Museum since 1810.

10. It fetched £1029 in this sale. HW noted in his copy of the Sale Catalogue, p. 194: 'As the Duchess paid £2000 for the Vase, the Jupiter, the Augustus and the Hercules, and the Duke bought the Vase and the Augustus for £1265, and as the Jupiter and Hercules produced but £220, the Vase and Augustus really cost the family £3045.'

11. Lord Orford.

12. Catherine II.

13. The picture is now in the Hermitage Museum, Leningrad. The 'two Emperors' are Ivan VI and her husband (Peter III), whose executions were attributed to Catherine.

14. Jean-Balthazar d'Azémar de Montfalcon (1731–91), Comte d'Adhémar, ambassador to England 1783–7.

15. See *ante* 27 March 1764.

16. D'Éon 'told people in the park t'other day that Madame de Guerchy, who is remarkably plain, was going to Paris to take Madame Pompadour's place' (HW to Mann 14 May 1764, MANN vi. 239).

17. HW's *Essay on Modern Gardening*, 1785, first printed in the fourth volume of the *Anecdotes of Painting* (Hazen, *SH Bibl.* 129–32).

18. Catherine Margaret (1756–1816) and Elizabeth (1759–1842); 'Miss Walpole' appears in HW's list of presentation copies (BERRY ii. 260; H. S. Vade-Walpole, 'Notes on the Walpoles,' *Genealogical Magazine*, 1898–9, ii. 435).

one, have told you. My Strawberry editions, merely from their scarcity, sell ridiculously dear. I was forced to pay thirteen guineas yesterday for the *Anecdotes of Painting* in quarto for the King of Poland,[19] who had sent to me for them, and I had not a spare copy left. It is hard to pay almost treble the value for my own impressions! If collectors are fools, it is a comfort at least that the works of great authors are common and cheap.

Lady Di[20] has painted a new room at her cottage since you saw it, with small pictures of peasants and children in rounds and squares, that are chained together by wreaths of natural flowers that exceed her lilacs—and all flowers that ever were painted. What pity that they are in water-colours, and consequently almost as perishable as their originals! Vanhuysum's[21] finical and elaborate works will pass for standards, because Lady Di's bold characteristic touches will not exist! They are like the excellence of a great actor or musician, whose perfections live only in tradition and cannot be compared with the merit of prior or subsequent performers. If the Apollo Belvedere were not extant, who would believe that it has never been equalled?

I am sorry your residence is so unentertaining, but I rejoice that all around you is so tranquil. I hate the authors of big news, who precipitate the bills of mortality and rival a pestilence. It is better to be occupied about a Déon and a Cagliostro than about a hero.

Adieu! dear Sir,

Yours most sincerely

H. W.

19. Stanislas II (Stanislas Augustus Poniatowski) (1732–98), K. of Poland 1764–95. HW at the same time sent him a copy of Nivernais's translation of the *Essay* (Berry ii. 260).

20. Lady Diana Spencer (1734–1808), m. 1 (1757) Frederick St John, 2d Vct Bolingbroke (divorced 1768); m. 2 (1768) the Hon. Topham Beauclerk. The room was one of several she painted at her villa, Little Marble Hill, and is described in HW's MS note to the Postscript to 'The Parish Register of Twickenham,' in his *Des. of SH*, 1774, now WSL; it is printed in Ossory ii. 472–3, n. 35.

21. Jan Van Huysum (1682–1749), fruit and flower painter; his brother 'lived a year or two with Sir Robert Walpole at Chelsea' (NBG; 'Anecdotes of Painting,' *Works* iii. 421).

To LADY WALDEGRAVE, July 1786

Missing; answered *post* 7 July 1786.

From LADY WALDEGRAVE, Friday 7 July 1786

Printed for the first time from a photostat of the MS in the possession of Lord Waldegrave.
Address: The Honourable Horace Walpole Strawberry Hill near Twickenham.
Postmark: 8 IY ONGAR.

Navestock, July 7, 1786.

My dearest Sir,

I RETURN you many thanks for your kind letter: hearing from you is always a great satisfaction to me as you are the only friend whose affection has been invariably the same for me through life[1]— I have a happiness which I believe no woman possesses to so great a degree as myself, which is being married to the best as well as the best tempered man that ever lived, indeed his goodness of heart is not to be equalled: the patience and resolution with which he bears his unpleasant state of dependence when it is so little suited to his inclinations,[2] for the sake of his wife and children, must of course add to the gratitude which I feel towards him whenever I reflect upon his affection for me—You are so partial to him that I know you will excuse my expressing my sentiments with regard to him.

Mr Damer[3] left us this morning; he has been with us a few days, otherwise we have had no company with us since we have been here. Our neighbourhood is so large that we by no means live alone and as they are in general very good sort of people I like their society. Our children have all been troubled with colds and Johnny's has

1. HW bequeathed Strawberry Hill to Mrs Damer with a remainder to Lady Waldegrave. Mrs Damer resigned it to her in her lifetime, and Lady Waldegrave lived there from 1811 onwards (Percy Noble, *Anne Seymour Damer*, 1908, pp. 147, 202).

2. HW commented to Lady Ossory on Lord Waldegrave's penury: 'I am pleased too that she has a boy, as it pleases her and Lord Chewton; nor do I wish her to encumber him with a bevy of indigent infantas—but alas! what is an heir, where there is so little to inherit?' (19 June 1784, OSSORY ii. 435).

3. Presumably one of Mrs Damer's brothers-in-law: the Hon. George or the Hon. Lionel Damer.

been accompanied with a cough, but they are all now pretty well—
We are much obliged to you for your kind invitation to Strawberry
which we hope to be able to accept of in the course of the next two
or three months, at present we are engaged to races, quarter sessions
and assizes[4] which I believe will fill up our time entirely for four
weeks to come—The only news I have heard has been the report of
the Duke of Dorset's[5] marrying Lady Anne Westley,[6] but his family
I find do not give credit to it. I think 25 years is too great a disparity
in their age.

I am, my dearest Sir

Your dutiful and affectionate niece

E. LAURA WALDEGRAVE

From THOMAS WALPOLE THE YOUNGER, October 1786

Missing; referred to *post* 25 Oct. 1786.

To THOMAS WALPOLE THE YOUNGER, Wednesday 25 October 1786

Printed from a photostat of the Holland MS; first printed, Sir Spencer
Walpole 96–9; reprinted, Toynbee xiii. 412–14. For the history of the MS see
ante 18 July 1766.
Address (torn): Monsieur . . . ⟨Thomas Walpole⟩ fils No 26 . . . 15 ⟨P⟩aris.
Postmark: 27 OC.

Strawberry Hill, Oct. 25th 1786.

IT would be most unreasonable, dear Sir, if so superannuated a
correspondent as I am should expect you to write frequently to
me. In winter the gout commonly prevents my using my fingers, as

4. Lord Waldegrave had been made
Master of the Horse to Queen Charlotte
in 1784, and filled the office till his death.
5. John Frederick Sackville (1745–99), m.
(1790) Arabella Diana Cope (1769–1825).
6. Lady Anne Wesley (later Wellesley)
(1768–1844), m. 1 (1790) Hon. Henry Fitzroy; m. 2 (1799) Charles Culling Smith
(Collins, *Peerage*, 1812, viii. 544; Sir
Bernard Burke and A. P. Burke, *Peerage*,
1928, pp. 2140, 2380). She was a sister
of the Duke of Wellington.

was the case of the two last; and in summer I live here where I know nothing worth repeating, as the newspapers, which are not reserved, must have proved to you. They lie or blunder, but somehow or other

They catch the Eel of *Science* by the tail.[1]

You have had a material event in Germany, the death of the King of Prussia.[2] I do not perceive that it made much public sensation here, even amongst the pamphlet-shops; not so much as Dr Johnson's —but of him there is an end too—his devotees have convinced the public what fools they were for idolizing him as they did. We have had a slip of Germany here that awakened some attention, the Archduke and his wife;[3] but they are gone and forgotten too. In my own connections there has been an agreeable event; the Duke of Grafton has seen Lady Euston[4] and treated her very kindly: she is in return going to make him a present of another grandchild,[5] which is not the greatest desideratum in that family. Some of your relations I suppose have told you that Dr Hor. Hammond[6] is dead. So, no doubt you know, is, my good old friend and your acquaintance, Lord Dacre; and Princess Amelie is not expected to live a week.[7] Such are the events only with which I could fill my letters, as they affect me, and reduce my very contracted circle; but are little interesting to you; and consequently I could not expect you should draw upon me for such intelligence. Your sisters, who write so well, have certainly supplied you better, and with younger intelligence.

I am much obliged to you for offering to trouble yourself with commissions at Paris; but if all my objects are narrowed here, they are almost totally so there. At most I shall beg you just to inform yourself how many numbers of the *Voyage pittoresque de la Grèce* have

1. 'Yet holds the eel of science by the tail' (*Dunciad*, Bk I, l. 280).

2. Frederick II (1712 – 17 Aug. 1786), the Great, K. of Prussia 1740–86.

3. Ferdinand Karl Anton Joseph (1754–1806), D. of Modena, 1803, m. (1771) Maria Ricciarda Beatrice (1750–1829) of Este. They visited SH (HW to Lady Ossory 28 Sept. 1786, OSSORY ii. 530).

4. Lady Charlotte Maria Waldegrave had married Lord Euston (see *ante* 25 May 1776, n. 1) without the consent of his father, the 3d D. of Grafton, but he was

later reconciled to the match (OSSORY ii. 451–2, 457).

5. Lady Georgiana Laura Fitzroy (15 Jan. 1787 – 1855) (Collins, *Peerage*, 1812, i. 220; Sir Bernard Burke and A. P. Burke, *Peerage*, 1928, p. 1054).

6. He died 11 Oct.; he was prebendary of Norwich cathedral, rector of Heysley and Great Boreham, co. Norfolk (GM 1786, lvi pt ii. 910–11; *ante* 15 May 1745 OS, n. 7).

7. She d. 31 Oct.

been published; and when you arrive, I will trouble you to send for those I want, as I have received none a great while; and I will desire you to pay for what numbers I am indebted of the *Bibliothèque des romans,* for which I will repay you. Should you see Dr Gem,[8] might I ask you to inquire whether Mr Selwyn has repaid him, as I desired, for *Les Mœurs des François.*[9] If not, shall I beg you to discharge that debt also?

Madame de Cambis is in England, but I have not yet seen her, but hope I shall. My good Duchesse de la Valière I never can forget, and the old Maréchales[10] and Madame de Jonsac,[11] I should wish to be mentioned to, if you see them—of the last I have heard nothing a great while. The Duc de Nivernois has done me too much honour not to be sure how much I respect him: vanity never forgets obligations.

You will find Tonton in as good health and spirits as ever, and so entire a favourite, that I doubt I cannot impute my fondness to gratitude too. I hope he will show you that his memory is as perfect as his other perfections, and that he is much yours, as, dear Sir,

Your affectionate humble servant

Hor. Walpole

PS. Will you be so good as to inform yourself whether Beaumarchais's edition of Voltaire[12] is totally stopped?

From Lord and Lady Waldegrave, ca Friday 3 November 1786

Missing. 'Lord and Lady Waldegrave . . . today have sent me a confirmation of several of Princess Amelie's legacies as you have seen in the papers' (HW to Lady Ossory 4 Nov. 1786, Ossory ii. 534).

---

8. Richard Gem (*ante* 31 July 1781, n. 1).

9. The volumes were probably *Histoire de la vie privée des français,* 3 vols, 1782, by Pierre-Jean-Baptiste Le Grand d'Aussy (1737–1800); HW's set is Hazen, *Cat. of HW's Lib.,* No. 3226 (see HW to Selwyn 5 July 1786, Selwyn 279).

10. Mmes de Luxembourg and de Mirepoix.

11. See *ante* 15 Oct. 1769, n. 11; she d. 1786.

12. HW owned 70 vols, ed. by Pierre-Augustin Caron de Beaumarchais (1732–99), printed 1784–9, sold SH v. 164 (Hazen, *Cat. of HW's Lib.,* No. 3057).

To the Hon. Thomas Walpole, Sunday
12 November 1786

Printed for the first time from a photostat of the Holland MS; for the history of the MSS see *ante* 18 July 1766.

Address: To Thomas Walpole Esq. in Curzon Street Mayfair London.

Postmark: 13 NO ISLEWORTH.

Memoranda (in an unidentified hand): Thomas the Scriven

St James Street

Oxford Street

Strawberry Hill, Nov. 12th 1786.

Dear Sir,

I SHALL have a bed at your service if you will dine here on Friday next. I name the earliest day, because I have sent to Park Place that if they would let me know when they like I should come, I would go thither for a few days; and as Gen. Conway is to be in town for a day this week, I am not likely to go before Saturday or Sunday.

Yours without compliment

H. Walpole

From Lady Euston, June 1787

Missing. 'I have been sending some layers of clove-carnations to Lady Ravensworth, for which Lady Euston wrote to me' (HW to Lady Ossory 28 June 1787, Ossory ii. 567).

From the Duchess of Gloucester, Tuesday
26 June 1787

Missing; answered *post* 9 July 1787.

To the Duchess of Gloucester, Monday 9 July 1787

Printed from a photostat of the MS in the possession of Lord Waldegrave; first printed, Biddulph 195–7.
Endorsed (by the Hon. Mrs William Waldegrave): Addressed to her R. H. Maria Dss of Gloucester then abroad.

Strawberry Hill, July 9th 1787.

I AM happy, Madam, at receiving your R. H.'s letter of the 26th as it was a great while, I thought, since I had the honour of hearing from you. Not that I blamed anybody but myself. I am sensible how unentertaining my correspondence must be. Almost a whole winter of gout[1] has thrown me more out of the world than ever; and as I am Methusalem when compared with the present actors, of both parties and sexes, on the stage, I have not only little connection with any, but should think myself ridiculous, if I had more. I do not know whether even my zeal for your welfare, happiness and glory, have not sometimes made me transgress the respect I owe and have for you. Yet if on late or former occasions I have used too great freedom, it has never been without sacrificing myself for your sake; that is, I may have risked displeasing you, only in order to serve you. My late time of life and my disinterested character made it impossible, that, with a little portion of common sense, I could have any view but your interest, and I knew that your conviction of my attachment to you, would authorize me in saying what no one living else would venture to say to you. I had a still better warrant—perhaps not a generous one—I was sure that your excellent heart would always make you forgive, and what is more uncommon, forget the trespasses of a true friend. Yet should I have been unpardonable even to the partial eyes of self-love, had I once presumed on your indulgence when strong circumstances and the duty I owe you, did not call on me for rigid truth. I have always severely weighed the crisis of the moment, and the hope of serving you has always preponderated against the fear of offending you. It was no insolent idea of having the smallest right to advise you,[2] Madam, that dictated

1. His 23d attack; see Ossory ii. 551.
2. The advice was doubtless in regard to the rift between her and the Duke, who wrote the King 22 June that 'the very unfortunate turn of mind and temper of the Duchess and her evil representations to them [the children] on every possible subject, makes it absolutely necessary for me to put them quite out of her hands.' He requested the King's permis-

my conduct—no, far from it; I may compare myself in a small degree to faithful servants who have received arrows in their own breasts to intercept them from the bosoms of their sovereigns. The same respect makes me silent, rather than be over-officious—and I am sure I wish infinitely more that you may have no occasion for my zeal, than I have any vanity in making a tender of it. Indeed I might flatter myself that should any new occasion arrive, your R. H. has good sense equal to any difficulty, fortitude enough not to be depressed, and piety enough to submit to the thorns[3] which Heaven often blends with the ermine of Princes.

I hope, Madam, you are quite easy about the poor girl who suffered by your coach. You think she had never before heard the voice of pity—I am sorry for human nature to be forced to reply, who almost ever did hear of a Princess weeping over a beggar wounded by accident? Heaven that has given you ermine, gave you a better gift, the best of hearts, and you have kept it incorrupt. That heart will secure for you more durable happiness than a crown itself could confer.

Lady Lincoln[4] has taken a house at Putney Common till October, and as her brother[5] and Lady Horatia have promised her a visit there,

sion to 'have a person appointed to attend my daughter . . . and keep her clear of the Duchess but at meals and in the evening society.' He felt he had been 'severely punished' for his 'juvenile indiscretion,' that is, his marriage to Maria. 'I have told her that if she lets the children from this time alone, and behaves more respectfully to me before the world, she may remain in my house,' although once (ca 1774) 'she threatened me with leaving me' (Biddulph 191–2, which contains a long discussion of the quarrel, pp. 186–202). The King acceded to the Duke's requests, appointing Miss Leonora Dee (see *post* 22 Sept. 1787) as governess to Princess Sophia, giving permission for Prince William to be entered at Cambridge, and granting the Duke of Gloucester an additional £4000 per annum for the children's education (Biddulph 199). HW after this avoided the Duke, 'whom I should be as sorry to meet . . . as he could be to meet me' and referred to him as 'my royal nephew, who I have reason to wish had never been so, and did all I could to prevent his being' (HW to Mary

Berry 3 July 1790, 11 March 1791, BERRY i. 80, 219; see also ibid. ii. 46; Sir Horace Mann the Younger to HW 5 April 1787, MANN ix. 674; Coke, 'MS Journals' 5 Oct. 1783; MORE 298).

3. A particular thorn was the Duke's continuing liaison with Lady Almeria Carpenter (1752–1809), 2d dau. of George, 1st E. of Tyrconnel. Lady Almeria had been lady in waiting to the Duchess. She gave birth 6 Jan. 1782 to an illegitimate daughter by the Duke, Louisa Maria, who was entered in the registry as 'daughter of Farley Edsir' (steward to the Duke and tenant of a dairy farm near Hampton Court). She was later given the surname of La Coast or Laccoast and m. (1803) Godfrey Macdonald, 3d Bn Macdonald of Slate in Ireland (GEC viii. 340, n. *b*, xii pt ii. 127, n. *f*; see also Appendix 5; Biddulph 181–5, 197).

4. Lady Frances Seymour-Conway (1751–1820) m. (1775) Henry Pelham Clinton, E. of Lincoln.

5. Lord Hugh Seymour-Conway, m. Lady Anna Horatia Waldegrave.

I shall be so happy as to see them. He is an incomparable young man. Mr and Mrs Fitzroy[6] and their little girl[7] are with Mrs Keppel[8] at Isleworth. I am sorry to say I scarce ever saw anybody look so ill as Miss Keppel.[9] I hope the air of the country, and Cheltenham, whither they are to go in August, will restore her. Sir Richard Jebbe is dead,[10] of a fever he contracted by sitting up with the Princesses in the measles at Windsor.[11]

Sir Horace Mann[12] has called on me and gave me vast pleasure by telling me of your R. H.'s charming looks and unaltered beauty.

It is very natural for an old man to moralize on events, and still more so for me who have seen Houghton plundered.[13] Claremont[14] has just now been sold in parcels, and bought on speculation. Sir Gregory Page's, which you once inhabited,[15] Madam, is pulling down. Cannons[16] was demolished a few years ago. Such is sublunary grandeur—my morality is, that if everything is transient, misfortunes must be so; and if magnificence is transient, unhappiness is so too. No cup is unmixed.

That monster Lord George Gordon is fled—I am surprised it is to Holland,[17] for though he might delight in an opportunity of burning a street or two, he is such a poltroon as not to like personal danger;

6. George Ferdinand Fitzroy, m. Laura Keppel.

7. Georgiana Maria Fitzroy (ca April 1785–1830), m. (1814) Capt. John Horace Thomas Stapleton (MANN ix. 571, n. 7).

8. Mrs Fitzroy's mother was HW's niece, Laura Walpole, widow of the Hon. Frederick Keppel, Bp of Exeter.

9. Anna Maria Keppel (*ante* 17 June 1759, n. 1).

10. 'Yesterday morning died Sir Richard Jebb, Bart, physician to their Majesties. . . . The specific cause of his death, was an asthmatic attack of peculiar violence, which first assailed him on Thursday last' (*London Chronicle* 3–5 July 1787, lxii. 16, *sub* 5 July). He attended the Duke when he had been ill in Italy (see *ante* 10 Aug. 1777).

11. They had recovered by 5 July. 'The Princesses accompany the King and Queen on their approaching little tour to Blenheim, Nuneham, and Castle Howard' (*London Chronicle*, loc. cit.).

12. The *London Chronicle* reported his arrival on 28 June. The Gloucesters and Lady Almeria had treated him badly in Italy, but changed their manner to him, and HW is here being propitiatory.

13. See *ante* 8 April 1786.

14. Near Esher, Surrey, the seat of the late Duke of Newcastle (COLE i. 44, n. 4).

15. 'Wricklemarsh, at Blackheath, where the Duke and Duchess of Gloucester lived in 1779 for a time' (Biddulph 197, n. 1).

16. The magnificent seat of James Brydges (1673–1744), 1st D. of Chandos; near Edgware, Middlesex, built ca 1712 at an estimated cost of £200–£250,000, sold by auction in 1747 for the materials, largely bought by William Hallett, who erected a new house on the site (COLE ii. 275, n. 16).

17. 'A gentleman, just arrived from Amsterdam, saw Lord Gordon there.' Gordon told one of the magistrates 'that having been most cruelly persecuted in England, he had retreated to a country very dear to him, as being the land of Protestantism and of liberty' (*London Chronicle* 3–5 July 1787, lxii. 10, *sub* 4 July).

and when Dutchmen are roused, they are very much in earnest. Our papers talk much of war—I hope without authority.

I have the honour to be, Madam,

Your R. H.'s most faithful humble servant

HOR. WALPOLE

From GEORGE, 4TH EARL WALDEGRAVE, Saturday 22 September 1787

Printed for the first time from a photostat of the MS in the possession of Lord Waldegrave.

Navestock, September 22d 1787.

My dear Sir,

LADY Waldegrave has received a message from the Queen to go to Windsor on the first of October if she finds herself well and strong enough. The Princess Royal['s][1] birthday is to be kept on that day.

Lady Waldegrave is perfectly well, except being wcak, and I doubt very much if she will be strong enough to go to Windsor. If she does not go, I will have the pleasure of waiting upon you at Strawberry Hill either going or returning from Windsor. I will write to you as soon as Lady W. has determined. She received a letter from Mr Shields[2] to tell her they were to come to England next month. The Duchess writes in good spirits. Miss Dee,[3] Mrs Johnston['s] sister, is to be with the Princess as her governess. I am dear Sir

Your most obedient

Humble servant

WALDEGRAVE

1. Charlotte Augusta Matilda (29 Sept. 1766–1828), George III's eldest daughter.
2. Servant of the Duke of Gloucester (see *ante* 26 July 1777).
3. Leonora Dee, sister of Deborah Charlotte Dee (Mrs George Johnstone). She lived in Portugal until 1782, when she accompanied her sister to England. She had been appointed Sophia's governess by George III at the Duke's request (see *ante* 9 July 1787, n. 2; HW to Mary Berry 12 May 1791, BERRY i. 264, n. 22).

To the Hon. Thomas Walpole, Sunday
9 December 1787

Printed from a photostat of the MS owned by H. Jack Lang, Cleveland, Ohio; first printed, Sir Spencer Walpole 99–103; reprinted, Toynbee xiv. 35–6. The MS was on deposit in the Harvard College Library; sold Sotheby's 11 April 1921, lot 400, to Maggs; offered by them in their catalogues 405, 445, and 474 (June 1926); offered by Charles Hamilton, 13 April 1960; acquired by Robert Black and sold Sotheby's 25 July 1961, lot 498, to Bernard Quarrich, Ltd; resold Aug. 1962 (no. 832); sold Christie's 18 Dec. 1968, lot 9, to Francis Edwards; sold by Ian Murdoch, London, to Paul Richards of Brookline (Nov. 1969), who sold it to Mr Lang.

Address: À Monsieur Monsieur Thomas Walpole.

Strawberry Hill, Dec. 9th 1787.

IT was not at all extraordinary, dear Sir, that I should tell your daughters[1] that I thought your marriage with Madame de Ville-gagnon[2] very sensible: I have long had great respect and esteem for that lady, and have no doubt but her virtues and understanding will make you very happy: and since you despair of returning[3] to your own country, so creditable a match in France seems a very wise measure, and the alliance will replace agreeably the friends you have left in England. I should have been very glad if your affairs would have allowed your bringing Madame Walpole over, and consequently, my making my court to her in person; but though I should hope the former may still happen, I am much too old to form any projects at all distant, and therefore must beg you, Sir, to offer my most respectful compliments and congratulations to her.

I am exceedingly glad of peace: I always wish for it for the sake of others, and *now* very interestedly, as my late time of life makes me desirous of perfect tranquillity, and of not suffering uneasiness for any of my friends, or on their account for their friends.

Whether the treaty of commerce[4] will be advantageous or the contrary, to this country, I do not pretend in the least to judge. You

---

1. See *ante* 8 April 1786, n. 18.

2. Jeanne-Marguerite Batailhe de Montval (1731–1821), m. (1755)—Durand, Marquis de Villegagnon; m. 2 (1787) Hon. Thomas Walpole. 'My elderly cousin Mr Thomas Walpole has espoused . . . Madame de Villegagnon, at Paris, who is no infant neither—but that is their affair'

(HW to Lady Ossory 15 December 1787, Ossory ii. 587).

3. On 1 August 1790 Thomas Walpole and his wife dined with HW at SH (HW to Mary Berry 2 Aug. 1790, Berry i. 108).

4. A treaty of commerce between France and England was signed in September 1786. It was initiated by Pitt, and op-

know, I think, how utterly ignorant I am of all matters of trade—and may say truly of anything useful. I never had a head or an inclination for business, and have passed an idle life in amusing myself with trifles: nor do I regret my option. The abilities, integrity and temper of my father seldom meet; and without them all, ambition, I believe, is no path to much felicity, or to solid reputation.

I am not better acquainted with the present internal politics of France, with which I have had little or no correspondence since my dear friend Madame du Deffand's death. I did cast my eye on M. de Calonne's book,[5] but not understanding the finances or terms of finance of France, I was little the wiser. The part I did understand, I admired very moderately. Eloquence has advanced with us to such masculine superiority, even in the youngest men, that studied flowers and affected pathos composed by the pen, are in my eyes quite puerile. Calonne's apostrophe to the manes of his father[6] made me smile, instead of touching me; and when I recollected the anecdote of La Chalotais,[7] my smile was converted into an emotion less tender.

For my own amusement I am sorry the press of Paris is so barren of everything but politics, unless it were to send us more Figaros and Tarares! Our own press produces full as little entertainment: we lived two years upon the dotage of Dr Johnson and his foolish biographers[8]—yes, I have seen one French book, which I should be glad to have and cannot get, Monsieur d'Argenson's (I think it is called) Loisirs.[9] There is much good sense in it, and many anecdotes; and I do not dislike it for *not* resembling what he calls his model,

posed by the Whigs, who saw it as an attempt by France to increase her power in Europe. The treaty established liberty of navigation and commerce on all but a few articles between the two countries, reducing the duties on many of the principal products (*Cambridge History of British Foreign Policy 1783–1919*, ed. Sir A. W. Ward and G. P. Gooch, New York, 1970, i. 167–70).

5. Charles-Alexandre de Calonne (1734–1802), made controller-general of finance in 1783. The *Correspondance de Necker et de Calonne* was printed in 1787, and Calonne's *Réponse* to Necker at London in 1788 (NBG). HW had no copies.

6. His father had been premier président of the Parliament of Flanders (*Dictionnaire de biographie française*, 1933– , vii. 922).

7. Louis-René de Caradeuc de la Chalotais (1701–85), champion of the Breton parliament against the Duc d'Aiguillon, governor of Brittany. They quarrelled, and in 1765 the King received anonymous and seditious letters about the disturbance. M. de Calonne identified the handwriting as that of La Chalotais, and was thus instrumental in obtaining his arrest; he was thrown into prison, together with his son and four other members of the Breton parliament (DU DEFFAND i. 109, 151, v. 371).

8. See *ante* 8 April 1786.

9. René-Louis de Voyer de Paulmy, Marquis d'Argenson, *Les Loisirs d'un ministre, ou essais dans le goût de ceux de Montaigne*, Liège, 1787. HW's copy is Hazen, *Cat. of HW's Lib.*, No. 2997.

Montaigne, who surfeits me with his own vanity—I cannot conceive why Montaigne is so much admired, unless by people who would like to talk as much of themselves. Adieu! dear Sir,

Your most obedient

humble servant

Hor. Walpole

From Thomas Walpole the Younger, July 1788

Missing; answered in the following letter.

To Thomas Walpole the Younger, Monday 21 July 1788

Printed from a photostat of the Holland MS; first printed, Sir Spencer Walpole 103–6; reprinted, Toynbee xiv. 60–2. For the history of the MS see *ante* 18 July 1766.

Address: À Monsieur Monsieur Thomas Walpole à Munich.

Memoranda: 57

13
──
70

Strawberry Hill, July 21st 1788.

Dear Sir,

I CAN but too easily excuse myself for being so irregular a correspondent, as I have had two fits of the gout since last Christmas; and as my hands are always the most affected, it is no wonder that so old a man is willing to indulge them. I did indeed answer Lady Craven's[1] last letter in November, though I have reason to think she did not receive it, as I have before heard she complained of me. It is very true that I have not been eager to revive that commerce, both from the lameness of my hands, and from my apprehension of her Ladyship's literary alacrity, having no ambition to figure in *les Mémoires de l'Académie d'Anspach,* of which she was pleased to enroll me.[2] I am moreover of opinion that a veteran author[3] ought to

1. See *ante* 13 March 1783, n. 18.
2. Lady Craven had written, 12 Aug.

1787, to Lord Harcourt that she was founding a literary academy at Ansbach,

take out his quietus as much as the superannuated of any other profession; and with so much more reason, as every man can be sure of having lost the use of his limbs, but is not so good a judge whether he has lost the use of his head or not.

I mightily approve Lady Craven's blending the dairy with the library as an example to her sex, who at present are furiously apt to abandon the churn totally, like the abominable milkwoman at Bristol,[4] who has been so ungrateful and abusive to her kind benefactress Miss Hannah More.[5] We have hen-novelists and poetesses in every parish, and Lady Craven might institute a whole academy of her own gender.

I am very glad, dear Sir, that your situation is improved: a more active and animated scene would be certainly more amusing; but to be comfortable is the first step to amusement. You can at least make more frequent little excursions; and, if little courts are not interesting, their mimicry of grander follies is diverting and various— diverting to anybody but to their plundered subjects; who, even so, are lucky, if they are not sold as mercenaries! I, you know, do not lament that your great neighbour[6] makes so poor a figure in his campaign. His female ally seems to be still more embarrassed. Her memorial in answer to the Swedes[7] is not at all in the stout Semiramis-style she had assumed.

Our summer, usually dull, is enlivened by the royal journey to Cheltenham[8] and another Westminster election[9]—at least the newspapers are not reduced to mere invention and lies from Ireland; but as those influences do not reach to Twickenham, my letter receives no aid: nor have we had any event but a great cricket match at Moulsey,[10] which was interrupted by St Swithin.[11]

---

in which she wished to enroll HW as a member (HW to Harcourt 1 Sept. 1787 and nn. 1, 2).

3. The *Morning Herald*, 30 June 1786, called HW 'the Veteran of Strawberry Hill' (Ossory ii. 516, n. 1).

4. Ann Cromartie (1752–1806), m. (1774) John Yearsley; milkwoman, poet. She had quarrelled with Hannah More (see HW to Hannah More 1 Jan., 15 June 1787 and Hannah More to HW October 1787, More 244, 247, 253).

5. (1745–1833), HW's correspondent.

6. Joseph II.

7. Catherine II of Russia, allied with Joseph II against Turkey, ordered her ambassador to present a rescript, dated 18 June, to the Swedish court, protesting against hostile acts (GM 1788, lviii pt ii. 644–5).

8. Where George III took the waters, doing him 'great service' ('Mem. 1783–91'; Ossory iii. 47, n. 3).

9. 'The great contest . . . between Lord Hood . . . and Lord John Townshend'; Townshend was returned (ibid. iii. 11, n. 3).

10. In Surrey, in HW's neighbourhood: from Strawberry Hill, HW was able to see a balloon ascend at Mr Dodswell's gardens, Moulsey-Hurst (Mann ix. 579).

11. I.e., rain; see Berry i. 37, n. 51.

Lord Frederic Cavendish[12] has succeeded my poor old friend the Duchess of Montrose[13] at Twickenham Park,[14] but I much doubt whether he will reside there. The Duke of York[15] has bought Oatlands[16] for three and forty thousand pounds. My neighbour Sir George Pococke[17] was much obliged by your civilities to his son.[18] What can I tell you more from hence? and why should one write more than one has to say? Adieu! then, dear Sir, and be assured I am with great regard

Your affectionate and obedient humble servant

HOR. WALPOLE

From GEORGE, 4TH EARL WALDEGRAVE, Monday 27 October 1788

Printed for the first time from a photostat of the MS in the possession of Lord Waldegrave.

Navestock, Oct. 27th 1788.

My dear Sir,

LADY Waldegrave was this morning brought to bed of a boy[1] and I have the happiness to inform you that I never saw her so well, so soon after lying-in as she is at present.

I am, my dear Sir

Your most obedient

Humble servant

WALDEGRAVE

12. (1729–1803), M.P.; Field Marshal.

13. See *ante* 19 Feb. 1785.

14. An ancient estate once owned by Francis Bacon, lying partly in Twickenham parish and partly in Isleworth (R. S. Cobbett, *Memorials of Twickenham*, 1872, pp. 224–36).

15. Frederick (1763–1827), Bp of Osnabrück 1764–1802; cr. (1784) Duke of York and Albany; George III's second son.

16. Oatlands Park, in Weybridge, Surrey, about nine miles from SH, purchased from the D. of Newcastle. The Duke of York took possession 11 July (OSSORY iii. 7, n. 13).

17. Sir George Pocock (1706–92), K.B., 1761; naval officer.

18. George Pocock (1765–1840), cr. (1820) Bt.

———

1. Hon. William Waldegrave (27 Oct. 1788–1859), their fourth son; 8th E. Waldegrave, 1846 (succeeding his nephew, George Edward); naval officer.

To Mrs Horace Churchill,[1] Wednesday 11 February 1789

Printed from the MS now wsl; extract printed in Sotheby's Cat. 10 June 1909, lot 371; Maggs Cat. 253 (1909), item 794; Maggs Cat. 299 (1912) lot 4214; Maggs Cat. 343 (1916) lot 564; Maggs Cat. 394 (1920) lot 1803; extract reprinted (from Sotheby's Cat. 10 June 1909) Toynbee *Supp.* ii. 29. Damer-Waller; sold Sotheby's 10 June 1909, lot 371 to Maggs and offered by them in several catalogues until they sold it to A. B. Triggs of Sydney, Australia; resold there by Messrs J. R. Lawson, 27 Nov. 1945, to Maggs, who sold it to wsl, 1946.

Address: To Mrs Horace Churchill.

Berkeley Square, Feb. 11, 1789.

My dear Madam,

I CANNOT employ my pen and your ink better than in thanking you for your very kind present[2] for which I am much obliged; and though I am not likely to prove the length of the ink's duration, my gratitude shall last as long as I do, and such a pretty memorandum will always revive your idea agreeably.

Yours most affectionately

Hor. Walpole

To the Duchess of Gloucester, ca July 1789

Missing; acknowledged *post* 28 July 1789.

---

1. Harriot Ann Modigliani (d. 1840), m. (1783) Horace Churchill, son of Lady Mary Churchill, HW's sister. Her husband was a captain in the army, becoming Maj.-Gen. in 1811 (Berry i. 264).

2. Presumably ink.

From the DUCHESS OF GLOUCESTER, Tuesday
28 July 1789

Printed for the first time from a photostat of the MS in the possession of Lord Waldegrave.

Address: The Honourable Horace Walpole.

Endorsed (by HW): From the Duchess of Gloucester July 1789.

Pavillions, Tuesday.[1]

I FIND this poem[2] to be one of the very few, which after striking prodigiously at the first hearing, improves upon the second! It is indeed charming and I return you many thanks for it. I wish I had wrote it.[3]—

The Divine[4] is come, so, I can write no more—

Yours, my dear Sir, ever and ever.

1. This must be the letter referred to by HW in his letter to Hannah More 9 Aug. 1789 (MORE 318) and sent with it to her as an enclosure.

2. *Bishop Bonner's Ghost* by Hannah More, printed at SH July 1789 (see HW to Hannah More 23 June 1789, MORE 301, n. 5).

3. 'Everyone is charmed by your poem: I have not heard one breath but of applause. In confirmation I enclose a note to me from the Duchess of Gloucester, who certainly never before wished to be an authoress' (HW to Hannah More 9 Aug. 1789, MORE 318).

4. Rev. William Pennicott (see *ante* 16 Dec. 1772; *post* 10, 12 Oct. 1789).

From LADY WALDEGRAVE, before Tuesday
22 September 1789

Missing; mentioned *post* 22 Sept. 1789.

From LADY WALDEGRAVE, Tuesday
22 September 1789

Printed for the first time from a photostat of the MS in the possession of Lord Waldegrave.
Address: The Honourable Horace Walpole Strawberry Hill near Twickenham Surry.
Postmark: SE 23 ‹89› COVENTRY.

Packington, Tuesday.

My dearest Sir,

I PROMISED that I would write to you again about Lord Waldegrave and I wish that I could give you a better account of him, but though if there is any alteration I must say that it is mending yet it is so very trifling that I acknowledge I am very uncomfortable about him[1]—His languor and lassitude continue, he gets scarce any sleep in the night and has at that time a great oppression on his breath—He has no fever: his looks are those of a person with the jaundice as he is very yellow—Dr Withering[2] a physician at Birmingham attends him and he appeared to think that when he is rather better that the Cheltenham waters would be advisable: I do not know whether Lord W. will consent to go there—

I am, my dearest Sir

Your dutiful and affectionate

E. L. WALDEGRAVE

1. 'Lord Waldegrave is ill of the jaundice at Lord Aylesford's [Packington Hall, near Great Packington] in Warwickshire. He is rather better than he was, but I believe it is a disorder never cured expeditiously—I am sure not so soon as I wish, who interest myself exceedingly about him' (HW to Lady Ossory 26 Sept. 1789, OSSORY iii. 68–9).

2. William Withering (1741–99), M.D., 1766; botanist and mineralogist; chief physician of the Birmingham General Hospital.

To LADY WALDEGRAVE, ca Thursday
24 September 1789

Missing; answered *post* 25 Sept. 1789.

From LADY WALDEGRAVE, Friday
25 September 1789

Printed for the first time from a photostat of the MS in the possession of Lord Waldegrave.

Address: The Honourable Horace Walpole Strawberry Hill near Twickenham.

Postmark: SE 26 89 COVENTRY.

Friday, September 25–89.

My dearest Sir,

AS no post goes from hence till Sunday I write today to return you my thanks for your kind letter[1] and for your anxiety upon Lord Waldegrave's account. I wish I could give you more satisfactory news concerning him for I do not think he is much mended since I wrote last. Dr Withering is here now who says he is rather better, but his nights are so bad with difficulty of breathing that he scarce gets sleep. I hope he will attend to his health when he gets the better of this attack: I find it is a violent bilious complaint but not a confirmed jaundice: Bath has not been named to him, but I should think very probably may if the Cheltenham season is over before he gets stronger—I shall be too late for the post if I do not put up my letter, therefore must bid you adieu.

I am your affectionate and dutiful niece

E. LAURA WALDEGRAVE

To LADY WALDEGRAVE, ca Tuesday 29 September 1789

Missing; answered *post* 2 Oct. 1789.

1. Missing.

From LADY WALDEGRAVE, Friday 2 October 1789

Printed for the first time from a photostat of the MS in the possession of Lord Waldegrave.

Address: The Honourable Horace Walpole Strawberry Hill near Twickenham.

Postmark: OC 3 89 COVENTRY [another illegible].

Packington October 2, '89.

My dearest Sir,

I AM much obliged to you for your kind letter,[1] and as I think Lord Waldegrave rather better I write to inform you of it—Since my last he has been considerably worse, his breath being oppressed to that degree that he appeared every instant as if going to die, and his retchings without vomiting were very painful: therefore as with these symptoms he could get no sleep, and that with difficulty he could be moved from his couch to a chair, I requested to have another physician sent for which was done the night before last: He agrees entirely with Dr Withering in the nature of Lord W.'s complaint and method of treating him excepting that he has recommended strengthening the medicines, which the other I suppose from being unacquainted with his constitution was timid about giving with the force required—They have so far proved effectual that he yesterday slept or dozed the greatest part of the day and his retchings have almost ceased, while the bile has been carried off in a much greater quantity than before—Dr Withering and Dr Johnson[2] sleep here alternately and the apothecary stays in the house—

I am much obliged to you for your kind hints, Sir John Eliot[3] was Lord W.'s physician and he has consulted nobody since. And I do not think either Mr Yonge[4] or Mr Livett,[5] the apothecaries whom he has sent to at different times for medicines for himself, know much about his habit of body, as he seldom has taken more than a dose of physic from them—I mentioned the James's Powder,[6] but as he has had no fever during the whole illness they do not think it advisable

1. Missing.
2. Perhaps Robert Johnson (ca 1749–93), M.D., of Mansfield, Notts (GM 1793, lxiii pt ii. 1155).
3. Dr John Elliott (1736–86), Kt, 1776; Bt, 1778; physician.
4. Not identified.

5. Probably John Livett (d. 1791), 'eminent apothecary in Albemarle Street' (GM 1791, lxi pt i. 286).
6. See *ante* 27 March 1764. HW believed it might have saved Lady Waldegrave's father, although he died of smallpox (HW to Mann 10 April 1763, MANN vi. 127).

particularly as Dr James's Analeptic Pills which he took before we sent for Dr Withering disagreed with him—The season is now over for Cheltenham and I fear it will be so long before he recovers strength sufficient that if Bath waters are reckoned advisable, which Dr Johnson seemed to think they would be some time hence, that we shall have time to consult other physicians when we return home—

You may conceive, my dearest Sir, how much I am agitated and suffer, I have more time to write as they think that he is quieter when I am absent than present, as from the extreme low spirits that accompany this disorder he apprehends himself to be worse than he is—

I am, my dearest Sir, your dutiful

and affectionate

E. L. W.

Lord and Lady Aylesford[7] are so attentive to us that I cannot say enough about their kindness: Lord Aylesford is almost constantly with Lord W. and studies everything that he thinks may be wanted that he may not feel distressed at being from home—

From the DUCHESS OF GLOUCESTER, Thursday 8 October 1789

Printed for the first time from a photostat of the MS in the possession of Lord Waldegrave.
Address: The Honourable Horace Walpole Twickenham.
Postmark: OC 8 89 ⟨I⟩E.

London, Thursday.

PERHAPS you have heard[1] from my poor dear child—Lord Waldegrave is alive, at least he was so yesterday when she wrote but I fear there are no hopes—God help her. By Lord Aylesford's

7. See *ante* 11 Nov. 1781, n. 16. Lord Waldegrave fell ill while visiting the Aylesfords at Packington. For Lord Aylesford's guardianship of the Waldegrave children, see HW to Lady Ossory 29 Oct

1789, OSSORY iii. 74 and n. 2, and *post* 30 Oct. 1789.

———

1. HW had not heard how grave Lord Waldegrave's condition was: 'I was thunderstruck by a note from the Duchess

not coming to the Drawing-Room, he must think him in the greatest danger—

God protect my poor dear child—I do not know what I write—how sorry you will be!

From the DUCHESS OF GLOUCESTER, Saturday 10 October 1789

Printed for the first time from a photostat of the MS in the possession of Lord Waldegrave.

Address: The Honourable Horace Walpole.

Saturday.

My dear Sir,

I LEAVE this[1] as I go by, that you may see what she says—I shall call upon you tomorrow. I should have wrote yesterday but the Thursday's letter only came with the Friday's—

I own I have no hopes—his constitution was broken up—why, why will people be above taking care of the health which God has given 'em. As you may suppose I am very very miserable.

MARIA

Will you send to Mr Pennicott *not* to come to the Pavillions tomorrow—I am too unhappy to rout myself up in the morning for prayers—and therefore may as well save him the trouble of coming.

with an account of Lord Waldegrave's extreme danger—I cannot describe the alarm it gave me' (HW to Lady Ossory 9 Oct. 1789, *sub* 13 Oct., OSSORY iii. 72).

1. Probably a letter from Lady Waldegrave to the Duchess (see *post* 11 Oct. 1789).

From LADY WALDEGRAVE, Sunday 11 October 1789

Printed for the first time from a photostat of the MS in the possession of Lord Waldegrave.
Address: The Honourable Horace Walpole Strawberry Hill near Twickenham.
Postmark: OC 12 89 COVENTRY.

Packington, Sunday, October 11, 1789.

My dearest Sir,

I BEGGED of the Duchess to inform you of the dreadful state Lord Waldegrave has been in, thank God the physicians have now hopes of his recovery—I have wrote the Duchess a very particular account of him and do not doubt she will give you all the information about him: after an uncommon discharge of bile on Friday evening he began to mend and yesterday grew gradually better—Pray, my dearest Sir, send Nancy[1] word of his amendment—

I am most dutifully and affectionately yours

E. L. W.

From the DUCHESS OF GLOUCESTER, Monday 12 October 1789

Printed for the first time from a photostat of the MS in the possession of Lord Waldegrave.
Address: The Honourable Horace Walpole Strawberry Hill.
Memorandum (a genealogical sketch):

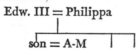

Monday.

THE servant is returned so late my dear Sir, that I cannot bring you the *good news* myself, as it will be your dinner time before I get to you.

My dearest child has wrote to you,[1] but I fear you will not have the

1. Her cousin, Anne Clement. HW's   1. *Ante* 11 Oct. 1789.
letter on this occasion is missing.

letter till tomorrow, but that will be time enough to know the particulars, as I can with God's blessing put your heart at rest—I now dread that he should not be sufficiently careful of his recovery—I send a note to poor Nancy—

Yours ever and ever

MARIA

From the DUCHESS OF GLOUCESTER, Wednesday 14 October 1789

Printed for the first time from a photostat of the MS in the possession of Lord Waldegrave.

Address: The Honourable Horace Walpole Twickenham.

Postmark: OC 14 89.

Wednesday.[1]

My dear Sir,

I HAVE just got two letters from my *happy daughter*. My son goes on well, so much so that he has sent me word that he has had a delirious bilious fever but hopes now to live to see me again[2]— This change is *happiness,* a feel[ing] I did not think I ever should know again.

I hope you mend accordingly. Will you be so good as to let Mr Pennicott know that next Sunday, if he can come to the Pavillions at nine o'clock I shall be obliged to him. I am, dear Sir,

Ever affectionately yours

MARIA

1. Biddulph mistakenly dates this letter 11 Oct. (p. 331).

2. Lord Waldegrave d. 17 Oct.; the Duchess arrived at Packington about 21 Oct. and stayed until about 20 Nov. (see OSSORY iii. 75, 83; MORE 334 and n. 3).

From the HON. WILLIAM WALDEGRAVE,[1]
Tuesday 20 October 1789

Printed for the first time from a photostat of the MS in the possession of Lord Waldegrave.

Packington October 20th 8 o'clock.

My dear Sir,

YOU are like myself, unhappily, but too well acquainted with the melancholy event that has lately happened here,[2] but as there are circumstances attending it that may serve to lessen the affliction of those most nearly concerned, I think it a duty I owe to my brother's dearest friends to communicate them as soon as possible. You will readily conceive, my dear Sir, how painful this task is to me, but 'tis a debt due to those who were sensible of my poor dear brother's merits, and cost what it will, it shall be paid.

As I have been long acquainted with my brother's tender regard for you, and I have every reason to suppose it to have been reciprocal, 'tis to you, my dear Sir, that I first address myself on this melancholy occasion, and I pray to heaven that the bitter moments this painful task will cost me, may serve in proportion to lessen yours. My head is at present too much confused to arrange my ideas in any degree of order, you will therefore pardon any incoherencies you may observe, and I will endeavour to express my thoughts as clearly as I am able.

In the first place you will learn with the greatest satisfaction, that from the first moment of the physicians[3] being called in to visit my brother to the moment of his decease, his case was clearly understood by them, so that every assistance that art could afford has been administered. As a confirmation of what I have advanced, the body has been opened, and with one exception, found to be precisely in the state in which it was conjectured to have been. Lord A[ylesford] who is in possession of the report of this examination, shall give me a copy of it for your inspection. The exception above alluded to, was that upon opening the body, the heart was found to be of an unusual figure and size, the first supposed to have been from its original

1. (1753–1825), 2d son of the 3d Earl Waldegrave; Capt. R. N., 1776; Vice-Adm., 1795; Adm. of the Blue, 1802, of the White, 1805, of the Red, 1810; cr. (1800) Bn Radstock. He was younger brother of the 4th Lord Waldegrave who had just died, and first cousin of the bereaved Lady Waldegrave.

2. Lord Waldegrave's death 17 Oct.

3. See *ante* 22 Sept., 2 Oct. 1789.

formation, the latter, from occasional inflammations. This circumstance alone, must have in the course of a few years brought on an untimely death, previous to which, the bodily pain that my poor brother has of late endured, must have increased to the most violent degree, therefore, this being the case, it is surely better for us that the event should have terminated as it has done. To have dragged through a few years of pain and misery and then to have ended by a sudden death, which the physicians say must inevitably have been the case, is surely infinitely more dreadful than the event, however cruel, that has happened; therefore we ought to be rather thankful than ready to condemn the ways of Providence upon this trying occasion.

Thus you perceive, my dear Sir, that we have at least the satisfaction of knowing that as far as human skill can be depended on, my poor brother has had every assistance that this world can afford. This same assistance he might have received in London or perhaps elsewhere, but there are other circumstances attending his being here, that I will take upon me to say have been providential to the greatest degree, and to which alone I will venture boldly to affirm, Lady W. owes her present existence. These are, my dear Sir, the unparalleled kindness and attention of Lord and Lady Aylesford. Oh, my dear Sir, 'tis not in words to communicate their angelic conduct upon this heart-rending occasion. Lord A. is all perfection. No, never did I see, no, never could I ever figure to myself that tenderness and manly fortitude that constitutes his character. His kindness and unwearied attention to my poor sister are not to be told. May heaven reward him with every comfort and blessing in this life and in that also to come—for the present I must quit my pen.

11 o'clock.

I am now more composed, and will continue what I have to say in as few words as possible, as I find my mind unequal to the sad task I have imposed on myself. My head is even at this moment so distracted, that I fear you will almost find parts of my letter unintelligible.

I am now going to communicate to you what will equally astonish you and give you pleasure. Alas! 'tis now the only sad consolation that remains for us! This is the wonderful composure in which Lady W. remains. 'Tis not the effect of stupor, but that of reason founded on religion. Till this morning, I have not seen her shed a single tear since my brother's death, and she talks of him with a degree of composure not to be described. She visited the body twice, without expressing much emotion, and had his picture brought into the room yesterday without its having any visible effect on her. When she is talking of him, she is as calm as if she was conversing about a common acquaintance, but when she is silent, her looks but too well express the agony of her mind. Never did I behold a human being so seemingly attached to her duty as she seems to be, and this alone supports her, and will support her, if anything can. She says her only prayer is that God will give her strength to overcome this severe trial that she may live to do her duty by her children.[4] During my brother's illness, she was almost frantic with anxiety, but from the moment of his decease, she seems to have been inspired with a calmness which God alone can bestow. Heaven grant this may continue. It seems that my poor brother has suffered as much bodily pain during his illness as possible, and that he was in a violent delirium for some days previous to his death. I fear he has left no will,[5] which leaves poor Lady W., as I understand, in some very unpleasant circumstances. As his death was in some degree unexpected, I was not sent for till too late, the express not reaching my hands till sixteen hours after his death.

The Duchess of G[loucester] is now on the road hither, as is, I flatter myself my eldest sister.[6] Poor Lady W.'s situation[7] renders the assistance of women more necessary to her at present than that of men.

I have now, my dear Sir, fulfilled my task with as much accuracy as my poor distracted brain will permit. Should it afford you the consolation I wish, I shall not think it has cost me too dear. Surely death may be considered as the mirror of perfection, as it hides even each little blemish in the character, whilst it magnifies every virtue and estimable quality. My poor dear brother required not this mirror, judge then what I must feel for so invaluable a loss. How true is it alas, that we are never truly sensible of the value of any object whilst it is in our possession!

I intended writing to our worthy friend Lord Ossory, but you will

---

4. At this time she had five, the eldest six years old: Maria Wilhelmina, George, John James, Edward William, and William (see *ante* 7 Feb. 1785, n. 1; 14 Aug. 1785, n. 1; *post* 22 Sept. 1795, n. 2).
5. See *post* 30 Oct. 1789.

6. Lady Elizabeth Waldegrave (1758–1823), m. (1791) as his second wife, James Brudenell, 5th E. of Cardigan, 1790.
7. I.e., her advanced pregnancy; see *post* 23 Nov. 1789, n. 1.

readily conceive how incapable I am at this moment of the task. As I know that he ever possessed the strongest regard for my brother, it would probably afford him much consolation to see this letter. Will you then, my dear Sir, have the goodness to enclose it to him.[8] I trust it will have two good effects, the one to convince him that my brother has had every assistance that this world can afford, the other, it will convince him of my most affectionate regard and esteem.

Allow me, my dear Sir, to subscribe myself with every regard and esteem.

Your very affectionate humble servant

WM WALDEGRAVE

To the HON. WILLIAM WALDEGRAVE, ca Thursday 22 October 1789

Missing; only the cover (in HW's hand) has been recovered; it is now in the Osborn Collection, Yale University Library, MS d 64, f. 71.

Address: To the Honourable Captain Waldegrave at the Earl of Aylesford's at Packington near Coventry.

Postmark: OC 22 89.

Endorsed (in an unidentified hand): Horace Walpole.

From ANNE CLEMENT, ca Sunday 25 October 1789

Missing; answered *post* 30 Oct. 1789.

---

8. HW wrote an account to Lady Ossory 29 Oct. 1789 (OSSORY iii. 74–5).

From the DUCHESS OF GLOUCESTER, ca Wednesday 28 October 1789

Missing; mentioned *post* 30 Oct. 1789. See also OSSORY iii. 75.

To ANNE CLEMENT, Friday 30 October 1789

Printed for the first time from the MS now WSL; acquired in September 1959 (in a collection) from Miss Eleanor Forster of Tynemouth, Northumberland.
Address: To Miss Clement at Hamhouse.
Endorsed (in an unidentified hand): Mr H. Walpole 1789 October.

Oct. 30, 1789.

Dear Miss Clement

I HAVE been in town for a few days, and at my return found your long letter,[1] for which I thank you.

I had a letter from the Duchess on yesterday,[2] who is charmed with the attentions and goodness of Lord and Lady Aylesford. The Duchess thinks Lady Waldegrave will go a week longer,[3] and as she has had time to be more composed, I hope it will secure her safety. She has indeed in the midst of her deep affliction, behaved with so much pious resignation and patience ever since the fatal day, that the Duchess is transported with her. Her circumstances her R.H. says will be very comfortable, which I did not expect,[4] and you will be glad to hear. There is no will. Lady W. has very properly chosen Lord Aylesford guardian of her children, and he has been so good as to accept it. He was so attentive too as to attend the burial with his own brothers.[5]

The Duke has given the Duchess leave to stay as long as she is necessary to her daughter.

If Lord Dysart wishes you to go anywhere with him,[6] I hope you will oblige him. He has shown[7] so much sincere regard for dear Lady

1. Her letter and the one from the Duchess of Gloucester are missing.
2. 'Thursday' altered to 'yesterday' in the MS.
3. See *post* 23 Nov. 1789, n. 1.
4. HW sent her a gift of money, acknowledged *post* 23 Nov. 1789.
5. Listed in OSSORY iii. 74, n. 3.

6. Since Lady Dysart's death 5 Sept. 1789, Anne Clement had come to help Lord Dysart in his affliction (OSSORY iii. 63; see the Ds of Gloucester's letters to Anne Clement at this time).
7. 'Chosen' crossed out and 'shown' written above.

Dysart,[8] that all her family owe it to him to endeavour to make his life as comfortable as we can. Time, I hope, will do more.

I am much better than I was, and hope to get abroad next week.

Adieu, my dear Madam,

Yours most sincerely

H. Walpole

From Lady Waldegrave, Monday 23 November 1789

Printed for the first time from a photostat of the MS in the possession of Lord Waldegrave.

Packington November 23, 1789.

My dearest Sir,

I HAVE been under the necessity of writing a letter upon business this day, therefore I should feel very ungrateful if I did not address a few lines to you, whom I have such obligations to and for whom I feel so great an affection—The regard you had for my dearest Lord when living and the affliction his death caused you makes me feel an attachment and love for you that I cannot express: indeed my heart is so oppressed with sorrow that I cannot attempt describing what passes in it, you knew his worth, you knew his merit, therefore must be sensible that his loss to me is irreparable. I am so convinced that those are favoured by the Almighty who are released from this world of misery, that the severity of my punishment will I hope plead in my favour at the last day, and that God may have compassion on me and grant that I may join my dearest husband in a joyful resurrection never more to be separated from him—I saw him after his death, his countenance placid and serene as when he was alive, I thought then that it could not be Heaven's will that an affection so strong as ours was for each other could then be at [an] end, but that we should meet in those mansions where holy souls rest and

8. The Duchess of Gloucester wrote Anne Clement 26 July 1790, 'The attentions you meet with at Ham, are proofs of esteem people had there for my dear sister [Lady Dysart]' (MS now wsl).

weep no more; this reflection supports me, for with five (I might say six) infants[1] it would be impious to wish to die. And therefore I think that a few wretched years will soon be past, that keeping constantly in my mind to accomplish, as far as I can, what were his wishes and intentions respecting them and other things will be the best preparation for the next world. The look forward to Eternity is such, that the space that there may be for me to pass between this life and that appears short, and my prayers are hourly offered up that I may so live and perform my remaining duties that when I am called away I may be fit to die—

Your generosity[2] has enabled me to settle many pecuniary affairs and to reward those who were unremitting in their attendance upon him; for I must say that not only Lord and Lady Aylesford[3] and their brothers showed an uncommon friendship for him, but every servant in the house appeared so anxious and were so careful of him that an indifferent person might have imagined that each had no other concern than waiting upon him—

If I survive my lying-in, you are one of the few I shall wish to see, for my affections are so entirely fixed upon his grave that those who most loved him are those who I am most interested about—You, my dearest Sir, I reckon one that loved him most.

Adieu, my dearest Sir,

Your truly

affectionate and unhappy niece

E. LAURA WALDEGRAVE

---

1. Her daughter, Lady Charlotte, was born 2 Dec. (see MORE 334, n. 2; OSSORY iii. 72, n. 12). HW wrote Pinkerton 15 Dec. 1789 that Lord Waldegrave's death 'left me in the greatest anxiety for his widow, who thought herself at the end of her pregnancy, but was not delivered till (above two months after his death) a fortnight ago' (CHATTERTON 310).

2. This is the only reference found to HW's timely gift.

3. See *ante* 30 Oct. 1789.

From the Hon. William Waldegrave,
Wednesday 3 February 1790

Printed for the first time from a photostat of the MS in the possession of Lord Waldegrave.
Address: The Honourable Horace Walpole Berkeley Square London.
Postmark: FE 4 90 WALTHAM CROSS

Claramont Waltham-Cross February 3d.

My dear Sir,

IT is with the most sincere satisfaction that I acquaint you, that I yesterday left Lady Waldegrave in a far more tranquil state than I had heretofore observed her in.[1] Not that I by any means flatter myself that my poor sister will ever entirely recover the cruel blow which has caused her affliction, on the contrary, I am thoroughly persuaded this will never happen, but it is with the most heartfelt pleasure I behold in her the beginning of that serenity of mind, which once attained, is all that can be hoped for after such a loss, from a person of her natural melancholy disposition.

When sorrow is not deep-rooted, the having, what is generally termed the pleasures of life, within our reach, quickly makes us forget our misfortune; but my poor sister's grief is of that poignant nature, that she seems to have totally renounced all worldly joys, so that her sole comfort is now drawn from the divine contemplation of a future state. The numerous books she has of late read upon this sublime subject, have already wrought her mind to that wonderful pitch of serenity, that I scarce believe any one misfortune in life that might befall her, could extract from her a tear.

Thus we see, my dear Sir, in spite of all Voltaire's wit and Mr Hume's philosophy, that religion alone can produce in a young mind the same effect, as all the boasted reasonings of the philosophers united. I am well aware that were all persons to testify their grief in the same manner as my unhappy sister, that the world would soon be annihilated; nevertheless examples of this kind held forth now and then, may certainly be considered as a benefit to the rest of our

---

1. On 4 Jan. 1790 the Duchess of Gloucester wrote Anne Clement, 'Poor dear Lady Waldegrave goes to Southill today! It will be terrible for her, the first meeting with her still happy sisters—may they ever remain so—but, now that the felicity of my children is broken into I never can feel secure' (MS now wsl).

fellow creatures, and as such, no doubt, are wisely ordered by the supreme disposer of all things.

I take for granted that you have been already informed that all my sister's children[2] are confined with the whooping-cough. As they were yesterday better, I trust their disorder is of the mild kind.

I was astonished to see their mother's composure upon this trying occasion, which only serves to prove how entirely insensible she is grown to the miseries and blessings of this world. However as this state of despondency cannot but be highly detrimental to the poor children, with so powerful an argument on our side, it is to be hoped that in time we may conquer it.

Believe me to be,

My dear Sir,

Most truly and affectionately yours

WM WALDEGRAVE

From LADY ANNA HORATIA SEYMOUR-CONWAY, ca Thursday 4 February 1790

Missing; mentioned *post* 6 Feb. 1790.

To the HON. WILLIAM WALDEGRAVE, Saturday 6 February 1790

Printed for the first time from the MS now WSL. Sold Sotheby's 11 Dec. 1957 (Lady Davidson's Sale), lot 728, to Francis Edwards; resold Christie's 18 Dec. 1968, lot 10, to Seven Gables Bookstore for WSL.

Address: To the Honourable Captain Waldegrave at Claremont near Waltham Cross.

Postmark: FE 6 90.

Berkeley Square Feb. 6, 1790.

I AM much obliged to you, dear Sir, for the kind account[1] you have given me of Lady Waldegrave and her children, and I am very

2. See *ante* 20 Oct. 1789, n. 4.   1. *Ante* 3 Feb. 1790.

glad of the visit you have been so good as to make to her, as I know what comfort she has in your company and advice. By a letter[2] I received from Lady Horatia yesterday I had the pleasure of hearing that all the children are mending. Your own children[3] and Mrs Waldegrave[4] I hope are quite recovered.

Lady Waldegrave's great piety is in every light, Sir, the most fortunate circumstance that could have happened to her, for though it does not diminish her loss, it enables her both to bear it with submission, and makes[5] her neglect none of her duties. Providence has graciously decreed that time should soften the greatest griefs. The acuteness of memory too[6] is blunted by lapse of time; and it is the nature of an affectionate heart to want an object of its tenderness: and thence I conclude that Lady Waldegrave's attachment to your brother will insensibly devolve to his children, though at present the sight of them only seems to renew her sorrow.

I am glad, as you approved of that plan, Sir, that she has determined to let Navestock,[7] and till all her necessary business is finished, will take some house not far from London. Indeed all her conduct is so guided by reason and advice, that I flatter myself all the friends of the Excellent Man she has lost, will think she acts as he would have wished she should.[8] I have the honour to be with great respect and gratitude, Sir, your most obliged and obedient humble servant

HOR. WALPOLE

2. Missing.

3. Granville George (1786–1857), 2d Bn Radstock, 1825; William (1796–1838); Emily Susanna Laura (d. 1870); Isabella Elizabeth (d. 1866); Harriet Anne Frances (d. 1880); Caroline (d. 1878) (Sir Bernard Burke and A. P. Burke, *Peerage and Baronetage*, 1928, p. 1914).

4. Cornelia Jacoba Van Lennep (d. 1839), dau. of David Van Lennep, chief of the Dutch factory at Smyrna, m. (1785) William Waldegrave, cr. (1800) Bn Radstock.

5. Originally 'to make'; 'to' crossed out and 's' added to 'make.'

6. An extra 'too' crossed out before 'too.'

7. The Duchess of Gloucester wrote Anne Clement 10 Aug. 1790, 'Tomorrow I go to Lady Waldegrave for two days. She now wishes to live on in Essex [at Navestock]—I knew it would be so, but she would not attend to my advice' (MS now WSL).

8. The Duchess of Gloucester wrote Anne Clement 10 June 1790, 'I passed two days last week with Lady Waldegrave; she is well in health—it is the will of heaven that she should be left to deplore the loss of a man who is a loss to the world—it must be right because it is so, but I must forever wish it had not been right' (MS now WSL).

To George, 5th Earl Waldegrave, ?Sunday 21 March 1790

Printed for the first time from a photostat of the MS in the possession of Lord Waldegrave.

Dated conjecturally by the reference to the box of papers which HW left to the Earl Waldegrave; see n. 1.

Address: To George Earl Waldegrave.

My dear Lord,

WHEN you shall have time to read over the mass of papers contained in this box,[1] you will find that they are not proper to be seen by anybody at present; and therefore I trust that you will not mention the contents to anybody, but reserve them in your own custody. They are most imperfect both at the beginning and end; nor do I wish *ever* to have them published;[2] but as they contain a great deal of curious matter, you may like to have them preserved in your family; but I am sure will give strong injunctions against their being made public in any manner. I have so high an opinion both of your good sense and honour, that I trust them entirely to your discretion.

HOR. WALPOLE

1. HW in a memorandum dated 21 March 1790 and countersigned 19 Aug. 1796 instructed his executor to 'cord up strongly and seal the larger chest, marked with A, and deliver it to the Honourable Hugh Seymour Conway, to be kept by him unopened and unsealed till the eldest son of Lady Waldegrave, or whichever of her sons, being Earl of Waldegrave, shall attain the age of twenty-five years; when the said chest, with whatever it contains, shall be delivered to him for his own' (MANN i. p. xliv, n. 6). It appears that HW's letter should be dated between the death of George, 4th E. Waldegrave in 1789 and 1791 when HW became E. of Orford. George, 5th E. Waldegrave was born in 1784 and died in 1794; his brother John James, 6th E. Waldegrave was born in 1785; he inherited the manuscripts in Chest A in 1810, on reaching the age of 25, and later turned them over to his trustee the 3d Lord Holland (ibid. i. p. xlviii).

2. Lord Holland made a list of the contents of Chest A 'as I received it from Sir James Mackintosh' in 1820 (Holland to Waldegrave 22 March 1820), when the publication of some of the manuscripts was being considered. Of HW's letter of instructions Lord Holland wrote Lord Waldegrave ca 1821, 'The letter which I re-enclose is most unaccountable and quite at variance with the appearance and in some instances with the text of the Memoires as I will show you when you come here' (MSS now WSL).

From the Hon. Thomas Walpole, April 1790

Missing; answered *post* 9 April 1790.

To the Hon. Thomas Walpole, Friday
9 April 1790

Printed from a photostat of the Holland MS; first printed, Sir Spencer Walpole 106–7; reprinted, Toynbee xiv. 248. For the history of the MS see *ante* 18 July 1766.

April 9th 1790.

Dear Sir,

I WAS obliged to go out just as I received your obliging communication, which I now return with many thanks. The letter is uncommonly sensible, clear and descriptive, and paints not only what is, but what certainly will happen, the last confusion[1]—and though the nation does not yet seem to turn, I am persuaded that it will, as soon as any considerable convulsion happens, and common sense tells one what numerous thousands must be ready to join and promote a re-revolution. How that will terminate, no foresight can predict—much less in favour of whom—not, I fear, of liberty, for however active patriotism may be at the outset of reformation, self-interest and ambition are endowed with much more perseverance.

My poor lame fingers cannot well say more, and they produce daily so much chalk, that I could write with it on black paper,[2] as easily as on white with ink.

Your much obliged

humble servant

Hor. Walpole

1. The French Revolution.
2. 'Soon mayhap I must write upon a slate; it will only be scraping my fingers to a point, as they will serve for a chalk pencil' (HW to Lady Ossory 15 Nov. 1781, Ossory ii. 310).

From the Duchess of Gloucester, Friday
5 November 1790

Missing. 'Last Friday the Duchess of Gloucester sent me one [an account of Hugh Conway], something better' (HW to Lady George Lennox 10 Nov. 1790, More 356).

From Thomas Walpole the Younger, ca Tuesday
11 October 1791

Missing; answered *post* 12 Oct. 1791.

To Thomas Walpole the Younger, Wednesday
12 October 1791

Printed for the first time from a photostat of the Holland MS. For the history of the MSS see *ante* 18 July 1766.
Address: To Thomas Walpole Junior Esq. in Stratton Street Piccadilly.

Strawberry Hill, Oct. 12, 1791.

Dear Sir,

I RECEIVED the favour of your kind letter but too late this evening to answer it by accepting your proposal.[1] I have frequently inquired of your father about you and when I should be likely to see you here. I do wish it could have been sooner, as you will not see my house in good order. I am sorry too, that I cannot name a precise day directly, because in this numerous neighbourhood our parties are begun, and I am engaged every evening till Wednesday. If that day should suit you I will keep myself entirely free; or if you would like to come sooner, I will propose to you to come on Saturday morning early and dine with me, and in the evening I will carry you to Madame de Boufflers[2] at Richmond and bring you back hither; or the

1. Apparently to visit SH.
2. Marie-Charlotte-Hippolyte de Cam-

pet de Saujon (1725–1800), m. (1746) Édouard, Comte (Marquis, 1751) de

same on Monday to Lady Mount Edgcumbe[3]—and I own I should rather prefer the latter, as the Duchess of Gloucester generally comes to me on Saturday morning, and I should have less time to walk about with you. I hope some one of these proposals will not be inconvenient to you; and I will beg you to let me know which by a line.

I am dear Sir

Yours most sincerely

Hor. Walpole

From Lord Cadogan, ca Saturday 19 November 1791

Missing. 'Nor should I have known a syllable of his [Lord Orford's] disorder and danger, had not Lord Cadogan,[1] who lives in the neighbourhood, sent me word of it, the persons in the house with Lord O. and his servants totally concealing his situation from me, and from both his steward and his lawyer in town, who knew it but not from me' (HW to Lady Ossory 23 Nov. 1791, Ossory iii. 129–30). See Appendix 6.

From Jane Clement, ca Tuesday 6 December 1791

Missing; answered *post* 10 Dec. 1791.

Boufflers - Rouverel. She had come to England in 1789 (Ossory i. 14 and n. 11; iii. 68 and n. 12).

3. Emma Gilbert (1729–1807) daughter of the Abp of York, m. (1761) George Edgcumbe (1720–95), 3d Bn Edgcumbe, 1761;

cr. (1781) Vct and (1789) E. of Mount Edgcumbe.

———

1. See *ante* July 1775, n. 1 and 7 Aug. 1777.

To Jane Clement, Saturday 10 December 1791

Printed for the first time from the MS now wsl. Sold Christie's 28 Nov. 1960 (Property of a Gentleman), lot 131, to Maggs for wsl.
Address: To Mrs Clement at Windsor Castle.
Postmark: 10 E < > 91.
Endorsed (in an unidentified hand): Ho. Walpole.

Berkeley Square Dec. 10, 1791.

THANK you a thousand times, my dear Madam, for your kind letter;[1] it has obliged me extremely, as coming from a true friend, though I am far from having the least pleasure in a title at my age;[2] and for the estate, it may give me a great deal of trouble, and probably not much advantage. However I am quite content with the poor man that is gone, not having passed me over.[3] I knew not a tittle of the contents of his will[4] till yesterday noon, and now very confusedly. He has given me the whole Norfolk estate, but with great encumbrances on it,[5] so that from prudence as well as inclination to a private life at my age, I shall not make an alteration of a shilling to my usual expense till after a whole year, when I may judge what I can call my own—and then I believe you know me too well to think that I will launch into any parade of equipages and show, so unsuitable to my age as well as disposition.

I hope you continue as well as when I had the pleasure of seeing you; and allow me as long as I can without affectation to sign myself

your obliged and

obedient humble servant
HOR. WALPOLE

1. Missing.
2. On the death of his nephew 5 Dec. 1791, HW became 4th E. of Orford.
3. HW wrote Lady Ossory 10 Dec. 1791, 'I had reason to think that he had disgraced by totally omitting me—but . . . he has restored me to my birthright' (OSSORY iii. 134).
4. There were two wills, one dated 25 Nov. 1752 (P.C.C. 166 Fountain) and another dated 31 March 1756; a codicil dated 4 Dec. 1776 refers to the will of 1752 but does not mention that of 1756. The will of 1752 with five codicils was

probated at London 7 March 1792; the descent of the Houghton estate was first to Sir Edward Walpole, second to HW, third to the Cholmondeleys, and fourth to the Walpoles of Wolterton (see Appendix 1, n. 1; 'Joseph Farington's Anecdotes,' DALRYMPLE 323–4 and nn. 52, 53).
5. The total indebtedness charged on the estate is not known, but when HW made his will 15 May 1793 the two mortgages then outstanding amounted to £17,500 (SELWYN 345). Orford after his mother's death had mortgaged the Norfolk lands for £12,000, which could not

DOROTHY CLEMENT, BY AN UNKNOWN ARTIST

To Anne Clement, Saturday, 10 December 1791

Printed for the first time from the MS now wsl; acquired in September 1959 from Miss Eleanor Forster of Tynemouth, Northumberland.
Address: To Miss Clement in Bury Street St James's.

Berkeley Square, Dec. 10, 1791.

Dear Miss Clement

I HOPE Miss Keppel[1] told you how much I wished to see you, any morning that you pleased. Nay, I am persuaded she did tell you, and that you who are always kindly partial to me, only kept away from tenderness for me, knowing in what distress and fatigue I was involved by my late nephew's illness.[2] The anxiety has fatally ceased by his death: trouble I must have by succeeding to his estate[3]—but as I can now pay no more attention to his preservation, I must gratify myself by seeing a few of my best friends; and as you are in that number, I shall be happy if it will suit you to call on me as soon as you come from church tomorrow—I love you too well to finish by a compliment, when I am

dear Madam

Yours most affectionately and sincerely

Orford

From Thomas Walpole the Younger, June 1792

Missing; answered *post* 26 June 1792.

be paid off until the other debts and legacies had been paid (see Ossory iii. 134, n. 3; 136, n. 2).

———

1. Charlotte Augusta Keppel, HW's great-niece.
2. Lord Orford had become violently ill at Brandon, Suffolk and HW had sent Dr

Monro to him (Ossory iii. 129–30). HW wrote Lady Ossory 23 Nov. 1791, 'I have been entirely shut up with my own family since Lord O.'s illness' (ibid. iii. 132). See Appendix 6.
3. See *ante* HW to Jane Clement 10 Dec. 1791.

To Thomas Walpole the Younger, Tuesday
26 June 1792

Printed from a photostat of the Holland MS; first printed, Sir Spencer Walpole 107–13; reprinted, Toynbee xv. 113–16. For the history of the MS see *ante* 18 July 1766.

There is a sketch, presumably by Thomas Walpole, on the back of the letter: a man's head, with cap, improvised upon an accidental ink blot.

Strawberry Hill, June 26, 1792.

I AM much obliged to you, dear Sir, for the trouble you have taken to clear up the matter of Monsieur d'Ormesson's[1] letter. You cannot wonder that I concluded it was not meant for me, when you find it was to thank me for a present made to the library of the late King of France six and twenty years ago! was it possible for me to suppose that the present reigning powers at Paris were busying themselves in paying debts of their quondam monarchs?—indeed they do pay them in their present coin, paper! This reminiscence puts me in mind of Tiberius's answer[1a] to the Trojan ambassadors who were sent to condole with him on the death of Augustus long after his exit—he condoled with them in return on the loss of so excellent a citizen as Hector—if I live six and twenty years longer, and the House of Bourbon is reestablished, I will send an answer to one of Monsieur d'Ormesson's successors.

To be sure I have been singularly circumstanced about presents of my editions to royal personages! Never having been an officious Royalist, my offerings have always been solicited, not obtruded. In 1766 the royal librarians desired to have my editions for the Bibliothèque du Roi. On my return to England I did send a set complete to that era,[2] handsomely bound, as M. d'Ormesson testifies—and I did receive a letter of thanks—from the under-librarian[3]—so M. d'Ormesson's is supererogation of gratitude. I did imagine they might have given me a set of the Louvre prints of Louis Quatorze's vic-

1. Anne-Louis-François de Paule le Fèvre d'Ormesson de Noyseau (1753–94), keeper of the King's library; Greek scholar (NBG). His letter to HW is dated 5 April 1792.

1a. Suetonius, *Lives of the Cæsars*, iii. 52. 2.

2. Fifteen volumes bearing the SH im-

print are in the Bibliothèque Nationale (DU DEFFAND i. 262, n. 8).

3. Possibly Jean Capperonnier (1716–75), keeper of books at the Bibliothèque du Roi (NBG); see HW's letters to him 17, 21 Nov. 1766. His letter to HW is missing.

tories, palaces etc.—a common present for contributions to their library,[4] and I should not have haggled about receiving a compliment from a crowned head, when the overture had issued thence. Some years afterwards,[5] Count Potocki[6] brought me a message from the present King of Poland,[7] with whom I had been acquainted when he was in England,[8] desiring my *Anecdotes of Painting*—It distressed me, as they were out of print—and I had only my own set. In short, I was reduced to buy a second hand set (yet in good condition) and though the original set sold for less than thirty shillings, I was forced to pay thirteen guineas, from their scarcity. In return, I received a letter of thanks[9] in his Majesty's own hand—if the Russians depose him,[10] and destroy that really noble new constitution,[11] which I shall lament as much as I detest the French anarchy, perhaps some Muscovite librarian of Catherine Slayczar will a few years hence send me duplicate thanks.

My third royal tribute has been still less acknowledged. A Dane or Islander,[11a] sent over hither to collect books and MSS for the Prince of Denmark[12] and for the illustration of their history, came to me, and, in the name of his Royal Highness, requested my editions, and offered me for them their splendid book of shells[13] (which, by the way, your father, dear Sir, gave me many years ago) I said I did not *sell* my editions; it would be sufficient honour if his R.H. would condescend to accept them. The emissary then proposed medals to me, or any thing I should like. I adhered to my refusal, and at last said earnestly, I did not sell books. A larger set I did send, as I had printed other editions, as you may imagine, splendidly bound—Several months afterwards the negotiator told me with some confusion

4. HW already owned 8 volumes of these prints, listed in Hazen, *Cat. of HW's Lib.*, No. 3591, two of them being now wsl. They were erroneously described in the SH sale catalogue, ix. 1189–96, as a gift from Louis XVI.

5. In 1786 (HW to Stanislas II 7 April 1786).

6. Probably Comte Ignace Potocki, grand marshal of Lithuania, son-in-law of the Princess Lubomirska who was Stanislas II's cousin, and who had visited HW at SH (Stanislas II, *Mémoires*, St Petersburg, 1914–24, i. 699, ii. 213, 566–7; Ossory ii. 565, n. 27).

7. See *ante* 8 April 1786.

8. In 1754 (HW to Chute 14 May 1754).

9. Stanislas II to HW 7 June 1786.

10. Catherine II's ultimatum of 22 July 1792 stripped Stanislas II of power. He was forced to abdicate in 1795 (Hannah More to HW ca 18 Aug. 1792, More 371, n. 4).

11. There was a 'state revolution' in the government of Poland 3–5 May 1791 (see Berry i. 286, n. 21).

11a. I.e. Icelander (oed).

12. Since 1784, Frederik (1768–1839) had been prince regent of Denmark for his father, Christian VII, whom he succeeded in 1808.

13. See *ante* 26 Oct. 1778, n. 1.

that he had received a letter from the Danish Prime Minister,[14] telling him that the Prince Royal would write to me himself by the next post—which post is not yet come in, though due three years ago. I have met the man several times since, who is always in confusion and trying to make awkward apologies—whether really blushing for his principal, or for having played me a trick for himself, I know not—but at last, I told him, I desired to hear no more about the matter—and I do hope never to be honoured again with parallel commands, which have cost me much more than vainglory is worth.

I thank you for your inquiries after my health—I am free from pain, and am content. I did not at past seventy-four expect to recover —I ought rather to say, gain strength, of which mighty little ever was my lot. I still creep about as nimbly as a tortoise; and wishing to do nothing more than I do, my situation is comfortable enough; and I take care not to look forward, not only because there may be no *forward* for me, but because at my age any alteration must be for the worst. I should be still more in the wrong to trust to amendment from fine weather. If I turn to the left, I see my hay yonder soaking under the rain; and on the right I have a good fire—'tis pity we ever imported from the continent ideas of summer: nature gave us coal mines in lieu of it, and beautiful verdure, which is inconsistent with it, so that an observation I made forty years ago, is most true, that this country exhibits the most beautiful landscapes in the world when they are framed and glazed, that is, when you look at them through the window.

With lawsuits I thank my stars and myself, I am not disturbed—I gave up everything that I could have contested; and though a vast deal of the vast injustice I have suffered came from the suggestions of lawyers, who were malicious, even out of their profession and without interest, I have not put it into their power to plague me by employing them. I am merely a peg on which the issue of a lawsuit hangs;[15] and as I do not take part in it, it does not molest my tranquillity. I

14. The Greve Andreas Peter Bernstorff (1735–97) had been restored as prime minister, in the reorganization of the Danish government in 1784 (*Dansk biografisk Leksikon,* Copenhagen, 1933–44, ii. 507–20).

15. The descent of the Houghton estate had been settled by the third Lord Orford's will, but a suit was under way between the Cholmondeleys and the Walpoles of Wolterton on the right of succession (SELWYN 344, n. 1, 372, n. 68). See *ante* 10 Dec. 1791; Appendix 1, n. 1.

wish you as long and as quiet an old age, and any thing you wish in the meantime.

I am, dear Sir,

Your most affectionate humble servant

Orford

PS. I am still in the dark, and to guess who the Horace Walpole, *homme âgé* was, who Monsieur d'Ormesson says was frequently at the Royal Library, but has not been seen there for a whole year—It is most sure that an old Horace Walpole has not been there in seventeen years—and if M. d'Ormesson can make an anachronism of 17 years, it is not so wonderful that he should thank me in 1791, for a present I made in 1766, and which was not made *progressivement* but at once. It is like one of the mad rants in Lee's[16] plays where a lover begs the Gods *to annihilate Time and Space*, that he and his mistress may meet incontinently, at the expense only of many years and miles![17]

From Lady Waldegrave, Wednesday 4 July 1792

Printed for the first time from a photostat of the MS in the possession of Lord Waldegrave.

Navestock July 4, 1792.

My dear Lord,

WHEN I was in town ten days since you were then settled at Strawberry Hill which deprived me of the pleasure of seeing you, therefore I cannot resist writing to know how you do?—I passed three or four days in London as I was on my way to Eton whither I took my two eldest boys[1]—they are now established at that school; they live in the house with Mr Boggust[2] a clergyman

16. Nathaniel Lee (?1653–92), dramatist.

17. 'Ye Gods! annihilate but *Space* and
    Time
    And make two Lovers happy.'
(Pope, *Of the Art of Sinking in Poetry*, Chapter 11). The quotation has not been traced to any of Lee's plays.

1. George, 5th E. Waldegrave, and the Hon. John James Waldegrave.

2. Thomas (Peter) Boggust (1765–17 Nov. 1792), fellow of King's College, Cambridge 1787–92; d. at Eton where he was Assistant Master 1791–2 (Venn, *Alumni Cantab.*; R. A. Austen-Leigh, *Eton College Register 1753–1790*, Eton, 1921, p. 56).

whom my Lord and myself saw three years since at Scarborough with Lord Holland;[3] he pleased us both so much that upon finding after very particular inquiries that he is a worthy and respectable young man, I determined to place my boys under his care—George likes school very much; Johnny says 'it is a very *odd* place that it is so full of *boys* and *Latin* and that he only likes it *middling*.' Maria[4] and I think we are rather uncomfortable without these two dear boys, but indeed while we live we are obliged to suffer the deprivation of our greatest comforts, in another world I have no doubt that we shall all meet where there will be no separation, and that the society of those dearest to us will constitute great part of our felicity—

The Duchess has been with me a week, she left me yesterday, I really think she is now getting well, her complaint[5] abates and she looks better, her spirits are much mended, therefore I trust she will now be restored to good health—I yesterday received one of the kindest of letters from Lord Cornwallis.[6] He was one of the friends whom my Lord loved the best, Lord Cornwallis writes with the greatest affection and regard for the memory of his friend and assures me for his sake that while he lives he will be every assistance in his power to his children—The loss I have sustained is one of those inflictions of Providence that is grievous to bear, but I have the consolation to experience proofs of regard for his sake that are strong marks of the veneration he was held in—I saw Lord Thurlow when I was in town who notwithstanding the events that have happened to himself[7] appeared as warmly interested about my children's welfare as ever—indeed he is a worthy good man and although he has not met with the reward due to his merits in this life, yet I hope he will be happy in another—

Adieu, my dear Lord

Wishing you all health and prosperity

I am your affectionate and obliged niece

E. LAURA WALDEGRAVE

3. Henry Richard Fox (1773–1840), 3d Bn Holland, 1774.

4. Lady Maria Wilhelmina Waldegrave.

5. Apparently erysipelas (Biddulph 333). The Duchess wrote Anne Clement ca Sept. 1792, 'I am better of my cold, but my face is hideous and uncomfortable' (MS now WSL).

6. HW wrote of this letter, 'How very amiable in the moment of victory to find Alexander the Conqueror of India thinking of writing a consolatory letter to a widow at the other end of the world' (to Lady Ossory 7 July 1792, OSSORY iii. 147).

7. Under Fox and North, Thurlow was compelled to retire in April 1783, but was

There is a gap in the Duchess of Gloucester's correspondence with HW from 1790 to 1797, but the Duchess's letters to Anne Clement contain several references to him, of which the most interesting is in a letter of July 1793: 'I went to Strawberry Hill yesterday evening; and found him just as all single people are in the summer; that is, not knowing what to do with himself between his very bad dinner, and the time of going out: in the winter fire and candle, with a book, makes up for solitude, but in the summer reading does not do forever, and ever and amen.'

From Lady Waldegrave, Friday 12 September 1794

Printed for the first time from a photostat of the MS in the possession of Lord Waldegrave.

Enclosure: The epitaph for the 5th Earl Waldegrave, in his mother's hand.

Navestock. September 12, '94.

My dear Lord,

I SEND you a copy of the epitaph[1] which I propose to have inscribed upon the monument that is to be put up in Eton Chapel. I hope you will approve of it—

Since Mrs H. More[2] has returned to her home she wrote me word that she had passed two mornings with your Lordship at Strawberry Hill and she was much pleased with your having asked her to write a sermon to vindicate the honour of Divine Providence, which it is the fashion boldly to arraign, on occasion of the supposed triumphant success of French wickedness[3]—Miss More says she wishes to see it

restored by William Pitt, and presided at the trial of Warren Hastings (1788). He was finally removed by Pitt in 1792 with the King's approval.

1. Her eldest son George, 5th E. Waldegrave, drowned in the Thames at Eton, 29 June 1794. He 'had come out of the water, and was putting on his clothes, when his two companions thought proper to swim across the river. He stripped himself again, and plunged into the water to follow their example, when he unfortunately sunk [sic] and never rose again' (GM 1794, lxiv pt ii. 673).

2. Hannah More admired Lady Waldegrave's 'exemplary piety.' She wrote to the Duchess of Gloucester in April 1794: 'The little I lately saw of her had convinced me of the soundness of her principles; that her religion flows from an internal principle of divine grace, and was not a transient impression excited by the heavy pressure of some mere casual feeling' (William Roberts, *Memoirs of . . . Hannah More*, 1834, ii. 397). See also Ossory iii. 203.

3. Lady Waldegrave wrote to her mother after the execution of Louis XVI: 'I have made the servants put on mourn-

executed by better hands than hers; but I sincerely desire as she approves of the idea that she would comply with your request—Among the very few people I see, I have observed the circumstance you allude to, and I think it is presumptuous of beings who cannot know the reasons that the Almighty has for his dispensations to arraign them. The Scriptures inform us that 'the wisdom of man, is foolishness with God!' The whole Gospel speaks of this life being a state of probation, and that the afflictions of this world are not to be considered when we think of that future state of being, when we shall no longer 'see through a glass darkly.'

If I continue writing in this strain, your Lordship will think I am sending you the sermon you desired Mrs More to compose. Therefore I will now conclude with assuring you I am, with respect

Your obliged and affectionate niece

E. LAURA WALDEGRAVE

[Enclosure]

Near this Spot is deposited
all that was mortal
of
George 5th Earl of Waldegrave:
who was born June 13th 1784
and unhappily drowned, when bathing in the Thames
June 29th 1794.
His strict application, even at this early period of his life;
United to uncommon Abilities,
afforded the best grounded hopes that he would have become
an Ornament to Society,
and an honour to the Place of his Education.
His amiable Manners and the sweetness of his Disposition
conciliated the affection of all who knew him.
Such was the exemplary docility
of his temper,
that he never gave his Friends
cause of grief or regret,
till the fatal Moment
which put a period
to his Life.

ing; that is the only mark of respect I can pay to the King of France's memory' (Biddulph 335).

From the Duchess of Gloucester, Thursday 2 October 1794

Missing. 'I have had a note from the Pavilions with a letter to be franked, and as the Duchess tells me nothing new, I suppose there is nothing' (HW to Mary Berry 1 Oct. 1794, postscript 2 Oct., Berry ii. 121).

To Lady Waldegrave, before Sunday 7 December 1794

Missing; answered *post* 7 Dec. 1794.

From Lady Waldegrave, Sunday 7 December 1794

Printed for the first time from a photostat of the MS in the possession of Lord Waldegrave.

Navestock, December 7, 1794.

My dear Lord,

I HAVE not troubled you with a letter from me for some time; I have indeed been very unwell, the shock I received the beginning of this summer has left a kind of terror upon my spirits that to a degree has affected my health—[1] I am rather better now and trust that by change of air and scene I shall get well—Tomorrow I propose going to Culford[2] for a short time, all my children accompany me— Lord Cornwallis is so very good to them and says while he lives he shall do his utmost to supply the place of a father to them: he had indeed the strongest affection for my Lord which he proves by his conduct to us—

Mrs Fitzroy[3] has been with me these five weeks, she is truly amiable and good: she intends going to town tomorrow and is to be at Lord Euston's[4] in Conduit Street, her stay in London is very uncertain—

1. See Ossory iii. 199–200 and n. 5.
2. Culford Hall, Suffolk, Lord Cornwallis's country seat.
3. Mrs George Ferdinand Fitzroy, formerly Laura Keppel.
4. The husband of Lady Charlotte Maria Waldegrave (*ante* 25 May 1776, n. 1).

she is in great hopes Mr Fitzroy will return home soon to her, which I earnestly hope he will, for she suffers so much anxiety about him— My poor sister Lady Horatia has for these five weeks past undergone much; during Lord Hugh's absence upon this last cruise two of her children have had most violent fevers, attended with excruciating pain and danger, they are now convalescent, but she is afraid another child[5] has caught it: I fear it is epidemic as Lady Louisa Atherley[6] (a married daughter of Lord Lothian's) and one of the nursery maids are lying ill of this distemper. The physicians say it is the most alarming complaint they ever before witnessed—I do most anxiously hope that neither my sister nor Lord Hugh will catch it—They are all at Lord Bathurst's[7] in Sussex, his and Lady Bathurst's friendship and kindness to them is most consolatory—I flatter myself, my dear Lord, that you keep your health and have had no attack of the gout—

Maria Sibly[8] is a very good girl and gives me great satisfaction—

I am

My dear Lord, with truth

Your obliged and affectionate niece

E. LAURA WALDEGRAVE

I sent your last letter[9] to Mrs H. More who writes me word she wishes much she were able to do as you desire,[10] but (her expression is) she does not find she has a vocation for it—

5. Lady Horatia had four sons: Sir George Francis Seymour (1787–1870); Hugh Henry Seymour (1790–1821); Horace Beauchamp Seymour (1791–1851), and William John Richard Seymour (1793–1801). Three other children were born later.

6. Lady Louisa Ker (1768–1819), dau. of William John Ker (1737–1815), 5th M. of Lothian, 1775, m. (1793) Arthur Atherley (*Scots Peerage*, ed. Sir James B. Paul, Edinburgh, 1904–14, v. 481–3).

7. Henry Bathurst (1762–1834), 3d E. Bathurst, 1794; m. (1789) Georgiana Lennox (1765–1841), dau. of Lord Lothian's niece, Lady George Lennox (who was HW's correspondent). He was M.P.; lord of the Admiralty 1783–9; of the Treasury 1789–91; foreign secretary, 1809.

8. A domestic, perhaps a daughter to James Sibley (d. before 1793), HW's second footman, who is listed among HW's servants in HW to Charles Bedford 18 June 1781. HW's will (15 May 1793) specifies a legacy of £100 to 'Ann Sibley of Teddington, widow of my late footman James Sibley' (SELWYN 362).

9. Missing.

10. HW had apparently renewed his request to Hannah More (through Lady Waldegrave) for a sermon (see *ante* 12 Sept. 1794). HW referred to his arrangement of a meeting between Hannah More and Lady Waldegrave as 'pimping between two female saints' (HW to Hannah More 27 April 1794, MORE 394).

From the DUCHESS OF GLOUCESTER, before Saturday 24 January 1795

Perhaps two letters, missing: 'I sent one [a prospectus of *Cheap Repository Tracts* by Hannah More] instantly to the Duchess of Gloucester, whose piety and zeal imitate yours at a distance, but she says she cannot afford to subscribe just at this severe moment, when the poor so much want her assistance' (HW to Hannah More 24 Jan. 1795, MORE 396).

To LADY WALDEGRAVE, September 1795

Missing; answered *post* 22 Sept. 1795.

From LADY WALDEGRAVE, Tuesday 22 September 1795

Printed for the first time from a photostat of the MS in the possession of Lord Waldegrave.

Navestock, September 22, 1795.

My dear Lord,

I RETURN you many thanks for your most kind letter[1] which I have received with the warrant for venison—The first buck was so excellent that I feel much indebted to your Lordship for this second, as it would have been an acceptable present to many of your friends—

Your affectionate expressions of regard towards me arrived most opportunely, I was very low. My two eldest sons[2] were setting out for Eton and after what happened last year, you are assured that I do feel the separation very keenly—I had intended writing to your Lordship last week to propose making you a visit *now*, but some business occurred which prevented my putting my design in execu-

1. Missing.
2. John James (1785–1835) and Edward William (1787–1809) see *ante* 14 Aug. 1785, n. 1 and OSSORY ii. 565, n. 23).

Another son, William (1788–1859) and a daughter, Maria Wilhelmina, were still at home (ibid. iii. 74, n. 4).

tion—I shall be happy to hear from you when it will suit that I should pass a day or two at Strawberry Hill and it will give me great pleasure to wait upon you—

My Lord whom you so tenderly regret, I may truly say had not his fellow—indeed as Hamlet observed

> He was a man, take him for all in all,
> I ne'er shall look upon his like again!

Everything in this world is so unsettled and imperfect, that that circumstance points decidedly towards a happier state of existence, where we shall learn the reason of those providences which now are beyond our comprehension—When I say this I do not allude alone to the loss of those dear to us, but to the pain which friends frequently cause (perhaps without intention) but which wounds severely—Your friend Mr West[3] remarked that

> Pain is our lot, and patience is our praise.[4]

Homer made nearly the same observation[5] some thousand years before—Therefore to *bear* and to *forbear* is I believe nearly half of what we have to practise, to enable us to struggle through this life of short continuance—

My children are all well, you are very good to think so much about them—

I am, my dear Lord, your much

obliged and affectionate niece

E. LAURA WALDEGRAVE

3. Richard West (1716–42), HW's correspondent.

4. A quotation from West's 'Ad Amicos' enclosed in his letter to Gray 4 July 1737 (*Correspondence of Gray, Walpole, West, and Ashton*, ed. Toynbee, Oxford, 1915, i. 141).

5. 'The gods have so spun the thread for wretched mortals that they must live in pain' (*Iliad* xxiv. 525–6) or 'The lot of man; to suffer and to die' (*Odyssey*, iii. 117, Pope's translation).

To the Hon. William Waldegrave,
Friday 2 October 1795

Missing; only the cover (in HW's hand) has been recovered; it is now WSL, the gift of the late R. W. Chapman.
Address: To the Honourable Admiral Waldegrave at Portsmouth.
Postmark: OC 2 95. ISLEWORTH.
Franked: Free Oxford.
Endorsed (by HW): Isleworth October the second 1795.

To Rachel, Lady Walpole of Wolterton,[1]
?June 1796

In Kirgate's hand, printed for the first time from a photostat of the MS kindly supplied by the Earl of Leicester at Holkham.
Dated conjecturally by a contested election in Norfolk (which contains both Crostwick and Houghton) at this time; Thomas William Coke's seat was being contested. 'I have [been] forced to get Sir Charles [probably Blagden] to write letters to Norfolk where there is started up an opposition to Coke and Wodehouse whom I must support' (HW to Mary Berry 30 May 1796, BERRY ii. 184–5).
Address: To the Right Honourable Lady Walpole.

Lord Orford begs Lady Walpole to acquaint Mrs Coke,[2] that he has sent the same orders to his steward at Crostwick[3] as at Houghton, to engage the tenants to vote as she desires.

1. Lady Rachel Cavendish (1727–1805), m. (1748) HW's cousin, Horatio Walpole ('Pigwiggin'), 2d Bn Walpole of Wolterton, 1757; cr. (1806) E. of Orford, n.c.
2. Thomas William Coke (1754–1842), cr. (1837) E. of Leicester, was M.P. for Norfolk. He m. (1775) Jane Dutton (1753–1800), sister of James, 1st Bn Sherborne, probably the Mrs Coke of the letter.
3. Now called Crostwight, about 16 m. NE of Norwich. Sir Robert bought the property ca 1720 from the LeGros family (SELWYN 344, n. 1, and reference cited there).

To the Duchess of Gloucester, Monday
6 February 1797

Printed for the first time from a photostat of the MS in Kirgate's hand in the possession of Lord Waldegrave.

Monday, Feb. 6th.[1]

Madam,

THE abscess that has been so long under my left arm[2] has broken this morning, and has made a very proper discharge, so I hope now to be quite delivered from it.[3] I have the

honour to be, etc.

Orford

1. The Duchess added, '1797 when he was dying.' HW died Thursday 2 March 1797 at 5 P.M. This is the last of all his surviving letters.

2. 'An abscess under his Lordship's arm very painful; another in his neck broke inwardly, yet the fever is abated and he can eat. No recovery is expected but he may linger for some time' ('Joseph Farington's Anecdotes,' Dalrymple 336).

3. During his illness the Duchess of Gloucester had written to Anne Clement: 'Lord Orford is so much mended that he was to go out tonight! to be sure it is wonderful! I was with him last Friday and he seemed very glad to see me' (1 Jan. 1797) and on 19 Feb., 'he is recovering; it is wonderful!' (MSS now wsl).

APPENDICES

APPENDIX 1

CASE OF THE ENTAIL OF THE ESTATE OF
SIR ROBERT WALPOLE EARL OF ORFORD

Printed from the MS, now WSL; acquired, 1937, from the estate of the younger
Richard Bentley whose grandfather presumably acquired it from Lord Euston
as executor to the 6th Earl Waldegrave (see Appendix 3 below). See *ante* 10
April 1756.

WHEN Sir Robert Walpole succeeded to his father in 1700, the
family estate was nominally £2300 *per annum* encumbered
with a considerable debt. He afterwards paid off the debt and raised
the estate; and in 1724, on marrying his eldest son Robert to Miss
Rolle, a great fortune, he settled his then estate on the issue of that
marriage, and on failure of such issue, on his other sons Edward and
Horace: but living till the year 1745, he made several additional
purchases.

About the year 1743 or 44, his eldest son Robert having but one
son, a youth, and being separated from his wife, and without any
prospect of more issue; and Edward Walpole being unmarried, and
about the age of 37, and having some natural children of whom he
was very fond, and consequently not likely to marry; and Horace
Walpole the third son, about the age of 26, being of a very tender and
weak constitution, and unmarried; Sir Robert Walpole proposed to
his own brother Horatio a mutual entail of their estates on the sons of
each other, in case of failure of issue by their own sons. It will be no
derogation to Mr Horatio Walpole to say, that he undoubtedly owed
the greatness of his fortune to his brother Sir Robert; and it must be
observed that at the time mentioned, Mr Horatio had four sons, all
very healthy, and who from the good education he had given them,
and from their dutiful dispositions it was to be presumed would
readily marry whenever or whatever wives he should order. And it is
moreover to be remarked that when Sir Robert made this offer to
his brother, Sir Robert's estate was near £8000 *per annum* and Mr
Horatio's not above £4000 *per annum* from all which considerations
it is obvious how greatly the advantage lay on the side of Mr Horatio
and his family; the proffered estate being near double his, and of
the four lives on one side, one was a man separated from his wife, one
a youth of about 13, one an unmarried man of 37 with illegitimate
issue, and one an unmarried man of 26, of a constitution that in

appearance promised a very short life: the four lives on the other side were young men or youths, all healthy and likely to marry. But Mr Horatio Walpole the elder, being a very affectionate father, and not to be moved by interest or the consideration of how greatly the advantage was in his favour, refused to come into any such agreement, alleging that he had three daughters, on whom he intended to settle his estate after his own sons. This was so natural and paternal a motive, and which ought so reasonably to take place even before his gratitude to his brother, that nothing could be said in answer—It was even a reproof to Sir Robert for overlooking his own daughters—accordingly, in IMITATION of, and in effect indirectly, by the advice of his brother, Sir Robert Walpole immediately entailed his estate (after his own sons and their issue) on George Lord Malpas and Robert Cholmondeley, his grandchildren, the offspring of his late daughter Lady Malpas, on their male issue, and after them on his own surviving daughter Lady Mary Walpole, since married to Mr Churchill.

Sir R. Walpole died in March 1745; and his eldest son Robert Earl of Orford in March 1751, by which means, George now Earl of Orford, being born after the marriage-settlement between his father and Margaret Rolle, had a power of cutting off the entail (I mean of the estate settled on that marriage, for there is a doubt whether he has a power of cutting it off with regard to the later-purchased lands) and he accordingly (his father and grandfather having left large debts) has very prudently cut off the entail in order to raise a necessary sum of money.

Finding the entail cut off, Mr Horatio Walpole the elder has *proposed to Lord Orford a mutual entail of their estates in the manner offered by Sir Robert Walpole;* and Lord Orford has accepted it!—on which proposal and transaction it is necessary to make some remarks.[1]

Mr Walpole is near fourscore, Lord Orford twenty-six. The age, rank, riches of the former must impress an idea of respect on the

---

1. After his father's death, George, 3d E., borrowed £4000 from 'Old Horace' who then proposed to make the settlement originally suggested by Sir Robert. Orford would not make the settlement immediately, but wrote a will consenting to it. It was this will and its codicils that HW is here disputing ('Joseph Farington's Anecdotes,' DALRYMPLE 323–5, 332). According to the *Gentleman's Magazine,* Orford 'left two wills, the first executed . . . [25 Nov.] 1752 and the second in 1756. The limitations of the first will were, 1st to Sir Edward Walpole, his uncle; 2d to Horatio Walpole [HW] . . . ; 3d to the Cholmondeley family;

latter, and prevent his suspecting anything improper or interested in his uncle; especially as his father in his will had recommended to this Lord to take the advice of his old Uncle Horatio, and of his uncles Edward and Horace. It seems, Mr Horatio the elder thought that in an affair of such moment his single advice was sufficient! and accordingly kept the transaction an entire secret from Sir Edward and Mr Horace Walpole.

When entails are cut off for the mere raising of money, it is usual and seemly, to reestablish them in the same manner, if those who were in the entail are the nearest of blood, and have done nothing to forfeit the good will of the person in possession. (It is not even pretended that the persons in question have disobliged Lord Orford). It is undoubtedly very unusual and uncommonly generous to place in the room of such near relations others more distant, who had even refused to accept the entail, and who, as Mr Horatio did, had refused to let the persons in possession have any chance of being benefited by his fortune. This opinion is not only most natural, but what Lord Malpas, Mr Cholmondeley, and Lady Mary Churchill might expect would be represented to this Lord Orford by old Mr Horatio, whom it so much became to disclaim accepting the entail of an estate which he had refused on fair terms, and whose extreme obligations to his brother Sir Robert, and the kind of monitorship which he had accepted from his nephew the second Lord Orford, and most willingly executed over the present Lord, made it incumbent on him to dissuade this Lord from doing so unkind and so unmerited an act, and to endeavour to prevent a disposition so prejudicial to the grandchildren and to the favourite daughter of his brother and benefactor.

and, last of all, to the Walpoles of Wolterton. The limitations of the second will differed from the above, by postponing the interest of the Cholmondeley family to that of the Walpoles of Wolterton. By a codicil, executed in 1776, he leaves £10,000 to Horatio, the eldest son of the present Lord Walpole ['Pigwiggin'], and refers to, and recognizes, the will of 1752, without mentioning the will of 1756. On this circumstance arises a question, which of the two wills is to be considered as his Lordship's last will, of no importance during the life of Horatio, the present Earl of Orford; but if he should die without issue, involving no less than whether the Cholmondeleys or the Walpoles of Wolterton shall succeed' (GM 1791, lxi pt ii. 1165). The eventual settlement, in a suit between Lord Walpole and Lord Cholmondeley in February 1797 before a special jury in the Court of Common Pleas, as directed by Court of Chancery, found in favour of Lord Cholmondeley; this decision was confirmed in a suit between Lord Walpole and Lord Orford in June 1797, which re-established the will of 1752 (Lord Walpole versus the Earl of Cholmondeley, English Reports, 1900–32, ci. 897–904; Lord Walpole versus Lord Orford, English Reports, xxx. 1076–85; GM 1797, lxvii pt i. 260).

But when we come to look nearer into the situation of both families, the case is infinitely more striking! Twelve years at least are lapsed since Mr Horatio's refusal, and Sir Robert's entail. Lord Malpas etc. have a prescription of twelve years. The present Lord Orford refused unseen to marry Miss Nicholl, a fortune of £150,000 and has constantly refused to listen to any proposal of marriage. Sir Edward Walpole is now 49, Mr Horace Walpole 38, both unmarried. On the other hand, of Mr Horatio's sons, the two elder are married to young women, who breed frequently, and the eldest has a son: his two younger sons are very healthy young men. Why should Mr Horatio be so willing to exclude his own daughters *now?* Does he love them less than he did? or does he love this Lord Orford better than he loved his brother and benefactor Sir Robert? has he contracted more affection for his nephews Sir Edward and Mr Horace? Is it not evident that his being so willing *now* to pass over his own daughters, is from the great probability that his own estate will never come even to his own daughters? and if he thinks so, *must not he by consequence see that his offer to Lord Orford is captious and by no means an equivalent?*—But these twelve years have made *another* material alteration; his three daughters are grown up, are not handsome women, and as he finds by various trials are not likely to be married—*so that he is not likely to exclude any posterity of theirs.* And the circumstances are the more unequal, as there are numerous descendants of Sir Robert Walpole's daughters, all which innocent children are injured by this bargain.

If these facts are true—and they are undeniable, with what justice can Mr Walpole offer or accept the mutual entail in question? has he a right to accept or refuse it just as it suits his convenience? Can he with any equity renew a bargain, offered by Sir Robert, when Sir Robert is dead, and when by his refusal a pretension was vested in Sir Robert's representatives? Can he *now* recall his own refusal? Shall he refuse when the chance was more equal, yet even then in his favour; and shall he be at liberty to accept when twelve years have made the balance so immeasurably in his favour? Has Lord Malpas, or Mr Cholmondeley or Lady Mary Churchill been acquainted with his retractation? have they had any opportunity to plead against so hard a decision? Was this a transaction to be done in secret? or was it not a transaction *only* to be done in secret? Why did Mr Walpole wish it buried in darkness, but because he was aware that the first friend of Lord Orford that should come to the knowledge of it would necessarily represent to him, how hard a thing he would do by his nearest relations, in favour of a more distant relation, who deserved so little from him? Have not the pretensions of Lord Malpas etc. been abrogated by the man from whom they ought to have expected protection and support? Can Mr Walpole ask for Sir Robert's estate in prejudice to Sir Robert's grandchildren, when he refused to let any part of Sir Robert's family have any chance of benefit from his?—or does his heart relent towards them, only, when there is no chance of their being benefited by his repentance?

Let it not be alleged that Mr Walpole's estate is increased, and Lord Orford's diminished—what does that prove but that Mr Walpole is convinced how little likely his own estate is to pass from his own descendants! When he would not entail an inferior in hopes of a greater, would he offer an enlarged estate for one decreased, unless the stability of his own, and the instability of the other had increased in proportion?

As Lord Orford was by no means obliged to old Mr Walpole for the original refusal of entailing his estate on him, so has he not much more reason to thank him for the present offer. Mr Walpole's proposal was to entail their estates only by will; but how triflingly does this differ from an irrevocable settlement, considering the vast disproportion of their ages? Is Mr Walpole's life worth two year's purchase? if he dies in a year or two, does not Lord Orford as a man of honour remain tied up to all intents and purposes from making any new disposition of his estate?—no wonder such secrecy was used! —Mr Walpole thinks himself at liberty to retract his refusal when Sir Robert Walpole is dead; but would my lord Orford think himself equally at liberty to violate an agreement made with a man who shall be dead? and did not Mr Walpole by this artful proposal as far as in him lay (for probably if the secret had been kept a year it had been sufficient) prevent the effect of any repentance in Lord Orford hereafter in favour of Lord Malpas, Mr Cholmondeley, and Lady Mary Churchill? Had this mysterious transaction not come to light most unexpectedly before Mr Walpole's death, Lord Orford (as he owns) contrary to his intention, and through mere want of consideration, the effect of want of other advice, had found himself no longer master of the disposition of his estate; and Lord Malpas etc. had been defeated of a succession intended for them by the person who acquired the fortune, when it would be too late to reproach the man to whom they would owe so irreparable an injury. Happily Lord Orford (who has been almost as ill-used as Lord Malpas) has been made sensible how much he has been overseen, and has protested that he will declare off the mutual entail; though he has not yet determined to restore Lord Malpas etc. to their place in his succession. His equity and good nature will no doubt prevail at last in favour of his nearest relations.

It is necessary to make but one more remark: old Mr Walpole is on the point of being created a peer: he takes the style of Lord Walpole, the title peculiar to the eldest son of the Earls of Orford; a confusion which it would rather be natural to avoid than affect. He may plead that this Lord Orford's son may become Lord Clinton —but if Sir Edward or Mr Horace succeeded to the earldom, that would not be the case. Is not it reasonable to presume that he, supposing that Lord Orford, Sir Edward and Mr Horace will not marry, takes that appellation, as an inducement to Lord Orford to let the estate accompany the title?

Upon the whole: there may possibly be men who in the worldly wisdom of their hearts will secretly think that old Mr Walpole has acted a very prudent part—but is there one man living who will avow that he would have acted as Mr Walpole has done?

LORD MALPAS TO HORATIO WALPOLE SENIOR

Printed from HW's MS copy, now WSL.

Gerard Street
April 10, 1756.

Sir

WITH all the respect and duty I owe you, it is impossible, if I have any regard for myself or my children, not to complain of the cruel and unmerited injury you have done me, and of which I had not the least warning given me, nor an opportunity of taking any steps to prevent it. What I mean, Sir, is being cut entirely out of the reversion of Lord Orford's estate, which you know my grandfather had entailed on me, after this Lord Orford, my uncles and their children; and which I hear, alas! too late, you have persuaded his Lordship to entail on your family. His Lordship has undoubtedly power to cut off the entail of what was settled on his father's marriage, and as I most heartily wish him well, and am an older man, it would have been neither affectionate nor decent in me to have expressed any expectation of a succession which I could not in reason think would fall to myself: but as neither his Lordship nor my uncles are married, nobody can blame me for thinking the reversion might regard my son: and as he would be the nearest relation to Lord Orford, and can have done nothing to offend him, as I am conscious that I myself never have, it was no great presumption in me to flatter myself that Lord Orford would not deprive my poor boy of what his grandfather had intended for him. However, I should have rested this hope in silence, trusting to his Lordship's equity and good nature. Indeed had I thought of making any interest for my son, to whom could I rationally have addressed myself so soon, Sir, as to you, whom I looked upon as a venerable parent, as the best representative of my grandfather, and whose peculiar kindness to me and my wife this winter encouraged me to expect all manner of friendship from you. How cruelly, Sir, are all my hopes blasted! Forgive me if affection for my son makes me forget a little of the duty I owe to my uncle—but, Sir, what shall I say, when I understand that our disappointment is owing to you? and can I help thinking it hard, that you, from whose refusal of the offer made by my grandfather, of a mutual entail, our hopes were derived, should be the very person to overturn them? Shall I not call it hard, that you should refuse the mutual entail, when you thought my grandfather's succession uncertain, and that you should think yourself at liberty, to claim it now, when it approaches so near? When you would give your brother's line no chance of your fortune, is it just to snatch his from his grandchildren?

I could say much more, Sir; but I hope it is sufficient to awaken your justice, and not necessary to take it by storm. From your venerable age, from your character, from the ample fortune you can leave your children, without obtaining Lord Orford's, from the regard I am sure you bear to your brother's disposition of his estate, from your gratitude to his memory of which I as little doubt, and from the goodness and friendship you have shown and of late increased to me, from the influence you have over Lord Orford, I will still believe that you will represent to his Lordship, that he has no

reason upon earth to be offended with me and my son, and I believe
not with my brother and his son, nor with Lady Mary Churchill
and her children, all whose cause I am pleading as well as my own;
and I think it more decent and respectful both to Lord Orford and
yourself, Sir, to trust our cause in your hands, than impertinently
presume to interfere with his disposition of his affairs; and though
you, without our knowledge, have intercepted our succession, I
choose to use no advocate against you but yourself, and I think you
have no reason to be angry with me for giving you this opportunity
of displaying your disinterestedness, your paternal justice to us, and
your gratitude to your brother. In hope of that generosity I am

Sir

your most dutiful

and affectionate nephew

MALPAS

HORATIO WALPOLE SENIOR TO LORD MALPAS

Printed from HW's MS copy, now WSL.

Cockpit April 11th 1756.

My Lord

WHAT has passed between Lord Orford and me relating to the
reciprocal entail of our respective estates, is a thing so entirely
in our own power, and judgment, that nobody has any the least pretence to call it in question, much less to complain of it in such
extraordinary terms as your Lordship has done by your letter to me
of yesterday.

Your Lordship is pleased to call Lord Orford's free, voluntary,
deliberate, legal and rightful act on this occasion, *a cruel and unmerited injury done by me to you;* which is an unjust imputation
of weakness in him, and of something worse in me, and deserves
contempt rather than a serious answer; and it should have had none,
had I not seen with great concern, that what you write so unkindly
to me, is conceived in a style and spirit entirely opposite to the

known candour and justice of your Lordship's own natural disposition, which I flatter myself you will upon cooler reflection resume again.

I have heard and believe, that my late dear, good and great brother, after having entailed his estate on his own sons, gave the reversion of it to your Lordship and your heirs male, and in default of such issue to Lady Mary Churchill etc. And the reason your Lordship gives for his having done it, is the strongest justification (if it wanted any) of what Lord Orford has now done.

Your Lordship owns that your grandfather's entail of the estate upon you etc. arose merely from my refusal of the offer he made me, of a mutual entail of our estates upon our two families, which I own I declined coming into at that time, not because, as your Lordship says, I thought the succession to my brother's estate more uncertain, and not so near as it approaches now (which are very indecent surmises to be made by anybody in cases of this nature) but because I could not agree at that time to a settlement upon such very unequal terms, as might hazard the doing a most irreparable injury to my own family, for had I come into it then, it would have been in the power of the present Lord Orford, when he came of age, to have defeated any settlement, that could have been made, with respect to me and my family; whereas the entail which would have been made by me on my brother's family, would always have stood good, and no son of mine could have altered or cut it off, although the very foundation and consideration of these reciprocal settlements would have been destroyed: Lord Orford therefore in this proceeding has strictly pursued the great object and original intention of his grandfather, in the disposition of his Norfolk estate, as I have consented to make the same disposition of mine, which my brother had so much at heart, and more than once proposed to me, by which I think I show the greatest regard and gratitude to the memory of him who was so near and dear to me.

I cannot conclude this letter, without taking some notice of a most remarkable paragraph in yours, which is in the following words: 'I could say much more, Sir, but I hope it is sufficient to awaken your justice, *and not necessary to take it by storm.*' What the last words mean I neither know nor care; and as I am not conscious of having done anything inconsistent with honour, probity or justice, I shall defy and despise all storms that may threaten me at this time of day, from whatever quarter they may come. In the meantime I shall continue to show you and your family, as I have ever professed, all possible marks of kindness and friendship, being with the most

affectionate respect

My Lord

Your Lordship's

most obedient and most

humble servant

H. WALPOLE

APPENDIX 2

THE DUKE OF GLOUCESTER TO SIR EDWARD WALPOLE, TUESDAY 25 May 1773

A copy in Sir Edward's hand, now WSL; first printed, as a footnote, in *Last Journals* i. 222–3: 'Sir Edward Walpole, who seldom went out of his own house, wrote to the Duke of Gloucester, condoling with and congratulating him on what was passing. The Duke returned this very sensible and pathetic answer.' See *ante* HW to the Ds of Gloucester ca 28 May 1773.

Address: To the Honourable Sir Edward Walpole.

Endorsed (by HW): From the Duke of Gloucester. This is a copy in Sir Edw. Walpole's hand.

Gloucester House, May 25, 1773.

Dear Sir,

I AGREE entirely with you, that our talking over together the subject of this last week's transaction[1] would be too affecting for either of us to have chosen; I am therefore sincerely obliged to you for having taken this method of easing your mind, which gives me so good an opportunity of doing the same.

Now I have had a little time to recover myself from the various feelings I have been agitated by for a long time past, I can reflect upon the real joy you must feel in seeing how the character of my amiable Duchess has shone through the cloud, I myself from duty to the King, was forced to permit to hang over my own wife for so long a time. And yet I have the secret satisfaction to believe that [when] his Majesty considers the variety of events that had happened during my last absence from England, he must allow that my public declaration of my marriage at my return, was a debt due to my country, my Duchess, myself, and to posterity.

Your compliments to me upon my management I would thank

---

1. The Duke and Duchess had met on 23 May with the committee appointed by the King to inquire into the legality of their marriage (see *ante* ca 28 May 1773, heading). HW wrote in *Last Journals* (i. 211–12) that on 21 May the Duke had sent Bishop Keppel 'to my brother Sir Edward Walpole and to me, to make excuses for not having acquainted us sooner with what had passed between the King and his Royal Highness, but the Duke said he had determined the Court should not have it to say that he had been governed by the Duchess's relations and had not acted from himself.' On 26 May the Council made their report to the King (ibid. i. 223).

you for if I felt I deserved them, but your approbation, as an honest man, of my conduct, I feel grateful for.

I am, dear Sir, yours

WILLIAM HENRY

THE DUKE OF GLOUCESTER to SIR EDWARD WALPOLE, Wednesday 12 March 1777

Printed from the MS, now WSL; first printed, Hist. MSS Comm., *Stopford-Sackville MSS*, 1904, i. 346–8. See *ante* the Ds of Gloucester to HW 10 Aug. 1777.

Address: To the Honourable Sir Edward Walpole Pallmall London Inghilterra.

Endorsed (by Sir Edward): Received in London on Sat. March 29, 1777; (by Edward Roberts): Pell Office Exchequer April 3d 1777. The above letter and postscript is accurately copied from the original one, written by the Duke of Gloucester, to Sir Edward Walpole, by me, Edward Roberts.

Rome, March 12th 1777.

Dear Sir,

YESTERDAY'S post brought me your letter of the 18th of February, the contents of which have given me not little uneasiness. I am truly sensible of your affectionate meaning in writing to Lord George Germaine,[1] but I cannot but heartily wish your warmth of heart had not led you to take that step, it having been my plan for these last two years not to trouble the King in the least with anything that concerns me, as I have too great reason to see how obnoxious I am unfortunately grown to him; besides, in the repeated applications I have made to the King[2] through Lord Rochford and Lord North, my whole idea and wish has been to get a provision for the Duchess and my children in case of my death; a request that appears to me so much my duty to have made, and of so little trouble to the Crown to grant, that it preys much upon my mind my having as yet failed in, as it is surely both just and moderate.

As to the getting any debts of mine paid by Parliament,[3] it has ever been far from my thoughts, knowing full well the little claim I

1. Sir Edward to Lord George 4 Feb. 1777, now WSL, printed in Hist. MSS Comm., *Stopford-Sackville MSS*, i. 344–5.

2. See Geo. III's *Corr.*, ed. Fortescue, iii. 50, 97–8, 101, 164–5, 536–7.

3. Sir Edward had asked Lord George Germain to use his influence 'to get the Duke's debts included in the Bill . . . for the payment of the King's debts' (letter cited in n. 1 above).

could have for such an application; and being ready enough to confess my follies ought only to be redressed by my future economy. I am now ten years older than I was, and as my only object in life is the care and education of my children, I have long bid adieu to views of ambition. Mistake me not in this point, for whenever the King or my country call for me, I shall stand as forward as ever and shall let all paternal affections sleep for that moment. But till that time comes, it is my firm intention to pursue a retired and economical plan.

I am as much at a loss as you are, Dear Sir, to explain Lord George's meaning where he says that *he trust my judgment* will lead *me* to pursue every method which may speedily produce *that happy union, etc., etc.*[4] I know of no fresh offence I can have committed since my first declaration of my marriage; and I had flattered myself that I had clearly proved to the King the absolute necessity I was under of making that public declaration at that time: if ill-minded people have misrepresented me to the King since that time, it is totally out of my power to know what effect that may have had. I have never troubled the King but for a provision for the Duchess and my children, and I must again repeat it; that its not having been granted me yet, grieves me to the soul. This application is misunderstood by the ministers, and the King is led to believe that the granting it would be a mark of his approbation of my marriage; whereas it would really be but an act of justice. The late King of France in '72 gave the Duke of Orléan[5] leave to marry, but required the marriage to be kept secret until the Duchess should be with child, in which case the King would have received her at Court, but nevertheless immediately empowered the Duke of Orléans to provide for this Duchess.

The King of Spain[6] last summer, though he had just made a new law[7] to hinder the Infants of Spain marrying without the consent of the Crown, in *imitation* of the *Royal Marriage Bill* in England,

---

4. The Duke is quoting from Lord George's letter to Sir Edward, dated before 18 Feb. 1777, in Hist. MSS Comm., *Stopford-Sackville MSS*, i. 345. The Duke mistakenly wrote 'wish' instead of 'which.'

5. Louis-Philippe de Bourbon (1725–85), Duc de Chartres; Duc d'Orléans, 1752; m. 1 (1743) Louise (1726–59), dau. of Louis-Armand de Bourbon, Prince de Conti; m.

2 (1773) Charlotte, dau. of Jean Béraud de la Haye (Isenburg, *Stammtafeln* ii. taf. 19, 32; MANN vii. 453).

6. Charles III (1716–88), K. of Naples 1735–59; K. of Spain 1759–88.

7. The 'pragmática relativa á los matrimonios desiguales,' 23 March 1776 (Conde de Fernan-Núñez, *Vida de Carlos III*, Madrid, 1898, i. 269–71).

suspecting his brother's[8] intention of marrying, yet gave his consent to a private marriage, and allowed the Archbishop[9] to marry them, and also immediately empowered his brother to make very great settlements upon his wife and children. I am further assured that the King intends soon to receive them publicly at Court. The Infant has been twice with the King since his *marriage*.

I have now fully explained my reasons for wishing you had not wrote to Lord George Germaine; but at the same time must desire you to be assured I am truly sensible of the warmth and zeal you have ever shown towards me.

Yours,

WILLIAM HENRY

PS. As I do not by any means feel myself so well as I did last winter, I propose if I am not wanted at home to pass another winter abroad; and as I had the King's leave of absence brought me by Lord North,[10] I cannot suppose Lord George Germaine conceives my being abroad can offend.

THE DUKE OF GLOUCESTER to SIR EDWARD WALPOLE, Friday 16 May 1777

Printed from the MS, now WSL; first printed, Hist. MSS Comm., *Stopford-Sackville MSS*, 1904, i. 349. Copy by Sir Edward Walpole enclosed in his letter to Lord George Germain 1 June 1777 (now WSL). See *ante* the Ds of Gloucester to HW 10 Aug. 1777.
Endorsed (by Sir Edward): To Sir E. W. from the D. of G.

Venice, May 16, 1777.

Dear Sir

I RECEIVED your letter of the 15th of April two days since. I am most sincerely obliged to you for it, as it gives me fresh

8. Luis Antonio de Borbón (1727–85), 8th son of Philip V; cardinal 1735; resigned, 1754; m. (28 Jan. 1776) María-Teresa de Vallabriga y Rozas (b. 1758), Condesa de Chinchón, 1776 (*Diccionario de historia de España,* ed. Germán Bleiberg, 2d edn, Madrid, 1968, ii. 809–10; Isenburg, *Stammtafeln* ii. taf. 50).

9. Francisco Antonio de Lorenzana y Butrón (1722–1804), Bp of Plasencia, 1765; Abp of Mexico, 1766; Abp of Toledo, 1772; cardinal, 1789 (Bleiberg, op. cit. ii. 793–4).

10. See Geo. III's *Corr.,* ed. Fortescue, iii. 164–6.

proofs of your affection and zeal. Lord G. Germain's conduct towards me is truly uniform and handsome; if you should find by him that it would be pleasing to the King that I should come over now, I will set out immediately, to show how desirous I am to give the King every mark in my power of duty and attachment.

At so great a distance it is impossible to discuss every point, or enter into a minute defence of my conduct; however, I must say I have been misinterpreted. If the coming over now should be approved of I will leave my family at Verona and return to them, as I feel it necessary, if I am not wanted, to pass another winter at Rome.

I must repeat my warmest thanks to you for the very friendly part you have taken. As to Lord G. Germain, I must leave it to you to assure him how very sincerely I am affected with his conduct towards me.

I remain

Dear Sir

Yours

W. H.

APPENDIX 3

Dispersal of the Manuscripts of Walpole's Correspondence

THE introductions to Walpole's correspondences, as published in the Yale Edition, always indicate the provenance of the texts of the letters included in each volume or group of volumes. These introductions, however, are so numerous, and in places so inconsistent, that a comprehensive account of the entire subject seems desirable.

Tracing each individual letter here would entail a useless duplication of space and effort: in our edition, the headings of the individual letters always give their histories when these differ from the general provenance as outlined in the introduction to each series. Every correspondence contains at least a few letters which strayed in some way from the main group. The present account is concerned only with the main groups.

Walpole kept a great many letters which he received during his long life, and he arranged to have certain packets of his own letters returned to him by the recipients—his letters to Sir Horace Mann and to Madame du Deffand are the outstanding examples of this practice. When some of his correspondents died, their heirs doubtless returned to Walpole the letters which he had written to the deceased. Nevertheless, the greater part of his letters were undoubtedly kept or destroyed by the recipients, and never again came into his possession. His letters to Cole were left by Cole to the British Museum;[1] the letters to Zouch went to the Lowther family;[2] the correspondence with Lady Suffolk was inherited by her nephew and passed to John Wilson Croker whose executors gave it to the British Museum; his letters to Anne Pitt went through Lady Grenville's hands to the Fortescues; most of the letters to Lady Browne remained in her family although a few were turned over to Miss Berry for possible inclusion in Walpole's posthumous *Works;*[3] the letters to Henry Fox, Lord Lincoln, George Selwyn, and Sir Charles Hanbury Williams passed to their heirs.[4] Walpole's letters to George Montagu were returned to him by Frederick Montagu, but were given back

1. COLE i. xxxvi.
2. CHATTERTON ix.
3. The correspondence with Lady Suffolk is described in MORE xiv–xv, that with Anne Pitt ibid. xii; that with Lady Browne ibid. xv–xvi.
4. See SELWYN xxxi–xxxii.

again, along with George Montagu's replies, and were inherited by the Dukes of Manchester.[5]

In spite of all these exceptions, the number of letters still in Walpole's possession at the time of his death in 1797 must have been in the thousands. His last will and its codicils made specific directions about some, without any blanket disposal of the whole. Letters from living persons were to be returned to them; trunks of papers relating to family affairs were to go to his nephew Lord Cholmondeley at Houghton; Box O containing his literary MSS was left to Robert Berry to be edited by him and his two daughters.[6] Walpole knew that Mary Berry was the one who would actually perform this task.

Walpole's personal property at Strawberry Hill was left, with the house, to Lady Waldegrave, his grandniece, subject to Mrs Damer's life use, and then to the eldest Waldegrave son, to remain as permanent heirlooms to that property.[7] The effects at Walpole's house in Berkeley Square likewise went to the Waldegraves but not with restrictions, except that certain pictures and family papers were to go to the Cholmondeleys.[8] Manuscripts, unlike books, are never specified as part of the general furnishings of the houses though it might be argued that their inclusion was tacitly implied.

On the other hand, it might have been asserted that since manuscript letters (apart from the three groups specified by the will) are never particularly distributed, they would form part of the residuary estate, and therefore would belong to Mrs Damer, daughter of Walpole's cousin, Henry Conway, and sole residuary heir under the last codicil to Walpole's will.[9]

Walpole, however, made further complications by leaving mem-

---

5. See MONTAGU i. xxvii–xxix.

6. Walpole's will of 15 May 1793 stipulated the return of letters from living persons (SELWYN 367–8); the disposition of Box O was decreed in the last codicil (27 Dec. 1796, ibid. 373). A codicil of 23 May 1796 bequeathed to Lord Cholmondeley 'two small red trunks in my bedchamber at Berkeley Square and the large one in the dining-room there . . . as they contain material papers relating to the affairs of our family' (ibid. 372), and the last codicil of 1796 added that 'All the family papers in the library in Berkeley Square with those which I have lent to Mr Coxe for my father's life I would have sent to

Houghton in the boxes in which they came' (ibid. 377).

7. This was a provision of the will of 15 May 1793, ibid. 351–3.

8. The furnishings in Berkeley Square were likewise disposed of by the main will, ibid. 355–6, but an apparently undated memorandum between the codicils of 5 June 1793 and 9 Feb. 1796 listed the pictures in Berkeley Square which were to go to Houghton if Lord Cholmondeley won possession of it—if he did not, they were to go with the other furnishings of Berkeley Square (ibid. 370–1); for the family papers see n. 6 above.

9. Mrs Damer by the last codicil of 27

oranda concerning manuscripts which were in certain receptacles (other than the Box O, and the red trunks of family papers, which the will had mentioned).

The letters from Madame du Deffand, with her other MSS and some of Walpole's letters to her, were in a cedar chest, to which instructions were probably attached although they have not survived. They presumably would have told Miss Berry to print Madame du Deffand's letters and to destroy Walpole's after they had been used for the annotation—at least, this is what seems to have happened. Miss Berry kept a few of Madame du Deffand's letters, which the Marquis de Sainte-Aulaire acquired, but the rest remained in the cedar chest and were sold at the Strawberry Hill Sale, 30 April 1842 (sixth day, lot 107) to D. O. Dyce-Sombre. At the Parker-Jervis Sale, 12 March 1920, they were dispersed, and Madame du Deffand's letters to Walpole ended in the Bodleian Library.[10]

The original letters to Sir Horace Mann had been kept in a japan cabinet in the Blue Room at Berkeley Square, and Walpole's memorandum of 21 March 1790 stipulated that they were to be turned over to the younger Sir Horace, but that Walpole's transcripts from them were to be kept in the Library at Strawberry Hill. The original letters were never turned over to the Manns, but were left by Mrs Damer to Sir Wathen Waller and then disappeared, possibly destroyed by Lord Cornwallis (heir to the Mann estate), or by Sir Wathen Waller on Lord Cornwallis's instructions.[11]

Besides the cedar chest, the japan cabinet, and Box O, there were also Box A and Box B. The contents of Box B are not known but it could possibly have been either the cedar chest or the japan cabinet. On Box A there is more detailed information. By another memorandum of 21 March 1790, endorsed 19 Aug. 1796, Walpole decreed that this box was to be corded and sealed by his executors at the time of his death, and kept until whichever of Lady Waldegrave's sons was then Earl Waldegrave and had reached the age of twenty-five.[12]

After John James, 6th Earl Waldegrave, became entitled to Box A in 1810, he turned its contents over to the third Lord Holland, who made a partial list of the contents.[13] Besides the numerous drafts of

Dec. 1796 (SELWYN 376) was appointed 'my residuary devisee and legatee.'

10. See DU DEFFAND i. xxxvii–xliii.
11. See MANN i. xli–xlviii.
12. This memorandum was first printed

in Lord Holland's edition of the *Memoirs* and reprinted in Lord Dover's edition of the letters to Mann (see paragraph below).

13. See MANN x. 38–9. Lord Holland's list is entitled 'Contents of Lord Orford's

Walpole's historical memoirs, it included the letters from William Mason, and a bundle of 'private and family papers' (perhaps Walpole's correspondences with his brother, Sir Edward, and with Sir Edward's daughters and granddaughters), and Walpole's transcripts of his letters to Sir Horace Mann. These transcripts were not listed by Lord Holland, but Lord Dover in a preface (i. pp. v–vi) to his edition (1833) of the letters to Mann quotes from Walpole's memorandum of 1790–6 as printed in Lord Holland's introduction to Walpole's *Memoires . . . of George II,* 1822. Lord Dover says (i. pp. vii, ix–x) that the letters to Mann (the transcripts, that is) were in Box A, and that Mann's replies 'are also preserved at Strawberry Hill.'

It is uncertain whether any letters were included in the literary MSS which the Berrys received in Box O for publication. Volume V of Walpole's *Works,* published in 1798 by Mary Berry, included Walpole's letters to Henry Conway (and his wife), Bentley, Gray, Chute, Lord Strafford, Lady Hervey, and Hannah More, besides miscellaneous letters of literary interest (such as the correspondence with Voltaire), and Gray's letters to Walpole. All these letters may have been in Box O. Most of them have disappeared, but several of those that survive were in the collection which Sir Wathen Waller inherited from Mrs Damer. Either Mary Berry turned them over to her as residuary heir, or returned them to Strawberry Hill when Mrs Damer was living there. A group of letters to Conway, which had been intended for *Works* but were not printed in it, stayed at Strawberry Hill until acquired by the Bentleys; a few other letters to Conway were kept by Miss Berry, who may have felt that her position as editor and literary executrix entitled her to keep certain souvenirs.[14] Gray's letters to Walpole were in the Waller Collection, and are now at Pembroke College, Cambridge.[15]

These, then, *may* have been among the contents of Box O. The history of the family papers which were returned to Houghton, as stipulated by the will, is even more nebulous, but they must have

Box A as I received it 1st March 1820—from Sr James Mackintosh—Vassall Holland.' It was endorsed in Lord Holland's letter to the 6th Lord Waldegrave, 22 March 1820, now at Chewton. Walpole's memorandum is apparently the first of the papers in Item 22: '1st. Copy of paper in handwriting of Horatio Earl of Orford —2d. Ld Hugh Seymour's engagement to

deliver over Box A to an Earl of Waldegrave.'

14. White the bookseller sold the MS of Walpole's *Supplement* to *Historic Doubts* which he had bought 'of Miss Berry into whose possession it had come with many other MSS and printed books from Horace Earl of Orford' (BERRY i. xxxiii).

15. See GRAY i. xxxiv–xxxv.

been concerned with business affairs of the Houghton estates because, if Houghton had gone to Col. Horatio Walpole of Wolterton, these family papers were to have gone to him, too.[16]

Many letters must have been returned to their writers who survived Walpole; the will instructed that this be done. The Berry sisters got their letters back; Walpole's letters to them passed through Sir Frankland Lewis to Lady Theresa Lewis and Sir Thomas Villiers Lister, and are now in the Pierpont Morgan Library or in the British Museum.[17] The Thomas Walpoles kept their letters.[18] Lady Ossory would have had her letters sent back (the sole survivor of them was not; it, and probably others too, were used by Walpole for scrap-paper). She kept his letters to her, which descended through her family connections.[19] The Harcourt, Mrs Dickenson, and Lady George Lennox correspondences remained in the possession of their respective families.[20] The letters to Pinkerton stayed with him.[21] Mason barely survived Walpole, and his letters to Walpole were claimed by his heir, the Rev. Christopher Alderson—in vain, since Walpole had already locked them up in Box A, so that they stayed at Strawberry Hill with the Waldegraves. The Aldersons kept Walpole's letters to Mason until they were published by the Rev. John Mitford; then they disappeared.[22] Since Conway's widow and daughter survived Walpole, Conway's letters to Walpole came back to them, and were inherited by the niece of Lady Ailesbury, Conway's wife; many of them were taken to Ceylon until acquired by W. S. Lewis.[23] Lord Hertford died before Walpole, and it is not certain how Croker obtained Hertford's letters, which are now in the British

---

16. Walpole's codicil of 23 May 1796 explained that 'I had directed that the two small trunks . . . at Berkeley Square and the large one . . . there should on my death be delivered to Mr H. Walpole, but as the law has decided that he is not to have the estate at Houghton, I now order that the said three trunks should be delivered to my great-nephew the Earl of Cholmondeley, who is to succeed me in that estate and that they should be preserved in the library at Houghton as they contain material papers relating to the affairs of our family' (SELWYN 372).

17. See BERRY i. xxxiii, xxxiv, 376, n. 2. Bentley (the publisher)'s advertisement, April 1848, to Walpole's *Letters Addressed to the Countess of Ossory* stated that the letters to the Berrys published by him in 1840 were 'most kindly presented to the publisher by Miss Berry.' This must have meant a loan since the MSS did not remain with Bentley.

18. *Some Unpublished Letters of Horace Walpole,* ed. Sir Spencer Walpole, 1902, pp. 1–7.

19. For the history of HW's letters to the Ossorys see OSSORY i xxxvii–xl.

20. As described in CHUTE (introduction) and in MORE xv.

21. See CHATTERTON x–xii.

22. See MASON i. xxxi–xxxiii.

23. The history of these letters will be given in the introduction to our forthcoming CONWAY-HERTFORD correspondence (Vol. 37 of the Yale Edition).

Museum. Walpole's letters to Hertford were printed in Vol. IX (1825) of Walpole's *Works,* and have disappeared.

Two folio volumes of letters to Walpole about artists were sold in 1842 at the London sale of Strawberry Hill's contents, lot 1121, and were later at Nostell Priory.[24] Lort's letters to Walpole were sold at the Strawberry Hill Sale, 1842, sixth day, lot 118, to the British Museum, when many other letters to and from Walpole, were also sold, lots 112, 114–17, and 126–41.

Even with the subtraction of all the letters covered by Walpole's will or by his memoranda, there remained a considerable number for which there was no specific directive. Some of these, such as the surviving MSS from Walpole's *Works,* and three portfolios of miscellaneous letters to Walpole were taken from Strawberry Hill by Mrs Damer, perhaps in her capacity as residuary heir and executrix, and were left to the first Sir Wathen Waller when she died in 1828. The Waller Collection was dispersed in two sales, at Sotheby's 5–6 Dec. 1921 and at Christie's 15 Dec. 1947, and included not only Gray's letters but Richard West's, some early letters to Mann, Hillier's letters to Walpole, the Middleton correspondence, a number of Henry Fox's, several letters to Lort, and most of Walpole's letters to Lady Ailesbury, besides many miscellaneous ones, most of them now owned by W. S. Lewis.

The other great collection of Walpole's correspondence remained at Strawberry Hill with the Waldegraves, and except for the volume of letters about artists, and Cole's, Lort's, and the other letters sold on the sixth day, did not figure in the Strawberry Hill sale catalogues of 1842. This omission from the sale was not because the Waldegraves wanted to keep them, but because Lord Euston as executor of the sixth Earl Waldegrave hoped to get a better price for them at a separate sale; this was achieved in 1843 or thereabouts, as we have explained in Appendix 12 in our Vol. X of the Mann correspondence, when Richard Bentley the publisher acquired the transcripts of the letters to Mann, the MSS of Mann's letters (including many of Chute's), the letters from Mason, the letters to Jephson, and a good many family letters especially those centered on the Nicoll Affair of 1751 and the Case of the Entail in 1756.[25] The Dalrymple corre-

24. See CHATTERTON ix, x.
25. Bentley, in the advertisement (26 June 1843) to his edition of Walpole's

later letters to Mann wrote that 'the Earl of Euston, surviving executor of the late Earl of Waldegrave, has placed the whole

spondence was likewise in this collection, and scattered letters to many other correspondents. Bentley's grandson, the younger Richard Bentley, sold Mann's letters in 1934 to W. S. Lewis, who bought Mason's letters in 1935, and the miscellaneous ones (from Bentley's estate), 1937.

By these transactions, the Waldegrave family were left with almost no Walpole letters. Frances, Lady Waldegrave, tried to rectify this loss, however, and bought back from Bentley the transcripts of Walpole's letters to Mann, together with Walpole's historical memoirs;[26] these were removed from Strawberry Hill to Chewton Priory and then to Chewton Mendip, the transcripts of the letters to Mann having been acquired by W. S. Lewis in 1948.

The reader is referred to the introductions of the several correspondences in our edition for more specific details about provenance, with the warning, however, that in some of the introductions, the manuscripts in the Bentley collection are said to have come from Mary Berry; they almost certainly came from the Waldegrave collection at Strawberry Hill.

of Walpole's unpublished manuscripts, including his letters, memoirs, private journals, etc., in the hands of Mr Bentley.' In April 1848 Bentley's advertisement to Walpole's *Letters Addressed to the Countess of Ossory,* ed. R. Vernon Smith, stated that 'The remaining letters to Sir Horace Mann . . . were published by Mr Bentley in 1843; the remaining works in manuscript having been purchased by him of the present Duke of Grafton, [formerly Lord Euston] as executor of the late Lord Waldegrave.' Mitford in his preface, 1 May 1851, to *The Correspondence of Horace Walpole Earl of Orford and the Rev. William Mason* stated that 'The letters of Mason, now first printed, formed part of the collection of manuscripts purchased of the Duke of Grafton, as executor of the late Earl Waldegrave.'

26. See MANN x. 40–2, 43–4.

APPENDIX 4

Jane Clement (ca 1722–98) was the sister of Dorothy Clement, Sir Edward Walpole's mistress (*ante* 15 May 1745 OS, n. 9). She lived in Sir Edward's household, where she was apparently for many years a supernumerary housekeeper. She also paid the Duchess of Gloucester's bills while the Duke and Duchess were abroad. In his will dated 17 May 1782 Sir Edward left an annuity of £400 to 'Mrs Jane Clement (now residing in my house)' in Pall Mall, and also the life-use of his house in Ryder Street after the death of her sister-in-law Margaret who was living there (OSSORY i. 412, n. 4).

SIR EDWARD WALPOLE to JANE CLEMENT, Tuesday 28 October 1766

Printed from the MS now WSL. This and the following letters were acquired in September 1959 (in a collection) from Miss Eleanor Forster of Tynemouth, Northumberland.

There is a slip in Sir Edward's date: Tuesday was 28 Oct. and Wednesday was 29 Oct. in 1766.

Tuesday October 29, 1766.

Madam

THE many indignities I have suffered through your pride and insolence, have at last brought me to the following resolutions, much against my will and very reluctantly, although you was pleased to say yesterday, in opposition to my word honour and assurance to the contrary, that you would prove to the Bishop[1] at a proper time that there was a concerted plan of some standing, to remove you from my house.

Madam, you are the first person that has even questioned my word and honour, which stands as fair in the world as any man's living, and is too dear to me to be forfeited through fear of what Mrs Clement may be able to do against me.

No—I do assure you and all the world upon my word and honour that the person[2] whom you wish to charge with practising against you, never in his life was your enemy or wished to show you disrespect or ever tried to animate me against you or to excite resentment in me or increase any displeasure which I conceived against

1. Frederick Keppel, Bishop of Exeter.
2. William Collier, son of Sir Edward's housekeeper, Susan Collier; Sir Edward left him an annuity in his will. He is mentioned *post* 31 Dec. 1766 and 2 Jan. 1767.

you. But on the contrary has frequently, when our quarrels have
been known in the family, has as far as became a person in his situation, used his endeavours to conciliate matters and produce peace
and harmony between us, frequently using these expressions, *'How
happy a family this would be if Mrs Clement and you could agree!
and I am certain that there is not a servant in the house but is
desirous of serving her and showing her all the respect that is possible.'*

This has frequently been his language, with much more both
words and deeds, that whenever they shall be known, will show him
to be no such person as you represent him most cruelly and unjustly.
And as to paying my bills; had it been possible for you and me to
agree, I must be mad if I did not choose they should be in your hands
sooner than anybody's, if you would take the trouble. And I am of
opinion that he does not wish to have that charge again, as he has
suffered greatly in his reputation concerning my accounts, through
the report of those who did not and could not know the truth, although they meant well.

Moreover I shall for the future always pay my bills myself.

To say that he is desirous I should, would be useless; because it
would not be believed by those that would be sorry to believe so
well of him, and would be needless to those that are inclined to
a fair story: which mine (as well as his) will I hope appear to be
when they are told.

And now I come to my conclusion and final resolution—First,
That I will live with you no longer.

Secondly, That I will never speak to you again as long as I live on
no account whatever, nor ever stay in a room where I find you. And
therefore I shall transact all business (whatever may necessarily
occur while you are under my roof) by some other person that may
go between us; it is indifferent to me by whom.

Thirdly, as to an allowance to you, which I do not choose to bind
myself to by any writing under my hand, I shall give to my daughters
for you whatever I intend to allow you.

It is to be presumed that it will be what was agreed upon between
us. And I shall not be the first that has supported such geniuses as
yours, whose pride would not let them thank him and whose malice
would study falsehoods to excuse them from it—Therefore I desire

you will, whenever it may best suit your health and be most easy and convenient to you, leave me forever.

Signed Ed. Walpole

PS. I keep a copy of this.

Sir Edward Walpole to Jane Clement, Thursday 6 November 1766

Printed from the MS now wsl.

Shooters Hill, Nov. 6, 1766.

Madam

I HAVE once more for your sake taken our quarrel into consideration, and as it is impossible for you to live so well by a great deal upon a hundred pounds a year as you do with me, I once more will permit you to stay if you choose it.—Your maid must go, as soon as you can possibly get another, and I will have no lady's woman, no double-ruffle-second-table-gentlewoman.—You must take one that will have to attend you, to take care of your apartment, clean your stove etc. and in the country (not in town) help to make the beds, but not help to clean the house anywhere or to sweep any room but yours.

I need not say that my servants all of them shall and will and always did show you all the respect that is possible and always wished to recommend themselves to your favour.—

If you do not choose to stay after this offer, and take the accounts into your hands as you did before, you may let it alone, and proceed on your expedition as fast as you please—I keep a copy of this paper to show in my defence.

It is certainly in your power without any diminution to your honour, your dignity, your credit in the world or your peace at home, to make yourself and me and my servants all happy as far as domestic comfort goes, for you certainly live with honest people that want to show you respect if you will give them leave, and have in me neither a rascal nor a fool.—Why is it not as easy and as just to suppose that you are imposed upon and governed as me.

                                              Answer that if you can.

Sir Edward Walpole to Jane Clement, Wednesday 12 November 1766

Printed from the MS now wsl.
Address: To Mrs Clement.

                                        Wed. November 12, 1766.
Madam

AS you leave me tomorrow and go to my house in town in order to take your things away, I require you to leave that house likewise by Sunday next at noon, because I propose being in town next Sunday by two o'clock, and I will not stay in it, if I find you there, but shall go immediately to some lodgings till you are so obliging as to let me have my house to myself.

You will please to ask Lady Waldegrave for the five guineas which I paid the other day for Mary Wright and deduct so much from your next quarterage that you are to receive from me at Ladyday. And I hope care will be taken that no more of Mary Wright's draughts be brought to my house.

                                              E. W.

Sir Edward Walpole to Jane Clement, Wednesday 31 December 1766

Printed from the MS now wsl.
Address: To Mrs Clement at Mr Reeds at Hatton Wall.

                                          December 31, 1766.
Mrs Clement

YOU are permitted to return to my house at the earnest requisition of the Bishop and my family, but much more through the persuasion of my friend Mr Reid;[1] for the Bishop and my family have used me too ill throughout the whole affair, for me to have complied with them.

When you arrive, I shall take no notice of what has passed nor exchange a word with you concerning the quarrel but let everything appear as if you had only been out and was come in again, that there may be room for you to recollect where you are and what you are about, and I shall for the future command my temper so as to say no uncivil thing to you, but if we can't agree, desire you quietly to take your allowance and leave me.

By way of postscript, I must observe to you that it was no way necessary for you to say to Mr Reid that in respect to Collier and my servants in this dispute, I had lost all honour and veracity.

Just so I have been treated in all the Bishop's letters in effect though not in words. Therefore I sum up the whole as follows—I suffer you to return, rather than make a private family quarrel the talk of the whole town, and I shall (I hope) always be civil to you. But to esteem you or bear you the least degree of kindness or good will is I fear out of my power. And a great deal must be done on your part for me ever to forgive you, much more than ever I shall require of you or in any degree be solicitous that you should do.—As to the Bishop and the family, he has treated me so unfairly so insolently and so injuriously, that I believe he may have in futurity to thank you for a very heavy mischief. And so I am

your humble servant

Ed. Walpole

The Bishop of Exeter to Jane Clement, Friday 2 January 1767

Printed from the MS now WSL.

Windsor, Deanery, Friday January 2d 1766 [1767].

Madam

I FIND (by a letter you wrote to Lady Waldegrave) that you are once again in Pall Mall, which I rejoice at, not that I think it will

1. Lancelot Reed, Esq. of Hatton Wall, Middlesex, is named as an executor and legatee in Sir Edward Walpole's will.

contribute to your happiness, or that peace and quietness will long subsist between you, but that it may be an inducement for Sir Edward Walpole (if you cannot live well together) to part with you in good humour, and allowing you an annuity, and such an one that may make you (with your pension, which, that you have got, for goodness sake never utter the least word about) comfortable. Now you are with Sir Edward Walpole, let me give you this advice, never contradict him in trivial matters, where it can answer no end, never find fault with Collier, or any other of his servants, though you even heard them yourself abuse their master—if you cannot agree with him in opinion, hold your tongue—Now that I have said this, I beg leave to add, that if you find his temper, his ill usage too much for you, you had best desire to part with him, and do it as amicably as you can, and if he does not think proper to allow you anything, you never shall want, while I live, and I think I may answer for Lady Waldegrave; but you must give us notice of such your intention before you put it in practice, that we may have some place ready for your reception, and not suffer you to go to aliens for protection.

I am

Madam

Your most obedient servant

FR. EXETER

APPENDIX 5

EXTRACTS FROM THE DUCHESS OF GLOUCESTER'S LETTERS TO JANE AND ANNE CLEMENT

To Jane Clement, St Leonard's Lodge, 3 Oct. 1772:

Mrs Craster is dead, so now the Winchester Tower is yours, for I have had a letter from Lord Hertford this moment to confirm his promise, but you know he must take some proper method of telling it to the King without naming me—I hope you will suffer my dear children to be in it this winter. . . . I must say I am very lucky—for even my children's not living with me is I suppose best, *for* if they did I should have nothing to wish for, and should be too happy, which in this world must *not be*. . . . You have been misinformed about my uncle, the Queen had said she should like to see his new room but this affair [the Duchess's marriage] coming out, has put him quite in disgrace. . . . Apropos if I thought my father would come and see us there [the Pavilions] I would write to him, and ask him for you know he could make it a morning's drive, and if he did not like to dine with us, could return to his dinner—but, if you think he would not come I will not ask him, for I do not like to lay the Duke open to any more refusals.

To Jane Clement, 27 Oct. 1772:

Mr Walsingham was at the levee last Friday, and to the surprise of *all* courtiers spoke to *most graciously,* although he is so declaredly one of *my party:* so are all our friends received—why will not the Northumberlands be wise in time—or Alnwick Castle will never see us within its walls.

To Jane Clement, 19 Nov. 1772:

Lord Cholmondeley was here last Sunday; therefore Lord Ch. I shall look upon as a cousin; but *no Conway* shall I or mine ever acknowledge, *nor Waldegrave.* They will all be sorry sooner than they think for I can tell 'em; they forget the bouncing difference between the two Dukes: the King never was so civil to Mrs Onslow in his life as he is now—and Lord North says that although the King has never named us to him, he knows the King likes those best who show attention to the Duke of Gloucester—poor Lord Hertford!

To Jane Clement, 18 Dec. 1772:

Pray, have any of the Walpoles been to my father or said anything of waiting upon the Duke? I hope they have *not*, for then they shall with all the Conways and Waldegraves be people my child, shall *never* know for relations or connections. Lord Cholmondeley has behaved as he ought, therefore I shall always look upon him as a relation; so I shall upon Lady Powis—but Waldegraves and Conways, *never never* shall I know again—Now, they do not care but our cards will sometime or other turn up trumps—notwithstanding the King's false and trumpery heart. . . .

I wish my father would come to the deanery for a day that he may wait upon the Duke, for I can tell him the Duke, stands upon form and will *never* enter his house till he has been to him, or at least offered it.

To Jane Clement, 19 July 1774:

I am very much flattered, upon account of my girls—I do not know what they do, but their behaviour is so admired, that Lady Dy[sart] and Mr Walpole hear of nothing else; poor dear things, it is better their behaviour should please than their beauty; for when such very young people are greatly admired their beauty seldom answers when they come out; their conduct can't addle.

To Jane Clement, Lyndhurst, 5 Sept. 1774:

The Duke ordered Stiel to supply my father with game and venison, I hope he has so done? The Duke has not recovered so fast as I should wish, he has bathed but three times, but I hope will now be able to continue it. Caroline is dipped in a tub of sea water, and it is surprising how she is improved by it, she grows very pert, poor little soul, there never was so quiet a child: as to Sophia her sauciness is above measure great.

To Jane Clement, Lyndhurst, 8 Sept. 1774:

Some time ago I sent my father a pie made of the black cock: it is so difficult to get that sort of game to London sweet that I thought a pie the best way, as we think our cook makes those pies remarkably well.

My poor dear little girls will not see me so soon as they hope; now, do you think my father would let 'em make him a visit for a day or two? Madam Vatas wants to go to town for two or three days, which I have refused, but if they could be at my father's two or three days, she would go to her sister's, and they would be very happy: and by that time the plays would be begun, so that you could take 'em to one play. . . . they need not have any of their maids with 'em, as Dothwaite can dress their hair—Horatia can sleep with Nancy and the other two together: you will sound *Me Dady* upon the subject and if he don't approve of it let it drop.

To Jane Clement, Lyndhurst, 3 or 10 Oct. 1774:

Your letter made me very happy: to hear that my poor dear girls please and are admired gives me an inexpressible joy: poor things, their not living with me is in some degree an advantage to them as it makes them exert themselves to make friends. I hope they will have many friends, but never be much talked of; may they only be admired where they are seen, and loved where they are known; that is enough for women. The Duke finds so much benefit by bathing that he will stay as long as ever he can; indeed his recovery is miraculous; I did not dare allow to myself how ill I thought him when we came down here; but God be thanked he is now very well, and by staying late in the season he will prepare a stock of strength, for the many vexations he will have to encounter in the winter. . . . Caroline is above measure improved by bathing, she is really now a very pretty child: extremely lively and never out of temper.

To ?Jane Clement, ca April 1776 (fragment):

Mrs Keppel writes me word that Lady Laura does not look well, on account of those nasty worms which teased her so much. If she does not look well it would be pity she should go to Court this spring. However, all that must be determined by her Aunts from the letters I have wrote upon that subject; I own I wish very much for her to come out, young as she is, because it will put her and her sisters upon a more comfortable footing. She is too old to be treated quite as a child, although much too young to run about, and be looked upon as her own mistress, even though she has been at Court and may go once or twice to Almacks.

To Jane Clement, Rome, May 1776:

Mrs Keppel is very good to my girls; but oh! my dear Aunt, why will Mrs Keppel always suppose that girls are disposed to do wrong? She writes me word that four girls are *too much* for any one person to take care of: *four bad girls* are certainly too great a charge, but *four such girls as* the Cousinhood, might be a pleasure instead of a constant state of anxiety as Mrs K. makes it. She writes as if they showed a perpetual propensity to behave ill! Sometimes Lady Laura is accused of not suffering herself to be amused: *now* Mrs K. says that Lady Laura's spirits she fears should run away with her when she is in company: I dare not tell Mrs K. but Lady Laura lamented to me in one of her letters, Mrs Keppel's manner of giving advice; she says that she always *seems* in a constant apprehension of Miss Keppel's doing some very bad thing. *Now,* I do think it a great pity that Mrs [K.] does so, as it really is unjust to girls who behave so very well. I fear, that without intending it Mrs K. will tease Laura a good deal this summer; for my sister certainly has not a good temper. My poor girls would never have had any vexations could they have lived with me.

To Jane Clement, Rome, before 28 Nov. 1776:

The Bishop in his letter calls our being out of England a sort of banishment—so it is, then why will not my friends in England lessen the disagreeableness of such a situation by the kindness of their letters, and not like Mrs Keppel fill her letters with panegyrics upon Lord Talbot; for no reason that I can find out, but his having behaved so uncommonly impertinent and insolent, to the Duke and me! . . . I must say for Mr Walpole that his letters are very constant, very friendly, and very respectful, he cannot be more so, should we ever again hold up our heads: of that however I have no hopes. . . . The Duke's health is so perfectly good here, and his spirits, and his attention to me so great, and his love for his children so unbounded, that if my dear girls were with me, and my infants secured from beggary, I suppose, I should be *too* happy. Before I finish my letter, I must assure you that whatever I say of Mrs K. I have no reason to complain of her behaviour to Lady Laura, for to her, she is everything that is obliging and kind, and as Laura expresses it herself, 'She treats me as an Earl's daughter in company, in private as her own child.'

To Jane Clement, Rome, 4 Jan. 1777:

Lord Dysart has behaved in his brutal manner to my girls, which has hurt me very much, they never had a cross word from me, and to have them treated like Charity Girls by him hurts my pride not a little. I wrote to Maria to leave Helmingham if his insolence continued—I shall rejoice when they are again in town, and they shall never go into his house again (when he is at home) to make any stay.

To Jane Clement, Rome, 4 April 1777:

But, my dear Aunt let me entreat of you not to talk of our debts, it is not debt, which makes us live out of England, it is the Duke's health first, and then the constant persecution we meet with from the King, who will never be at rest whilst one person of quality comes to Gloucester House. You cannot imagine how the Duke fretted at my father's writing to Lord George Germaine about his debts: had he wrote about a provision there would have been reason in it; but we have no pretence to expect to have our debts paid. I have often uttered it to you as a wish but never as an expectation: and it must have rendered the Duke ridiculous to Lord George; and what have we got, but a proof that Lord George is *now* quite a minister, and no longer the Duke's friend? I hope in God my father will not show his correspondence with Lord George to Mr Walpole, or the Bishop, for as *all my* friends are of a particular cast, instead of being sorry that we have lost Lord George they would rejoice— for they always have *triumphed* upon the failure of any friend to us: it is not that they do not wish us well but then it must be through the people they like. The Bishop would have us obliged to no one but Lord Rockingham who never means to serve us, and Mr Walpole through Mr Conway, who hates us.

To Anne Clement, 21 July 1778:

You should not have told Sir Edward, that I had borrowed £200 of Mr Walpole, for it is not to me that it is lent. Lady Laura borrowed it and I have nothing to do with it: to be sure Lord Thurlow is a man of great virtue to refuse so reasonable a demand as money to set the young ladies out. I write this to you not to be seen, for I assure you I think it not fair to say any more; I am sure he will lend it if he can, and if he does, I hope he will be repaid part of it at Christmas, because that money will put them beforehand with the world and as soon as they are clear, they will pay as they go, which will keep them with my help very well for the future. Was Lady Laura married we should all be so much set up that we would not care about money. That rogue Mr Barn will I hope pay back the £50 which will help us much—and we will not pay so exorbitantly for an house as we did last winter: masters must go on the same, for the girls are too well educated to give up that: but although they will certainly pay Sir Edward, they need not be distressed about paying him as they are about their tradespeople: Mr Suckling has left Sir Edward £100 which you know will be a great help, and reduce the difficulty about raising the £400. You are a very good girl, and I only write this to thank you for the trouble you have had.

To Anne Clement, 30 June 1790:
   I was yesterday at Strawberry Hill: Mr Walpole says that Lord D[ysart] has been twice to visit the Beauclercs! I wonder at that; yet, if he does marry I think he would choose something young unless it is (as I have always supposed) that he knows he never can have a child, therefore will let it appear to be equally the woman's fault— I do not understand why Lady Frances [Tollemache] wishes him to marry? but *I* do not care what they do.

To Anne Clement, 26 July 1790:
   The attentions you meet with at Ham, are proofs of esteem people had there for my dear sister [Lady Dysart]. I do not know how it is, but I am more overcome today with thinking of her, than usual! I have paid her a tribute of tears—I was not meant to be allied to a Brunswick, for *they can* only love what they see every day; and every minute! *I never* forget.

To Anne Clement, 9 December 1790:
   My illness is all bile—when that is eradicated my face will recover, at least for some time; but, as day after day passes without a probability of any change in my uncomfortable way of living, the bile will accumulate, and sometimes break out—if I get the better of this attack I shall be constantly attentive to my diet, and hope by that means to prevent its ever getting such a head again.

To Anne Clement, 4 February 1791:
   My face is now all scabby, so I suppose it will get well in time.

To Anne Clement, 22 Aug. 1793:

Sophia goes tonight to the Princesses at Kew, my son and I have a little party of casino. I once feared that *they* and *their* friends, had lessened his affection to me, but I have no reason to think so at present, he is very attentive to me, and as he is now old enough to judge for himself, I hope he will never be shook. As to his father, I do not think he is so much with *his* jade as he used to be; but that helps nothing; *she* began her attacks upon *him* by setting *him* against me; therefore nothing that happens to *her* will ever make *him* behave to me like a gentleman and that is all that I desire. I own fairly, that I am woman enough to wish to see *her* humbled before I die; and if *he* neglected *her*, *she* would be neglected; but *he* will never do anything of that sort, for fear it should be any gratification to me! *He* has not that greatness of soul that would guide *him* to say *he* wished to make me some atonement by the humbling of that *woman*.

To Anne Clement, Navestock, 3 July 1794:

My poor Lady Waldegrave is better than she was, when I arrived; but she is very unhappy for she never can forget that angelic boy; yet I think that John will be a great comfort to her: he is a sweet affectionate boy, and is very unhappy at his brother's death. I wish Lady Maria showed as much feeling as both he and Miss FitzRoy do.

The King told my Sophia that my dear boy was teased by some of his playfellows and that made him rush into the water? I hope that is not so; but if it is his poor mother must never know it. Everybody is very sorry for him. I shall stay here till the middle of the week.

To Anne Clement, ca December 1794:

Lord Orford is still at Strawberry Hill—he desires me not to begin the monument yet—but, I shall begin it when I have got the money ready for the first payment—it is a thing that cannot be done in an hurry. Lady Mary Churchill has been very ill, I believe she frets about her daughter; who is now at Monmouth with Mr Cooper, who is in jail there, for Lord Cadogan has arrested him for the £2000 and as he and she were at Monmouth he has got into that jail—I pity his father and mother very much indeed.

To Anne Clement, 27 Dec. 1794:

Since my last illness, I have a feel of comfortable resignation, that surpasses everything; I do not pretend to feel any affection for my husband, therefore *now* his society would be no satisfaction to me. I have the best of daughters always with me; and as I may *now* take her out to air with me whenever I like it, I do not want any change; her goodness makes her pleased with the solitary life she leads; but when the Princess of Wales comes, she will have some gaiety to compensate for all the dull hours she passes.

To Jane Clement, 30 August 1796. *Address* (in HW's hand): To Mrs Clement at Windsor Castle. *Endorsed* (by HW): Isleworth August the thirtieth 1796. Free Orford.

I will carry this letter to Lord Orford, for him to frank. Lady Waldegrave has been with him two days; I believe nothing particular passed between them.

To Anne Clement, 23 November 1796:

Lady Waldegrave does not intend to come to London this winter. She says she cannot afford it; she is the best judge, of her own affairs. She writes to me; but, if she had humility to write as she ought to do; we should both go on better. As she has read so much piety, I wonder that she has not detected that a *proud heart* and a religious one, are incompatible? A *proud heart to a parent* is to me incomprehensible; especially in a person who thinks herself very devout? I shall answer her letters, but they will be very cold—I can never again write to her as I used to write. I wonder, what friend she will find to make up for her loss of my affection, which she has contrived to get rid of, almost entirely: I have been many years, coming to this indifference; for it is *many* years, that she has behaved ill to me; I suppose she wished to provoke me, by the pains she has taken—and at last she has succeeded.

APPENDIX 6

LORD ORFORD'S ILLNESS

First attack

Between 29 Jan. and 12 Feb. 1773 six letters from William Moone, Lord Orford's steward, to Thomas Walpole from Great Chesterford, Essex, describe Orford's first attack of insanity (MANN vii. 460, nn. 4, 5; 463, n. 3):

29 Jan. 1773. 'Half past twelve at noon': 'Yesterday morning about 4 o'clock I received an express from Chesterford, acquainting me that Lord Orford lay extremely ill there. I immediately set out, and arrived there about a quarter after eleven. I found his Lordship in a very bad state of health, but last night the doctors thought him much better. About two this morning his Lordship grew worse, and still continues exceedingly ill. He is attended by Dr Glynn and Dr Plumptre, who think him in a very dangerous way.'

30 Jan. 'Half past one': 'His Lordship's disorder was a kind of delirium. . . . They [the physicians] were unwilling I should mention the disorder, fearing it would give too great an alarm to the family.'

1 Feb. 'My Lord slept a great part of the night, but at intervals rambled . . . about eight in the morning . . . his Lordship grew extremely outrageous, and it was with the utmost difficulty he could be kept in bed.'

2 Feb. 'Yesterday . . . in the evening, his Lordship was very outrageous for about two hours.'

12 Feb. 'My Lord was thought to be better yesterday all day than he has been for many days past.'

14 Feb. 'Lord Orford had a tolerable day yesterday, and last night his Lordship slept several hours . . . upon the whole the doctors think his Lordship, etc., etc., etc. better, and intend, if no unforeseen alteration happens, to remove him to town Tuesday [16 Feb.] or Wednesday next.'

17 Feb. HW wrote Mann of this attack, 'I have a melancholy tale to tell you of . . . my Lord Orford. He had a cutaneous or some scorbutic eruption. By advice of his *groom* he rubbed his body all over with an ointment of sulphur and hellebore. This poison struck in the disease. By as bad advice as his groom's, I mean, his own, he took a violent antimonial medicine, which sweated him immoderately—and then he came to town, went to Court, took James's pills, without telling him of the quack drops, sat up late, and though ordered by James to keep at home, returned into the country the next day [26 or 27 Jan.]. The cold struck all his nostrums and ails into his head, and the consequence is—insanity!' (ibid. vii. 460).

12 March. 'The physicians have fancied my poor nephew cured; but yesterday he wrote a letter that proved the very reverse' (ibid. vii. 467).

2 April. 'My brother and I are very earnest to have her [Lady Orford] come over. . . . I doubt very much of her son's recovery, though as the physicians say they expect it, at least intervals of sense, I have given her those hopes' (ibid. vii. 471).

27 April. 'Lord Orford continues as he was; that is, sometimes very well; sometimes very sullen and suspicious—I doubt much of his recovery. I wish for some answer from his mother; . . . I fear she will not come over herself. This will be a great distress to my brother and me, who are most unwilling to take the direction of his affairs' (ibid. vii. 476).

ca 19 May. 'I wish, alas! I could give her Ladyship better hopes of such amendment, but am sorry to let her know that the physicians have little expectation of it. Lord Orford has sometimes good intervals, but relapses so often, that they, from experience in such vicissitudes, conclude he is likely to continue in that alternate state. . . . I hear the physicians wish we would give them authority to use more restraint, an ill occasion having been taken by some of his friends to visit, and even once to carry him into company, extremely with the disapprobation of his physicians' (ibid. vii. 482).

29 May. 'Lady Orford distresses us much by not writing. Her son is very bad, and something must be done—but who will do it, I know not' (ibid. vii. 485).

15 June. 'All we can do is to watch over my Lord's person and to take care that every attention of humanity and tenderness be paid to him, and that his unfortunate life may be made as comfortable as possible. The recovery of his senses, is, I fear, hopeless; his constitution is robust, and his health perfectly good. The physical people that attend him say, he may live these forty years' (ibid. vii. 489).

13 July. 'Her son has had a terrible relapse, and for above a fortnight kept me under dreadful alarms by attempting to destroy himself. He is now quieter, and is settled at Hampstead in a house I have taken for him, and with which he is pleased. . . . Dr Jebbe reckons this relapse favourable, as opposite to idiotism, into which he seemed sinking. It may be so—but idiotism would guarantee his life, and such relapses, (after recovering from the immediate cause of his malady, the violent quack medicines) indicate strongly to me a radical cause' (ibid. vii. 495).

15 Aug. 'My Lord seems to me to grow so much worse. The people about him call it *his fit,* and fancy he is worse periodically once a month. The great and uncommon heats we have had lately, may have contributed—but this fit, as they call it, has lasted longer than the month. He is forced to be confined in his bed at night, and pinioned in the day, as he incessantly tries to escape, or to do himself mischief. He swallows nothing but broth, and that by force; consequently you may imagine, falls away. . . . I do not find the physical people under apprehension for his life, if he can be kept from hurting himself' (ibid. vii. 505).

4 Oct. 'My poor nephew is at present quite furious, as he is at the beginning of every month, and apt to attempt mischief. At best he seems to have quite lost his head, knows nobody, is restless, and walks incessantly' (ibid. vii. 521).

28 Nov. 'Her son grows worse, for he is more furious and mischievous, and for longer seasons' (ibid. vii. 529).

30 Dec. 'My nephew, after being for nine weeks at the lowest pitch of deplorable frenzy, has suddenly emerged to a strange degree of reason, and has written three letters with more coolness and clearness

than he did almost when he was, what was called, in his senses' (ibid. vii. 539).

31 Dec. 'Doctors Battie and Jebbe . . . confirmed the wonderful recovery of Lord Orford, and though so contradictory to the sentence they had pronounced on him three weeks ago, have the fairness to own their mistake and surprise. He is in fact come to his senses so much, that they have opened his whole case to him, and told him they expect he will be quite well, if he keeps himself cool and quiet for some time, neither writing letters nor seeing company, which he has promised' (ibid. vii. 540).

19 Jan. 1774. 'Lord Orford is amazingly recovered—that is, has a most lucid interval, though neither I nor his own friends whom I have made visit him, look on him as perfectly in his senses. Dr Battie, however, has been so precipitate as to promise to quit him in a month if he does not relapse, and he counts the hours eagerly and exactly, which makes us suspect that the temper he shows is but pretended. My situation will be frightful when the day shall come, if he is neither quite well nor worse, for nobody can restrain him, if the physicians pronounce him in his senses; and if he does mischief to himself or others, there will not be wanting kind friends to blame me for setting him free' (ibid. vii. 546; see also HW to Mason 14 Jan. 1774, MASON i. 126).

2 Feb. 'Her son is recovered entirely' (MANN vii. 548); he was in London and planned to go to Court 5 Feb. (Lord Hertford to George III, Geo. III's *Corr.* ed. Fortescue, iii. 60).

23 Feb. 'I have taken care not to be too sanguine about the continuation of my nephew's recovery—and yet it begins to flatter me with a prospect of its duration' (MANN vii. 554).

28 March. 'I have been with him at Houghton, and am returned full of sorrow; convinced on one hand that if he remains in what are called his senses, his conduct will not be more reasonable than formerly; and on the other, expecting a relapse. In one word, he observes no regimen, eats intemperately, and drinks above a bottle a day' (ibid. vii. 560).

Second attack

21 April 1777. HW arrived at Eriswell; 'my Lord was in bed, and is
very mad. . . . He has got the waistcoat on' (*ante* HW to Sir Edward
Walpole 21 April 1777; OSSORY i. 349–50).

28 April. 'After an interval of three years, in which my nephew remained as much in his senses as he was *supposed* to be before his
declared frenzy, he was seized a fortnight ago [ca 14 April] with a
fever that soon brought out the colour of his blood. In two days he
was furious. The low wretches with whom in his *sensible* hours he
has always been surrounded, concealed the symptoms till they were
terrifying. I received no notice till the sixth day' (MANN viii. 293).
'Dr Jebbe pronounced that he had neither fever nor understanding.
He has had a slight return of the former, and no delirium. Yet
both his physicians, the apothecary, and even his mistress, think his
disorder will still last some weeks' (ibid. viii. 294).

2 May. 'The Norwich physician said he found my Lord so much
better that I left him two days ago, though his mistress desired I
would leave the keeper, at least for a month. Thus his life will be
safe' (ibid. viii. 296).

15 July. 'Lord Orford is no better, and everything is in confusion'
(OSSORY i. 365).

1 Sept. 'My poor nephew remains in the same undecided state, sometimes furious, sometimes sullen' (MANN viii. 324).

18 Sept. 'My nephew remains quiet, but gives no prospect of amendment' (ibid. viii. 327).

26 Oct. 'Lord Orford seems to be growing childish, which is the most
eligible state for him, as the safest: but I depend on nothing' (ibid.
viii. 332).

4 Jan. 1778. 'Lord Orford has been in a most hopeless way for above
three months; but last week, though the weather was severe, he had
a furious fit, which the faculty reckon more likely to indicate an
interval of sense, than quiet and settled irrationality' (ibid. viii. 349).

27 March. 'Dr Monro . . . came to tell me that Lord Orford is come to himself' (ibid. viii. 367).

31 March. Lord Orford wrote Lord Hertford, 'I have now the pleasure to inform you that I have the pleasing prospect of a speedy recovery—I find my health increasing daily . . . I ride two or three hours every day' (Geo. III's *Corr.,* ed. Fortescue, iv. 89).

9 April. 'His recovery was as marvellous. He waked, could scarce articulate, and thought himself paralytic. The keeper gave him a common apothecary's draught. In a quarter of an hour he said, "What have you given me? It has removed a weight from my head" —and thence talked rationally. . . . It even looks in him as if it took the same time to come to maturity. Last fit lasted under or about thirteen months; this not quite twelve—I hope the next will be as long gathering as the last, three years!' (MANN viii. 372).

Third attack

23 Nov. 1791. '. . . in what distress I have been from a new fit of frenzy of Lord Orford, attended by total insensibility, and so violent a fever, that from seven o'clock on Friday evening [18 Nov.] when Dr Monro, whom I had sent down to him, returned, I had dreaded an express with an account of his death; till the post came in very late on Monday; nor should I have known a syllable of his disorder and danger, had not Lord Cadogan, who lives in the neighbourhood, sent me word of it . . . the fever is in a manner gone, and his senses so far returned, that I conclude it will again be said, as it has been the fashion to say, "that he is as well as ever he was" ' (OSSORY iii. 129–30).

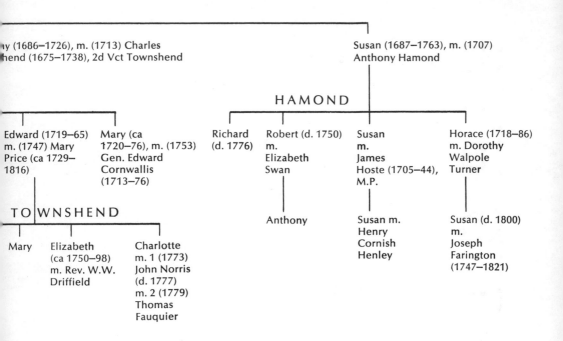

y (1686–1726), m. (1713) Charles
hend (1675–1738), 2d Vct Townshend

Susan (1687–1763), m. (1707)
Anthony Hamond

HAMOND

Edward (1719–65)
m. (1747) Mary
Price (ca 1729–
1816)

Mary (ca
1720–76), m. (1753)
Gen. Edward
Cornwallis
(1713–76)

Richard
(d. 1776)

Robert (d. 1750)
m.
Elizabeth
Swan

Susan
m.
James
Hoste (1705–44),
M.P.

Horace (1718–86)
m. Dorothy
Walpole
Turner

TOWNSHEND

Anthony

Susan m.
Henry
Cornish
Henley

Susan (d. 1800)
m.
Joseph
Farington
(1747–1821)

Mary

Elizabeth
(ca 1750–98)
m. Rev. W.W.
Driffield

Charlotte
m. 1 (1773)
John Norris
(d. 1777)
m. 2 (1779)
Thomas
Fauquier

WALPOLE GENEALOGY
Names of Horace Walpole and his correspondents
are printed in bold-face type.
Illegitimate descents are marked by broken lines,
the names of the mothers being indicated in
square brackets.

F GLOUCESTER

ta Maria

William Frederick (1776–1834),
2d D. of Gloucester, m. (1816)
Princess Mary (1776–1857)